Ann Sophia Stephens

The Gold Brick

Ann Sophia Stephens

The Gold Brick

ISBN/EAN: 9783743313576

Manufactured in Europe, USA, Canada, Australia, Japa

Cover: Foto ©ninafisch / pixelio.de

Manufactured and distributed by brebook publishing software (www.brebook.com)

Ann Sophia Stephens

The Gold Brick

THE GOLD BRICK.

BY

MRS. ANN S. STEPHENS.

AUTHOR OF "FASHION AND FAMINE," "MARY DERWENT," "THE OLD HOMESTEAD," "THE REJECTED WIFE," "THE HEIRESS," "THE WIFE'S SECRET," "SILENT STRUGGLES," ETC.

> His was the deepest sorrow, for it grew
>   Out from his crime, a night-shade of the soul.
> There, fed on poison—bathed with bitter dew,
>   She found the evil thing. Her sweet control
> Unearthed the root, and softly planted there
>   A tiny germ, all white and pure as snow,
> And then with tears, and smiles, and silent prayer,
>   Through grief and darkness, watched the lone plant grow
> A stately tree, rooted so deep in Love,
> That its best fruitage must be found above.

Philadelphia:
T. B. PETERSON AND BROTHERS;
306 CHESTNUT STREET.

Entered, according to Act of Congress, in the year 1866, by

MRS. ANN S. STEPHENS,

In the Clerk's Office of the District Court of the United States, in and for the Southern District of New York.

TO

MY DEAR FRIEND,

MRS. BENJAMIN F. LOAN

OF ST. JOSEPH, MISSOURI,

THIS VOLUME

IS AFFECTIONATELY DEDICATED.

ANN S. STEPHENS.

NEW YORK, *March*, 1866.

CONTENTS.

CHAPTER I.
THE MASSACRE.. 27

CHAPTER II.
THE JEWEL BOX.. 33

CHAPTER III.
THE BURIAL... 39

CHAPTER IV.
THE FAITHFUL SLAVE.. 46

CHAPTER V.
THE SEARCH FOR GOLD....................................... 54

CHAPTER VI.
THE FLOGGING... 61

CHAPTER VII.
A REBELLIOUS SPIRIT.. 67

CHAPTER VIII.
THE BOX OF JEWELS... 76

CHAPTER IX.
CHAINED IN THE HOLD.. 81

CHAPTER X.
THE HOUSE IN THE PINE WOODS........................... 92

CHAPTER XI.
KATHARINE ALLEN'S VISIT TO THE WHITE COTTAGE...... 97

CONTENTS.

CHAPTER XII.
HOME FROM SEA.. 104

CHAPTER XIII.
THE WAY-SIDE MEETING.. 110

CHAPTER XIV.
THE OLD HOME AND THE OLD PEOPLE.................... 116

CHAPTER XV.
BREAKFAST IN THE OLD HOMESTEAD...................... 125

CHAPTER XVI.
A PAINFUL INTERVIEW.. 135

CHAPTER XVII.
JEALOUS PANGS REGARDING MRS. MASON................ 139

CHAPTER XVIII.
MRS. MASON'S RICH UNCLE IN THE SOUTH................ 144

CHAPTER XIX.
MRS. MASON LEAVES THE PINE WOODS.................... 152

CHAPTER XX.
ANOTHER SEPARATION... 160

CHAPTER XXI.
THE MINISTER AT BAYS HOLLOW GETS A WIFE......... 164

CHAPTER XXII.
THE MINISTER'S WIFE TAKES PUPILS...................... 171

CHAPTER XXIII.
THE VILLAGE DOCTOR IN A SNOW-STORM................ 175

CHAPTER XXIV.
THE GRANDMOTHER RELENTING............................. 183

CHAPTER XXV.
A GRAVE IN THE SNOW... 190

CHAPTER XXVI.
A CROWD UNDER THE BUTTERNUT TREE.................. 195

CHAPTER XXVII.
THE SAILOR AND HIS TWO COMPANIONS 201

CHAPTER XXVIII.
OUT OF HER DELIRIUM... 207

CHAPTER XXIX.
STRANGERS IN THE VILLAGE.................................... 214

CHAPTER XXX.
THE WELCOME LETTER... 223

CHAPTER XXXI.
THE RED SCHOOL-HOUSE AT SHRUB OAK................. 232

CHAPTER XXXII.
A TERRIBLE DISCLOSURE... 239

CHAPTER XXXIII.
THE OLD COUPLE ON THEIR SHADOWED HEARTH-STONE.. 244

CHAPTER XXXIV.
THE SNOW FRESHET... 248

CHAPTER XXXV.
ALL SORTS OF TREASON... 254

CHAPTER XXXVI.
MRS. MASON AT HER STUDIES.................................. 265

CHAPTER XXXVII.
SETTLING THE WEDDING DAY.................................. 272

CHAPTER XXXVIII.
A DOUBLE GUARD... 280

CHAPTER XXXIX.
OUT IN THE DEPTHS OF THE NIGHT........................... 284

CONTENTS.

CHAPTER XL.
TAKEN IN FROM THE COLD. 293

CHAPTER XLI.
THE MARRIAGE CERTIFICATE. 298

CHAPTER XLII.
ON THE FIRST STAGE TO PRISON. 307

CHAPTER XLIII.
FRIENDS IN COUNCIL. 313

CHAPTER XLIV.
THE SEPARATION. 319

CHAPTER XLV.
PAUL FINDS A NEW HOME. 326

CHAPTER XLVI.
JUBE FINDS HIS WAY TO BAYS HOLLOW. 331

CHAPTER XLVII.
A CHILDISH CONSULTATION. 336

CHAPTER XLVIII.
PAUL SEES HIS MOTHER'S NECKLACE. 341

CHAPTER XLIX.
A PALACE READY FOR ITS MISTRESS. 348

CHAPTER L.
COMING HOME OF THE BRIDE. 351

CHAPTER LI.
THE DAY BEFORE TRIAL. 355

CHAPTER LII.
THE STREETS AND THE COURT HOUSE. 362

CHAPTER LIII.
THE DOCTOR'S EVIDENCE. 367

CHAPTER LIV.
THE VERDICT.. 372

CHAPTER LV.
THE TRAIL OF THE SERPENT............................. 376

CHAPTER LVI.
LOVE'S GOLDEN HARVEST................................. 382

CHAPTER LVII.
ONE HOUR OF SHAME...................................... 386

CHAPTER LVIII.
THE MOTHER AND SON.................................... 390

CHAPTER LIX.
THE EMPTY HOUSE... 397

CHAPTER LX.
TOM HUTCHINS' LETTER................................... 400

CHAPTER LXI.
UNSATISFIED VANITY....................................... 404

CHAPTER LXII.
ARTFUL FASCINATIONS.................................... 409

CHAPTER LXIII.
GATHERING APPLES... 417

CHAPTER LXIV.
MARRIED AGAIN... 423

CHAPTER LXV.
THE FANCY BALL.. 427

CHAPTER LXVI.
STRANGE GUESTS... 431

CHAPTER LXVII.
TOGETHER, YET SEPARATED.............................. 439

CONTENTS.

CHAPTER LXVIII.
THE TREASURE VAULT... 445

CHAPTER LXIX.
SIMSBURY MINES... 448

CHAPTER LXX.
THE PRISON ANGEL... 455

CHAPTER LXXI.
THE SWEATING OVEN.. 460

CHAPTER LXXII.
UNDER THE APPLE TREE... 468

CHAPTER LXXIII.
OUT OF A SCRAPE.. 474

CHAPTER LXXIV.
THE LONELY HOUSE... 481

CHAPTER LXXV.
THE MANIAC'S TOILET.. 486

CHAPTER LXXVI.
THE DOCTOR'S RIDE.. 491

CHAPTER LXXVII.
THE CONVICT'S RETURN... 498

CHAPTER LXXVIII.
TOM HUTCHINS' QUARREL.. 500

CHAPTER LXXIX.
THE WEDDING AND THE BAPTISM.................................... 508

THE GOLD BRICK.

CHAPTER I.

THE MASSACRE.

A LOW coast, burdened in every foot of its soil with the luxuriant growth of a tropical climate; a large town, straggling and flat, swarming like a hive of bees with turbulent life. Lights flickering wildly from the windows and dancing with a fantastic and red glare up and down the streets. A dull, hollow sound rolling constantly out upon the stillness of the waters, broken now and then with sharp shrieks as lightning cleaves the thunder gust.

This was the scene commanded from the deck of a New England brig, lying in the harbor of Port au Prince, on one of those terrible nights in the end of the last century, when the horrible passions that had rioted through France, like wild beasts ravening for blood, fled across seas and fired themselves anew in the hot life of the tropics.

The contrast between the stillness of the harbor, where the starlight fell smilingly, and the waters rippled like kisses around the vessels, and that demon riot on the shore, was awful. To lie so near, with death shrieks cutting the air every instant, with murderous yells chasing them, like fiends, was enough to drive men mad. The iron-hearted New England sailors on that deck, grew restive as caged lions, while the tumult swelled louder and louder around them. The young captain turned white as he took short marches up and down the deck. The men drew close together, eyeing each other with fierce glances. A word from the captain would have sent them headlong into the massacre, in a wild effort to save the women and children, whose shrieks, even from the distance, drove them frantic.

But what could they do?—a handful of men against thousands on thousands of brutalized blacks, swarming in that doomed city. It was terrible to remain, but madness to go. The captain ground his teeth and clenched his hands in the agony of this restraint. Every cry that reached the ship pierced him like a sword; every fresh gleam of light quivering across the waters seemed to lure him to the rescue.

"Oh, my God! my God! I cannot bear this!" he cried, as a group of wooden buildings near the shore burst into a volume of fire, and one appalling shriek told that scores on scores of human beings were engulphed in the flames that danced and leaped and shed floods of fiery gold far out on the harbor. "Neither my owners nor my Maker could wish me to stand still now."

Going up to the group of sailors, he called out, "All hands to work, my boys! lower the boats. Such of you as want to help the poor wretches they are murdering yonder, come with me."

"Aye, aye," broke in a smothered shout from the sailors, and each man sprang to his duty—from cabin boy to mate, not a soul lagged behind. Yes, one man, the first mate, he neither repeated his superior's orders, or moved toward the boats, but stood near the captain, looking quietly unconcerned, with a half smile on his lip.

"You will not go, Thrasher," said the captain. "I am glad of it; some one must take charge of the ship. Stay on board, and be ready to lend a hand—we may bring back some of those poor creatures."

"And if your men are killed, who will work the ship, Captain Mason? Remember the craft belongs neither to you nor me."

"They shall not be killed, Thrasher, these brutes have plenty to do without minding us; besides, I'll keep off shore, and only lie to, ready to haul any poor creature in that takes to the water. They are sure to try, if they think of the ship."

"Well, well, captain, you command here, and know your own business best," answered Thrasher, with that same smile creeping across his lips; "for my part, I stand by the ship."

"That's right; I won't risk the men—never fear! As for the brig, what can harm her?"

"Nothing, while I'm aboard," answered the mate, turning suddenly townward, where another broad sheet of smoky flame blazed forth. "There," he cried, almost with a shout, "there goes another bonfire. The whole town will be roaring hot at this rate. Ha, look at that flock of women rushing out of the smoke like rats—hot work that—how plainly you can see 'em with their hair in the wind, turning and rushing hither and yon, between fire and water! Ho, ho, the black rascals are after 'em —Lord, how they run!—how they fling up their arms toward the ship—scatter on the beach—take to the water—they're on 'em—the nigger hounds are on 'em tooth and nail. What an infernal yell!"

Even that hard man turned away and covered his face with both hands; when he looked again it was with wild, heavy eyes.

"Heavens and earth," he muttered, "how still it is in spite of the roaring pit behind. The brutes have done their work, and gone into the smoke again. How softly the waves lick up the dead bodies from the sand and sweep 'em under. But they'll come to daylight again; perhaps here under our bows, a hundred women—who knows how many—with long hair, weltering up and down like sea-weed after a storm. Faugh! the dread of it makes one childish. I wonder if they are all gone. What, ho!"

Two persons, the cook and cabin-boy, had been left behind by the boats, much against their will. They, also, had witnessed the fearful scene on the beach, and shuddering with terror, crouched together behind some barrels that stood upon the deck. One of them tried to answer Thrasher's shout, but his voice broke in a hoarse whisper, and he really had neither the strength nor courage to move.

By this time the captain's boat was nearing the shore rapidly. If the scene of revolt had been terrible from the distance, it was crowded with horrors now. The fierce, hot breath of the fire came surging toward the coast like a sirocco. The roar of that infernal massacre, the pleadings and shrieks, the moans and shouts, horribly mingling and rising above each other, oppressed the very air. Out of the reeking melee of the town human beings darted like scared birds, and hid among the chaparral or rushed madly toward the beach.

The captain was brave and humane, but he was honest too, and in the midst of all this gave a thought to the obligations he owed to his command. He would go close to the shore, ready to save those who fled to the water for death or refuge. If it proved possible for the nature within him to resist the temptation to offer more, he would resist; if not, he was but human, and life was a precious thing to every breathing being; God would forgive him for saving it, though his owners might not.

As he neared the shore, that portion of the town which lay close to the water was in a bright blaze; the boat, the wharves, and the foam-fringed waves reddened and glowed under the hot smiles of the fire. Deep into the lurid caves made by the whirl of glowing smoke men and women struggled madly, and tore at each other like wild beasts, smothering their yells beneath the tumultuous elements.

From this lurid torrent the people scattered, both pursuers and pursued, out upon the open country. The poor wretches who were to die sought the darkest spots, hiding behind clumps of aloes and cactus hedges, or creeping under torn masses of wild vines, panting with terror and dread, and striving to hold the very breath that threatened to betray them.

Secure of their victims in the end, the triumphant hordes of negroes came huddling forth like demons, hooting, dancing, and rioting in the brazen light their own fiends' work had kindled. A group of palm trees stood close to the shore a little distance from the town, and to that point the insurgents swarmed in hundreds, dragging the pale beings whose death was to be their sport, brutally after them. When they reached the palm trees there was a rush from the crowd, and a score of dark objects leaped upon the slender stems, struggling upward, hustling over each other, the lowermost seizing his neighbor by the bare, glistening shoulders and hurling him down to the crowd amid wild shouts and stormy oaths.

At last the palms swayed and bent almost double under the burden of fiends, who dropped off by dozens into the yelling crowd. The beautiful trees, relieved of their weight, swayed back and penciled themselves against the flaming sky, not green and free as they had appeared a moment before; but with the bark torn from their delicate trunks, and the symmetrical foliage broken and ragged. From the point of each leaf flaunted a gorgeous scarf or tawdry ribbon—red, orange, purple, and flame colored—which fluttered wildly in the hot draughts of wind that swept over them from the burning town.

Out from the crowd, like sharks leaping in the black waves of a tempest, the negro women sprang upward, seizing the ribbons, tearing them away from the leaves, or bending down the stately trees until they took uncouth forms, and seemed tortured like the group of women and children whose death cries rang out from the midst of the fiendish dance. The mingled mirth and horror grew more and more maddening, till the sand all around refused to soak in the blood they had shed, and the naked feet of the dancers plashed to their own barbarous war cry, or stumbled over the dead bodies of the slain; for with every turn of the dance, an axe had fallen, and a soul gone shrieking up to its Maker.

Captain Mason saw all this from his boat, while it was far out in the harbor; with a cry of horror he seized the oars and worked them till they bent like saplings under his iron handling. But human strength was not equal to human cruelty. While he was yet some fathoms from the shore, the demons under the palm trees, scattered back to the town in search of fresh victims, leaving the dead and the dying to their agonies, with those mocking ribbons waving fantastically in the wind, as if a May dance had just passed beneath them.

Panting and breathless, their hearts burning with indignation, the captain and his men rested on their oars; their work of mercy cut short, for alas! rage is quicker than charity. They could see the pale, dead faces of the white women and children that had been murdered under the palm trees, with terrible distinctness. Their rich garments and delicate features, bespoke them of the higher classes, but there they lay, like soldiers heaped on a battle-field, with nothing but the stars of heaven to pity them—the pure stars that seemed affrighted by the tumult, and grew pallid in the smoke.

CHAPTER II.

THE JEWEL BOX.

As the captain sat with his face toward the palm trees, he saw a woman rise up from among the dead, and turn first toward the town, then seaward, in a wild despairing search for help.

The captain stood up in his boat and shouted aloud, while all hands pulled for the shore.

She heard him, reeled back against the stem of the
2

nearest palm tree, and clung to it, waving her hand toward the boat. But as they looked, a young boy was standing at her side, grasping her garments with his hand, while his face was turned toward the boat. He seemed urging her to flee. Twice her arm was unwound from the palm, and a step tried, but she fell back again, as if severely hurt or frightened out of her strength. The boy still pleaded. They could see it in his gestures, in the eager hand that motioned toward the shore, which the boat almost touched.

He pointed this out; he pulled frantically at her garments; he fell upon his knees, lifting his clasped hands toward her imploringly.

Something gave her desperate strength. She left the palm, staggered, and sprang forward, more than keeping pace with the boy, who, clinging to her hand, rushed on with his great, wild eyes, uplifted to her face.

The captain sprang on shore, and met them on the verge of the surf. The woman reeled toward him blindly, with both hands outstretched, and fell into his arms headlong, as she must have fallen on the sand but for his presence.

He gathered her to his broad bosom, and wading through the surf, waist deep, laid her in the boat, upon a pile of jackets that his men hurriedly took off their persons, and cast at his feet.

She was coldly pale, and did not seem to breathe. But the captain had no time to remark this or any thing else. A group of negroes who had been pursuing their death work among the cactus hedges, saw the boy and turned upon him.

The lad saw them, and with a desperate bound, leaped into the surf—struggled, lost his foothold, and was in the very sweep of the undertow, when the captain snatched him away. The savages hurled their sharp missiles after him, which the water swallowed instantly. So, as they were without firearms, the boy was saved, while his pursuers raged and hooted on the shore.

When the boy saw his mother lying so pale and still in the boat, he struggled from the captain's arms, and kneeling by her side, pressed the beautiful face—for it was beautiful—between his little trembling hands, while in the purest and most pathetic French he besought her to look up. He told her that they were safe now—away on the sea, where nothing could hurt them. He entreated her to wake up, only for one minute, just long enough to kiss him, and then she might go to sleep again for ever so long.

The touching anguish in the boy's voice would have called any mother back to life. She opened her eyes; a look of divine tenderness came softly to her face, and died in a smile upon her lips, as the boy bent down with a gush of tearful gladness and kissed her.

"There," he said, touching her raven hair with infinite tenderness, "go to sleep now. Paul will sit by and watch."

She seemed to understand him, for a serene smile beamed on her face, and softly as white rose-leaves fall, the lids drooped over her eyes.

The child was satisfied, and looking up at the captain, said—"Yes, yes, she will have a sweet, long sleep. We will not wake her—I promised, you know. If I forget, and begin to kiss her, don't let me, please, sir, for she always wakes, and smiles, when I do that. How softly the boat rocks! Oh, it will make her well."

The captain turned away his face, for he knew how long that sleep would be.

Slowly and sadly they rowed toward the ship. Fire and massacre raged behind them, but there was safety and solemn stillness on the waters. The boy clung to his mother's garments, and drooped his head wearily. The motion of the boat—the soft stars, smiling down, and scattering their broken images on the waves—affected him peacefully. He longed to fall asleep with his mother; but somehow the idea that she needed his care, kept the lids from sinking entirely over those beautiful eyes.

At last the boat drew close to the sides of the brig. The captain attempted to take the boy in his arms and carry him on board. But the little fellow struggled manfully, and insisted that his mother should be carried up first. Captain Mason, with his imperfect knowledge of French, understood this, for the child's face was more eloquent than words; but the men only comprehended his gestures, and interposed their superstitions against his generous wishes.

"No," they protested, with sullen determination, "the woman is dead—what have we to do with a corpse on board the brig? Ain't the signs agin her bad enough, without that one? Hoist the youngster aboard, captain, and let us row the boat over to White's Island, and bury the poor critter there!"

The child turned upon the sailors and searched their faces eagerly, as if he guessed that they were planning something against him. The men dropped their gloomy eyes beneath his glances, but were not the less resolved.

Captain Mason knew the superstition of his men too well for any idea of opposing it while his ship lay in that dangerous neighborhood. He cast one pitying look on the beautiful young woman who lay at his feet, in her

calm, eternal slumber, then tenderly addressed the boy:
"Your mother is asleep, let her stay here," he said,
in very confused French. But the attention of the boy
was keenly directed; he understood clearly, and sat
down, folding his little arms with a pleading smile.

"Me too?" he said.

"No, my child, you shall go on deck and wait while
the boat rocks here. All shall go, and leave your mother
to sleep alone."

"Is it best?" inquired the boy; "will she sleep
longer if we go?"

"Yes, poor orphan, her sleep will be long enough,"
cried the captain, all his generous sympathy bursting
forth in English.

"What!" said the boy, gently, "will her sleep be
sweeter—did you say that? Lift me up, I will go. Let
one of those big men put me on his shoulder. I shan't
be afraid. My father is—oh, how brave!—so am I."
The captain lifted the little fellow in his arms, and held
him against as good and true a heart as ever beat in
man's bosom—a heart pained with many compunctions
by the humane deception he was compelled to practice.
The men made the boat fast, and came up the side of
the brig, leaving it rocking softly on the water.

"Wait till he is asleep," the captain said, as they
stood in a group, anxious for orders. "Then we will
take her to the island."

The men retired, somewhat dissatisfied at any delay,
but made no further protest.

"Let me sit here, please, where I can look over and
see her face as she sleeps," said the gentle child, in a
sweet, pleading way, that went to that captain's heart;
"besides, I want to watch for papa. When the negroes

dragged us away, mamma and I—he followed after a little while, and when I looked back and he was lying on the ground, tired with running, I suppose; but he'll come, so if you don't mind, monsieur, I'll just wait here."

The boy had clambered up to a cask that stood near the side of the vessel, as he spoke, and folding his arms on the bulwarks, looked down with touching watchfulness upon the face of his mother, which lay, white as marble, in the starlight.

How beautiful, and how patient was that childlike watch. Sometimes the boy would lift his eyes with a troubled look, and turn them toward the town, which, still glaring and riotous, kept up its atrocious noises. Then he would search the harbor for some boat, and finding none, sink to his patient watch again, murmuring, "Oh, but he will come, when it is daylight—when it is daylight."

At last the struggles of nature were too strong for a child so delicately nurtured, and with his little arms folded on the bulwark he dropped into a profound sleep. But it was almost break of day before he became thus unconscious, and the captain had no time to spare. Taking the little fellow once more in his arms he laid him on his own bed, and going instantly on deck, summoned his men. With eager alacrity they descended to the boat. The captain followed with a large cloak over his arm, with which he reverently covered the dead. One man brought a pickaxe and spade, which he had taken from the cargo, and sat them in the stern of the boat; now that all danger of a dead person being carried aboard was over, they went quietly and seriously to their duties. As they gave the boat to her oars every arm fell softly to its work, it seemed as if they feared that a single splash of water would be followed by wails of pain from the poor child whose mother was floating away into eternity while he dreamed.

Across the waters and through the gray gleams of early dawn the boat cut its way to White's Island—which as yet was calm and peaceful. In a jungle of roses, where lofty cedars sheltered the beautiful coffee trees, the sailors dug a grave, leaving the murdered woman in the boat till their work was done. The captain, saddened by this individual instance of wrong, sat down upon the bank watching the boat, while his men completed their task. Once or twice he heard a movement in the chaparral, as if some wild animal were disturbed by his presence, but he took no heed, and at last his men came back.

CHAPTER III.

THE BURIAL.

Captain Mason would not leave that delicate creature to his men, but folding his cloak carefully around her, supported her head as she was lifted from the boat. Under the bending trees and through the fragrant shrubs they carried her, with hushed voices and cautious steps; for wrapped in the stillness of the morning there was something awful in that hastily prepared burial which penetrated to the hearts of those New England sailors as no ceremony could have done. But the vines, that fell in garlands from the trees, and the flowering branches which they were compelled to sweep aside, made the passage difficult. Once a patriarch aloe, which had shot up its great spikes of yellow blossoms for the first time in that year of blood, caught an ornament of the cloak on one of its sharp leaves and tore it from the dead, leaving the beautiful face and the long, sweeping hair exposed.

That instant there arose a fierce, rustling sound in the chaparral, followed by a cry that made the sailors pause in their holy work. The captain, pained by this sudden exposure of the dead, stooped, and with one hand strove to gather up the cloak which was now drawn entirely away, and trailed like a pall along the path they had taken. But at that instant a powerful negro tore a passage through the chaparral, and throwing himself on the ground, seized upon the garments of the dead lady, and broke into a passion of grief so wild and poignant that the sailors looked at each other awestricken.

"Is she dead—is she dead?" cried the negro, in wild, broken French, which the captain could hardly understand. "My mistress—my beautiful—beautiful mistress. They have killed her—why did she send Jube away?—where is the little master?—where is monsieur? All dead, all murdered, burned, trampled in the ashes."

"Did you know this lady?" said the captain, in his broken French. "Did you know her?"

The man looked up; tears rained down his face, and he sobbed out an incoherent answer amid plaintive moans over his mistress, for such evidently the lady had been.

"Me know her—me that swung her first hammock on

the mangoe trees—me! ah, strange master, tell me, is she dead? gone forever and ever? no more smiles, no more sweet words for Jube when he brings her fruit."

"Get up, poor fellow, get up, and let us pass," said the captain, in a kindly voice. "She is dead, and it is dangerous to wait."

The man drew back, but still kept on his knees. "And the master," he said piteously.

"I can tell you nothing of him," said the captain; "but the boy, the little one, is safe in my ship yonder."

The negro sprang to his feet, searched for the ship with eager glances, and began to clasp and wring his hands in alternate paroxysms of grief and joy.

"The little master! The poor, poor mistress!" he kept exclaiming.

"Come, let us pass," said the captain, a little impatiently, for the morning had dawned, and rays of soft, rosy light flushed the sky, and fell trembling on the water. "Let us pass, we are not safe a minute here."

The negro stood aside, shaking with grief, and when the funereal group had passed him half a dozen paces, he followed it with his head bowed down, and his clasped hands falling heavily before him. Thus he stood till the body was placed in its shallow grave, but when the first shovelful of earth was lifted, he came forward with both hands extended imploringly, and pushed the spade back. An orange tree stood near, on which the yellow fruit and white blossoms hung clustering together among the fragrant leaves; the negro went to this tree, seized one of the most richly laden boughs, and tore the blossoming branches away with both hands. Then he gathered them eagerly up, carried them to the grave, and over the body of his mistress he scattered the flowers till the turf all around was flooded with fragrance, like an altar at some holy festival.

When this was done the poor fellow drew back, and covering his face with his hands, stood trembling in all his limbs till the sailors had done their work, and dragged some shrubs and vines over the earth under which his murdered lady—more fortunate than thousands massacred that fatal night—had found a death shelter.

The sailors moved away from the grave they had made, but the negro did not look up, and they started for the boat, leaving him behind. Then the stillness aroused him, and as the party neared the shore, he followed with a look of painful entreaty in his face, begging to go with them to the ship.

The captain made a prompt motion for him to come on; but gesticulating energetically for them to wait, he ran back to the spot where they had first seen him, stooping downward, he began to tear up the earth with both hands, flinging the leaves and sods on one side in wild haste, only pausing to entreat their patience, with a pitiful glance of the eyes. At last he dropped on his knees, lifted something from the hole he had dug, and came forward with the moist soil dropping from his hands, which were clutched tightly around a bronze box. He followed the men into the boat, and sat down hugging the box to his bosom, and muttering to himself in hurried, eager words, which no one present understood.

When they reached the ship the negro climbed up the sides like a cat. Once on the deck, he ran back and forth, searching every corner. Then, with a despairing cry, he sprang upon the bulwarks, lifted the box over his head, and poised himself for a plunge.

The captain saw this desperate attempt, threw both arms around the negro, and dragged him back upon the deck.

The poor fellow scrambled to his knees, and looking up with pitiful abjectness, said:

"He is not here—the young master is not here; you said he was."

"Get up and come this way, my poor fellow!" said the captain, touched by the humble pathos of his disappointment.

The negro sprang up and seized the box, which had fallen with a crash on the deck.

"I come, master, I come."

"Hush!" said the kind-hearted sailor, pointing to his berth as they entered the cabin. "Hush! and tell me if that is your young master."

The negro drew in his breath with a sob, and scarcely seemed to respire after that. He crept close up to the berth, and looked down upon the boy with a glow in his black face that it is impossible to describe, for every ugly feature quivered with tenderness, while his eyes filled with light, like those of a Newfoundland dog when he has done brave work for his master.

"What will you do with us, strange master?" he said at last, addressing the captain in a humble whisper. "Not send us back yonder?"

He made a motion toward the town with his hand, and a slow horror crept over his face.

"No, my poor fellow, I will take the child to my own thrice-blessed land, if there is no one left to claim him."

"And Jube—let him go too. If the strange master wants a slave, Jube is strong, like a lion, and honest as a dog."

"Poor fellow!"

"See if Jube is not honest," he added, pressing the bronze box between his hands, and forcing some secret spring to recoil. "They told Jube to keep them, and he did. The master went back after mis—went after them. Jube wanted to go with him, but the master said, 'No, stay on the island, and guard that;' so Jube staid, waiting—waiting—waiting for master to come with mistress and the little boy. He never come—never—never will come again. The mistress sleeps! but where shall Jube go to find him, and give back the box?"

"My poor fellow, I fear your master is dead, from some words I gathered from the boy; I am almost sure of it."

"You will take the little boy and Jube away?" said the negro, anxiously, still holding the box half-shut between his hands.

"If no one comes to claim him or you, I will."

The lid of the box flew open, and a ray of sunshine from the cabin window flashed upon the jewels with which it was filled—diamond necklaces, bracelets flaming with rubies and emeralds, ropes of oriental pearls, and armlets flashing like rainbows, broke the sunshine into sparkles of fire.

Mason looked wonderingly on the eager face of the negro.

"And this treasure—did it belong to your master?" he questioned. "Was it to guard this, you hid in the chaparral at White Island?"

"All his; more, more, much more in the great house out there; but heavy gold—too heavy—we had to leave it and go back. He went—wouldn't take Jube—master went, but never he comes to see if Jube is faithful!"

"And all this belongs to the little fellow yonder. God help him!"

"You take little boy—take the box, and take Jube; he gives you all!"

Jube closed the box, dropped on both knees, and held it up.

Captain Mason hesitated, looked at the sleeping child and its strange guardian, shrinking from the trust which chance had imposed upon him. But he felt that a sacred duty was placed before him, from which no honest man should wish to retreat.

He took the box, but as his hands touched the metal a cold chill crept to his heart, and a mist floated before his eyes—an unstable, reddish mist, such as floods a room when the light is filtered through crimson drapery.

Perhaps the red curtain had fluttered before the cabin window; but if so, he felt the startling effect without knowing its cause, and the box shook in his hands, till the jewels within gave forth a faint sound.

"You will take us," pleaded the negro, frightened by the change in Captain Mason's countenance.

"Yes," answered the brave man, casting off the feeling that had seized upon him; "I accept the trust; God has placed it in my hands. As I discharge it, may he prove merciful to me and mine."

The captain spoke to himself, and from the feelings that filled his heart, rather than in reply to the negro; but the expression of his face was full of grand resolve, which the slave could read better than language. So he looked on with a glow of satisfaction while the box was packed up among the most valuable property the captain possessed.

All this time the cabin door had been ajar, and but for the excitement consequent to the scene, Captain Mason might have heard cautious steps creeping down the stairs, and the suppressed breathing of a man who skulked on the lowest steps, with his greedy eyes fixed on the jewels, as they flashed that one minute in the negro's hands. The listener waited until he saw the treasure put safely away, and heard the captain's promise. Then he went up the steps, two at a time, with soft, cautious leaps, like those of a fox, and when the captain came on deck, his mate was busy superintending the boat, as it was hauled to its fastenings.

CHAPTER IV.

THE FAITHFUL SLAVE.

In France, the awful strife of the Revolution had sprung out of oppressions heaped by one class upon another, from century to century, until the people began to comprehend the powers that lay in mere physical strength, and hurled themselves in a phrensy of hate on their oppressors. But even Paris, whose awful example had run like wildfire all over France and its dependencies, plunged into its carnival of blood with far less ferocity than marked this outbreak of Negroes in St. Domingo. In Paris, it was an upheaving of classes, marked and established by men of kindred blood, and born to the same soil. A struggle of men clamorous for their birthright of freedom, which they were determined to wrest from the strong hand of power.

Ages of oppression could not be hurled off thus suddenly, without horrible carnage. But there, it was the people against a government—white men struggling against white men. In a mighty effort to upheave the foundations of despotism, the people grew mad. In their ardor for liberty, and in the ignorance of her very visage, they trampled her in the dust, setting up red handed murder in her place, dealing death on every hand, as they hurled themselves with mighty force on their oppressors and trampled upon them with that ferocious hate continual wrongs will ever engender. But in the hot tropics, this struggle became a war of races, the most fierce, terrible, and relentless that humanity has yet known. It became a war of blacks against whites. Slaves against their masters. Where hate and ignorance hurled their massive strength against luxurious refinement. The brightest features of this horrible struggle were, the murders that gave Paris so many blood red pages in history, pages that all her after greatness and glory will never have power to wash white.

The massacre of St. Domingo was one of intense hate. The black slave, brutalized by the chains he wore, stood on every hearthstone ready for revenge on his white master. That which followed was not merely a massacre but a hurried carnival of ruin, a riot of awful passions, of atrocities for which there is no language, and from which the imagination revolts with sickening inability of comprehension.

Of all the horrors perpetrated in the French Revolution, which was one great horror in itself, that of St. Domingo was the most brutal the most demoniac. And such a war of races—a war between white men and negroes must ever be. With the despotism of long established power, luxurious ease, and pampered intelligence, opposed to the hot blood of Africa, scarcely subdued from its first savage state, fired by the memory of slave ships, chains, starvation, barter, and above all, the wild freedom which preceded these wrongs, who can wonder at the scenes which made that lovely island a purgatory of crime.

But these scenes no human being can ever describe. It would require a pen of adamant and the heart of a fiend to depict a single act of that fearful outbreak.

All the night, and deep into the sweet rosiness of the morning the terrible strife raged on in that doomed city. But in the broad day these black savages began to retreat from their ghastly orgies, and, for a time, the delirium of murder waned from its climax. The thirst for rapine slackened to a degree, and the monsters who had found this ferocious pastime full of intoxication, grew sluggish like wild beasts satiated with blood.

Some of these wretches lay down in the public streets, and fell asleep in the hot sun; others huddled together in torpid masses and sunk into stupor, dreaming of coming nights, which should give them a new riot of blood and fire. Stumbling over these, fierce crowds of untired demons kept on their work, stabbing right and left in brutal wantonness, for a lack of victims, and sickening the air with boasts of hideous acts performed in the night, and which another night should witness. Never on this earth had a scene more revolting presented itself to the beautiful sunshine.

But human nature is not all vile, and even among those ignorant, ill-used blacks, germs of compassion, tenderness, and good faith are found, redeeming, in a degree, the harrowing cruelties of the many. Among these good men—good in spite of ignorance and wrong endured—was the black man Jube. If ever faithfulness, natural feeling, and a simple sense of honor, dwelt in a human being, these feelings throve in the broad, cloudy bosom of the slave, and many another household servant became a household saviour in that cruel time.

While his little master was wrapped in the deep slumber which follows exhaustion, the negro had besought permission to go on shore and search for his master. Captain Mason, in his generous pity of the poor fellow, sent the boat back to the place it had reached the night before, to lie in wait for the negro while he searched around the palm trees and the neighboring chaparral for some traces of the noble master who had won his whole savage heart by great kindness.

The men who waited in the boat saw him wandering along the shore in a dejected attitude, for a long time. At last he came near a great spreading aloe, whose broad under leaves were half buried in the sand. Those who watched, heard a low, wailing cry, and saw the negro fall upon his knees, and rock to and fro in an agony of grief over some object concealed behind the aloe.

"He's found something that's cut him down like grape shot," said one of the sailors, flinging a quid of tobacco, which he had just cut for himself, back into his box, and closing it softly.

"Such a scream as that is enough to take a man off his tobacco for a month," answered another tar, taking off his tarpaulin, and wiping his bald head with the sleeve of his jacket.

"Supposen we pull in and see what it is?" said Rice.

"No; the captain told us not to go ashore. Some of

them tarnal niggers 'ed get hold of the boat, spite of us," answered the old tar.

"But we'll row up into shallow water, and one of us can go see what's the matter, and the rest 'ell take care of the cutter. Every thing seems to be still along there, not a nigger in sight," answered Rice, who commanded the boat.

The boat was urged into water so shallow that one of the sailors rolled up his duck trousers and stepped in, wading easily ashore. With a long, rolling step he swung himself forward up the beach, and soon found Jube on his knees by the body of a dead man, who lay in the gaunt shadow of the aloe, pierced through the heart, with a spear broken short in the wound.

Jube looked up, his black face wet with tears, his great hands clasped and pressed downward in the sand.

"It is him. Me has found the master," he said in broken English. "Cold! cold! oh, so dead!"

The sailor looked down into the calm, aristocratic face of the dead patrician—for such the man evidently was—no marble could ever have been more finely cut, or coldly pale than those features. But for the masses of glossy hair and the black eyes, that remained partly open, the idea of some perfect specimen of sculpture would have been complete.

Jube unclasped his great hands, and with a reverential touch attempted to close the eyes.

"It's of no sorts of use," said the sailor, "you poor heathen nigger you. It ain't possible to shut them eyes now; they'll stay wide awake till the judgment day. All we can do is to dig a trench here, close by this thing with the notched leaves, and lay him in. Come, bear a hand, and I'll help you, if you are black; this ain't no time to be perticular, besides I've kinder took a notion to you, anyhow."

Jube did not comprehend many of the words, but he understood the gestures, and went to work, raining great tears on the sand as he scraped it up.

The sailor fell to, and worked vigorously, comforting the negro, in his rough way, all the time. At last a trench of some depth was dug, and the sailor bade Jube help him lift the body into its poor resting-place. Then Jube began to sob, and tremble through all his massive frame, but he obeyed meekly. The garments upon the body were rich and of value. That sailor only got ten dollars a month for his hard labor, but he never thought of taking a fragment of those rich clothes, nor attempted to examine the pockets, though a clink of gold, as they lifted the body, told him that what might have been wealth to him was there. As for Jube, poor fellow, he scarcely knew what money meant, and if he had, would have guarded that about his master's person with his life.

So they lifted that proud and noble man from the red sand where he had been murdered, and laid him in the best grave they had the power to make. Jube tore away one of the great aloe leaves, and laid it over the white face, moaning like a wounded creature, as he shut it out from his own sight; but he shook so violently, that the sailor, with rough kindness, bade him go away, while he filled in the grave, and evened the sand. So Jube sat down in the shade of the aloe, and covering his face with his hands, sat still waiting.

When that boat neared the vessel, Jube saw his young master leaning over the bulwarks, and watching it with longing impatience.

"Jube, oh, Jube! why did they not come? I thought they would both be with you!" he cried, in a voice of keen disappointment. "Come up, come up, and tell me; the time has seemed so long."

Jube climbed up the rope ladder very slowly, with his black face bent toward the water. At last he stood on the deck, his heavy shoulders drooping, his eyes cast down, and his great bare feet trembling on the boards they pressed.

"Jube, Jube! tell me where they are? Why did mamma go away, and not call me? It wasn't kind, Jube."

"Mistress always kind, very kind, little master," stammered Jube, trying hard to control the tremulous motion that contracted his heavy lips.

"But where? Is she with papa?"

"Yes, little master. She—she is with papa, sure."

"Jube, did they both go home and leave me?" questioned the child, with tears in his eyes. "Did they, Jube?"

"No, little master, they didn't do that; how could they?"

"Well, then, where are they?"

"Not in the old home, be sure, not there; bad slaves, bad negro there."

"But are they safe?"

"Yes; safe."

"On shore?"

"Yes, little master, safe on the shore."

"But when will they come after us, Jube? I do so want to see them. Mamma was so tired she couldn't say good-night, and papa—I feel very, very unhappy about papa; he never left me so long before."

"But he couldn't help it, little master; sure he couldn't."

"I know that. Of course he couldn't; but, oh! when will he come? Jube, Jube, my heart aches so!"

"Jube's heart aches, too."

"Does it, Jube, like mine—heavy, heavy; and when I ask you about them, it aches worse? Dear old Jube, I won't do it. You shall see how bravely I can wait."

The child took one of Jube's hard hands in his, as he spoke, and led the negro away.

"Why, how you shake, Jube! What for? I never felt you shake so before!" he said, laying his other delicate hand caressingly over that of the black man's.

"Jube helped row the boat, little master, and it is hard work."

"But you are so strong, Jube; strong as a lion, and as brave; papa said so."

"Did he say that, little master; did he?"

"There, you are shaking again! Sit down, Jube. Don't be afraid; I won't ask any thing. There, lean your head against the mast; I will watch for them while you rest."

"No, don't watch. They won't come yet—not yet."

"Not before night, perhaps."

Jube closed his eyes heavily, and groaned.

It was mournful—the sight of that strange child, sitting upon Jube's knee and watching the shore with a trusting, earnest hope that his father and mother would seek him over the water where she had fallen asleep and floated away, but would be sure to come back when papa was found. The child said this a hundred times, as he patted the hard palm of the slave with his little hand, while Jube answered bravely, each time, "Oh, yes,

Master Paul, sometime they shall see us again. That's what the captain was saying to me just now. I hope it's true, little master; for your sake I hope he knows."

When he had done speaking, Jube would turn his head quite away, and shake the tears from his eyes, while the boy fell to his patient watch again.

CHAPTER V.

THE SEARCH FOR GOLD.

PAUL saw that questions wounded his black friend, and fell into silence, thinking of his parents with mournful yearning, but not mentioning them again.

It was a long, dreary day; but the sunset came at last, flooding the harbor with crimson, which made the water look ensanguined like the land. One by one the lights of the town began to flame out again, and hoarse sounds mingled with the surf of the tide. Now the boy became restless, and his eyes began to gleam impatiently.

"Jube, dear Jube, let us go ashore with a big boat, and bring them away! don't you hear the noise—don't you see how the fire flashes. They'll be hurt, Jube, and we shan't be there to help them."

Thrasher, the mate, was passing as the boy said this; he paused, and patted the little fellow's head.

"Who is it you want to help, my little man?" he said.

The child shrunk against his black guardian, and

looked up with such gentle earnestness that Thrasher's eyes fell under the glance.

"We want to go after *them*, monsieur. My papa and mamma; she couldn't wait for me, because papa wanted her, and so rowed away after him. But she sent dear old Jube to stay with me, didn't she Jube?"

He lifted both hands, and pressed the palms lovingly against the black cheeks of the slave, with a childishness which was the more touching because of its mournful trust.

"So you think your mother has gone back to the shore again?" said Thrasher, whose attention to this child was singular, for he was in no way a man of fine sensibilities, and had received the boy, and, afterward, the slave, rather grudgingly.

"Yes," answered Paul; "after papa lay down to rest, you know, mamma wanted to go back there, and struggled, and cried; but they wouldn't let her. You might know she'd be off the minute she woke up and found the captain had left her with a boat all to herself; but she's a long time. Don't you think it's a long time. I'm so tired of waiting."

"And who was your mamma, my little man?"

"My mamma! she was a beautiful lady, oh! *so* beautiful! I know that's true, because papa told her so every day, when she put the red roses in her hair that Jube brought. You remember, Jube?"

"Yes, little master, I remember; but turn your eyes away, I can't bear 'em just now."

"And where did your father live?" persisted the mate, feeling his way adroitly, as a pointer scents his game.

The child pointed toward the town.

"In a large house?" said Thrasher.

"The biggest house on the island," answered Jube, true to the instincts of his class.

"And they drove your master away like the rest?"

"Like the meanest of them all. It was his own slaves began. They knew of his gold, and that he wanted to send it off to some other country."

"He was rich, then?"

"Rich—no man like him in all Domingo! It was a great family—six brothers; they all gathered up their gold and brought it to my master's, ready to be put on board some ship—this one it may be. I had care of the gold, but the boxes were heavy, and the other slaves guessed what was in them, and told about it. But they did not know where it was hid, for my master and his brothers only went with me to the cellar. It was a heavy lift for gentlemen like them, but we got it all into the vault, and heaped stones and rubbish against the door. They meant to move it that very night. A boat was ready to carry it to White's Island. The day before, masters and I went there, and dug a pit to bury it in."

"And did you take it there?" asked the mate, with suppressed eagerness.

"No, surely—no!" answered the slave, with a sudden gleam of caution. "The patriots fell upon us—they began to burn and kill without warning. My master sent me to the boat, and told me to wait till he came with the mistress; but they fired the wharves, which made the water one blaze of light; and I could not come near the shore, try as I would. So at last I went to the island, and waited; but instead of my master—oh! you know what came there!"

"But the gold—did any one find the gold?"

"How do I know?"

"And the house—was it burned?"

"No; little master says they were dancing, and shouting, and drinking wine from the cellars when the family was driven out."

"And your master, where is he—his brothers, what became of them?" questioned the mate, so excited that his voice grew hoarse.

"Hush," said Jube, glancing at the boy.

"All?" whispered Thrasher.

"All, master."

"Where did you say the house stood?"

"Yonder, on the edge of the town; you can see its white walls in the sunset behind the mango trees."

"What, that house? I know it, I have passed its gardens a hundred times."

"Oh, I shall never pass them again," said Jube, with tears in his eyes.

"Oh yes; papa will come after us, don't say that, Jube," whispered the boy.

The mate, who had taken so much interest in them both, now turned abruptly away, and began to pace the deck, with the quick, heavy tread of a man who thinks excitedly. At last he paused, stood looking over the bulwarks awhile, and then went below.

The captain was in his cabin when the mate entered rather abruptly.

"Captain Mason," he said, "you had the luck to do some good on shore last night, what if I take a turn with three or four of the men? The black rascals will be at their work again, no doubt

The captain looked up surprised. It was the first instance of humanity he had ever known in his mate.

"Go by all means," he said; "pick your men and God speed you!"

Thrasher did not start so promptly as his eagerness seemed to promise. He was a long time lowering the boat, and paused more than once to cross-question the slave and the little boy, always managing to gain some fresh knowledge with every innocent answer he received.

At last, after the night had set fairly in, he descended to the boat, followed by four stout men, selected from the crew. The boy watched his movements with anxious eyes, and Jube seemed troubled as the boat glided off into the twilight.

They reached the shore, Thrasher and his crew, without molestation; a broken attempt at riot had been made early in the evening, but the blacks were besotted with a carousal of blood which had now lasted forty-eight hours, and fell into sluggish inactivity; so the band of sailors, always popular men with the blacks, made their way safely enough up to the walls of the white villa, which Jube had pointed out from the ship. It was a vast pile, built low on the ground, but covering a spacious area, and enclosing a court, overrun with flowers, that filled the air with fragrance, trampled and torn as they had been.

It was one vast scene of desolation. The broad gates were flung open, the trees that overhung them were broken, and their branches trailed on the ground; while a host of rude feet had trampled the luscious fruit upon the pavement of the court. Among the roses, and passion-flowers, and cape-jessamines that trailed along the court, a fountain flung up jets of pure water; but its basin of white marble was clouded with broad crimson stains, that all the crystal springs on earth would never wash out. Over the arched entrances that led to the separate apartments of the house, lamps of colored glass were swinging exactly as they had been lighted when the family were surprised by the murderers, fleeing from them only to meet a more terrible fate outside the walls. No one had cared to put the lamps out, so they burned on through the daytime, and into this second gloomy night.

The mate and his men stood a moment in the court, not to breathe its delicious atmosphere, but to take their bearings, as he said, with unseemly spirit. Lights burned in a few of the windows, and he saw by the gossamer draperies, and silken gleam within—for the latter shone richly through a lattice-work of flowers which filled the verandas—that he was near that wing of the vast building usually occupied by the family, now utterly dispersed, save one little child and a single slave.

"From these rooms there should be some passage leading to the cellars," reasoned the mate, as he mounted a flight of marble stairs that led to the first gallery, and was followed by his men, whose heavy footsteps broke the bell-like fall of the fountain with their coarse noise.

The work of desolation was complete in those vast saloons. The broad silken divans were trampled over by the tracks of naked feet, left on the delicate fabric in long trails of soot. Chandeliers of frosted silver, and lamps of delicate alabaster, were torn down and overturned, with their wax candles, broken and trampled upon the floor, and perfumed oil dripping along the pure marble. Many of the lace window-curtains were torn to shreds; others were gathered up and twisted in soiled wisps over the cornices; some still floated in gossamer softness over the windows, through which orange branches, heavy with bloom and golden with fruit, looked in, rustling to the night wind with sweet, lulling sounds.

The men passed through these saloons, trampling many a precious thing under their feet, which a delicate feminine taste had gathered to beautify the dwelling. They rushed through the broad saloons, and into the more private apartments—apartments in themselves so pure and spotless, that the insurgents had turned from them, as fiends might be supposed to shrink away from the resting-place of angels. The couches were untouched, and white as snow; flowers stood, but half withered, on the marble consoles; a few ornaments, dropped on the floor, bespoke some haste, but no violence. One of the sailors crushed a string of pearls under his foot, and ground it to powder upon the marble floor. Another tangled his boot in a web of costly lace, that had been hastily taken from a drawer and dropped in the terror of a sudden assault. The man tore it away from his boot with a smothered growl, and the party went on, looking cautiously back to be sure that no one followed.

The mate had guessed well. He found a passage leading from one of the lower galleries into the cellar, which was now half flooded with wine that had been left to flow from the reeking casks without check. Here the blacks had held a grand carouse after the massacre under the palm trees. Bottles had been dashed against the walls, and the fragments were trodden into the earth, which sent up mingled fumes of wines and liquors, with a strength that almost stifled even those tough sailors.

Plashing across the moist floor till his boots were red with wine, the mate found a pile of rubbish heaped against the wall. He held up a little silver lamp, which had burned its perfumed oil long after the fair hand was cold that filled it, and bade the men go to work. He spoke in a hoarse whisper, that almost startled himself.

The bricks and loose stones flew right and left, revealing a low iron door. The foremost man swung the crowbar over his head to dash the door in, but that instant Thrasher seized him by the arm. The man turned angrily around. Then, struck by the dead whiteness of Thrasher's face, glanced over his shoulder, and the iron fell heavily from his grasp.

CHAPTER VI.

THE FLOGGING.

They were far out to sea, the New England brig which lay in the harbor of Port au Prince on that terrible night, with the unhappy and helpless creatures who had found protection under its flag. Thrasher, who was the commander now, sat in his cabin at breakfast. He held a cup of coffee in one hand which seemed to have excited his disfavor, for setting it on the table and dashing the spoon so angrily into the coffee that it scattered the drops all around, he called out,

"Come here, you brat."

Paul, the little boy whom Captain Mason had saved, came reluctantly forward, his black eyes heavy with fear, and his delicate limbs trembling, as you see those of an Italian greyhound when driven into the cold.

Why don't you move—what do you stand there shaking like a thief for?"

These coarse words were made even more brutal by the base French in which they were uttered. At any time the boy could with difficulty have understood them; in his fright he could only stand still, with his terror stricken face turned away from the man who persecuted him.

"Why don't you move, I say?" repeated the commander.

"What for, monsieur—what shall I do?" asked the child.

"What shall you do?" answered the man, mimicking the gentle terror in the child's voice with a rough drawl of mockery. "What shall you do? why go to Jube, your father, and tell him to come here this instant! I'll teach him to send coffee like that to a gentleman's table. Bah, it's bitter as gall and thick as mud. Go call your father, I say."

"My father!" said the boy—"my father!" and his beautiful eyes were instantly flooded with tears.

"Yes, that nigger, Jube."

"But Jube is our slave, not my father."

"What! don't let me hear you tell that again or I'll give you a taste of the cat-o-nine-tails, no humbug with me, now I tell you "

The boy shrank back, but gleams of fire shot through

the tears that still trembled in his eyes; he felt that the man was insulting him, but did not quite comprehend how.

"Go call your father, I say," repeated his tormentor.

"I'll call Jube if you want me to," said Paul, with the dignity of a little prince, "but if I were to call ever so long my father—oh, my father!—will never, never come."

The pale face of the child burned red as he began to speak, but it was pallid again before he closed, and his proud voice broke into sobs.

"Take that, and mind how you howl when I speak to you again," cried the tyrant, giving that pale cheek a blow with the palm of his hand.

The little fellow staggered back and uttered a faint cry, but in an instant the dignity of blood aroused itself even in that childish heart. He stood up bravely, pride of race sparkling through his tears.

"I am not a slave, and you have struck me."

The mate laughed.

"Well done, my little bantam rooster, give us another fling."

The boy's face flamed red under the insulting laugh.

"I am only a little boy; besides, papa says gentlemen never fight with their fists, so if I were a man it would be all the same—but Jube can fight like you—he knows how—yes, I'll call Jube."

"Not till I've knocked all the infernal pride out of your little body," exclaimed Thrasher, starting up and making a dash at the boy.

He was too late. The little fellow had cleared the cabin stairs with the leap of a fawn, and rushing across the deck where Jube was standing, seized him by the garments.

"Jube, good Jube, you can fight—that man downstairs wants you—he struck me here on my face, the very spot my mother kissed—with his hands so—he struck me."

There was no need for the boy to say this, for three blood red finger marks glowed like living fire across his delicate cheek.

The gladiator broke into Jube's eyes as he saw these marks. His hand clenched and unclenched itself, and he ground his white teeth in ferocious rage. The savage African was fully aroused in him then.

"Look," he said, towering upward, till his athletic person was revealed in all its powerful proportions—"look, your master has struck my master's son—I'll kill him!"

"You will, ha!" cried the loud voice of Thrasher, who had followed the boy on deck. "You will, lump of ebony, will you? Well, let's begin at once. I say, Rice, take that fellow to the rigging, and give him a couple of dozen. I'll let him know that white folks have the say here."

Jube did not understand this order, for it was given in English, but he guessed something of the truth when the group of sailors, that had stood looking on, broke up in a commotion, and two of the strongest came toward him menacingly.

"What is it, tell me—what are you going to do with Jube?" inquired the boy, going up to Rice, who, with all the men who had been trading to St. Domingo for years, had a rude knowledge of French.

"Go away, shaver, get down below, nobody wants to hurt you, and if they did I wouldn't let 'em by jingo!

but the nigger there, mutinied, and he'll have to catch it."

"Don't, don't hurt Jube," cried the boy in an agony of fear, "what has he done?"

"He's threatened the captain—that is, he's threatened the one who took the captain's place, and that 'ere's mutiny on the high seas, do you understand?"

The sailor put Paul aside as he gave the desired information, and joined his comrade who had seized upon Jube, who inquired fiercely what they wanted with him.

"Don't stand to talk, but lash the nigger up, and give him an extra dozen for his impudence!" shouted the captain; "no parley, but go to work."

While Jube stood half at bay, doubtful of the evil that threatened him, the two sailors sprang upon him, and began to take off his outer garments, while half a dozen others stood ready to aid them, should the poor fellow resist. There was a desperate struggle, but it lasted only a few moments; great as Jube's strength was, it proved nothing opposed to the powerful force arrayed against him. In a few moments the poor fellow stood with his bare shoulders glistening in the sunshine, and all his muscles quivering with the fierce restraint that had been put upon them. Each hand was manacled by the iron gripe of his captors, who were stern but not mocking, while Thrasher, who looked on with a cold smile, muttered:

"Yes, my fine fellow, we'll teach you the difference between this deck and Port au Prince—here white folks are white folks."

Paul stood looking on, wild with terror. "What

were they doing? Would they kill Jube before his eyes? Had he been the cause of this?"

The men dragged Jube away, heedless of his broken cries. With them a punishment at the rigging was no very extraordinary occasion, and when exercised on a negro was not altogether a disagreeable excitement But Rice, more merciful than the rest, came back, and attempted to persuade the child away from the deck, but Thrasher confronted him at the gangway, and ordered him back.

"Let the youngster stay and see the fun; it'll do him good," he said; "if he keeps up that whimpering I'll give him a dose, too."

Rice stood a moment with something of revolt in his eyes, but seemed to think the question not worth a quarrel, and slowly retreated, dragging the child with him. The mate did not deem it prudent, perhaps, to urge the seaman too far, so Rice withdrew to the remotest part of the deck, and lifting the child in his arms, pretended to point out a ship which he persisted was hovering on the line of the horizon.

But this humane ruse was of no avail. With the little heart quivering in his bosom like a wounded bird, and every sense awake to the danger of his friend, Paul was not to be interested in any thing. His white face was turned anxiously over the sailor's shoulder, and he listened keenly.

It came at last, a sharp, cutting twang. The boy uttered a shriek, and struggling from the sailor's arms, fell upon the floor, shuddering all over. Again, again, and again; harder, fiercer, and with a biting sharpness that made the blood curdle in that young heart, the blows fell, then a cry, shrill with agony.

The boy leaped to his feet, and breaking away from the kind hold of the sailor, went staggering across the deck, pale and wild, stung almost to death with the pain of those lashes.

The captain stood near the masthead, smoking a cigar. He did not lose a single puff—nay, between the lashes he would sometimes retain the smoke with his lips, and emit it enjoyingly, as the blows fell, thus keeping lazy time with the torture he was inflicting.

Half blind, almost dead, the boy came toward him, and fell at his feet, clasping his hands and holding them up in dumb, pitiful entreaty, for the voice was dead within him, and his pale lips uttered moans instead of words.

"Ha! you have come to, have you?" exclaimed the mate, taking the cigar from his mouth, and winding a loose fragment of tobacco leaf around it. "I thought as much. Well, never mind, the music's nearly half over now—then your turn shall come."

Those little hands dropped, and the child fell forward on his face; a faint quiver which followed each crack of the lash was all the sign of life he gave.

CHAPTER VII.

A REBELLIOUS SPIRIT.

THE threat of violence which Thrasher uttered against the delicate creature at his feet, might have been only an ebullition of his dormant hatred of the boy—the bitterest and most deadly hatred known to humanity—that of a bad man for the object he has wronged; but wanton or earnest, the threat had its effect, for Rice strode to Thrasher's side, and bending to his ear, whispered.

"I say, captain, we've had enough of this ere, I reckon. Jest order the men to unsling that nigger, or I will."

Thrasher took the cigar from his mouth, and held it smoking between his fingers.

"What's the meaning of this, Rice?" he said, mildly, knocking the loose ashes away with his little finger, as he eyed the seaman with a keen side glance.

"What I said afore; we've had enough of flogging for one day, at any rate."

"I'd do anything to oblige you, Rice, be sure of that, any thing but give up my authority before the men."

"The men don't know what I'm saying to you. Anyway, jest give orders for 'em to wait till we understand one another."

The mate lifted his hand, at which signal the man who had just raised the lash, which was growing red and wet in the sunshine, dropped it heavily. The thong fell upon the deck, leaving a crimson trail along the white boards, while its holder stood panting and out of breath from the violence of his exercise.

"Well now, Rice, what is the meaning of all this?" said the mate, a little anxiously.

"It don't mean nothing, only this, captin—I won't have that ere nigger struck another blow in this child's hearin'. As for the nigger hisself, I don't care a quid of tobaccer, but human natur' can't stand that sight—at any rate, I can't and won't—so if you expect me to keep a close jaw, order them to let the nigger down at once."

"Hush—speak lower, Rice. You see I must keep up my authority. You can understand that. I'd give the fellow up with pleasure to please you, Rice; but this is the first punishment on board since I came into the command."

"Since you came into the command—jest so."

"And if I give up now, it'll be all day with my authority; and that'll never do."

"There's something in that ere," answered Rice, with an uneasy hitch of his garments, "but then there mustn't be no more flogging afore this little chap, no how. I don't want to be obstroperous neither. Supposing you shut the fellow up, and keep him on bread and water a few days—I shouldn't mind that."

"But, he's a good cook—we can't spare him, Rice."

"Must," answered the sailor.

"Must," repeated the the mate, with a gleam in his side glance.

"Must," repeated Rice, settling his garments afresh.

The mate hesitated awhile, eyeing the sailor askance, but Rice stood solidly on the deck, looking him in the face as if certain of his answer.

"Very well, pass the order. Remember, I let off a dozen lashes, and give him irons, with bread and water, in exchange. Make that well understood."

"Aye, aye, never you fear," was the prompt reply.

"As for this imp of Satan," said the mate, spurning the prostrate boy lightly with his foot, "I'll deal with him."

"Don't do that, Mr. Thrasher; you've struck that ere

child once too often. Try it agin, and there ain't a man on board this 'ere brig as won't rise agin you."

"Indeed!" said Thrasher, closing his teeth hard, "and you——"

"I'll head 'em, and take you home in irons."

Thrasher turned a dull white, and, for an instant, a sound as if his teeth were beginning to chatter, came faintly through his lips, but he turned it off with a laugh.

"Hang me if I care what you do with the fellow or the boy. I only wish we had left them behind; that would have settled it once for all."

"But seeing as they're here, I won't stand by and have 'em murdered outright."

"Well, well, as you like; it won't pay for us to quarrel, Rice."

"Enough said, captain."

"Now I'll go down and finish my breakfast," said Thrasher, tossing the end of his cigar overboard. "Confounded coffee the fellow sent down; that was what commenced the row, I believe; but I'll try another cup."

"Aye, aye, better go down and leave the rest to me," said Rice, stooping tenderly over the boy. "Come, get up, my little chap; it's all over! No use wilting down in this way! poor fellow, poor fellow, how he shakes!"

The child, who had been lying with a hand pressed hard over each ear, lifted his head, and turned his white face on the seaman.

"Is it over? Have they killed him? Oh! Jube, Jube!"

This pathetic cry reached the unhappy man, who had just been taken down from his place of torture. With his helpless hands hanging loose, and the red drops falling from his shoulders, he came reeling across the deck, and lay down by the boy, like a great Newfoundland dog wounded unto death.

Paul received him with a gush of tears. He took the handkerchief of delicate cambric from his bosom, where it had rested sacred till then, for his mother had placed it there, and tenderly wiped the drops of agony that still hung on Jube's brow. The poor negro, always treated with gentle household kindness till then, moaned aloud, not with the pain—he was brave enough, poor fellow—but from a sense of the desolation that had fallen on his master's son.

"Oh, young master, young master, who will help you now when Jube has only the power of a dog left? never 'till now, never 'till now, was Jube striped with a whip! What will become of him? He had nothing but his strength, and they have taken that!"

"Come, come," said Rice, "it isn't all over yet, by a long shot."

The negro looked up with his heavy, bloodshot eyes, in which there was a gleam of patient heroism that touched the sailor greatly, while the boy grew faint and gasped for breath.

"Don't, don't," pleaded Rice, patting the boy gently with his rough hand. "As for you, cuffy, keep a stiff upper lip. I'm to put you in the hold, and feed you on bread and water; but I'll see that the handcuffs ain't too tight, and as for the grub, why some of us chaps will go on half rations to give you a meal now and then."

"I don't care about the place you put me in," said Jube, mournfully, "or what they feed me on. If they chain me down hands and feet I won't say one word; but the little master, what will they do with him?"

"Never you mind about that, cuffy; I'll see to him. He shall have enough to eat, any how."

"But that man—he'll strike poor little master again, and Jube chained down in the bottom of the ship."

The great tears rolled over Jube's face as he said this, and he shook violently.

"No," said Rice, with an honest sailor's oath, which was profane in its language, but noble in its meaning, "the captain shan't touch him agin, I give you my hand on it."

Jube took the rough hand in his trembling grasp and kissed it gratefully.

"Take me down, Mr. Captain, take me down; get out the irons; bring on the bread and water; you'll see that Jube will wear 'em, and sing like a bird, so long as you take care of *him*."

"That's hearty now," cried Rice, pleased to the depth of his really kind heart. "Just give up, and it'll be all the easier. I've had the bracelets on in my puppy days, over and agin. It aint nothing."

"I'm ready," answered Jube, making a brave effort to smile, and staggering to his feet, where he stood shaking all over from the shock of pain that had been given to his whole system. "I'm ready. Good-by, little master."

"Paul set up on the deck, and lifted his hands pitifully, while his pale, cramped features began to quiver with coming tears.

"Botheration, 'taint nothing. I'll smuggle the little craft down to see you every day, if not oftener. Do you hear that, shaver?"

Tears swelled into the boy's eyes, and he covered them with his hands, moaning painfully.

Rice was a good deal troubled that his efforts at consolation had so little effect, but all at once his face brightened, and thrusting a hand deep into the pocket of his trowsers, he brought forth a huge jackknife, and opened it temptingly.

"Look a here, little whipper-snapper, just look a here, no doubt about it, I'm a going to give you this very identical knife, I am, sure as a gun."

The boy took his hands away, and gazed wonderingly at the great, buck-horn handle, and the hooked blade, to which tiny fragments of plug tobacco clung lovingly.

"All right," he said, closing the blade with a jerk. "I thought you'd be surprised. Isn't it a sneezer? Where's your pocket?"

As Rice thrust the knife into the silken lined pocket of Paul's dress, the boy looked downward with vague interest; but, all at once, his face brightened. He snatched at the knife eagerly, and tried to open it.

"It's rather stiff, I reckon, for them little fingers," said Rice, opening the knife again; "but, never you mind, I'll drop a little lamp ile on the jint, and it'll open easy as whistling, it will."

"Is it strong—is it sharp?" cried the boy, touching the hooked blade with his delicate fingers. "Would it kill a man?"

"Why, Lord love yer eyes, yes! Jest turn the pint upwards, and it'd rip its way like blazes. But what der ye ask that for?"

"Jube," said the boy, in sad, earnest tones, holding up the knife, "if he strikes me again, and you are by, just take this and kill me at his feet. I'd rather die a thousand times than live to see you whipped for my sake."

"Give it to me," said Jube, with a gleam of his old African ferocity. "I'll use it, but not on you, little master—not on you!"

"Look a here," said Rice, hitching about uneasily in his clothes. "You jest let the boy's knife alone, will ye? I guv it to him for a plaything, and it's hisen, not yourn. Do ye want to be slung up again? Here comes the captin—now up with ye, for I must be cross as blazes, or he'll think we're confabulating something against him. Come, look sharp, nigger, I can't wait here all day for you to snivel over a flogging as you ought to be grateful for, 'cause you arned it." To this Rice added, in a low tone: "Look scared, as if I had been a worrying you tooth and nail, or he won't trust you with me." Then raising his voice, he went on abusing poor Jube, till the mate came forward with a smile upon his face.

"That's right, my good fellow, take him down. He'll be an example for the men. They're beginning to want one. Off with him—plenty of irons, and don't be too particular about the bread or the water either."

"Aye, aye, I'll see to him," cried Rice, ferociously. "Come, march, tramp—off with you, cuffy! You never seed sich a pair of bracelets as I've got for ye down below."

Jube kept his eyes bent to the deck, that no one might mark the ferocious hate that burned in them— hate that re-strung his nerves, and made them tough as iron.

"You'll learn to threaten me!" said the captain, scoffing at the negro, as he passed.

Jube did not lift his eyes, but passed on. Paul arose and followed.

"Hallo! what is the youngster after?" cried Thrasher.

"I want to go with Jube," said the boy, shuddering under the captain's eye.

"You want to go with Jube, ha!" cried the mate, mocking the gentle tones, which might have won pity from a Nero. "Well, you won't go with Jube, do you hear that? I aint likely to give up cook and cabin-boy, too, so just march for the caboose."

Rice turned back, leaving Jube near the gangway. "Look a here, captain," he said, in a low voice. "Don't put upon that little shaver so! It's too bad; he's a peaked child, just out of his mother's lap, and this ere sort of work will kill him sure as a gun."

"Well, if it does, Rice, what's the loss?"

"Wal, it'd be a good deal to me, anyhow. I've sort a took a shine to the boy."

"That's unfortunate," sneered the mate, "because I, being commander here, have just done the other thing."

"Hate him like pison—I knowed it from the first."

"Well, what of it?"

"Nothing—only as I've took a notion to him, and he kinder likes me, supposing you jest give in a trifle, and let the chap alone. I shall be much obleeged to you if you will."

Thrasher turned on his heel, saying, with assumed carelessness, for he did not like the gleam of those gray eyes, "Well, well, we'll talk about that another time."

"Aye, aye," responded the sailor, with a nod of the head, which had a meaning in it that Thrasher did not like.

CHAPTER VIII.

THE BOX OF JEWELS.

"I'LL have an end of this," said Thrasher, as he went into the cabin restless and anxious. Throwing himself on the locker, he began muttering to himself. "As for keeping this child to hang around my neck like a millstone, I never will. He's old enough to remember every thing; and if the negro tells tales he'll be sure to cherish them. What possesses Rice to rise up against me in this way? If he'd been quiet, I'd have had 'em both under water before half the voyage was over."

Thrasher lay awhile revolving these thoughts in his mind, without arriving at any satisfactory conclusion. At last, a new anxiety seized upon him; he started up, and went to the closet set into the wall, in which he had seen Captain Mason secure the box of jewels that Jube had placed in his keeping.

"It's fortunate I secured this," he muttered, taking a key from his vest pocket, and fitting it into the lock. "He didn't know I was on the watch, careful as he was. Ha, it's all here! and that nigger knows it as well as I do. He'll tell, and then Rice 'll take another hitch in the eternal rope that's being knotted around me. I would give any thing to know exactly what the fellow is at, but I won't ask questions, that's against my principles; they let out too much."

As he spoke, Thrasher sat down, placed the bronze box on his knee, and forced the lid open. Just as we have seen them before, the jewels lay huddled together, without cushions or caskets; but, here and there, a fragment of crimson or white satin clung to them as if they had been torn away from their cases in wild haste.

"Now, I dare say, this is worth lots of money, if one only knew about it," he said, taking up a necklace, formed in links of large, oblong opals, with rainbows breaking in fragments from their hearts, and rivulets of diamonds running around them. "How it glitters! This would be pretty for *her*. I wonder if she'd take it from me now? or warn me off as she did that evening? Well, I don't know about that—a poor wretch, with nothing but his good looks, and so on, to recommend him, is another thing from a fellow that can come to a woman with both hands full of yellow gold and such things as this. Wouldn't they blaze on that white neck! —such a neck, with shoulders that dimple like a baby's hand! I saw them once when she was dressed to go out with him. She little thought I was under the window, and that a corner of the paper curtain was turned up, just leaving a peep-hole. How softly the white dress was folded over her bosom. Lord, how my heart went down as she put on that lace cape, and fastened it with a wild rose that he had given her before my very face! No wonder I hated him! there isn't a man on earth that could have helped it. Handsome—was he really handsomer than I? did she love him so very much? Oh, how it blazes! These are real diamonds, no mistake about that. How the light rains from them! Oh, how I'd like to see it flashing on her neck, just as it was then, with two or three of these things in her yellow curls. Women like these gew-gaws; and she's fond of pretty things—like a child about them; besides, she'll be poor enough before I get home, she and the child— his child."

He crushed the necklace in his hand, as the image of a pretty, fair haired baby girl rose before him, and crowded it fiercely down into the box. "She'd be wanting some of them for her, I dare say. Well, perhaps that woman could do any thing with me; in fact, when I first knew her, any kind woman, from my mother down, would mould me as she liked, I was wax then; but after she married him—well, it's no use thinking what one has been, or how much better things might have turned out; there's iron enough in me now. Still, I loved her then well enough to go mad and run away from all that ever cared for me. I might have been a gentleman; the old folks educated me well enough for that or any thing else, but she drove me out before the mast. Storms and hardships was what I wanted; I got enough of it in the end. It made me tough and hard as the rocks we sometimes narrowly escaped. Cruel, too—every one says that—but I could be kind to her and the little girl, perhaps, if the mother loved me. If not, oh, how I should hate the blue-eyed imp."

These thoughts seemed to excite the man beyond any thing that persons knowing his stern character would have believed. His hands clutched and unclutched themselves in the jewels, his lips quivered, and alternate gleams of fire and clouds of mist chased each other in his eyes. He started up, thrust the box back to its closet, forgetting the fears that had urged him to seek for it, and putting the key back into his pocket went on deck. The first sharp gust of wind that swept his face carried off these feverish thoughts and he grew hard as rock again.

Paul was on deck, crouching down among the barrels and bales of merchandise that offered him friendly concealment. Wretched and heart-broken, the child watched for Rice. When he saw Thrasher, fear made him shrink together and hold his breath as if some wild beast were creeping along his path. After a little, the mate went down again and Rice appeared.

The boy crept from his hiding-place and came up to the sailor.

"What have you done with him? please tell me."

"Oh, here you are, as large as life," said Rice, who had missed Paul from the deck, and felt some relief at finding him alone and so quiet. "Done with him? why cleared out a snug harbor in the hold, and anchored him safe and sound. Come along, if you want to see."

"Oh, yes, yes, I want it so much. Is it dark?"

"Rayther, I should think."

"May I hold your hand?"

"Aye, aye, come along afore the captain knocks us all aback."

"Who goes there," cried out a voice from the cabin stairs.

"Nobody but Rice and this 'ere little shaver," answered Rice, facing round to meet Thrasher.

"Where are you taking him?"

"Nowhere just now—he wants to take a look out."

"Very well—pass on."

Thrasher went down to the cabin again; he had seen Rice as he led the boy across the deck, and understood the opposition which was going on to his wishes. The train of thought that had seized him while examining the jewels had not entirely passed away, but with it came others appealing to his worst passions, and mingling themselves, as evil things sometimes will, with much that was tender and pure in the man's nature. He was not all bad—what human being is?—but he was a strong man, and used his evil strength without scruple to secure the love, which was, in truth, wounding him daily with its hungry cries.

Thrasher was afraid of Rice, and with him fear was an incentive to action. Jube and the boy Paul were also sources of great anxiety. They might interfere with his one great hope, and utterly destroy the brilliant future that lay so temptingly before him. All this was food for thought, and made him more than usually morose.

The sensitive nature of the boy Paul had suffered acutely by the indignity that had been put upon him, and still more by the awful scene of Jube's punishment. But there was a noble spirit in that little frame, and though he shrank from encountering his enemy, it was not from a cowardly feeling, but as a brave man may evade a wild beast that possesses a hundred-fold of his own physical powers. No amount of punishment would have induced the child to submit meanly; but he was a creature of exquisite refinement, and had, all his little life, been shielded from the first approach of sorrow. Within the last few weeks, he had been cast headlong into the boiling vortex of the most terrible scenes that ever disgraced humanity—scenes that drove many a stout man insane, and left a whole population at the mercy of savage, maddened slaves. He, a young, sensitive child, brought up in luxury, shielded from the very breath of a flower if it was not grateful to his fine sense—loved by his parents—idolized by a host of servants—had struggled through death, and horrors sharper than death, to find himself worse off a thousand times on board that brig, than any of his father's slaves had ever been.

And now his only friend was torn away, and cast into the black depths of the hold, smarting with pain, writhing under the ignominy of a first blow, and chained hand and foot like a mad dog. If little Paul had known that the captain would kill him, I think he might have found his way to that poor friend.

At last they were together, down in the black hollows of the ship, with scarcely a breath of air, and surrounded by a host of uncouth objects, which appalled them like the walls of a prison. They had no light, and the rush and gurgle of the waves sounded horribly distinct. Jube held up bravely after his little master came to bear him company. No groan escaped his lips, but he insisted on sitting up, and made Paul nestle close to him, striving to soothe and comfort the child, spite of his own keen suffering.

CHAPTER IX.

CHAINED IN THE HOLD.

CHAINED in the hold, drifting away—it was only after dark that Paul could visit his friend without fear of detection. On the third night, they were together in the hold. Thrasher himself had been down just before, and finding Jube without irons, had riveted them on his limbs with his own hands, so the poor fellow was bowed down with the weight of his chains, and could not even hold the child to his bosom when he came to share his solitude.

It was very dark, and Paul was compelled to feel his

way through the freight heaped up on each side the place where Jube was confined.

"Jube, Jube! do you hear?" he called out, in a frightened voice.

Jube lay still, for he was afraid of frightening the boy by the clank of his chains, but he called out softly, "Yes, little master, here I am, just here, don't hurt yourself against the boxes."

"Can't you come and help me, Jube; it's dark as midnight."

"Well, little master, it ain't just convenient this minute; but if you'll listen while I talk, and come by the sound, it'll bring you right straight to Jube."

"Yes—yes, I hear; keep speaking, Jube, but not too loud. What a noise the water makes to-night, and the ship pitches so I can hardly stand. Oh, here you are, dear Jube; just hold out your hands, to steady me. What's that?"

"Only the handcuffs; but don't you mind, they don't amount to much after all—screwed a little tight—but not unpleasant, if it wasn't for that."

"Chained you—chained you!" said the boy, in a voice of such keen anguish that Jube forced a little, hoarse laugh, in order to convince him that being chained hand and foot, in the black hold of a vessel, was rather a refreshing amusement than otherwise. "Why, it ain't nothing, little master, just see here!"

He tried to lift his hands, but the iron galled his wrists, and forced a groan from his brave heart.

"Oh, Jube, Jube, they will murder you!"

"Not they—why it's nothing."

"Let me help you hold the irons up, they drag on your poor hands—there, does that make them lighter?"

"A good deal little master; every thing is light when you come to see Jube."

The gentle boy had knelt down in the darkness, and was striving to hold up the chains that dragged in rusty links from the poor fellow's hands.

"Are you hungry, Jube?"

"No, not at all, little master; had a splendid dinner just now."

The poor fellow had just eaten half a cake of hard sea bread soaked in water.

"Because I've saved my dinner," said the child, "and we'll eat it together."

"Oh, little master, there never was but one angel like you that ever I saw."

"Mamma!" said Paul, softly, "you mean her, I know."

"Yes; who else?"

"I shall never be beautiful and kind like her, Jube—never! but, when she finds us, you will tell her how I have tried to be good and patient, Jube?"

"Yes, little master."

"How mournfully you say that. Are you crying, Jube?"

"Crying? no, no; don't you hear how I laugh?"

"That's worse yet; the chains are breaking your heart, Jube."

"No, I like 'em; they're a sort of company."

"Company!"

"Yes; when I'm all alone in the daytime, you know, I can jingle tunes with 'em."

"It's awful music, Jube; my heart trembles when I hear it. Besides, I cannot get close to you, the iron keeps me off."

"Just creep up to this side, little master, and lean against my shoulder; the feel of you gives me heart."

Paul crept close to his friend, and passed one arm over his chest as his cheek rested on the shoulder turned lovingly for its reception.

"How the water beats and roars," said Paul, clinging close to his friend; "it sounds like that night."

"Yes, I've been listening to it all day; sometimes it seems close, too, as if it would leap in and tear me to pieces; but that is when you are not here."

"How it moans, Jube!"

"Don't tremble, little master, it's only the water, and that isn't cruel like men."

"Hallo, here, havn't you a voice, cuffy? Here's some prog, and I've brought something to rig up a light that you can see to eat by."

It was Rice, with a tin basin in his hand half full of lard, in which a twist of cotton lay coiled like a serpent.

"There, just wait till I set this down shipshape, and you shall see what I've got; some boiled beef and lashings of grog; havn't wet my whistle to-day. Hallo, cuffy, what's this—a cargo of iron on board!—who did that ere?"

"*He* did it," said Jube, while Paul lifted his head, with hope in his eyes.

"*He* did it, did he!" Here the sailor emitted half a dozen heavy oaths, in broad English, which neither the boy nor Jube understood. "Just give us hold here; if I don't smash every link on 'em afore ten minutes is over, call me a land lubber that's afraid of his mammy. Hold out them hands, blackball. By jingo! can't do it without a hammer. Yes, this'll do; smash, here it goes! You like that music, my little commodore, does ye? Now out with yer feet, blackball, and when the captain comes, tell him I did it."

Jube, who had been painfully cramped for hours, stood up and stretched himself, as the irons fell with a clank to his feet.

"It seems kind o' refreshing, I reckon," said Rice, bringing one keg forward, on which he placed his light, and another which was to serve as a table. "Where's that jackknife, whipper-snapper? Out with it, and cut up the grub. Set to, cuffy. Glory! how the ship rolls and pitches! We'll have work afore morning. The fellow will crowd all sail; he'll fetch the brig into the middle of next week at this rate. Never mind; set to, all hands, we may as well go to Davy Jones' locker with a full cargo on the stomach as with empty lockers."

Jube was nearly famished, notwithstanding his boasted dinner, and he accepted this hearty invitation with zest. Paul tasted a few mouthfuls of the food, but with strange hesitation, as if he were putting some restraint on his appetite. His own little store of provisions remained untasted, and he made no effort to bring it forth.

"Why don't you stow away?" asked Rice, cutting a lump of beef in two and splicing it, as he observed, to a piece of bread. "What are you afeared of?"

"I—I'd like to save a little, if you please," said Paul, timidly.

"Save a little! why, what's the use? There's plenty on board; I can get a double allowance any time."

"You can, and will you?" cried the boy, eagerly.

"Why, yes, but what for?"

"We may want it, who knows? The captain may forbid you to come here, and then Jube would starve."

"Well, that's sensible. It ain't likely to happen, but then there's no harm in a full locker. I'll bring down a bag of bread this minute if he's in the cabin—then there's plenty of oranges in the cargo; if you come to hunger, cuffy, you can stave in a box, and hide the boards. Now fall to, youngster. There's no fear of a famine."

The boy was very hungry, but it made him faint, rather than eager. Something seemed to excite him; perhaps it was the gathering storm, through which the brig labored heavily. Perhaps he had some vague, childish hope, scarcely understood by himself; certainly his eyes had never shone so brightly before. His face was that of a young hero preparing for battle.

The brig plunged and reeled more and more. Her timbers began to strain and creak; the waves leaped and howled against her sides like charges of cavalry in fierce action. The roar and boom of the storm was terrible.

The two men who sat together in the dim light, floating upon the basin near by, looked at each other. The negro's face was ashen gray; the sailor lost his ruddy color; but the boy's eyes grew bright as stars.

"It's on us—it's on us—and every stitch of canvas out!" cried Rice. "I knew he was acting like a fool, but didn't expect this. Splurge! heave! Crack—crack! Jerusalem! there goes the mainsail! Aye, aye."

The hoarse call of a trumpet rang through every corner of the brig.

"All hands on deck!"

"Aye, aye!" shouted Rice, kindling to his work; "keep a stiff upper lip, cuffy, and cheer the boy, for we are just as near Davy's Locker as any of us ever will be again!"

They saw him plunge onward through the reeling freight, and he was gone. The poor negro and the child were left alone, not quite in darkness, for the cotton wick still shimmered fitfully, and made the blackness beyond its little pale circle more dismal than ever. It seemed just enough of light to see each other perish by, and that was all.

Louder and fiercer grew the storm. The brig was tossed upon it like a handful of drift wood; every timber seemed to carry on a struggle by itself—every joint wrenched and tore against its fastenings. The strained rudder shrieked like a wild animal in the agonies of death. The hoarse cry of the trumpet sounded like a groan through the general turmoil. But all these sounds were nothing to the howl of the winds, and the great upheaving rout of the waters, as they swelled and mingled together in one tremendous uproar. The negro fell upon his knees, trembling and ashen; but the boy—the gentle, sensitive child—stood up, with a smile on his mouth and a beautiful brightness in his eyes.

"Don't be afraid!" he said, bending over the negro. "The God that took care of my mamma when she fell asleep, is here. Something tells me so."

The poor negro had no God of his own people to understand, so he hung upon the words that fell from those young lips with unreasoning trust. The dusky color came back to his cheek, and lifting his faithful eyes upward, he said meekly:

"If you say so, young master, I believe it. Jube go where you go; she'll be sure to want him, too."

A fierce plunge—a recoil—and the brig stood still, shivering in all her timbers, like a wild horse with its fore feet over a precipice. It was but an instant. Then a cataract of waters swept over her. She rolled upon her side, and could not right herself; a mighty throe, and she struggled back, working heavily. Another plunge—a crash—a despairing cry from overhead—and the boy started from his wrapt composure.

"Come, Jube, let us go up and tell them not to be afraid."

The crew had given up. One man, Rice, stood at the helm, resolute to meet death at his post when it came. Thrasher stood firmly, with the trumpet grasped in his right hand; but his face was like marble, and he gave no orders. The brig that he commanded was almost a wreck. The sails had been swept away; the mainmast was in splinters; not a vestige of her massive bulwarks was left. The men were grouped together in sullen despair. Nothing was to be done—they could only stand still and wait. With that tornado tearing through the mighty waters, and lashing them into great sheets of angry foam, there was no contending. They huddled together, that group of stout men, helpless as infants.

When despair was on every face, and the storm raged fiercest, that pale, Heaven-eyed boy, came up through the hatches, and stood among the sailors, smiling. He did not speak, but the sweet serenity of his face gave them courage.

The mainmast had fallen, dragging heavily on the ship. The last order of the mate had been to cut it away, but no one obeyed, and thus inevitable destruction lay before them.

"One more onset, my men!" cried Rice. "Clear away the mast and she will right herself."

"Jube, give me an axe, I will help!" cried Paul; and the beautiful courage that shone in his face inspired the men. They fell to work vigorously. The mast, with all its entanglement of cordage, plunged into the boiling sea, and the brig righted herself.

The storm was over, the dismantled brig still rode the waves, for the staunch timber of New England does not yield readily, and the strongest had been put to its test in that gallant craft. Jube was sent back to his imprisonment in the hold, where Paul sought him at every opportunity; but, from the night of the tempest, a strange animation had marked the boy, something which no one could understand.

"Jube," he said, having left the deck on the third night, when the sea was calm as if it had never known a tempest, and ten thousand stars broke their flickering gold on its waves. "Jube, it is time that we look for mamma. God has taken care of her, I know, but we must search and find her."

"Little master, I know where she is, we left her on White Island."

"And you did not tell me when I was so near; but we cannot be far off now, the storm drove us back. Jube, I've been watching for something to happen, for it is sure mamma wants us. Look behind that barrel, and see how much bread I've saved. Then the oranges Rice spoke of; he broke open a box, and I've got plenty."

"Well, little master."

"They've been working on the side of the ship to-day, and did not haul up the boat. That was what I've been watching for. Take the bread and the oranges, Jube, and let us go."

Jube arose, took up the little sack which the boy pointed out, and followed his young master without a question. They crossed the deck softly, dropped down the side of the vessel unseen, and with the knife which Rice had given him, Paul cut the boat loose from the ship.

The brig lay motionless, for she was still disabled, and the boat rocked lightly on the waves, breaking the starlight into golden ripples; thus the boat and the half wrecked vessel drifted apart. Three days of sunshine, and calm, lonely, bright days, in which these two child-like beings floated like people in a dream. The boy was in search of his lost parents, and looked out for them over the bright ocean with smiling and beautiful faith. The slave hoped nothing, sought for nothing. He was content by his young master's side. They had no compass, and but one pair of oars, which proved of little use, for the boat had no destination, nor its inmates the remotest knowledge of their own reckoning. Thus they drifted on three days without accident. No vessel hove in sight, and all was a clear, heavy calm. On the fourth day the bread and fruit were gone. Not a mouthful of food, not a drop of water, save the great deep, a draught of which would be delirium or death. The fifth day, and the pangs of hunger had crept steadily on, and gnawed at their vitals relentlessly. Paul no longer gazed abroad on the waters, but lay faint and ill in the bottom of the boat, looking up to the stars in the night time, as if missing his mother on earth, he sought her there. Thus they drifted on day and night, until the end drew near. Jube managed to catch a little dew at sunset, which he gave to the child. Rain fell once in small quantities, and refreshed them, but still the cry of famished nature went up for food, and there was nothing but the salt water and the rainless heavens to answer it.

Paul lay in the bottom of the boat, fading away, and moaning with the pangs of famine; Jube bent over him, breaking the hot rays of the sun from the white and sunken face with his body, for they had no other shelter. The boy moaned in his sleep, and called for his mother in feeble anguish. Jube was very weak, but he managed to lift that light weight so far as to lay the boy's head on his knee.

With a spasm of pain the child awoke.

"Little master."

Jube's voice was like that of an old man, hollow and broken. The boy looked up, tried to smile, and murmured,

"Yes, Jube."

"Would you like something to eat, little master?"

"To eat—to eat," whispered the boy, opening his eyes wildly.

"A piece of nice steak. You wouldn't mind its being cooked, would you?"

"Steak!—something to eat! Oh, Jube, we shall never eat again!"

"Look here, little master, now be still and hear what I say."

The boy made a struggle to collect his faculties.

"Little master, listen: when you find me lying here in the boat, and you can't feel my heart beat when you lay your hand here, just cut a slice out of my shoulder with the jackknife."

The boy closed his eyes, shuddering.

"It won't be very hard eating."

The slave was feeling for the knife as he tempted the famished child, who lay moaning across his knee. He found it at last; but his gaunt hands opened it with difficulty, for their strength was all gone.

The poor fellow felt for the spot where his heart beat strongest. Then he spoke to the child again.

The knife will be open, little master, don't forget what I tell you."

He lifted the knife feebly, a flash of sunshine on the blade gleamed across the half shut eyes of the boy. He comprehended the meaning of Jube's words. He sprang up, snatched the knife, flung it into the ocean, and fell senseless on the bottom of the boat.

Jube burst into childish tears, and with his head bent down to his breast, fell into a state of apathy.

When he looked up again a ship was in sight, coming gallantly toward them. He gave a feeble shout, and strove to arouse the child, but could not. Then he took the cotton bag that had held their bread, and fastening it to an oar, swung it wearily to and fro, crying out with all his strength, which left nothing but moans on his parched lips.

The ship bore down upon them, she came so near that Jube could see her crew on the deck, then veered slowly and faded away.

CHAPTER X.

THE HOUSE IN THE PINE WOODS.

Some four or five miles from that lovely spot, where the Housatonic and Naugatuc join their waters, stands a large manufacturing village of no inconsiderable importance. Iron foundries, paper-mills, India rubber and silk manufactories cluster around one of the finest waterfalls of New England. That waterfall is picturesque even now, spite of the cottages, boarding houses, hotels, railroad station, and tanneries, that have taken the place of green woods, richly clothed hills, and a valley so fragrant with wild flowers, that it was happiness to breathe its very air.

But it is hardly worth while to describe this town as it is. Every thing, even the name, derived from an old Revolutionary officer, is changed. My object carries me back to a time when it was indeed one of the loveliest spots in the world—a rich, deep valley, with a noble waterfall thundering at its heart. High, curving, and broken banks, almost mountainous in places, looming up or sloping back on either side, and two lovely brooks pouring their bright, fresh waters into the river above the falls.

One came winding around Rock Rimmond, softened and shadowed by its grim heights. The other, pretty, sparkling Bladens Brook, ran laughing and dancing through the Wintergreen woods, on the opposite shore, with a gush of cheerfulness that seemed like sunshine, and leaped into the river just where it began to gather up its waters for a plunge over the great falls, in one broad, rushing cataract of crystal. From the falls downward, the valley was choked up with noble forest trees, through which the river ran slowly and grandly till it swept around the shadowy base of Castle Rock, and disappeared on its way to join the Housatonic. This rock, high, precipitous, and picturesque, terminates all that we have to do with the valley, for its high cliffs cut off the prospect in that direction, and all the level space between it and the falls was one vast grove of white pines, which formed the grandest masses of trees I ever saw in my life.

A few hemlocks, a white poplar or so, with now and

then a magnificent oak variegated the woods, but great pines predominated everywhere. The earth was littered with their sharp leaves; the wind sighed among their branches as if it never could win a free passage through their greenness. As for the sunshine, it only reached the forest turf and velvet moss in a golden embroidery —seldom with broad gleams. Never were there such cool, green shadows as hung about those woods. The noises that floated through them were strangely bewildering; there was the roar and dash of the falls— the clatter of machinery—for even in that day one factory, among the first ever established in New England, stood by the falls, and the sound of flying shuttles and the beat of heavy looms, held a cheerful rivalry with the flow of the waters and the rush of the winds. Then came the bird songs, wild, clear, and ringing, lost outside of the woods, but making heavenly music if you but listened under the trees.

Just below the falls, so near as almost to be sprinkled with the spray, and to gather foam wreaths about its timbers, was a long, low, wooden bridge, linking two villages together.

These villages crowned the two lofty banks overlooking the falls, from which one took its name. Fall's Hill was rendered most conspicuous by a pretty, white church, with a tall, symmetrical spire, cutting sharply against the sky, added to a cluster of superior dwelling houses, and a country store. In front of this store, just on the fork of the roads, stands, I hope to this day, a magnificent old willow tree, under which people who came from afar sometimes tied their horses, while they went up to worship in the church, which stood on the very highest point of land to be found till you came to Rock Rimmond on one hand, or Castle Rock on the other. These crossroads cut in two directions, one led to the Bungy hills, and the other toward a red school-house and some straggling dwellings in shrub oaks: beyond this, the geography of the country is lost in a confusion of green hills and woodlands, which form a pleasant and prosperous farming country.

From Shrub Oak, the turnpike leads directly down Fall's Hill with precipitous steepness, across the old bridge, and through a sand hill, with a wall of white sand thirty feet high on either side, directly into Chewstown, on the opposite hill.

This cluster of houses took its name from some old Indian, forgotten by his tribe, who lived and died in a hut somewhere in the neighborhood, and at this day is probably forgotten in a town where a change of time-honored names seems to be a political fashion. At any rate, it was called Chewstown then, and a smart, active little village it was. For it had two crossroad taverns, a great, barnlike Presbyterian meeting-house, and a dashing, new Academy, which boasted of a pretentious little cupola with a bell in it, mounted on the highest point of land that side of the river, and contrasting itself saucily with the spire of the church on the opposite bank. Any number of roads crossed and recrossed over the hill at Chewstown. There was the Derby road, running along the banks of the river; the New Haven road, cutting through the sand banks in a parallel line, and crossroads from the farming districts intersecting them both. The fact is, Fall's Hill had a little more than its share of the aristocracy. Chewstown made up for that, by broader commercial opportunities. The taverns were always in a flourishing condition, and a blacksmith's shop, that looked like a foundry, brought the farmers from far and near to get their horses and oxen shod. Besides, there was a country store on the corner, and three white cottages with basements, built in a line like city houses, and the farmers on that side of the river were often heard to say that Chewstown could pull an even yoke with Fall's Hill any time of day, if they had not got a steeple to their meeting-house.

In this village, Captain Mason had left his wife and child, and here, also, Thrasher, the mate, was born. Down in the outskirts of the pine woods, on the Fall's Hill side of the Naugatuc, a river road ran along the curving base of the hill, and wound seaward with the stream. On this road, between the bridge and Castle Rock, there was but one house, a low, white cottage, with peach trees behind it, and lilac bushes in front. A great tulip tree sheltered the low roof, and behind the garden rolled the green billows of the pine woods. It was a lonely, but very beautiful spot, such as a man like Mason would be likely to select as a home for his beloved ones.

Here, in fact, this good man had left his wife and only child, the latter a charming little golden-haired creature of four years old, when he sailed for St. Domingo in the brig Floyd, which we know to have been left disabled and drifting on the ocean. The vessel had been absent six weeks beyond its time, and no intelligence had yet reached her owners or that anxious woman, regarding her fate. This voyage had been Mason's first experience as captain; his little savings had been invested in a private venture, out of which he hoped to provide something—beforehand, to use his own words—for his wife and little one.

Mrs. Mason was both sad and anxious—sad from the gloom of hope deferred, and anxious because the little provision made for her support had melted away, leaving her almost in want. She was sitting in her neat parlor, with one of the little girl's garments in her hands, sighing heavily with each drawing of the thread, when a knock sounded at the door

She stopped, with the needle half through her work, and listened. Of course, *he* would never have paused to knock at his own door, but then, the very thought of this wild possibility suspended her breath.

Again the knock sounded, and the young wife called out with her usual hospitable voice,

"Come in."

The door opened, and a female entered, wrapped in a dark red cloak—the hood of which she put modestly back, revealing as fair a face as you often look upon in an entire lifetime.

CHAPTER XI.

KATHARINE ALLEN'S VISIT TO THE WHITE COTTAGE.

"Oh, Katharine Allen, is that you?" said Mrs. Mason, with a touch of disappointment in her voice, which the girl noticed with a pang.

"Yes, Mrs. Mason, I had got through my day's work, and so ran down once more to see if—if you had heard any thing yet."

"Yes, I thought so—it must be a comfort to have some one to run to—I haven't a living soul!" said Mrs.

Mason, a little petulantly, for Katharine had been at the house more than once to ask these same questions, and the young wife always shrank from acknowledging that she had no good news. This feeling became more and more painful as the time wore on, and her own heart grew faint with apprehension.

"Not a word? Haven't you heard any thing?" faltered the young girl, sinking into a chair, and turning her great blue eyes on Mrs. Mason, with an intensity of suffering that startled the unhappy woman into a momentary forgetfulness of her own anxieties.

"No, Katharine, not one word. It breaks my heart to own it, but not a breath of news has reached me since the brig sailed."

"And she ought to have been in weeks ago! What can be the matter, Mrs. Mason? tell me, oh do tell me, if you have the least idea!"

"I can only guess like yourself, Kate. The ocean is a treacherous thing to trust those you love with. The storm of a single night may have made little Rose an orphan."

The poor woman began to cry as she said this, and calling the little girl to her knee kissed her with mournful tenderness.

"How fond you are of the little girl—it must be a great comfort to have his child looking into your face! One could endure almost any thing for that!" said Katharine, evidently trembling as she spoke.

"A comfort and a pain, Katharine, for if he never comes back—"

"Oh, don't—don't say that," cried the girl, shivering. "The thought is enough to kill one: words—I could not put that into words"

"I wish you would not take on so," said Mrs. Mason, sharply. "It's bad enough to wait and wait, and—oh dear, oh dear, what will become of us?"

Here the poor woman burst into a flood of tears, wringing her hands passionately.

"Mother," said little Rose, "are you crying because pa hasn't come back with my pretty dress?"

The mother could not answer for her sobs; as for Kate Allen, she sat looking at them with cold tears dropping down her white cheeks, as if she longed to fall upon her knees and ask them to pity her a little.

"What do you cry for, Katy Allen?" said the child, rather jealous that any other one should weep but her mother. "You have not got no pa, nor no husband out to sea."

"Oh, God help me! God forgive me! I haven't, I haven't," sobbed the beautiful girl, rocking to and fro on her chair.

Mrs. Mason checked her tears and looked on wonderingly. This strange outburst of grief almost irritated her, for, like her child, she rather craved a monopoly of suffering. All at once a wild apprehension seized upon her. What if Kate had heard—what if she knew that the brig had gone down with every soul on board, and had no strength to speak it out! Frightened by this new dread she started up and stood over the weeping girl.

"Tell me—tell me all you have heard," she almost shrieked. "If you don't want to see me drop dead at your feet, before the face of my child, speak out!"

Katharine looked up; amazement checked her tears, and the pupils of her beautiful eyes dilated.

"I have nothing to say, Mrs. Mason; I have not heard a syllable, how could I?"

"And are you so very sorry for us?"

"Does it make you angry, because I can't keep back the tears? Oh, it seems as if I could die, if any one would feel for me."

"Why, Katharine, what is your trouble?"

"Nothing—nothing—I'm not in trouble."

Mrs. Mason began to look serious, an old suspicion flashed across her mind. She was not a woman of much natural refinement, and the innate vanity of her nature more than compassion spoke out in her next words.

"Katharine, speak out—is it about Nelson Thrasher you are taking on so?"

The blood rushed over that white face like a sudden sunset, then the poor girl grew pale again, and purplish shadows came out under her eyes, leaving them, oh, how mournful.

"You need not look so frightened, Kate—there's no harm in it if you do love him, only you haven't got my spirit, that's all."

"What!—what do you mean, Mrs. Mason?"

"What do I mean? why nothing worth mentioning." A peculiar curve of the handsome lip, as Mrs. Mason said this, made the young girl shiver from head to foot.

"Yes, but you have a meaning when you speak of my not having a spirit. Oh, tell me what it is!"

"Why nothing, Kate, only I thought you would have more pride than to take up with another woman's leavings."

"Another woman's leavings!" repeated Kate, all aghast; "another woman's leavings!"

"That was what I observed," answered Mrs. Mason, with a slight toss of the head. "Boasting isn't in my line, or I could point out a certain person who gave Nelse Thrasher his walking papers more than once, as if I would condescend to him, when his superior stood hat in hand."

" You—you—was it so? when, when?"

" Really, Miss Allen, you take away one's breath; of course it was before I married John Mason, as if there could be a choice."

The poor girl was thunderstruck—that beautiful face drooped slowly to her bosom, and she seemed to be shrinking into a shadow. At last, she lifted her head with a wan smile.

" That was four long years ago, more than four years ago," she cried—" Four years ago."

" Well, what of that; four years does not destroy the truth."

"I don't believe it," said Katharine, very quietly, "there's some mistake."

" Mistake! what does the girl mean? as if I didn't know when a man persecutes me with his love. Makes me a point blank offer, and goes off to sea in despair when I marry his superior. Mistake, indeed!"

" No," persisted the girl, " I don't believe it; no woman could refuse him if he once offered. No woman on earth; it isn't in nature."

" Indeed, you have a mighty high opinion of Nelse Thrasher, as if he was fit to be mentioned in the same day with Captain Mason. I wonder at your daring to say these things to me."

Katharine did not hear her; she was searching the past, urged and goaded in her memory by keen pangs of distrust.

" Besides," she exclaimed, " he has been home since then, and never come near you, not even as a friend."

"I'd like to see him have the impudence," was the angry rejoinder.

Katharine seemed bewildered a moment, and then clasped her hands in passionate despair. "What's the use—oh, what's the use of saying this! It's terrible, and they both in the deep, deep sea."

Here Mrs. Mason's vanity broke down, and her true womanliness asserted itself.

"God forgive us for quarreling about them," she said, really penitent. "If they only come back, I shall be as glad for your sake as you will be for mine. Don't mind what I said, Katy, it isn't worth remembering. Tell me now, are you really engaged to Thrasher?"

"Yes." This little word came faltering through lips as cold and white as snow.

"And you never told of it?"

"What did I say—engaged! No, we are not engaged. How could I tell you so!"

"Well, well, there's no harm in it if you are. God send the Floyd and all hands safely back."

Those large eyes were lifted—oh! how pleadingly—to heaven, and then Katharine began to gather her cloak more closely around her.

"You're not going!" said Mrs. Mason, ashamed of her unwomanly outbreak. "Just take off your cloak, and have a cup of tea. Rose and I haven't had ours yet; I fell to thinking over my work, and forgot it."

"No," said Katharine, more quietly, "I must go now; mother will be anxious to hear. You forget, Mrs. Mason, that my half-brother is on board the brig."

"Well, true enough, my head was so full of that fellow, Thrasher, that I forgot that it might be some other person you were crying about. It's hard, waiting and waiting in this way; but we must have patience, I suppose."

"I'll go now," said the girl, rising.

Little Rose, with the sweet instinct of childhood, came up to where the young girl stood, and lifted up her arms for a kiss.

Katharine bent down, with a flutter of the heart, and left a kiss on the little rosebud of a mouth, but her lips quivered, and the child grew sad under the mournful caress.

When Katharine Allen was gone, Mrs. Mason sat down to her work again. She was a vain, self-sufficient woman, but not in reality an unkind one. The distress which she had just witnessed left her in low spirits. She was naturally of a hopeful disposition, and, in truth, was quite incapable of the deep feeling which had disturbed her in Katharine. Something would turn up and set all things right, she was sure of that; contrary winds, heavy freight—there was some such reason why the brig did not come to port; what was the use of fretting while these chances remained. As these consoling thoughts passed through her mind, she plied her needle with increasing diligence. Rose must have her new frock embroidered before her father came home. A few more leaves in the vine that enriched the skirt, and it would be completed. Mrs. Mason was almost out of bread, or any thing from which bread is made, but she was a woman to cover unsuitable garments with useless embroidery, rather than turn her hand to any thing by which her necessities could be supplied. She would rather have seen little Rose hungry a thousand times than ill dressed.

CHAPTER XII.

HOME FROM SEA.

WHILE Mrs. Mason sat plying her needle, little Rose wandered about the room, wondering what made pretty Katharine Allen so very sorrowful, but keeping the thoughts to herself. In the stillness, she heard a step on the gravel walk outside the house. Then a white lilac bush near the window was disturbed, and she saw a man's face close to the glass. The child would have cried out, but the tongue clove to her mouth, and she stood transfixed with fear. She saw the door softly opened, and a strange man step to the threshold. Then her voice broke forth, and pointing her finger at the stranger, she cried out:

"Mother, mother! it's somebody from the sea!" Mrs. Mason dropped both hands in her lap, and gazed breathlessly on the man. Every tint of color left her handsome face; she tried to speak, but could not. The man was so pale and so wild of countenance that she might well have been stricken with deadly fear.

"Nelson Thrasher," she faltered at last.

He took a step into the room, but did not speak.

"Nelson Thrasher!" she almost shrieked. "If you are a living soul, speak. Where is my husband?"

The man recoiled a step, and well he might. The question came on him so suddenly, it might have startled the boldest man on earth. It absolutely seemed to terrify him. He stood a moment staring at her, then answered in a low, hoarse voice:

"I come to tell you about him."

The little girl caught the meaning of his words, rose up and seizing his hand between both her dimpled palms cried out:

"He comes to tell about pa! Oh, please sir, where is he? Why don't he come home?"

Thrasher looked down in her face, and met the glance of those eyes—her father's eyes. He instantly shook her hands off as if they had been vipers, and with a gesture which seemed to cast aside some terrible feeling, threw himself on a chair.

"My husband!" said Mrs. Mason. "Tell me, is he coming?—is he well?"

"Your husband, John Mason, is dead!"

"Dead! dead!" The poor woman grew faint under the suddenness of this solemn announcement, and dropped helplessly into her chair.

Thrasher sprang up, and stretching out his arms, received her head on his bosom.

Little Rose stood in silent fear, watching them. After a moment she went close to Thrasher, and pulled at his coat.

"Let me hold mother—I don't want you there."

Thrasher pushed her away with one hand. The woman lay as if she were dead against his heart, which beat with iron heaviness, like the trip-hammer of a foundry.

Again the child pulled at his skirts. She was crying now.

"What is dead? I say, man, what is dead? I want to know!"

"See!" answered Thrasher, lifting the woman's white face from his bosom. "See!"

"And is that it?" whispered the child, through her hushed tears. "Mother! mother!"

The shock and suddenness of Thrasher's tidings had overcome Mrs. Mason, but she was not entirely unconscious. When the child called out in her sweet, pathetic voice, she staggered from Thrasher's hold, and falling back into her chair, held out both arms for Rose. The little thing sprang to her lap with a cry of joy, and instantly covered the troubled face with kisses.

"Now," she said, turning her face toward Thrasher; "now tell me about him, my dear, dear pa."

"Send the child away, while I tell you," said Thrasher.

Rose clung to her mother's neck.

"No," said Mrs. Mason, "she must learn all sometime, and I am stronger with her near."

There was a moment's silence, then Mrs. Mason said very faintly,

"Was the ship lost?"

"Almost—but it was not then it happened. We were on shore at Port au Prince. The blacks had risen, and a horrid murder of the white inhabitants was going on. Mason would go on shore. I warned him, but it was of no use. One night, when the massacre was at the highest, he took all hands except one or two, and left the ship. The negroes were hard at work, murdering and burning like demons. He *would* venture among them. It was dangerous—I told him so. Well he came back at last with a woman and little boy."

"A woman!"

"Yes, a beautiful woman, one of the handsomest you ever saw."

"Indeed!"

"He had saved her from a swarm of blacks, who had

brought her and her son out for a carouse, under the palm trees. The boy was brought on board, but they carried the lady off to one of the little islands in the harbor. Mason, with some of the men, went down the ship's side at night, and rowed off with her. After that Mason was never at rest, always going off on private expeditions. I did not like it, so one night, when he was determined to go, I insisted on taking a turn on shore myself. To own the truth, I had a little curiosity to see the house where the lady had lived, and to be certain that she was not there still. Well, he consented, and I went.

"It was a splendid house; covered an acre of ground. Such rooms, such gardens—I never saw any thing like it. The house was so large that we could not tell if it was inhabited or not, but while we were wandering around, a great noise in the lower rooms alarmed us; we hurried through the long halls down to the underground cellars.

"The negroes had been there before us. Every thing was in confusion; we waded ankle deep in red wine. The cellar was half full of negroes who had been wallowing there, and were now fierce with drunkenness. There was not much light, for the negroes dropped their torches, one by one, and the lees of the wine put them out. How your husband came there, I do not know. He must have followed us in one of the small boats. Certain it is, when I was half down the steps his face was the first I saw; he was struggling for his life—a dozen sooty rascals were tearing at him. I gave the cry and sprang down, cutlass in hand, but before I reached him it was all over."

"And they killed him? Oh, father of mercies, they killed him, and you saw it?"

"I have told you all."

The child had been growing pale as she listened, not that she quite understood, but because of the deadly whiteness which settled on her mother's face, and the hoarse voice of the man who was speaking. Mrs. Mason sat still. The shock of this wild story left her dumb. Thrasher cast anxious glances on her face, but if the child looked at him his eyes fell. At last, the woman found the power of speech:

"He sent no word—he died without thinking of us!"

"I cannot tell what his thoughts were, or any thing except that we found him fighting, and saw him fall."

"And who else saw him?"

"No one. My men went into another section of the cellar. The wine was good, and they were in no hurry to follow me."

"But some one saw him after—you did not leave the dead body of my husband to be trampled on by a band of negroes?"

"We could not help it—the blacks were ten to one."

"But did no one see him but yourself?" Did no one try to help him?"

"Yes, one man."

"And who was he?"

"A fellow by the name of Rice."

"What! Katharine Allen's half brother?"

Thrasher turned paler than he had done before that evening. "Her brother—I did not know that," he muttered, uneasily.

Mrs. Mason did not heed this; the conviction of her great loss grew more and more distinct to her mind; all the desolation that must follow the cruel news of that evening crowded upon her. She folded the little girl close to her heart, and began to weep over her in bitter grief.

"Are you sure that Rice is connected with Katharine Allen?" asked Thrasher, taking advantage of a pause in her sobs.

"Old Mrs. Allen was married twice," she answered, impatiently, for grief made her restive. "He was her only son by the first husband. Tell me where he is; I want to see him. I want to know every word and look of my poor, poor husband. Where can Rice be found?"

"I don't know; he kept with the ship. I came directly home, fearing to let any less friendly person tell you the sad news."

"You were very kind," sobbed the poor woman, "very kind; I shall never forget it."

"I always wished to be kind to you, Ellen," was the almost tender reply.

"I know it, I know it; but he always stood between me and any other man."

Thrasher arose, and would have approached Mrs. Mason; but Rose clung to her neck with one arm and waved him away with the other.

"She is my mother—you shan't touch my mother!" she cried, flashing angry glances at him through her tears. Thrasher looked upon the child with mingled hate and fear. It was wonderful how much power those deep blue eyes, sparkling with a thousand childish emotions, possessed over the strong man. There was something spirituelle in her loveliness that impressed him, as if an angel had been reading the record of his life, and rebuked him with those violet eyes.

Thrasher arose hesitating, and almost timidly; he

stood expecting Mrs. Mason to notice the movement; but she was occupied with her grief, and did not observe him.

"Mother," said little Rose, smiling through her tears, "look up, mother; the man who makes you cry is going away."

Mrs. Mason wiped her eyes, and strove to appear interested.

"Hush, Rose, hush, he has been very kind to come with this sorrowful news."

"Yes, mother, he's going right off, so don't cry any more."

Mrs. Mason reached forth her hand; she was a tall, fine woman, with bright eyes, that tears only softened; these eyes full of touching sorrow were lifted to his. All that was good in the man's nature arose in response to this look. His hand trembled as it grasped hers. He could have fallen on his knees and wept over it, so great was the power of love in a nature that had little else to soften it. But the eyes of the child followed his movements vigilantly, and he dropped the mother's hand with a deeply drawn breath.

"Give the gentleman a kiss, my little Rose," whispered the mother, touched by his humble demeanor.

Rose turned her face squarely upon him and lifted her eyes. He met their clear glance and dared not kiss her.

"Good-by," he said, standing before them uneasily.

"Good-by," answered Rose, eagerly.

"When you are better—when you are a little reconciled, Ellen, may I come again?"

"No, no," shouted Rose, waving her hand, "no, no, no."

"Be still, Rose, this is naughty. Remember he was your father's friend."

Rose hid her face and began to cry. Thrasher took the mother's hand again, dropped it, and went away, softened and almost remorseful.

CHAPTER XIII.

THE WAY-SIDE MEETING.

A FOOTPATH intersected the highway some few rods below Mrs. Mason's cottage, and ran off among the hills that lay behind Castle Rock. At this point, Thrasher paused. He had only reached town that day, and his first visit had been to the white cottage. Now, he thought of his parents, who lived on a farm among those hills, and of another person whose home he must pass in going there.

"I must see her, of course," he said, mentally; "but not at once. I have no heart for another scene. But the old folks—that will be all joy—no rebukes or entreaties ever came from that quarter. They will be hurt, too, if I sleep at a tavern, and the homestead so near."

With these affectionate thoughts urging him forward, he turned up the foot path and walked slowly on, wondering at the tender feelings that rose and swelled in his heart as he drew near the family home.

You would not have believed that the man who walked so quietly along the greensward with the moonlight on his face, could have been the same person who stood on the deck of that brig and superintended the number of lashes that should be dealt on the back of a human being. Once or twice, as his glance fell on some familiar object, a sweet brier bush, perhaps, or a cluster of tall mulleins that had grown by the footpath since he was a child, his eyes would fill with tears. There was something holy and homelike in the stillness that made a child of this cruel man.

The footpath led Thrasher into the Bungy road. He had mounted one hill and was descending into the valley which lay between it and another, when he saw some dark object sitting on a pine stump, from which he had gathered moss years before. His step was smothered on the sward, and the night wind, which made a rustling sound among the leaves of a neighboring wood, rendered his approach inaudible.

It was a woman shrouded in a cloak, but the light was so clear that he could see the outlines of her person, though her face was bent down and her limbs were drawn together as if she suffered from cold or sorrow.

Thrasher's heart told him at once who the woman was, and the knowledge made a coward of him. He hesitated, turned to go back, but resumed his course again, ashamed of so much weakness. The woman's face was bent down, her hands were locked around her knees, and he could hear the swell of her sobs as she rocked to and fro, as if the motion gave relief to some great pain.

Thrasher stood close by the unhappy creature, but she was lost in grief and did not look up.

"Katharine!"

She started to her feet with a cry that haunted his memory years after, and stood before him, shaking in all her limbs. Why did she not fling her arms about his neck as she had done at parting? Why did she shrink and gather the cloak so timidly around her? Did the shadow of some great wrong fall upon her with its sundering power?"

"Katharine, you know me, but don't seem glad that I have come."

"Not glad—oh, my heart is dumb with joy! I thought —I feared that you were dead, Nelson, and the idea was driving me crazy. I was trying to pray when you came up."

She stole timidly toward him and held out her hand.

"Is it real—are you alive and here? Oh how good you are, coming to our house the first moment to see me, for I know well enough you did want to see me— while I was doubting if you would care about me after being away so long, and wondering what I should do. You are not changed, Nelson; you love me yet as well —better than ever."

There was something in the girl's manner that Thrasher did not understand. She seemed frightened, and shrunk from approaching him. This was so unlike the childlike affection with which she had hitherto met him, that he stood looking upon her in surprise, mingled with a little irritation.

"Why, Katharine, what is the matter? You are so changed—it may be the moonlight, but your face seems thinner and less rosy.'

She turned her eyes upon him with a wan smile, but did not answer at once.

"You have changed, perhaps, and found some one you like better."

There was something in his tones that stung her; a hopeful questioning as if he wished rather than dreaded this change. She looked at him reproachfully, and her blue eyes floated in tears.

"Oh, Nelson!"

The words were uttered in a very low voice, but in their quietness lay deep pathos. She moved close to his side and laid one hand on his shoulder, waiting for him to return the caress. He placed his arm lightly, and it seemed half reluctantly, about her waist. She felt the chill at her heart.

"*You* are changed!" she said, in a loud, clear voice, that sounded to his ear like a challenge. "You come here not to meet, but to abandon me."

Thrasher tightened his arm around her.

"Is this the way I abandon you?" he said.

She withdrew herself quietly from his arms, and fixing her eyes on his face gave him a long, sorrowful look.

The moonlight lay full on his features. His dark eyes looked into hers; a smile, half mocking, half pleasant, hung on his lip. He was a tall, handsome man, and the moonlight refined his face into remarkable beauty.

"Are you trying me, Nelson?" she said, half returning the smile. "Don't—don't—I have trouble enough without that."

"Trouble—was there ever a girl of your age without it, I wonder? Come, take my arm, and as we walk along you shall tell me what great misfortune sent you here crying and rocking yourself like an old woman turned out of doors."

Katharine tried to laugh and took his arm, leaning on it with that half caressing, half dependent grace which a woman who loves from her soul assumes unconsciously. Formerly, when her arm touched his, he had, at a time like this, taken the willing hands in his clasp, but the touch of Ellen Mason's fingers thrilled his nerves even yet, and Katharine's hand drooped helplessly over his arm.

"Now tell me what this great, great trouble is?" he said, walking forward.

"Wait until we get into the shadow of the woods, and I will," she replied, in a low, choked voice.

They walked on in dead silence, entered the shadow of the wood, paused in the darkest spot, and talked earnestly together. When they came in the moonlight again, Thrasher looked pale and angry. He walked fast, sometimes forcing her on beyond her strength, and cutting up the silk weed and mulleins in his path with fierce dashes of his walking-stick. Katharine made no resistance, for a cold, dead silence, which shut out all joy, had fallen on her.

They came to a little brown house, under the shelter of a hill, and half covered with morning-glories—a pretty, rustic place in which Katharine lived alone with her mother. A board fence ran along the front yard, hedging in some lilac bushes and a huge snowball bush. A flower bed ran along each side of the walk, from the gate to the door. All this looked pretty and cool, in its night dew, and Thrasher recognized the familiar objects with something like a pang.

Katharine withdrew her arm from his at the gate; she tried to speak, and ask him to go in, for a light shone through one of the windows, and the old lady was evidently waiting for Katharine to come home before she went to bed; her lips trembled, but refused to utter the invitation; he read it in her eyes, however, and shook his head.

"Not to-night—another time we will talk this over."

They parted with these words, and Thrasher walked on at a more rapid pace than he had yet used. Katharine watched him mournfully as he disappeared, then, with a deep sigh, she entered the house.

CHAPTER XIV.

THE OLD HOME AND THE OLD PEOPLE.

A LITTLE way over the hill from Mrs. Allen's dwelling, stood a low, red farm house which covered a good deal of ground, and possessed many pleasant surroundings, such as marked the more thrifty class of farmers in those days. Rows of stiff, Lombardy poplars stood in lines before the house, looking more like mammoth umbrellas, verdant in color, and shut up for the season, than any thing else. Tall, cinnamon roses clambered up the front, while a whole forest of lilac and snowball bushes cast their shadows on the rich sward of the door yard. At the back was a fine apple orchard which filled the air all around with the delicate perfume of its blossoms in the spring-time, and gave out a rich, fruity odor in the autumn. A well sweep pencilled its slender shadow along the plantain leaves that grew rank at the back door, and beyond that, the distant outlines of a cider-mill could be imperfectly seen through the orchard boughs.

Every thing seemed natural to the stern man, as he drew near the homestead. He could not remember a time when the old place did not look thrifty and comfortable, as it appeared then. A few dry branches bristled here and there among the poplars, speaking of progressive age, like gray hairs in the head of a strong man, but they were scarcely perceptible in the moonlight, and Thrasher could see no change since the years of his boyhood.

The family sitting room was back of the house, and through the windows a gleam of light shot along the grass. Thrasher passed through the yard, and, pausing beneath the window, looked in. The paper blind was partly rolled up, and he thus commanded a view of the entire room.

Two old people sat together on the hearth, where a few embers lay smouldering. A round, cherry wood stand stood between them, from which towered a massive brass candlestick, supporting the only light that burned in the room.

The old lady was knitting. What a sweet, benign expression slept on her face! How softly the white hair was folded under her cap! The pure, healthy bloom on her cheek was something wonderful. It made you in love with the beauty of old age.

The old man was reading aloud; the great family bible lay open before him, and his deep, reverential voice could be distinctly heard through the imperfectly closed window. As Thrasher looked, the old man removed the spectacles from his eyes, and laid them on the page he had been reading, while he listened smilingly to some observation that his wife had made, but which, with her lower and softer tones, Thrasher had lost.

"How many times have we read this chapter together, Eunice—so many that neither you nor I can remember them; but every reading brings out something new—

something more holy than we ever found before. Isn't that your experience?"

"Yes," answered the old lady, taking a seamstitch with serene precision as she spoke. "It seems to me, husband, that one never learns really what is in the Bible till old age comes on. When we were young, I can remember being so tired when the morning chapter was read, and full of other thoughts, that I am sorry to remember now. That is the reason I always had so much charity for our Nelson. Poor child, he never could sit still through a whole chapter—boy or man!"

"I'm afraid," answered the old man, with a heavy sigh. "I'm a'most afraid, Eunice, that we neglected to perform our whole duty to the boy at the start. He was such a bright child, that we wandered off into ambition and worldly pride where he was concerned. Now, that we are getting old, and a'most as good as childless, this idea troubles me more than a little. Maybe, if you and I had been a little more strict with the boy, he'd have got over them roving notions, and stayed at home."

"I don't know," said the old lady, putting on her glasses to loop up a stitch, while a shade of trouble came to her face. "It seems to me as if nothing would ever have kept Nelson on the farm. He was too high strung for that. But what then? Every body isn't of the same idea, you know; and if the education we gave our son helped to unsettle him for our way of life, it fitted him for another. Remember, he went out first mate this time."

"He's a brave boy, any way," said the old man, kindling with the subject; "and if the season of grace has not reached his soul yet, we must only pray the more earnestly."

"Yes," whispered the mother. "Pray without ceasing, and in every thing give thanks!"

"If we did not kneel to the throne of grace in his behalf so often as we might have done in our younger days, we must make up for it now, for our son will some day make a shining light in the house of the righteous," continued the father. "I feel it. I know it, Eunice."

The old lady sighed.

"I'm afraid that even now I pray that he may come back to his home, before I think of his eternal salvation, for that wish is always uppermost with me."

The old man smiled reprovingly, and shook his head. "Ah, Eunice!"

"I can't help it," sighed the mother, confessing her weakness, with a deprecating smile. "He is my only child—all the precious, earthly blessing we have. I can't help being proud and fond of him."

"How could you, when I, a strong man—one that the brethren sometimes look up to, as all the church members will admit—can't keep back the pride of having a son like that. There's no denying it. Nelson is a young man that must put a temptation of pride into his parents' path. It seems to me as if I were a stronger man and you a handsomer woman for having a son like him."

"So honorable, so handsome," murmured the old lady.

"So strong and energetic," responded the father.

"Ah, if he would but come once more to see his old father and mother."

The old lady bent over her knitting, and pretended to search for a false stitch, but it was only to conceal the tears that swelled tenderly into her eyes.

Thrasher could bear no more. The man loved his parents, and those soft tears in his mother's eyes brought moisture to his own. How innocent and childlike the old people were, in comparison with him. Satan, when looking over the flow'ry walls of Paradise, must have felt as he did, listening to that household conversation.

The old man took up his glasses again, and began to read. The mother kept on with her work, listening, with meek faith, to the holy words that fell from her husband's lips. All at once she started, dropped the knitting in her lap, and listened.

"It is his step!"

The old man raised his face from the Bible, and listened, also.

"Yes, Eunice, it is!"

The door opened, and their son stood on the threshold —a strong, handsome fellow, such as the father had described him. There was no outcry of joy, no wordy demonstrations; but a tender gladness possessed the old people. The mother kissed him, almost timidly. There was something that awed her tenderness in this powerful young man, though he did tremble in her gentle embrace.

"My son, you are welcome home—oh, my son!"

There was something hearty and patriarchal in this welcome of the father. The noble old Christian that forgave his prodigal son must have spoken much after the same fashion.

They shook hands—the father and son—with a firm, lingering clasp, while the mother looked on, smiling through her tears. With your genuine New England housemother, hospitality is always the servitor of affection. The night dew lay heavily on her son's garments. He looked pale and tired. The mother's heart rose pitifully in her bosom; she insisted upon raking open the fire, and getting a warm cup of tea; even went so far as to offer a cider-brandy sling, with toasted crackers floating on the top.

Thrasher yielded himself to her tender care. It was wonderful how submissive and grateful that strong-willed man had become under womanly influences. He declined tea, but accepted the glass of smoking drink which the mother prepared. Soon the old man took a tumbler, also, and praised it greatly; for religious men and elders of the church, in those times, thought it no sin to make themselves comfortable with a glass of hot drink before bedtime, never dreaming that their limited indulgence might lead to excess in the coming generation—excess which even legal enactments have failed to remedy. Having no fear and no conscientious scruples on the subject, the old man enjoyed his glass, and filled that of his son more than once; for, somehow, the color would not come genially to the young man's face, and after the first glow of his reception had passed off, he seemed depressed, almost gloomy.

The old lady took her seat again on the patchwork cushion of blue and red cloth which Thrasher could remember from his childhood, and attempted to resume her knitting; but the plump little hands trembled so much that she gave it up, and drawing back into the shadow, had a sweet, motherly cry all to herself. It was pleasant to hear those two voices blending together in their talk. It was heaven to know that the whole family sat on one hearth again. She could not be thankful enough. What had she done to merit so much happiness at the hands of the Lord.

This pious under-current of feelings mingled with the conversation as it went on between the two men, leaping rapidly from subject to subject, as always happens when members of one family have been long separated. While the mother was wrapped in dreamy thanksgivings, the old man, not less grateful or affectionate, fell to questioning his son about his voyage, the fate of the ship, and the terrible scenes which had been enacted at St. Domingo, while she lay in the harbor of Port au Prince.

Thrasher went into the thrilling details. He was naturally eloquent, and the intense interest manifested by his parents, made his pictures as graphic as the reality; but another person might have remarked, though his parents did not, that he avoided mentioning either his own share or that of Captain Mason in these exciting events.

"But how long did this last, Nelson? Was the brig kept in harbor all the time? Some of the neighbors began to fear that she was lost; but your mother and I hoped and prayed, didn't we, mother?"

The mother smiled on her son, answering:

"Nelson always knows that we hope and pray when he is upon the great deep."

"But where is the brig now; at her port?" questioned the father, after a brief pause.

"No, we were compelled to abandon her; one of the most terrible storms I ever faced on sea or land, took us unprepared. It swept us clean from stem to stern. Another hour and we should have gone down like a handful of drift wood—for days and days we floated on the ocean, no sails, our masts gone, nothing to rig new ones with. The men were discouraged, some of them threatening mutiny; for a negro and a little boy that came on board at Port au Prince, the only creatures that I know of who escaped the massacre, were missing just after the storm, and the fellows would believe that I had something to do with it, so they sulked and threatened until I began to fear for my life. Nothing but our own great peril prevented them rising.

"At last, the brig sprang a leak, and what with working at the pumps night and day, hard commons and no drink—for I staved the casks in—they had plenty to do without turning on me. It was enough to put down any rebellion to hear the water rushing and gurgling into the hold, faster, a great deal, than all hands could pump it out. So, while working for their own lives, they forgot to take mine."

"Thank God for this great deliverance," said the old man, solemnly.

The son paused an instant, and then went on.

"The water gained on us; we worked desperately, but the brig sunk lower, and lower, till we had scarcely a hope left."

"Then," whispered the mother "you thought of us, my son."

"Of his God," said the old man, devoutly; "he prayed to God and so found safety."

Thrasher was no hypocrite; he remembered how different the scene had proved to any thing his parents imagined, and felt rebuked by their simplicity.

"Yes, mother, I did think of you both with an aching heart. As for prayers, we sailors have little time for them. But I was telling you of our condition; it was forlorn enough. The men gave out and refused to work. Persuasions went for nothing—threats were of no use. They were tired out and wanted to die. You have no idea, father, how reckless such men are."

"No, son; I couldn't imagine it."

"At last, when all was given up, and we had nothing to do but die, a sail hove in sight."

" Thanks be to God!" ejaculated the old man, lifting his clasped hands, while tears stole softly down the mother's cheek.

"' Sail O!' That was a shout which filled us with new life. We tore off our jackets, we searched for fragments of the old sails, our voices rose in wild, hoarse shouts, that sounded awfully along the waters. At first, she did not see us, but seemed steering another way. Our despair broke forth in one mighty shriek! It reached them—we could see a commotion on the deck. Breathless with expectation, grouped together like so many ghosts, we watched her slacken sail, and bear down upon us. Then the strongest man among us burst into tears! That moment I shall never, never forget!"

"Not while there is a merciful God to thank!" said the father, shaking the tears from his cheek as a lion flings dew-drops from his mane. Low sobs broke from the darkened portion of the room. During her son's narration the good mother had sunk unconsciously to her knees, and lay prostrate before her God, trembling with thankfulness.

Thrasher went on:

"We took to the friendly vessel, all but three persons. They would not leave the wreck. No persuasion could move them. It was a terrible thing, but the ship sailed away, leaving them to their fate!"

"And who were these men, my boy?"

"Rice, old Mr. Allen's son."

"God help the poor woman."

"With the negro and boy I told you of. They had taken the boat and put out to sea alone—after drifting five or six days hither and yon, they were taken up by the vessel that afterward saved us. They saw the wreck and came to her in the first boat. When Rice refused to abandon the brig they sat down by his side, and so we were compelled to leave them."

"And is this all?—did you never hear of them again?" inquired the mother, rising to her feet.

"No; we never heard of them after that. They drifted off with the wreck, and what became of them no one can tell."

"This will be sorrowful news for our neighbor. Husband, I wish some other person than our son had brought it."

Thrasher arose hastily.

"Good night, mother. Shall I sleep in the old room?"

His voice shook, and he seemed greatly disturbed.

"Yes, yes, my son. You are tired out. Go up to your old room."

CHAHTER XV.

BREAKFAST IN THE OLD HOMESTEAD.

Nelson Thrasher could not sleep under his father's roof. The neat, high posted bed, with its blue and white coverlet that he had slept under in boyhood, was so familiar that it seemed to reproach him in its homeliness for the great change that had fallen on himself. The little looking-glass over the cherry-wood dressing stand, flashed upon him like a human eye angry and fierce at the intrusion of a guilty man where an innocent boy had slept. As his foot touched the rag carpet, worn smooth by his light tread, years ago, the breath paused on his lips, and the stern face softened into sadness so deep, that his worst enemy might have pitied him.

That instant the old man's voice rose solemnly through the stillness of the night. From the depths of his heart, he was thanking God that his son had returned. Every word of that prayer rose to the son, rebuking him to the soul. He fell upon his knees, unconsciously occupying the very spot on which his first prayer had been learned from his mother's lips. Bitter repentance swept over him for the minute, and covering his face with both hands, he cried like a child.

But such feelings could not hold that stern nature long. When the old man ceased, Thrasher shook the tears from his eyes, and stood up, turning his face away from the glass, hating that it should reflect the workings of which he was even then ashamed. It was useless; the familiar things around him were full of associations that would make themselves felt. He put out the candle, and got into bed, his eyes filling in the darkness as he lifted the coverlet.

Still he could not sleep. The dear old objects were all shut out, but the home feeling was too strong. For that one hour he was almost a good man.

As he lay in the darkness, a soft tread came on the stairs, and the door of his room swung open. He knew all about it. The footsteps were his mother's. How often he had heard them, in childhood, coming up, because the kind woman fancied that he might be afraid, or ill, or that the coverlet had slipped from over him. Just as of old, she glided through the door and close to the bed. He feigned sleep, that she might not guess how much he had been acting like a child. She stood beside him, full of motherly tenderness, yearning for a few last words before she went to rest; but with gentle self-command, waiting for some sign that he was awake. When she found that his eyes were closed and his breath came evenly, she bent down and kissed him on the forehead more than once, whispering his name to herself, as she had done a thousand times over his cradle.

Still he did not move; the kiss stole like an angel's whisper through his heart. For the moment, it sanctified him, even in his own eyes. This did not appear to awake him, and the mother could attempt no more. Still she lingered, settled his pillow, delicately as a bird smoothes the plumage of its young, and tucked up the bed, blessing him the while. It was not chilly, but the action put her in mind of old times, and she loved it.

At last that gentle mother glided out of the room, and he drew a deep breath, longing to call her back, confess how far he had gone astray, and become as a little child again.

The night wore on, and he had not slept a moment. Many thoughts came crowding over the holy ones that possessed him, and finally overpowered them. He thought of Mrs. Mason—his first, his only love—for this truth he confessed to himself over and over again, in the stillness of that night, when the difficulties of his position crowded close upon him. He thought of Katharine Allen, not with solicitude, such as the poor creature's fate should have inspired, but bitterly, harshly, for she was a stumbling-block in his way, an object almost of dislike. Though a cruel man, Thrasher was not recklessly so to women—thoughts of his mother always kept him from that. Still, he almost cursed Katharine in the struggles of that night, for she stood between him and the great desire of his life—John Mason's widow. But for her, he could make a brief wooing, settle down by his old parents, and without temptations to evil courses, become a man of power, for he possessed that which enabled him to accomplish almost every thing, an unlimited control of wealth. But with this young creature in the way, what could he do but plunge into schemes that brought sin and peril with them, such as he shrunk from encountering. Abandon his father and mother—go off to some unknown country with the woman of his love—cast off all duties—leave that beautiful girl to die of grief—could he do that?

Thus the good angels and the evil spirits struggled over that man all night long. In the morning, neither had the mastery. On ship-board, the guardian angel would have been driven forth at once; but under his father's roof, there was something of heaven which would not let the seraph go.

After daylight the young man fell asleep, weary with thoughts that still left their shadows on his forehead. The mother came up twice to call him, but seeing the weariness in his handsome face, went away, holding her breath, and walking on tiptoe.

At last he came down-stairs, and found the old people, with the table spread and the breakfast dishes standing on the hearth, patiently waiting till he should join them.

It was of no use struggling. Over a breakfast table like that the good angels held control; nothing worse could hover near those blessed old people upon their own hearth-stone. There every thing spoke of the old time—the round table, covered with bird's-eye linen, homemade, glossy as a snow crust, and as white. The same sprigged china and quaint teaspoons. The silver teapot—old-fashioned even then—had been brought out for the first time in years, and stood emitting dainty puffs of steam between the andirons. The old lady looked at her son and at the teapot with conscious smiles, which said plainly as smiles could speak, "You see that I keep nothing back when my son comes home, not even that!"

Thrasher smiled as he gathered in this picture. It was the smile of a stern character, and changed his whole face. Rare must be the smile which makes a human heart leap. You never heed perpetual sunshine, but that which flashes through clouds makes itself felt and remembered.

"How much he looks like his father now," thought the mother, while the old man held out his hand, and grasped that of his son with a hearty "good-morning."

"Son," said the old lady, as she took up the teapot, with a little flutter, like that of a bird pluming itself, "now that we are all together—the whole family, you know—supposing we sit down at once. Your father usually goes to prayers before breakfast, Nelson, but we'll just put it off till afterward—don't you think so, husband?"

A strong sense of duty alone kept the old man from saying yes, at once; but he wasn't to be led into temptation by the fond designs of that precious little woman, not he; nor by the fear that his son would rather not. Morning prayers didn't happen to be duties so lightly disposed of, in his estimation. He motioned the old lady to leave the breakfast where it was, on the hearth, and taking the great Bible from its stand, began to read with solemn deliberation.

8

Thrasher liked this; had his father varied in any thing from the steady goodness of his character, it would have been a sad disappointment to the son; for such persons are generally the most keen-sighted in detecting the weakness of good men. Besides, there is something holy in the religious associations of an early home, which no man or woman can see disturbed without pain.

I am afraid that the old man, in compunction for a momentary impulse to yield, made his prayer a little longer than usual, and dwelt elaborately on that point which asked deliverance from temptation. Certain it is, that according to the habit of the times, he spoke of himself as a hardened sinner, and confessed to shortcomings and taints of original depravity that must have made the recording angel—who had set down nothing but good deeds to his account for many a long year—smile in benign patience.

Once, as the good Christian gave signs of prolonging his devotions, the old lady turned softly on her knees and pushed the dish, which contained a choice delicacy for her son, close to the fire; but she blushed in the act, and covering her face the instant it was accomplished, whispered "amen" at the end of a sonorous sentence in which her husband acknowledged the native depravity of every soul within the created world.

Still Nelson Thrasher was not impatient. Every word of the old man's voice thrilled him through and through. It would have taken something more than that to upheave the stern selfishness of his character to any purpose; but many a good feeling rose to the surface which, for the time, made him a better man.

They sat down to breakfast at last, and a right hearty

New England breakfast it was. The old man talked pleasantly on every subject that came up. He possessed a clear, energetic mind, and had read a great deal more than was common to his class. His intelligence was active to seize on any food that presented itself, and his son's adventures by sea and land, were as exciting as a romance; not that old Mr. Thrasher knew what a romance was, or would have allowed one to enter his door if he had. Indeed, the Pilgrim's Progress had disturbed his mind a good deal from the fact that it was not an actual, instead of an ideal truth. As a great many conscientious people condemn the theatre, but fill the boxes of an opera, every night, this old-fashioned Christian listened to his son's spoken romances with infinite zest. They appealed keenly to his imagination, which found little aliment in any book he read, except when it seized upon the grandest of all poetry—that of the Bible.

So the father asked questions, the son answered them pleasantly, and that dear old lady sat smiling upon them both from behind her silver teapot; convinced from the depths of her heart that she was the happiest and most good-for-nothing old mother that ever drew the breath of life, and ought to be ashamed of herself for not deserving all this joy more thoroughly.

After breakfast, Thrasher took his hat, and prepared to go out. The old gentleman, in the innocence of his heart, proposed to accompany him, but Mrs. Thrasher began to nod and signalize him across the table, and he sat down rather bewildered.

"Don't you see," said the old lady, with a sweet, knowing smile, "Nelson is sure to find his way down to Mrs. Allen's—he must have loved us very much to come by without stopping last night. I shouldn't wonder if that girl kept him at home?"

"You don't say so!" exclaimed the father, in blank astonishment; "well, I never thought of that."

"Why, don't you remember how often he used to go there the time he came home before this, and how he went to York State to see her when she was out there with her uncle that winter, going to school."

"Well, wife, I shouldn't wonder if there was something in it," said the old man, going to the window and looking after his son.

The mother emitted a low, mellow laugh; she was rather proud of her quicker penetration, and patronized the old gentleman accordingly.

"Why of course there's something in it," she said, nestling herself up to his side, and putting a lock of gray hair back from his temples with her finger. He'll hang round her a little while—go down the hill two or three times a day likely, while we don't seem to know any thing about it—and then think he's surprising us, when he says that he's going to marry Katharine Allen, if we've no objections. Of course we shan't have any—for she's a nice girl and handsome as a picture. Then there'll be a wedding down yonder. You'll buy the wine, and I'll find the cake. Mrs. Allen has got lots of homespun, and Nelson won't want much for a setting out, for this house isn't badly off for furniture, and I've been thinking of a new cherry-tree chest of drawers some time."

The old man laughed pleasantly.

"My wife, you've got them married and to housekeeping before he's crossed the top of the hill."

"But wouldn't it be nice? She's a smart girl, and might take a great deal of care off me. As for Nelson, if he once took to farming what a hand he would make at it!"

"And you believe all this?"

"Why shouldn't I? there's nothing unnatural about it, nor wrong either—besides I am sure Katharine likes him."

"Well, wife, any thing that keeps the boy at home will satisfy me. Marriage is an institution of the Lord, and no good man should say a word against it."

"Of course not, for that would be to slander our own youth. See, there is Nelson now, looking down toward Mrs. Allen's house. That's him under the but'nut tree. He's just stepped on the rock—you remember it. I wonder what he's flirting out his silk handkerchief for?"

"It's to scare off the crows, I reckon," answered the father, watching the movements of his son with some curiosity, "they're greater pests than ever, this year."

"No," said the old lady, "it's more than that. See, something moves on the other side of the stone wall. It's a woman—she's climbing over. Why don't he help her, I wonder? Yes, just as I thought, it is Katharine Allen. What do you say to that?"

"Well," answered the old man, flushing around the temples. "I say it isn't likely the young folks think that we are spying after them. If they want to have a talk by themselves, I'm sure we've no objections. You and I have been but'nutting together in our lives, haven't we?"

I am not sure that the old man did not kiss the face that was lifted smilingly to his. There was no one by, and he was so very happy all the morning—who could wonder at it? The old lady, at any rate, made no ado about the matter, but nestled a little closer to his side, and asked "if he saw Nelson and Katharine yet?"

"They are sitting on the rock together, wife, talking, no doubt; but we must not be watching them. Young folks don't like that, you know."

"Well, only just say that you think there's something in it, and I won't turn my eyes that way again; though it's a trial for a mother not to look on her son anywhere, after he has been away from home so long."

The father himself seemed to feel that it was a hardship, for, after walking across the room once or twice, he came back to the window where his wife still remained.

"See, husband, how Katharine jumps up and seems to be wringing her hands. What can ail her?"

"Maybe Nelson is telling her about leaving her half-brother on the wreck; that is enough to make the poor girl wring her hands—as for Mrs. Allen, nothing but the grace of God can carry her through this trouble. She hasn't seen her son for years, and was just expecting him home."

"Supposing I go right down and comfort her," whispered the good woman, her heart full of tender pity. "Or would she rather be left alone, I wonder?"

"Wait till the first grief goes off; after that, company may do her good."

"Poor girl, how she takes on, while Nelson sits there as if nothing was the matter. No, no, I am wrong; he's taken hold of her hands. He's talking to her—how kind of him. See, Katharine is quieter already. She sits down again; I know well enough, if any thing on earth could pacify her, he could. The dear boy!"

CHAPTER XVI.

A PAINFUL INTERVIEW.

TRULY, Catharine Allen had sprung to her feet, and was wringing her hands in wild, bitter grief, at the news of her half-brother's death, for such she considered the account Thrasher gave her. True, she had never seen Rice since she was a little girl, and he was scarcely known in the neighborhood, as Mrs. Allen had moved to her present home with her second husband, and her son had gone to sea long before that. In her second widowhood, he had sometimes sent her money and warm-hearted letters, written in a great, cramped hand, which no one but a mother could have read. In her retired life, Mrs. Allen, who was a middle-aged woman when Katharine was born, had looked forward to news from her son as the great event of her life. With only her house, a few acres of land, and her pretty daughter's labor to depend on for a livelihood, the twenty and thirty dollars which came to her from this son, at the end of each voyage, was a great help. Without it, the widow and her beautiful daughter must have come to want, especially when sickness was in the house.

Now he was dead—the brave, generous man, whom Katharine had been taught to love like a father; and even while Thrasher told his own story, and her loving heart was almost given up to fond credulity, she was not quite satisfied that Rice might not have been saved. To leave him on the wreck even at his own request, seemed to her a terrible cruelty.

"He was my brother," she said; "the only support we had. He was so generous—so good to us both! Oh, Nelson, you should have saved him!"

"How did I know he was your brother, Katharine? He never told me a word about it; and if I ever heard the name, it had escaped me."

"But he was a human being; a mother waited for him, somewhere. You should have remembered that."

"It is useless talking in this way, Katharine," replied Thrasher, striving to pacify her grief. "I could only have saved him by violence. He would not come with us, but stuck to the wreck, under some wild idea that she might yet be taken into port. I could have died with him, but nothing beyond that was possible."

"Oh, my mother! my poor mother! must I tell her this?" moaned Katharine.

"Perhaps it would have pleased you better had I gone down with him?"

"You!—you! Oh, that would have completed our desolation! The news would have killed me dead!"

"Then don't attempt to make me out a murderer."

"I haven't—I haven't!"

"Sit down, Katherine. These wild gestures will be seen from the house, and the old people won't know what to make of it. Sit down and compose yourself. This is not the only subject we have to talk about."

"I know it—I know it; but the thought of carrying the grief to my mother kills me."

"This is childish—I will submit to it no longer," cried Thrasher, beginning to lose patience. "Sit down, I say, and control yourself!" He took hold of her hands, grasping them till they burned with pain, and drew her forcibly to the rock. She looked at him breathlessly; the expression of his face frightened her.

"Now that you can be still," he said, sternly, "I have a great deal to say about our conversation last night. Will you try and listen like a rational creature?"

She was sobbing bitterly, and could only give an assent by a motion of the head.

"Well, regarding the senseless event which you make so much of——"

"Senseless, Nelson!" She looked up, as the words left her lips, and gazed at him reproachfully through her tears.

"Yes, senseless! What else could an act like that be considered? I was a man—and should have known better. What good has it done to be in such desperate haste?"

"What good?—what good? Did we not love each other?"

Something like a sneer came to Thrasher's lip. He longed to tell her the truth. It seemed the surest means of putting her out of the way.

"You don't speak, Nelson. You look strange when I say, 'Did we not love each other?'"

"No wonder, Katharine—why should you ask the question? If to make a fool of one's self is a proof of love, you have it!"

"To make a fool of one's self?" The poor girl turned white to the lips as she repeated these insulting words. "What does this mean, Nelson?"

"It means that you and I went off, like a couple of dunces, and got married!"

Katharine stopped crying. Surprise, for a moment, kept her mute; but directly there came into her eyes a proud, almost fierce determination, that Thrasher had never witnessed before.

"Do you mean this?" she said at last, in a low, clear voice, that made him start.

"Mean what?"

"That you are sorry for having married me."

There was something in her face that startled him—that woman's character had a depth and strength which he had not dreamed of until then. It was not his habit to evade or equivocate much, but now he saw the necessity.

"I haven't said that, and did not mean it, my sparrow-hawk. How could I?"

"Then, what did you say?—what did you mean?"

"Nothing, except that it was a great folly—but a very pleasant one—when we got married in that private way. It would have been better to have waited."

"But it was you that urged me."

"To the marriage, but not the secrecy, that was your own doings entirely, Kate. I wanted you to go at once and live with the old folks, while I went this voyage, but you begged and pleaded to stay with your mother, and what could I do but consent. Of course, as my wife, you must have lived with my family, so you preferred secrecy and your mother. It was a foolish arrangement altogether."

"My poor mother was so sad and lonely then, I could not bear to leave her; besides, I did not dare tell her about it while she was in poor health—she would have taken on dreadfully—for somehow——"

"Yes, I know she hated me."

"No, not that; but mother has strange prejudices."

"I should think she had. I have not forgotten her forbidding me the house; but for that——"

"What were you saying, Nelson? your voice is very husky."

"I was saying that we should not have been led into the weakness of this concealment if she had been more reasonable."

"Well, if it was a weakness or a sin I have suffered for it keenly enough, Nelson. While my mother had those hard feelings I could not tell her. Oh, Nelson, it seemed as if I should die when the time for your return came and we heard nothing of the brig. If you had been lost, what would have become of me? No one would have believed that I had ever been married, no matter what I had said."

"But you had the certificate?"

"Yes, but the people here don't understand those things. They're used to a publishment and all that. They never would see the difference between Connecticut and York State. Then, if they had sent to my uncle he knew nothing about it, you remember, and could not have helped me. Besides, I didn't even know where to find the people that stood up with us."

"Why, child, all these fears are nonsense. The certificate is enough."

"But it's all of no consequence now. You are here and we can speak out. It isn't like a poor girl being all alone without knowing any thing of the law."

CHAPTER XVII.

JEALOUS PANGS REGARDING MRS. MASON.

THRASHER sat with his hands clasped over one knee, looking thoughtfully on the ground as she spoke. Katharine had nestled close to his side, and was looking wistfully into his face.

"There isn't any trouble now, Nelson. Mother may be angry for awhile, but it won't be forever."

"I was thinking," said Thrasher, with his eyes resolutely fixed on the ground, "I was thinking that, as it had gone so far, we had better put off telling about it till after my next trip."

Katharine turned white, and suddenly shrank away from him. He did not seem to notice it, but went on in the same even voice.

"It will not be long—not more than two or three months at the most."

Katharine held her breath and listened, but sobs were gathering thick and heavy in her bosom.

"Three months!—three months! Oh, Nelson!" and now the sobs broke forth with painful violence.

"It may be less than that—I will get the shortest voyage that can be found. But for the shipwreck this might not have been so necessary; as it is, one must have a little money to go to housekeeping with. You wouldn't have me ask my father for that?"

"No, no. Besides, what would mother do without me just now—with this dreadful news to bear up against?" cried Katharine, hushing her sobs.

"I was sure you would see the whole thing in this sensible way, dear."

Katharine wiped her eyes and made a miserable effort to smile.

"Yes, I suppose it is best. But what if something happens to keep you away longer?—I should die! I should die!"

"But nothing can happen. If it should—that is, if I

do not come back in three months at the furthest—take your certificate, go up to my mother, show it to her, and tell the old folks to take care of you for my sake; for after that, you may consider yourself a widow!"

"A widow?"

"Yes, beyond a doubt; for if I do not come back in three months, be sure that nothing but death keeps me!"

"Don't! don't!" cried the poor wife, lifting her hands as if to ward off a blow.

"Well, well; there's nothing so dreadful about all this. One would think, by that face, you saw me in the water now, with a stone at my feet."

Again Katharine held up her hands and shut her eyes. The picture was too dreadful.

Spite of himself, Thrasher was touched by this evidence of affection; he changed his position, and stole his arm around her waist.

"There, now, we have settled all this terrible business, and can talk of brighter things," he said, caressingly. "Have you seen much of the old people since I went away?"

"I had no heart to go there often; but sometimes I saw your father at the gate. He always stopped if I was there when he rode by; and when mother was sick, Mrs. Thrasher always came."

"Dear old lady!" said Thrasher, with emotion. "When was she ever away when help could be given? Under all circumstances she will be good to you, wife or widow."

"Don't use that word widow; it makes me cold."

"Yet it is sometimes a pleasant word," said Thrasher, forgetting her presence in thoughts of another.

"A pleasant word, Nelson?"

"Pleasant!—did I say so? How strange that one's tongue will make such blunders."

Katharine was thoughtful for a moment. Something in her husband's manner brought back the feelings she had experienced at Mrs. Mason's house the night before. Vague spasms of jealousy, that culminated in a sharp pang when she remembered that the beautiful woman who had almost taunted her, was a widow now.

"Nelson," she said, awaking from her grief, for there was something of indignation mingled with it now, "last night I was at Mrs. Mason's."

"Indeed? Have you visited her often?"

"Only when I went to get news of the ship; for I don't much like her."

"Indeed?"

"No; she hurts one's feelings without meaning it, I dare say. Her haughtiness keeps every one at a distance."

Thrasher turned his face away, to conceal the proud smile that broke over it. He longed to defend the haughtiness of which Katharine complained—to say that it was the birthright of Ellen's great superiority over all other women. But he checked the impulse and only answered:

"Perhaps it is so. I have seen very little of her since she married that—that—I mean since she married Captain Mason."

"She told me something last night that surprised me."

"What was it?"

"She said that you had loved her before she accepted Captain Mason, and that she refused you."

"Ah, she told you that; and did her ladyship tell you why she took Mason instead of me?"

"Because you was a third or second mate, I forget which, and he was a captain; that was the reason she gave—but you speak as if it were true."

"Well, when I say that I had never been to sea in my life when John Mason married Ellen Palmer, you'll probably believe this nonsense."

"Then it was not true!" cried Katharine, smiling happily the first time that day.

"When women boast of their conquests, they seldom are true, Kate."

"But how unfeeling to say all this to me, your wife!"

"She didn't know that; with a secret like ours, one is always getting into trouble, Kate; as for this haughty woman, I would not go near her again—she'll find you out in no time."

Katharine smiled with a little bitterness.

"I suppose she would, for when the heart is full, it is hard to look calm. Last night I longed to tell the woman to her face, that I had a right to inquire after you—just as good a right as she had to be taking on about her husband."

"But you did not?"

"Certainly not. I only sat and cried. The little girl seemed to grudge me that comfort, for she said I had no husband nor father off to sea, and she couldn't tell what I wanted to cry for like her own mother."

"The little fool!" sneered Thrasher. "So they were having a general season of mourning, because Mason did not present himself?"

"Not exactly that," said Katharine; "still, I was sorry for Mrs. Mason and the little girl, for they felt bad enough; and now, when you are safe—when I ought to be so happy—it is a shame to talk over their faults. I dare say she didn't mean any thing. Such women sometimes fancy that men want to offer themselves who never had the idea. Besides, I told Mrs. Mason to her face that I didn't believe a word of it."

Thrasher laughed.

"And so you managed to get up a little sparring-match between you, and all upon my account?"

"Not quite that," answered Katharine, laughing also. "But I was so disappointed that every thing went wrong. Besides, it's no use denying it, Mrs. Mason made me angry. The idea of a married woman speaking of her offers! But then, you never did make her an offer—and I knew it."

"Well, any way, you have a pretty sure safeguard that I never shall make her one."

Katharine's face brightened beautifully. She looked toward him with a long, steady glance of affection. Tears trembled on her long lashes, and shone like dew where they had fallen on the damask of her cheek. But the smile upon her mouth, and the tenderness in her eyes, were enough to excuse any man for remembering, just then, that she was his own wife.

Thrasher drew her toward him, and kissed her with hearty warmth for the first time since his return home.

I am afraid the dear old people standing by the window saw it, for they looked at each other slyly and turned away.

CHAPTER XVIII.

MRS. MASON'S RICH UNCLE IN THE SOUTH.

"Mother!"

"Well, Katharine?"

"Nelson Thrasher came home last night."

"Better have stayed away!" answered the stern old lady, thrusting her knitting-needle into the goose-quill tube of her sheath, which was fastened, like the leaf of some great, red flower, on the right side of her waist. "No good ever followed his coming, that I ever heard of."

The color came into Katharine's face at this, for no woman likes to hear the man she loves spoken lightly of. Still she was striving to lead her mother's mind quietly to the bad news which lay heavy at her own heart, and did not feel the scornful tones in which the words were spoken, as she would have done.

For a little time there was no sound save the rattle of Mrs. Allen's needle in its sheath, which grew quicker and sharper each moment—a sure sign that the old lady was disturbed in her mind. After knitting twice round the top of a mixed stocking with unceasing vigor, amid a great click and rattle of the needles, she drew a length of yarn from the ball in her lap, with a jerk, and commenced again more deliberately. Katharine sat still, for she knew that this was preliminary to a renewal of the conversation. The first words, however, came out with a suddenness that made her start.

"Have you seen that fellow?"

Katharine could keep a secret, to her sorrow, poor thing; but she was incapable of a direct falsehood, so she answered truly, but with a quiver of fear in her voice.

"Yes, mother, he overtook me on my way home from Mrs. Mason's, last night."

"You saw him last night, last night, and got no word of my son. Where is he—when will he come, Katharine Allen? You could not have forgotten to ask."

"No, mother; but I—I was afraid to say any thing—

indeed, I did not know until this morning, for I saw him under the great butternut tree by the road, and went out—I did not know what sad news he brought."

"Sad news of my son!" cried the woman, drawing herself up as if to ward off a blow; "did you say sad news, Katharine?"

"Yes, mother," answered the beautiful girl, stealing close to the high-backed chair that her own face might be concealed, but her voice and limbs shook with the emotion she strove to suppress, and this the old woman felt to the core of her heart.

"Is my son dead?" she inquired, in a deep, hoarse voice.

"I fear so, mother."

"Fear! if you are not sure, speak out. Can't you see that I must know, or—or drop dead in my chair!"

"They were wrecked. My brother, my poor, poor brother would not abandon the vessel. They were compelled to leave him."

"They—who?"

"Every soul on board—no, I remember a negro and a little boy stayed with him."

"And the man Nelson Thrasher left my son on the stormy seas to die?"

"No, no, he only went with the rest; besides, he did not know, 'till I told him, that David was my brother, or your son."

"And they left him alone on the high seas to starve or drown," said the old woman, hoarsely. "Katharine Allen, never mention that man's name to me while you live. If you see him passing my house, give warning, that I may turn away and not curse him."

"Oh! mother, mother!"

"Be still, girl!"

The old woman's face was bloodless as parchment. She tried to go on with her work, but it fell from her hands, while she, unconscious of the loss, kept on with the motion of knitting, and looked down with her heavy black eyes as if she were counting the stitches that were only made in air.

"Mother, dear mother!"

The old lady did not speak, but the two hands dropped heavily in her lap, and her face fell down upon her bosom. The stillness of her grief was appalling. Katharine knelt before her, pale as death.

"Oh, mother, speak to me!"

All at once the old woman sat upright.

"Katharine Allen, tell me word for word what that man said to you of my son David."

"Be composed, don't look so hard, and I will—you shake so, mother."

"No, I do not shake. Pick up that knitting needle. There, do I knit evenly?" She placed the needle in its sheath, and began taking her stitches with slow precision.

True enough, her nerves were braced like steel, and like steel were her features locked. Katharine, poor soul, repeated what Thrasher had told her of the shipwreck, faithfully; softening it with the sweet tenderness of her voice, and putting in a word of excuse here and there. Then she came to the end, and told how that little boy and his noble slave insisted upon staying with Rice, after they had been saved from the very jaws of death—a terrible death—like that which threatened him.

Now the old woman's heart began to heave, and her great, heavy eyes kindled with living fire.

"Katharine," she said, "were these three martyrs alive when the cowards left them?"

"Yes, mother."

"Brave spirits," cried the old lady, rising suddenly. "They were in the hands of a merciful God, and he will save them! We will not mourn David as lost till that wreck is heard from. He is wise, and had courage. Had there been no hope he would have left with the rest."

Katharine's face brightened.

"Oh, mother, if it should prove so!"

"God did not inspire that brave child and the negro to stand by him for nothing. I *feel* that he is alive in the return of my own strength. When a strong man dies, his mother should feel weak, though he were a thousand miles off. But I, look, am I feeble and drooping, as if the staff of my age were torn from under me. If I stand upright, it is because he was, he *is* a good man. If I feel a power of vitality here, it is a proof that kindred life beats somewhere in response to it."

Katharine gazed at her mother in astonishment. There was something sublime in her great faith, a grandeur in her attitude like that which we give to a prophetess of the Bible. In her language and voice she seemed lifted out of herself.

Katharine always held her mother in profound reverence, in which love and fear were so equally blended, that she was seldom quite at rest in her presence. Now these feelings arose almost to religious exaltation. With all the softening influence of love and youth about her, she possessed many of the vigorous and noble traits which gave the old woman an acknowledged superiority in the neighborhood. With her mother's faith her hopes arose, and coming out of their deep grief the two sat down together, and strove to wrest some assurance of the son and brother's safety from the news that had reached them.

"He is alive—I feel that he is alive—my noble, strong boy!" said the old woman, as she laid her head on the pillow, but a heavy fear lay at her heart all the time.

"He was alive, and while there is life we may hope," whispered Katharine, sadly, as she sank to an unquiet sleep. A heavier sorrow, alas, lay upon her; the sorrow of a corroding secret which the last few hours had rendered almost a guilty burden from the new causes of detestation that had sprung up between her mother and the man she had so rashly married.

Thus every thing conspired to keep that young creature silent—Thrasher's request and the mother's prejudices, made more bitter by that man's desertion of her son in his hour of need, kept the secret weighed down in her bosom. True, this prejudice seemed very unreasonable; no one had compelled Rice to remain on the wreck. The same means of escape which brought the others home in safety was free to him; but a feeling stronger than facts possessed the old lady. Dead or alive, she believed that some treachery had been practiced on her son, and that the traitor was Nelson Thrasher.

Katharine remembered that the man was her husband —that in a few months she might be called upon to choose between the mother whom she regarded with loving reverence and the husband whom she almost adored. No wonder the poor girl shrunk from the moment which was to force the heart-rending decision upon her. It was a terrible position for one so young and so helpless. Between these two strong, positive characters, there was little hope of tranquillity for her, even though a partial reconciliation should take place.

One gleam of consolation did break upon her that night, when she remembered her mother's faith. David Rice was as good, as noble-hearted a man as ever drew breath. It was the forlorn hope that he yet lived, and would mediate for her and her husband with the stern mother.

It was impossible for Thrasher to visit Mrs. Allen's house; Katharine told him so on their next interview. Thus the young wife had no cause to complain that he spent but little time with her, and seemed both occupied and anxious when they did meet.

After the news which had disturbed her so, the old lady kept her room, and all the duties of the house fell upon Katharine, so that she had little opportunity to go any distance from home, and the gossip of the neighborhood seldom reached her.

Indeed, there was almost nothing for her to hear. Thrasher held very slight intercourse with the neighbors; and as his father's farm was, like Mrs. Allen's house, isolated among the hills, they knew little of his movements. That he occasionally was seen going down the footpath that led to Mrs. Mason's cottage in the pine woods, counted for nothing. Mason had been his captain, and it was but kind and right that he should offer sympathy to the widow. All the neighborhood was excited to pity in her behalf. What could she do, so proud and helpless, with that pretty child to support?

The widow was very desponding at first, and went about the house mournfully, her beautiful eyes heavy with tears, and her red lips ready to tremble if any one spoke to her. Compassion for her became general. The kind farmers stopped on their way from mill, and insisted on leaving a baking of flour at the gate. Pretty girls came with their aprons full of newly-laid eggs; and a little fellow, diverging every morning from his way to school, set a small tin pail, bright as silver, through the fence, and ran away as if he had been stealing. The pail always contained milk, with more cream in it than ever came there naturally, and sometimes, on the grass close by it, Mrs. Mason found a roll of golden butter folded up in a cool cabbage leaf.

Was it these kindnesses that softened the widow's grief, and brought the rich bloom back to her cheek so early after her loss? or had she some hidden source of consolation which kindled her face into more superb beauty, as the earth looks fresher and more heavenly after a tempest? Certain it was, her step soon regained its firmness, and her person its haughty poise. She spoke of Captain Mason less frequently, and there was in her manner something that surprised the good neighbors and repelled their sympathies. She seemed ashamed of the meagre attempts at mourning that she had been enabled to make; and exhausted quantities of vinegar and cold tea in refreshing bits of French crape and breadths of bombazine, which would look worn and rusty spite of all she could do, and this brought tears into her eyes when they had ceased to weep for deeper cares.

But, as I have said, after awhile all her beauty and animation came back. She began to talk hopefully of an uncle, who lived away off in the South, who would, perhaps, send for her and little Rose, when he received her letter, informing him of the helpless state in which they had been left. No one of the neighbors had ever heard of this uncle before, and her constant boasting about his wealth and the style in which he lived, rather set them aback. It cast their own little kindness quite into the shade. How could they offer fresh eggs and rolls of butter to a woman who wore her cheap black dress like a queen, and talked of pearls and diamonds all the day long, as if she had discovered a mine, and wanted to find out its exact value.

CHAPTER XIX.

MRS. MASON LEAVES THE PINE WOODS.

At last, Mrs. Mason announced that the expected letter had arrived, with money for her expenses to the South—she never told the exact locality—and that she and little Rose would set forth at once, taking the steamboat from New Haven to New York, where her passage southward was already engaged.

All this was very magnificent and almost startling, but corroborated by a supply of money which the widow evidently possessed, and by the disposition of her little household furniture, which she distributed among her friends with the careless prodigality of a princess.

The preparations for her departure went on spiritedly. With nothing to prepare; for all her new mourning dresses, she announced, were to be made in New York; it was only packing a small trunk, and taking leave of the old neighbors, and she was ready with little Rose to go forth into her new life. A neighbor had been engaged to take her to town in a dashing, one horse wagon, which he had just bought, and in this way the whole arrangement promised to go off with the eclat which the widow Mason always affected.

Thus time passed until the night before her journey. The furniture had not yet been removed, and every thing retained the old homelike aspect; from any appearance of confusion that existed, you would have fancied that the mistress of the house was only going out for a morning drive. She seemed rather elated than otherwise, and received her friends with half royal condescension, not absolutely offensive, but calculated to check the honest grief with which old neighbors parted on those days when a household was breaking up. Many kind wishes were, however, exchanged, little presents were brought in, such as patchwork holders, work bags, and pincushions, besides a pair of fine, lambs' wool mittens, knitted by the oldest woman in the town, was presented to her with a gentle message of farewell, followed by various other trifles, calculated to appeal eloquently to a kind heart. All these, the widow received with concealed and smiling indifference, thinking in her soul how paltry such things were to a person of her expectations.

But little Rose made up for all her mother's lack of feeling. She was broken-hearted at the thought of leaving her playmates, burst into tears when the old people patted her on the head, and refused to be comforted by all the promises of grandeur which were whispered in her ear, either by her mother or her friends.

That night—after the neighbors had gone away, and Rose was in bed hugging a home-made doll which one of the little girls had brought her—a boy who had been kept late with his lessons, climbed softly over the door yard fence. He was afraid that the gate would creak, and disturb the family if Rose should be in bed; so with a long string of robins' eggs held in one hand, he leaped into the grass and stole softly up to one of the front windows. A corner of the paper blind was turned up by the back of a chair which it had fallen against, and through this opening, our little adventurer saw clearly into the room. First, he looked for Rose, the object of his juvenile idolatry; but her little chair was empty, and her tiny morocco shoes and red worsted stockings lay in a heap on the seat, sure proofs that she had gone to bed.

This was a sad disappointment to the lad, but he soon forgot it in the surprise which followed. Mrs. Mason and some strange man were sitting by a work table, which stood near the window. A tallow candle shed its light on the widow's face, but the man sat with his back to the window, his features all in deep shadow. His hand was extended half over the table, clutching a quantity of gold or silver coins, the boy could not tell which, for gold money he had never seen, and the pieces that escaped between the man's fingers, and fell ringing on the table, might have been Spanish quarters, or guineas, for aught he knew. At any rate, that great handful of money seemed a marvellous sum to him, and when Mrs. Mason received it in her two hands, he wondered that she did not jump for joy. But instead of this, she took a variegated work bag from the table drawer, poured the money into it with some smiling remark, and crossing the room, unlocked her trunk and placed the bag in one corner.

While she was thus occupied, the lad observed a

strange looking box upon the table, which the person still sitting there had opened. A bright flash came out of the box, as if something had struck fire within. Mrs. Mason came back to the table. She had taken off her mourning dress, replacing it with a black silk skirt and dimity short gown, with loose, open sleeves that left her fine arms partially exposed, every time she lifted them. She came up to the table and seemed struck with wonder, for lifting up both arms, she uttered an exclamation of delight which the boy heard clearly.

The man snatched something from the box, arose, and seized her arm. A little struggle followed, quick, impassioned words, which the listener did not understand, but he saw that the man was pleading for something which she smilingly refused. That boy knew at last what it meant; he had begged and coaxed exactly in the same way for a good-by kiss, which little Rose resisted, almost as her mother was doing now. He had promised the very string of robins' eggs in his hand, as a temptation, and all to no effect. He remembered his own disappointment, and rather pitied the poor man, who, baffled and mortified, bent down and kissed Mrs. Mason's arm, just above a glittering band which circled the wrist, flashing there like a ribbon of fire.

Mrs. Mason was evidently angry and resentful, even of this liberty. She tore the bracelet from her arm, and tossed it haughtily into the box. Still the man's back was toward the window, so it was impossible to mark the effect this had on him, save by the droop of his shoulders, and a deprecating action of the hands. But the widow motioned him away, frowning heavily. The man sat down, closed the box, and bent his forehead upon it. She leaned over the table and spoke to him.

He started up with a suddenness that frightened the lad, who leaped the fence like a deer, and fled up the road.

It was a long time before the boy ever mentioned what he had witnessed that night. The remembrance of his own shy feelings about little Rose kept him silent. Besides this, he had a consciousness that there was something to be ashamed of in peeping through the windows of a neighbor's house, and so wisely kept his peace about what he had discovered in this surreptitous manner.

The next morning, a little group of neighbors gathered to see Mrs. Mason off. A light, yellow wagon, stood before the gate, a restive, gray horse, stamped and chafed beneath his harness till it rattled again. The widow was shaking hands in the entry, while the proud owner of that equipage carried out her little hair trunk, and put it behind the seat. Rose was crying bitterly over a gray kitten that came and rubbed itself against her ankles, and purred as if it rather enjoyed the unusual commotion. This pretty child really seemed to feel the parting from her home much more keenly than her mother.

It was the father of the bright boy that had so naughtily looked into the window—who owned the wagon. With his heart full of grief, the poor fellow had begged a ride, and stood dolefully by the gate, peeping at little Rose through an opening of the boards.

At last Mrs. Mason came forth into the morning sunshine, prepared for her journey. The earth was wet, and she gathered up the skirt of her dark dress, as a queen manages her train, revealing a finely shaped foot, with which she trod daintily through the grass. Really

It was difficult to say which struck the beholder most forcibly in that woman; the regal style with which she carried herself, or the marvellous physical beauty which gave grace to her very haughtiness. No one could deny that she was a superb creature, even in that cheap bombazine dress and gloomy black bonnet.

Mrs. Mason took her seat in the wagon. The owner placed himself by her side, and began to unwind the long lash from his whip handle, with the air of a man who meant to do the thing up handsomely. Little Rose had been lifted over the wheel, and placed into the centre of the seat, like an exclamation point in the middle of a short sentence. Thus they were all crowded together a little uncomfortably.

"Wait, wait," cried the lad, dashing into the house, and bringing forth Rose's tiny arm-chair with its pretty crimson cushion. "There," he said, choking back a great sob, "if pa brings it back in the wagon, maybe you'll let me keep it; nobody shall ever sit in it, Rose, 'till you come home again."

Then Rose covered her face with two dimpled little hands that were wet all over in a moment. "Oh, don't —la, don't!"

The lad sprang up on the hub of the front wheel, and laid the string of robins' eggs into her lap, his face all in a blaze, and his eyes full of tears.

"Don't forget me, Rose, don't—no boy will ever love you half so much as I do."

Rose dropped her hands, looked down at the blue eggs in her lap, and throwing her arms around his neck, kissed him three or four times.

The farmer and Mrs. Mason looked at each other, and laughed softly. The boy heard them, sprang down from the wheel, and dashed into the house, where no one could see what a great baby he was ready to make of himself. Then he watched the wagon drive off through a flood of blinding tears, while little Rose flung kisses back at random, sobbing as if her heart would break, and wondering if any of them would reach him.

When the farmer returned from his ten miles' drive into New Haven, he brought news that a steamboat lay at the foot of "Long Wharf," ready to sail in half an hour after Mrs. Mason reached it, and that he saw her go on board in great spirits, with Rose, who had cried all the way, but seemed a little pacified by the sight of the broad waters, and the great puffing boat in which she was about to cross them.

Nelson Thrasher happened to be standing near when the farmer said this, and one of the rare smiles I have spoken of crossed his face, but he made no observations, and soon took a cross-cut through the fields which led him by Mrs. Allen's, on his way home. Katharine was watching for him at the back window. She had heard of Mrs. Mason's journey, and exulted a little when Nelson passed the house on his way to Falls Hill, an hour after she had started. All that night she had been troubled lest he should wish to bid the widow farewell; for, spite of herself, a lingering distrust still kept its hold on her heart, when she remembered the conversation of that evening.

Thrasher saw her at the window, and made a signal, which soon brought her outside of the stone wall, and under a huge apple tree, which flung its branches across it and into the garden.

Never since his return had Thrasher seemed so cheer

ful. He even inquired after the old lady with something of interest, and spoke of the time when she would regard him with less prejudice. All this gave Katharine a lighter heart; her beauty, which had been dimmed by adversity of late, bloomed out again. If not so stately as Mrs. Mason, she was far more lovely, and her fair, sweet face was mobile with sentiments which the widow could not have understood. Compared to that woman, she was like the apple blossoms of May contrasted with autumn fruit—one a child of the pure, bright spring, appealing to the imagination; the other a growth of storm, sunshine, and dew, mellowing down from its first delicate beauty to a perfection of ripeness which sense alone can appreciate. There existed elements in that young creature's character from which the best poetry of life is wrought. Heroism, self-abnegation, endurance, and truthfulness—all these rendered her moral character beautiful as her person.

But, alas! our future pages will prove all this. Why should we attempt to foreshadow in words a destiny and a nature like hers? It is enough that she looked lovely as an April morning that bright day, as she stood under the apple tree, leaning against the mossy old wall, talking to her husband, sometimes with her lips, sometimes with her wonderful eyes, which said a thousand loving things that her voice refused to utter. He fell into the current of her cheerfulness, and chatted pleasantly, till the slanting shadows warned her that the tea hour had arrived, and that her mother would be impatient. With his kisses warm upon her mouth, she went singing into the house, happy and rich in sudden joyousness.

CHAPTER XX.

ANOTHER SEPARATION.

It was about two weeks after Mrs. Mason's departure, when Thrasher began to talk of going to sea again. This depressed his parents greatly. They had hoped that his attachment to Katharine Allen would have kept him at the homestead. Thus they had carefully avoided any allusion to the subject of his departure, satisfied that every thing was progressing to forward their wishes. When he spoke of going away in the course of another week, it was a terrible shock to them, and seemed a painful subject to himself.

Katharine had, from the first, expected his departure—its necessity had been urged upon her on their first meeting under the butternut tree. She acquiesced in his decision then, and never thought of disputing it afterward. But, as the time drew near, she became very sad—vague doubts beset her night and day—formless, reasonless, as she strove to convince herself; but the struggle was always going on—the feelings reasoned out of her mind overnight, were certain to return in the morning.

It was a sorrowful position for a young creature like her, inexperienced every way, needing counsel as no human being ever required it before, yet afraid to breathe a word of the trouble that oppressed her, lest it should alienate her entirely from her suffering mother, whom, next to Thrasher, she loved with the tenderest devotion.

It was an honor to this young creature that she bore

all this load of anxiety without a single word of complaint. She felt that all the concealment that followed her marriage had sprung from her own desire. But the dread of giving pain to her mother had exerted an overpowering influence over her. Thrasher had not seemed to care about the matter. Whether his marriage was proclaimed at once or not, had been a subject of indifference. If secrecy had become more important now, she did not realize it; but imagined that he was still indulging her fears rather than guiding them. The sad news that he had brought, the sickness it had inflicted upon her mother, were stern reasons why she should not speak then.

All this Thrasher knew, and was content to leave things to their natural course. So, instead of offering hindrance to his departure, Katharine was almost anxious for him to go, that his return within the promised time might be more certain.

Still the young man lingered at the homestead, though letters reached him from New York twice in one week, from ship owners, he said, urging him to be on hand for a fresh voyage, where, he could not exactly tell. The vessel belonged to no established line, but traded with the West Indies, generally.

The old people were inconsolable. It seemed, they both said plaintively, as if they were parting with their son forever. Why must he leave them again? The homestead and all they possessed in the world should be his if he would but marry and settle down. They only wanted a comfortable room in some corner of the old house, where, with a knowledge of his presence and happiness, their content would be perfect.

He could not answer these tender entreaties, but sat

moodily, striving not to listen. His mind was made up —his career marked out. The great loves of his life were antagonistic; one must be surrendered—the holy or the unholy. He turned from the wholesome fruit, and took that which was ashen at the core.

Thrasher might have avoided the last farewell; but painful as it was, he could not force himself to leave the old people unawares. The last evening must come, the last good-night must be said. He would listen to the old man's voice on his knees once more, and let his mother kiss him, as of old, before he went to sleep in that house for the last time. It was all very painful—worse than leaving his young wife; worse than death, he said to himself, a hundred times; all his innocent memories, all his household affections, to be torn up at the roots by his own hands. For what, and for whom?

Would other love come into his life and compensate for this which he threw away? His teeth were clenched, and great drops stood on his forehead, as he asked these questions. But his resolve was made; nothing could change that—not even the gentle old woman, with sweet motherly love in her eyes, who came and sat by him so meekly, and talked of the next thanksgiving, when he would be at home again, and they would have such a dinner. She had set aside the plumpest young turkey on the farm, and it should not be killed till he came back—thanksgiving or no thanksgiving.

God help the man! He stood out against all this; every affectionate string in his heart trembled in the struggle, but his bad, strong will, carried him through.

That night he met Katharine by the old stone wall, when they bade each other farewell. He was gentle to her then, and his voice was so full of anguish, that she gathered up her strength to comfort him. The poor girl spoke hopefully of the little time they would be apart, and how constantly she would think of him—pray for him. She dwelt, too, on other things—on the great happiness that would come in the future. Her voice grew soft with tenderness, and her sweet face looked heavenly in the starlight, as she made this womanly effort to console him; but his eyes were cast down, and a heavy, leaden feeling, weighed upon his shoulders. Dumb and granite-hearted, he listened, striving not to hear.

Katharine's time was up; in a few minutes her old mother would be calling for her. She already saw her tall person casting its shadow across the window, as she walked to and fro, impatient of her loneliness.

"Nelson, I must go!"

The anguish that broke forth in these words smote through his heart, making it leap and tremble, but leaving only a gleam of tenderness behind. The rock of his stern will was unbroken even by that cry, from a heart as true and loving as ever beat in a woman's bosom.

He trembled from head to foot, within the clasp of her arms; cold, spasmodic kisses were pressed on her face. The hands which grasped hers at last, were cold as ice.

They parted thus. He turned and walked heavily away, while Katharine went back to her mother, entreating God to help her bear this separation. It was only for a little time, she murmured over and over again; but even then, she had need of strength from heaven.

Few words were uttered in the Thrasher homestead that night. The old man sat upon the hearth, grave and heavy hearted, smoking at intervals, but quite unconscious when the pipe went out between his lips.

The mother held her knitting work—she would not have been herself without it—but her fingers rested motionless on the needles half the time, and she sat gazing wistfully upon the floor till the tears blinded her. Then she would start, look meekly around, to be sure that she was not observed, and wipe her eyes with the cotton handkerchief which she softly drew from her pocket.

Thrasher saw all this, and the iron heart almost melted within him. If the dear old people suffered thus at a temporary parting, what would the future bring them? Again the struggle commenced, battled, strove, tortured him, but ended as before.

In the morning, long before daylight, he arose, and with a valise in his hand, went away, leaving every thing behind him in darkness. When the old people missed him, they said very gently to one another, "He could not bear to say good-by. It was his kind heart. Our Nelson always was kind-hearted."

Katharine, who had watched at her window from dawn until the sun was high, growing pale and sad every moment, heard that he was gone, and whispered, amid her tears, "His heart failed him; he shrunk from seeing my poor face again—my own dear husband; how kind-hearted he is!"

CHAPTER XXI.

THE MINISTER AT BAYS HOLLOW GETS A WIFE.

I DARE say that the village to which I take my reader is a town of some importance now; but years ago, it was nothing but a cluster of houses snugly nested in a valley, through which a small stream wound itself, sinuously creeping through the meadows and along the base of the hills, in so many picturesque windings, that you really could not tell in what direction it was destined to run at last, north or south.

The village stood at two crossroads, which the river intersected three or four times; besides, a brook from the hills met it just below the corners, demanding a little plank bridge for itself, over which a clump of golden willows bent and sighed pleasantly all the day long. A great, square, barnlike meeting-house, with pews laid out like town lots, and aisles broader than any street in Constantinople, occupied the centre of the village. A range of wagon sheds stood behind it, and a small prairie of greensward lay all around it. There had been some vague attempt at a steeple, which the prejudices of the community had cut short at the belfry, and left without a spire, which gave the edifice a broad, flat look, which would have driven a modern architect mad.

On the top of a broad platform, which rose half way to the ceiling, and was approached by two steep flights of steps, was perched a little sentry box of a pulpit, surmounted by something in the shape of a huge toadstool, which the architects of that day called a sounding board.

In this pulpit, Sunday after Sunday, Mr. Prior, minister of the parish, held forth after the good old fashion, when sermons had more heads than a centipede has legs, and hearers got the value of the minister's salary in good, sound gospel. Besides, Mr. Prior had other sources of popularity—his doctrine was sound, and his sentences offered rare opportunities for short snoozes, which came oftenest between seventhly and eighthly, or thereabout. Not that minister Prior was dull—nothing of the kind; he was a very learned man, educated solemnly in a gloomy college, and lifted so completely out of the world during his clerical studies that he never quite found his way back again.

After Mr. Prior had settled himself in the ministry some ten or fifteen years, he married the most accomplished and correct person of all that region, a lady who had kept the district school, to general acceptance, six consecutive summers, had embroidered a cover for the communion table with her own hands, and was only prevented adding a gorgeous book mark and a pair of slippers for the minister, by the fear of what people might say.

I think it was one of his deacons who first put a vague idea of matrimony in the minister's head. One day the two were standing on a little swell of ground which overlooked the juncture of the mountain rivulet and the river. The clump of golden willows looked beautiful that morning; the yellow boughs and twigs glanced in the sunshine, and the thick leaves were all in a quiver under the kisses of the wind. Have I said that the brook clove one of the greenest meadows you ever set eyes on, before it crossed the road? If not, understand that pleasant fact now, and more, that groups of trees had been left near the brook, all along its banks, and one of its grand curves hedged in the loveliest spot for a house your imagination ever dwelt upon.

"I say, minister," said the deacon—this was some time before our story, remember—"I say, what if you get married, and settle down in that ere meadow?"

The minister blushed, and looked, as the deacon afterward said, every which way, before he answered.

"Me marry, Deacon Smith; me!"

"And why not? there's acres of Scripture for it, and not one word agin it; for how could St. Paul know any thing about it, never having had experience like us married men?"

"Us married men," how strange the words sounded. "Us married men." The minister turned the bow of his white cravat more in front and settled himself complacently in his rusty black clothes. "Us married men."

"We talked about it in vestry meeting t'other night, and the notion seemed to take wonderfully. We all agreed to a T about the person, but our land for a home lot, building the house, and all that, was rather a puzzler."

"I should think so," said the minister, taking out a broad silk handkerchief, and wiping his forehead, which was getting crimson again. "Then you agreed on—on—on the person."

"Unanimous," answered the deacon. "Not a dissenting voice."

"And—and—"

"Oh, yes, of course you've the best right of anybody to know first. It's Miss Bruce—salt of the earth—salt of the earth, minister."

"You think so?" said the pastor, meekly.

"We know it; trust the vestry for discretion and sound judgment too. Isn't that a building spot, now."

"Beautiful," said the minister, in a confused way; "but the lady, did you ask her?"

"Not exactly; agreed to put it to vote first. Then I promised to inform you of the sense of the meeting, and brother Wells will speak to Miss Bruce. It's all settled before this time, I dare say."

The minister drew a deep breath, as if he had just come out of a shower bath, and then, his vision being cleared, took a survey of the meadow lot. The deacon saw how his attention was directed, and went on.

"I agreed to give the lot, the bull meadow, understand. Deacon Styles will find the timber, and the rest 'll be divided up, sort of ginerally, among the congregation. Then the women folks are going to get up quiltings, and spinning frolics, and so on. In about three months, I reckon, all will be ready."

Again the minister gave a shower bath gasp.

"There is brother Wells coming now, on his black horse, all fixed up in his Sunday clothes," cried the deacon, triumphantly.

The brother rode up, looking as if he had something portentous on his mind. "Well," said the deacon, "how did you get along, brother Wells?"

"Tolerably, tolerably; she was a little sot on having the minister come over himself, but when I told her it was the solemn sense of the vestry, of course she gave in."

"And she—no objections," said the minister.

"Objections!" cried both the men at once, "how could she?"

"Well, I don't know," answered the pastor. "That is, I didn't know but she might think it a little sudden."

"Sudden! why it has been on our minds a whole year. It isn't just the thing for our minister to be boarding about like a schoolmaster. A servant of the Lord should set under his own vine and fig tree."

The minister wiped his face again, and cast a glance toward the meadow, which began to look like home already.

THE MINISTER GETS A WIFE. 169

"I stopped at the saw-mill and bespoke the timber," said brother Wells; "so if you'd just as lief, we'll go down and pick out the exact spot."

A smile glowed out on the minister's face. The deacons saw it, and nodded pleasantly one to the other.

"Minister," said Wells, leaning down from his horse, "if you should take a notion to go over yonder any time afore the house is built, just consider this ere black horse as your own."

"Thank you kindly, brother."

"And," said Deacon French, "I stopped at the tailor's coming along; he's got a firstrate piece of English broadcloth, but he says it's seven years since you have been measured, minister, and to make a good fit you'll have to go again."

"Doubtless—doubtless!" answered the minister, ready to cry under all this goodness—a house, a wife, and a new suit of clothes all at once! It really was too much of a mercy; he didn't know how to be thankful enough.

Well, they went down to the meadow, selected a lovely spot for the house, and stopped at the tailor's on their way home. That very week a little boy came over to Deacon Wells, and asked, in a mysterious way, if he would let the minister have his black horse to ride over the hill.

Deacon Wells smiled grimly, and brought out the horse himself, taking great pains to tighten the saddle girth and shorten the stirrup leathers properly, before he gave the bridle into the boy's hand.

It wasn't the last time that black horse was sent for to go over the hill, and the result exhibited itself, in the course of a few months, in a pretty, white house, with a porch and dormer windows, standing in the greenest curve of the brook; a thicket of wild roses, only half shutting out a view of the water; ducks were swimming up and down the little stream, and a flock of hens running riot in the meadow grass. Besides this, a neat, little body, with the quaintest bonnet and neatest dress in the world, came into the meeting-house with the minister, who appeared in a new suit of black, separated from him in the broad aisle in front of the deacon's seat, and while he mounted the pulpit stairs, she turned into a side pew, and listened to his discourse, from beginning to end, with unbroken interest.

But it is the weakness of vestry-men to vote money which they have not the power to collect. The minister was married, and his house built, but a debt lay on it, which troubled him as only studious men can be troubled by monied claims.

The little wife came to his aid. She was a highly accomplished, well educated woman, who had earned her own living from early girlhood, and was not ashamed or afraid to help her husband in any womanly fashion that presented itself. She had plenty of room, good health, and a clear brain, all sources of usefulness, which she was prompt to put into action. Teaching was her business. If she could obtain a couple of boarding scholars into her own house, at city prices, the debts upon their home would soon be removed.

The dainty little housewife began to talk with her husband about the project one morning just as he was resolving the fifth head of his next sermon, at which time he never heard a syllable addressed to him by any mortal being, but always assented blandly to every thing proposed.

So, under the full conviction that he approved her plan, she wrote to a friend in New York, requesting her to aid in obtaining the desired pupils.

When his sermon was over, the minister received the news of this arrangement with considerable astonishment, but he submitted without protest, as the letter had already gone.

CHAPTER XXII.

THE MINISTER'S WIFE TAKES PUPILS.

BAYS HOLLOW stands on the very boundary line which separates Connecticut from New York. Half the valley was in one State, half in the other; but the minister's house, in fact the whole village, lay in Connecticut. Persons acquainted with the geography of that part of the country, will understand that the easiest mode of access to this place before railroads threw their iron belts from State to State, was by the Hudson river. Indeed, between New York and the minister's house, there was scarcely half a day's land travel, and that was easily accomplished in a stage-coach that ran twice a week from the river.

One night, it was late in the autumn, this stage-coach stopped at the minister's house, and after great trampling of horses, crashing of iron steps, and unhooking of straps, a lady was assisted out. Her trunk was set on the turf, a basket, and after that, a charming little girl was lifted through the door; bang—crash—a shout to the horses, and off the stage thundered, arousing the whole neighborhood with its noise.

Mrs. Prior came out with a white sun bonnet shading her modest face, and a tidy, black apron tied over her calico dress. The rich travelling costume of the lady, her stately beauty, joined with a haughty pride of carriage, impressed her greatly. The little girl was, no doubt, to be her pupil. What a lovely little fairy she was, with her blue eyes so full of light, and her curls falling in waves and dancing in ringlets over her shoulders.

"Is it Mrs. Prior?" inquired the traveller, with a sort of unpleasant politeness. "Your friend in New York recommended this as a quiet place where I and my daughter could be made comfortable for a few months."

"Yes, madame," said the lady, somewhat disturbed; "I desired scholars, not boarders only."

"And I bring you scholars, madame."

"One—yes, I see, and a sweet creature she is," said the minister's wife, looking at the little girl, who was drawing slowly toward her.

"More than one," answered the lady, blushing crimson; "I wish to study myself, partly to encourage the child, partly because I require lessons almost as much as she does."

"You, lady?"

"No matter about explanations. I have really come to be your pupil with my daughter; my education is deficient—I wish to learn. I am a widow, and quiet is good for me. I am quick, have a fine memory, and am willing to study hard. This is my object in coming—will you take me?"

"If you wish it, certainly; but we are plain people—the minister and I; our way of living may not suit you."

"Do not trouble yourself about that. I shall content myself with any thing; it is knowledge I came after."

"I—I suppose my friend said something about terms," faltered the minister's wife, blushing.

"Certainly; but that was for children; of course I shall be more trouble. If I pay you just as much again will it answer?"

"It would be wrong to take it."

"Not at all; so if you will have the trunks carried in we can settle the terms comfortably. I am ready to pay half the sum in advance, and commence study at once."

Mrs. Prior called the hired girl to help carry in the trunks, and led the way into the parlor. Mr. Prior passed them in the hall and made one of his solemnly polite bows. The visitor answered it with a sweeping salutation, and entered the parlor a little discomfited.

"Your husband is a clergyman, as I understand?"

"Yes, he is the minister here; I hope you will like him."

"Oh, certainly."

The lady placed her travelling basket on the table, and opening it took out a heavy purse. Pouring out a quantity of gold she divided it without counting and pushed it toward Mrs. Prior.

"This will be sufficient to commence with, I fancy."

Mrs. Prior looked at the little pile of Louis d'or in absolute consternation. In her whole life she had never seen so much gold.

"It is good money," said the lady.

"Yes, doubtless," answered the minister's wife, examining a piece of gold. "French coin."

"You read French, then?"

"Oh, yes."

"And can teach it?"

"I think so."

"And how long will it take me to learn?"

"That depends on the—the powers of application you possess."

"Oh, never fear, I accomplish all I undertake—music too?"

"I have no instrument."

"But you can teach music?"

"Yes."

"Then if there is an instrument to be got we will have it. This is a nice, airy room, and a little more furniture would not hurt it."

Mrs. Prior was busy counting the gold; her face flushed, and she made sad mistakes.

"This is too much," she said. "It would cover board and tuition for a year."

"Well, perhaps we shall stay so long."

"But even then——"

The lady made an impatient gesture.

"Pray don't trouble me about the money. If it is enough, well—if not, I will give you more."

Here the minister came in. His wife moved toward him with the gold in her hands.

"See what the Lord has done for us through this lady," she said.

He glanced at the gold, smiled benignly, and with gentle politeness inquired the lady's name.

"Mrs. Mason—Ellen Mason, of South Carolina," she answered, coloring as she spoke. "Rose, my dear, come and shake hands with the gentleman."

Rose shut the fanciful little basket that she carried

on her arm and came forward smiling in all her features; but as she stood on tiptoe pursing her pretty mouth like a rosebud, her mother took up the basket. The little girl saw it, broke away from the minister's hold and ran back, crying out:

"Oh, ma—ma! take care or you'll break my string of robins' eggs!"

CHAPTER XXIII.

THE VILLAGE DOCTOR IN A SNOW-STORM.

Snow! deep, deep snow everywhere! It lay three feet on a level in the river vale. It spread a shining crust over the hills. It lodged in the branches of the densely green pine woods, and whitened the roof of every house in the neighborhood. The burying-ground on the hill, was wrapped so deep in a fleecy shroud, that you could hardly distinguish the marble grave-stones from its white surface, and the church, always a beautiful object, with its slender steeple and white walls, looked like a temple wrought from the snow itself—something that the angels had visited overnight, and left spotless as themselves.

With all this depth and volume of snow, crusted over as it had been by a sharp frost, it was almost impossible that the roads could be broken in a single day. Still, a few ox sleds had marked out the line of the turnpike, and some sleighs had followed in their track, with a wrangle of bells that told of the struggle made by the smoking horses which drew them. On the bank of the river, on the Chewstown side, the highway runs along the side of a hill, which terminates abruptly at the bridge, where the New Haven turnpike intersects it.

There is nothing very beautiful about the spot now, for the hemlocks, and young tamarisks are all cut down, the dog-wood and shad-blossoms cleared away, and the hill is almost left without a shade. But at the time of this snow-storm, the naked boughs and evergreens proved how thick and green the summer shadows must be, and if the "Rock Spring" sent its waters flashing through the snow, melting it softly away, you could, at least, imagine how cool and bright they were when ferns, mosses, and violets crept into the turf, and covered the rocks with the green and azure of a spring birth.

This road was not generally so much travelled as the one across the sand banks, but two or three loads of wood had passed that way, revealing the depths of the drifts without rendering them much more passable. Still a "solitary horseman" came out from the shelter of the hemlocks, and made his way very slowly toward the bridge. His horse, a stout animal, with any amount of mane and foretop streaming in the wind, came tramping heavily through the snow, emitting clouds of steam from his sides, while each labored breath bearded his under lip with icicles, and fringed his dilating nostrils with quivering frost-work.

The man who had braved that almost impassable road and cold day, was one of the most remarkable personages known in that portion of the country. His very eccentricities gave force and vitality to the general regard. Singular in person, singular in character, unlike all other men in almost every particular, he was, perhaps, somewhat for this very reason, looked up to and reverenced as the peculiar property of the neighborhood. Learned he certainly was; and neither before or after has another man been found who could, in all things, pretend to fill his place.

This man was the village doctor; no, the district doctor, rather, for his ride extended over thirty miles, and as a consulting physician over the whole State. With a huge bear-skin cap upon his head, and an ample brown overcoat, girded to his waist by a broad leather belt, and falling low on each side of his horse, he issued from behind the trees. Two crutches, worn smooth as glass, were crossed before him on the saddle bow. He held the bridle loosely in his hands and encouraged the horse with many a droll saying, as if the animal were human and could enjoy his quaint humor. At the "Rock Spring" there was a struggle between the doctor and his steed. For an unknown number of years the horse had invariably quenched his thirst in that particular place, and he was determined not to make this day an exception, though a deep round hole, scarcely larger than the doctor's cap, and a moist sinking of the snow across the road might have deceived a less sagacious animal into a belief that this old drinking place had been swallowed up by the storm.

There was no deceiving our doctor's brown horse in any thing, much less in a case of appetite like that. He was a dainty animal in the matter of drink, and water so pure and crystaline as that which lost its smothered music in the snow, was not to be found within twenty miles.

The doctor was in haste, or he never would have dreamed of contesting any thing with his faithful steed.

Indeed, the case must have been one of life or death which could bring any man on the highway at a time like that. He began to protest and reason with the horse after his eccentric fashion, and finally went so far as to gather up the bridle and tighten the bit, a procedure which so astonished the horse that he backed sideways into a drift, viciously slanted his ears, and subsided into a state of masterly inactivity, the most difficult thing to conquer that we know of, either in statesmanship or horseflesh.

The doctor chuckled, laid the bridle down caressingly on the neck that had made a lamentable failure in striving to arch itself, and folding his hands in the loose sleeves of his overdress, waited. Obstinate animals and obstinate men are apt to feel as if fighting the air when no one opposes them. The horse began to realize this sensation. The snow-drift into which he had backed was cold and deep. The waters of the spring murmured a soft enticement. First, he pointed one ear and turned his head with sly, compunctious timidity, as if ashamed to enjoy his own triumph. Then he pointed the other ear, shook himself a little, tramped heavily toward the spring, and thrusting his head deep into the snow, began to drink.

The doctor indulged in a laugh, and when the horse withdrew his head, shaking a storm of drops back into the spring, he patted him softly, called him a good fellow for having his own way, and appeared so much like the obliged party that the animal, to his dying hour, was never quite certain of his own triumph.

After all, this struggle had taken but little time. The horse breasted his work with fresh vigor after it. He pushed through and trampled down the snow until he reached the bridge, stalked over it, toiled through the valley and up Falls Hill, never stopping till he reached the huge willow tree which stood on the crossroad that led to Bungy. This was a farming district, back of Castle Rock, where the Thrasher farm and Mrs. Allen's place lay.

While the doctor was breathing his horse under the willow, a teamster passed with a large sled, on which some bags of grain were piled. He stopped his oxen with a flourish of the goad, and a storm of who—who-o-as, while he held a little conversation.

"Tough teaming this!" he said. "Hard on young cattle; but somebody must go first. Any of the neighbors dangerous out this way, doctor?"

"No," answered the doctor, with a twinkle of the eye.

"Then what on arth brings you out?"

"Wanted a ride, and thought perhaps I could hunt up a patient"

"Wal, now I shouldn't a thought it! Which way are you a going, if I may be so bold?"

"Haven't decided. If you've got a copper in your pocket, toss up. It's all the same to me."

The man took a new cent from his pocket, and balancing it on his thumb nail, he called out—

"Which'll ye have, doctor?"

"Heads."

Up flashed the cent into the sunshine, then down to the teamster's feet, where it made a deep, round hole in the snow.

"Heads it is, doctor," cried the man, fishing his coin up in a handful of flakes.

"True enough! then I will ride over the hill. That toss up decides it."

"You'll never get there, doctor; drifts over your head."

The doctor was ploughing his way up the Bungy road, and did not seem to hear this prediction. He was evidently very anxious to go forward, and encouraged his horse with sharp ejaculations, as they approached the hills. The animal understood it all, and lending himself to the work, stamped and pursued his way onward with the perseverance of a veteran; but his progress was necessarily slow, and the doctor's broad forehead gathered into an anxious frown under his cap.

"Poor thing—poor thing—she may be dead before we get there," he muttered more than once, and then he would commence expostulating with the horse, who, good fellow, was doing his very best. Just as they were ascending the brow of the hill, a woman was seen in advance, wildly pushing her way through the snow. She saw the doctor, and waved her arms in distracted haste, beckoning him to come on.

The doctor must have been insane with anxiety to have ventured on it. But he seized one of his crutches and gave the horse a back-handed blow. A plunge that almost unseated the imprudent man—a storm of snow about his ears, and the animal broke into one of the most extraordinary gaits that ever a horseman experienced—backing down, rushing forward, and making side movements that came very near landing the doctor head foremost in a huge wave-like drift that covered the fence close by to its topmost rail.

At last, with great coaxing and expostulation, this state of things was reduced to the most awkward attempt at a trot, which the exasperated animal persisted in, though his efforts were broken up at every other step.

The woman stood for a minute knee-deep in the snow. She only ceased wringing her hands to beckon him forward. When certain that he was doing his best, she turned and walked quickly up the road, and entered Mrs. Allen's house.

"I thought so—I feared it," muttered the doctor, "but who ever saw riding like this? It's like wading through a desert of cotton wool. Don't you think so, old fellow?"

The horse was indignant yet, and scorned to give any sign that he understood those conciliatory tones, even by a twinkle of the ear. On he scrambled, deeply injured in his feelings, but resolved to do his duty, and leave the rest on his master's conscience.

At last they reached the gate which led to Mrs. Allen's house. With his crutches making deep holes in the snow at every step, the doctor made for the door, which was opened hurriedly, and Mrs. Allen stood pale as death, with a wild light in her eyes, waiting for him to come in.

The door was closed, and only opened for a moment for the pale, stern woman to come forth, with a blanket in her arms, which she threw over the smoking horse, and went in again.

Then a dead, heavy blank came upon the house, and all that surrounded it. The horse fell into a doze under his blanket. Not a living thing was in view, nothing but the dreary white bosom of the earth, and a soft curl of smoke that rose from the Thrasher homestead, which was itself invisible, a little farther over the hill, though the naked twigs of the poplar trees in front could be seen against the sky. Once, the horse started, and pointed his ears, as if some familiar sound had reached him, but his head drooped again directly. The sound, if any had troubled him, was so indistinct that he rejected it as a delusion. When the doctor came out, it was with a thoughtful, anxious look that seldom visited his face. No one followed him to the door, and he sighed heavily while climbing to his seat on the saddle.

On his way home the doctor met several persons, who in the kind-hearted curiosity usual to the place, inquired who was sick enough to call him out in such terrible weather. He answered, with quizzical gravity, that he had been to visit old Mr. Lane over the hill, a man of ninety, who was suffering dreadfully with the whooping-cough.

"The whooping-cough, and he full ninety—why I never heard of such a thing," said one of the questioners; "I thought nothing but children ever had that disease."

"True enough; but you forget that old Mr. Lane is in his second childhood," answered the doctor.

The man's face brightened.

"Yes, yes," he said, "that accounts for it. I never thought of the second childhood. Does the old chap whoop much?"

"Awfully, awfully! Good-day!" and the doctor rode on, chuckling pleasantly to his horse; but the gleam of humor soon died from his features, and they grew anxious again—so anxious, that you might have fancied that his visit had been to a death-bed.

CHAPTER XXIV.

THE GRANDMOTHER RELENTING.

THE widow Allen sat by her kitchen fire, and a sterner, sadder woman never drew breath than she appeared on the day after that stormy visit from the doctor. She was waiting for him now. Her eyes, full of sullen thought, dwelt on the fire. Her feet were planted hard on the hearth—every thing about her looked unyielding and stiff—the high-backed chair, the full borders of her cap, and the white kerchief folded over her bosom— the very grief in her features seemed frozen there.

"Mother!"

This voice came from an inner room, the one which Mrs. Allen had occupied during her sickness. Its faint sweetness drew the old woman from her sombre mood. She arose and entered the apartment where her daughter lay.

The room was dimly lighted, for besides the usual blinds, a patch-work quilt, glowing with gorgeous colors, had been stretched across the only window it contained. As a great proportion of scarlet and green predominated in the quilt, it gave a richness to the atmosphere somewhat like that which streams through stained glass in a chancel window.

Katharine lay upon the bed among pillows, white as the snow drifting outside, and with a pretty cap shading her delicate features.

"Did you call, Katharine?" questioned the mother, in her clear, cold way.

"Yes, mother; my head begins to ache. A little while ago I was cold, now hot flushes are running all over me. Is this fever, do you think?"

The old woman lifted a corner of the quilt from over the window, and looked in her daughter's face.

Katharine shrunk from the glance.

"Oh, mother, don't look at me so—it makes me tremble!"

Mrs. Allen dropped the quilt, and, ignoring the fears of her child, answered to the first question,

"You are getting excited, but I think not feverish."

"Mother."

"Well, Katharine."

"I want—I wish—"

The poor thing made an effort to pull down the bed-clothes, but her hand trembled so violently that she could only make a faint signal before it fell.

The mother was touched. What woman, however aggrieved, would have resisted those mournful eyes? She went close to the bed, and turned down the blanket. A babe lay sleeping on that young creature's bosom, its little hand resting like a rose leaf, on her neck. A cloud of soft, golden hair covered its head. Mrs. Allen turned her face away, but the magnetism of those blue eyes drew it softly toward the child.

"You are its grandmother—and oh, tell me if I am your child yet?"

The young creature began to tremble as she uttered these words. This disturbed the infant, and the grandmother found a pair of soft, dreamy eyes looking into hers. The angels who guard little children may have thrown a heavenly earnestness into the child's look; I do not know—but it touched that stern heart more than the young mother's appeal had done. She stooped and took the babe in her arms; a thousand sweet, maternal recollections rose in her bosom as she pillowed it there, and laid her face against its velvet cheek.

Katharine smiled. "Mother, is it like me—like what I was once?"

"Yes."

The woman could not utter another word. When a rock is cleft, the fragments half choke up the waters that gush through them.

"Mother, my head troubles me, and I'm afraid if fever comes I may lose my senses; but I know every thing now, and want you to believe me. All that I have told you is true. It isn't because I am ashamed, but he will be here in a few days—I am sure of that. It is now more than three months, and he promised solemnly to come by that time. This is why we must not say any thing to the neighbors; they might not credit me, you know; but when he is here, who will dare turn against me? You believe that we are married, dear mother?"

"Yes, I believe it, Katharine."

"If I should be worse, you will find the paper in the garret, between one of the rafters and the shingles. Nobody must be allowed to say a word against this child when I am dead."

"Nor against *my* child while I live!" answered Mrs. Allen. "For this reason, it must be made known in the neighborhood that you are that man's wife."

"Not quite yet. It will be time enough when some one comes," pleaded the young creature. "Nelson may be on the road now. The doctor won't tell, he promised me."

She was getting excited with opposition; her cheeks were scarlet. The soft blue eyes began to glitter.

"Promise, mother! It kills me to think what the neighbors will say; but when he comes, I shall be so proud to take my baby in my arms—and—and—" She broke off, and lifting one hand to her head, began waving it to and fro.

Mrs. Allen saw that there was great danger in this agitation, and attempted to soothe it.

"Promise not to tell! promise not to tell!" cried the invalid, panting for breath, and moving restlessly on her pillow.

"Yes, Katharine; I promise not to say any thing for a week at least."

"He will be here in a week! he will be here in a week."

Katharine kept whispering this over and over again, until she fell asleep from pure exhaustion. It was some time before the crimson flush left her face, or the quick breath subsided to the calm respiration that followed; but at last she slept tranquilly as the infant which still lay on its grandmother's bosom.

Mrs. Allen sat down by the kitchen fire. She could not find it in her heart to put the babe away after its little face had once touched her own. Seating herself in the high-backed chair, she began rocking to and fro —and as the love of that little child crept, like a perfume, to her heart, hatred to its father slowly disappeared, as a kingly essence destroys all evil odors. She began to think how pleasant it would be to live in closer connection with the good old couple over the hill, and how much she had to be thankful for, that her daughter was not, in fact, the outcast she had almost believed her. As this spirit of gratitude took possession of her heart, she began to hum over a cradle song, which had almost died out of her memory, and tender dews stole into her eyes, of which she was quite unconscious, until the fire began to look hazy under her steady glance.

Our God uses little children as instruments of great tenderness. They want no key to the hardest heart; but go in, without knocking, and nestle themselves like birds in a strange nest, carrying gentleness and blessings with them. So it was with this little mite of humanity. In the helplessness of its animal life, it appealed to the stern woman's heart without challenging the stubborn pride that nothing could conquer. So she softened down, and from touching the little face, began to kiss it, and finally converted her lap into a cradle and commenced trotting the baby on her knees with the most womanly gentleness.

The doctor found her in this condition when he came in the afternoon. Katharine was still asleep, and the two held a confidential talk on the hearth-stone, in which the young creature's condition was thoroughly discussed. When told of the great dread which the young mother felt regarding any present publicity being given to her marriage, or the existence of the child, the doctor rather sided with that view of the question.

"The truth is," he said, "we should have gossip and questions, guesses and scandal, running through the neighborhood like wildfire. Let the young fellow come back and settle the whole matter for himself. There is no reason on earth why you should see company. Besides, the state of the roads will keep everybody away."

"I never have much company, and don't want any just now; as for explaining what——"

"Is nobody's business; why, it's just what you dislike, and the thought of it has, by your own account, driven the young creature half beside herself. Just let the thing alone, Mrs. Allen; where there is no one to talk with, there is nothing to tell."

"I will neither seek my neighbors, nor withhold the truth if they demand it of me," said the widow.

The doctor gathered up his crutches, with a show of impatience, and muttered something not over complimentary to the sea, and all that followed it.

His voice aroused the patient in the next room, who called out:

"Who is there, mother? Has he come?"

The doctor stumped across the room, and stood balanced on his crutches looking at her.

"Oh, is it you, doctor?" she said, in a voice that plainly spoke the disappointment that she felt.

"Well, it seems impossible to mistake myself for anybody else, or I should deny being fool enough to come this road twice."

"But you are here. It is very, very kind. You don't know how much I feel it; besides, I want to say something."

"Never mind, I know what it is; have been talking it over in the next room. Want to be quiet, natural; sick people always do. Hate to have a lot of old women screeching over the baby, and asking questions enough to drive a Christian mother into Bedlam—natural again, why not? nuisance—women ought to be prohibited as a sex by act of Congress—a few exceptions, no doubt; but patriotic women are ready to be flung overboard for the general good."

Katharine looked a little bewildered, and quite weary. She was thinking about her own troubles, and had not strength enough for any thing else.

"Did any one ask you about us, doctor?"

"About you? no—about where I was going, fifty."

"And you told them?"

"Yes, of course I told 'em; why not?"

Katharine turned very white, and gasped for breath.

"You told them about me—about my baby?"

"Bah child, no; but I told 'em old Lane had caught the whooping-cough, and that will keep the whole town in gossip at least a week."

Katharine began to laugh—she was but a young thing, and the idea amused her excessively.

"Stop that, or it'll end in hysterics," he said, frowning upon her with comical affectation; but she smiled yet, and her pale cheek flushed. Still, the anxieties that pressed upon her were too real, and she became grave again.

"You wont say any thing about it, please," she murmured. "The minute he comes, they shall know everything. I'm not very strong; if it wasn't for that you should read the certificate now; but it's up-stairs, and so we must wait."

"Never mind, my little Katy-did, I can wait, and so shall the rest of them; never fear."

"You're very good!" murmured Katharine, faintly; "I shall sleep without dreaming such frightful things after this."

She closed her eyes a moment, and then opened them with a start.

"Where's the baby?"

"In your mother's lap—don't you hear her buzzing over it like a bumble bee?"

"Is it—is that her?" whispered the young mother, and a beautiful smile stole into her eyes. "I don't re-member ever hearing her sing before."

"Oh, she'll soon break in—no fool like a grandmother."

"How pleasant it sounds," murmured the young mother, listening to the low hum which came from the next room, and ignoring the doctor's speech entirely. "I didn't know mother's voice was so sweet. It makes me sleepy."

"Then shut your eyes and go to dreaming at once; a good sleep will do you more good than I can," said the doctor, wheeling round on his crutches, and stumping off into the next room. Here he gave Mrs. Allen a quaint reprimand for allowing her patient to put herself into a fever, and warned her that the next excitement might go to the brain and raise the mischief. Then he chucked the baby under its mite of a chin, which the little thing returned with an incipient hiccough instead of a smile, which was altogether beyond its powers, after which he mounted his horse and rode off, chuckling over the mystifications which all questioners were sure to get, on his way home.

CHAPTER XXV.

A GRAVE IN THE SNOW.

It chanced, during the week, that another fall of snow blocked up the roads just as they were getting well trodden down. This kept the people in-doors, and Mrs. Allen was left to the entire solitude she so much desired. The doctor only came once after the visit we have mentioned. That time Mrs. Allen had been compelled to leave the house. Her firewood was out, and she had gone in search of a neighbor who had promised her to haul a load from the forest back of Castle Rock. The distance was considerable, and the walking toilsome, beside the neighbor she sought had gone out after his team and she was compelled to wait.

It was during her absence that the doctor went to the house. He found Katharine improving; still excitable on the subject of her husband's return, and listening for his step at every movement, but apparently so happy with the growth of her child, that even this craving wish could not materially impede her well-doing.

The doctor had a tedious ride before him, and only remained long enough to be sure that there was really nothing to require his stay, and rode off. He was in the more haste because dull, leaden clouds were gathering in the sky, and fine snow came down at intervals, threatening a heavier fall.

On his way down the hill he met the town carrier, a man who distributed papers, and transported parcels for the whole neighborhood, to and from New Haven, twice each week. Sometimes he brought letters from the post-office. Indeed, from a three cent whistle to a dressed pig in killing time, he refused nothing that came within the capacity of his one-horse wagon, or could be sheltered by its oil-cloth cover. This man nodded to the doctor, and after passing him, gave a little blast from his tin horn to notify the next house that he was about to stop there.

This house was Mrs. Allen's, Katharine was in her room, and was ignorant that her mother had not returned. She started up in bed at the first sound of the horn, and cried out:

"Run, mother, run. It is the carrier, he may bring news. Nelson has come passenger. I'm sure of it!"

The carrier drew up before the house, and waited a minute for some one to come forth. But no one appeared, and with an impatient growl at the delay he jumped out of his wagon, opened the street door, and flung a letter through, muttering that he would call for the postage some other time, a storm was coming on, and he was late already.

Katharine saw the letter, gave a cry of joy, such as those humble walls never heard again, and sprang to the floor, leaving her child asleep in the bed. She seized the letter and tore it open; three or four bank notes fluttered around her, falling unheeded, about the room. She strove to read, but the paper rattled in her hands—dizzy and weak she could not distinguish a word of the few that danced before her eyes. She went back to the bed, seized one of the posts of the bedstead, and steadied herself desperately.

"Katharine, it cannot be helped, I am going on a whaling voyage; nothing better presented itself, and I must not be idle. The ship will be gone three years at least, perhaps more, but there is a chance for making money. I send you all that has been advanced to me; when that is gone go to my father, as I told you.

"NELSON THRASHER."

She grew blind. A dull, sickening weight fell upon her. She strove to creep into bed, clambered to the edge upon her knees, and fell forward, with her face pressed to the pillow, which settled slowly down, and buried the sleeping child—a struggle—a faint, stifled sound—a scarcely perceptible upheaving of the pillow, and all was still.

There was no change in the mother; white as marble, she had fallen upon her face—lifeless as marble she lay until the great clock in the kitchen tolled the hour.

The struggle of her coming misery was terrible. She turned and sat upon the bed, with her white feet hanging over the edge. The shawl which Mrs. Allen had folded over her shoulders from fear of cold, hung loosely adown her long night robe. She began to shiver, and drew it around her, hugging it to her bosom, but some idea of its emptiness seized upon her. She opened the shawl and looked down upon her flowing night dress wonderingly, as if she had lost something. Then her eyes were turned vaguely around the bed. She lifted a corner of the blanket, and finding nothing, impatiently pushed the pillow aside.

There it lay—her little babe, asleep, and yet not asleep. Insane fire flashed to her eyes; fever leaped, and burned in all her veins; angry defiance blazed in her face. She was stunned before, but maddened now. Somebody had been trying to kill her babe with too much warmth. Her mother had done it. Her stern mother, who never would forgive, and had always hated the Thrasher blood. She would come back and try again. How flushed and hot its little face looked. How menacingly its tiny fist was clenched. Something very cruel must have been done before it came to that. How soundly she had slept to know nothing of this. But her mother should never harm it again. She knew of a nice cool place under the great butternut where it could have a beautiful blanket of snow, with light icicles shimmering over it from the branches. Nobody could find it there, and that strange look of pain would change to quiet sleep.

Prompted by these insane thoughts, the young mother seized her child, folded it closely to her bosom, under the shawl, and fled from the house. She hurried on, her white feet sinking in the snow at every step. The crust cut her ankles, but she was unaware of the pain. The wind whistled through her night dress, but she only laughed—its sharpness would drive that terrible red from her baby's face. She clambered the stone wall twice, into the orchard, and across another lot, until she reached the rock beneath the butternut branches, now without a leaf.

A shelf of the rock shot out from the drift that almost buried it. She took off her shawl, wrapped it tenderly about the child, laid it on this shelf, and began to work. She tore the glittering crust away, fell upon her knees, and commenced hurling the loose snow out with her hands, until a cradle was scooped in the drift. Then she gathered up an armful of the flakes, moulded and patted them into a pillow, and hushing the baby in her arms a moment, laid it down. She covered it with a soft blanket of snow, placed the icy crust carefully over it, and then stopped, and looked about bewildered, as if wondering what she could do next.

By this time the cold had pierced her to the vitals, but the fever met it fiercely and shook that delicate form like a reed. She sat down on the rock, gazing at the little white grave, as if she had just buried her heart there; and was afraid that some one would trample on it. The cold was doing its work; a few moments more and she would never have left the rock again. But some imaginary noise frightened her. She started up, forgot every thing, and flew toward the house—the light hair floating back from under her cap, and her thin garments fluttering through the atmosphere like shadows. The door was partly open—she darted in, crossed the kitchen, and springing to the centre of her bed, covered herself up with the clothes, shuddering and laughing in the same breath.

CHAPTER XXVI.

A CROWD UNDER THE BUTTERNUT TREE.

At last the old woman came in. With the sly instincts of insanity, Katharine lay still, holding the blankets over her head, pretending to be asleep.

The old lady did not attempt to disturb her, but merely looked in to see that all was quiet, and went to the kitchen. To her surprise, she found the outer door open. The wind had swept in, scattering snow and ashes over the floor. This had produced a draught down the wide-mouthed chimney, and filled the room with smoke. Mrs. Allen threw up a sash, which produced an eddy of wind and sent some loose papers flying toward the hearth—one, which seemed to be a letter, floated by her and was drawn up the chimney, catching fire as it went; another was following, but she grasped it in time, and found that the flimsy bit of silk paper was a bank bill of considerable amount. Two others she picked up from the floor.

Who could have been in her house? How was it possible for so much money to have found its way there? She went into the bedroom, resolved to question Katharine, who heard her coming, and crouched under the bedclothes.

"Katharine! Katharine!"

No answer.

The old lady, fearing she scarcely knew what, went up to the bed and turned down the clothes. There was a little resistance, and then Katharine looked up with a frightened smile, trembling terribly either with dread or cold.

"Who has been here since I went away, Katharine?"

"I don't know."

"But look! Where did all this money come from?"

"I don't know."

And, indeed, she did not know, never having taken a thought of that portion of Thrasher's letter; even the epistle itself only whirled through the chaos of her mind, like dead leaves in a tempest.

Mrs. Allen examined the money again, while Katharine eyed her with the sharp cunning of insanity.

"How you shake, child? The open door has given you a chill."

"It was too warm! too warm!" muttered the poor creature; "crimson hot, crimson hot!"

Mrs. Allen was so surprised with the money that she did not heed the strange murmur of her daughter. She put the bills away in an old teapot in the corner cupboard. Then something struck her as unnatural in the stillness of the room, and she went back again.

"Is the baby asleep yet?" she inquired, sitting down by the bed.

Katharine shrunk away from her; but answered in a quick, eager way:

"Yes; it sleeps sweetly, sweetly, sweetly."

This strange repetition of one word drew Mrs. Allen's attention more closely to the invalid. There was something strange in her face—a gleam of vigilant cunning in the eyes that made the mother anxious.

"How soundly the little thing sleeps," she said.

"Yes, soundly," was the answer.

"Move a little, and let me take it up."

"No!"

A look of defiance came into that beautiful face. Katharine was resolved to defend her secret to the last moment.

Mrs. Allen became frightened; forced the bedclothes from that feeble grasp, and stooped down to search for the child.

It was gone!

"Where—oh, Katharine—where is the baby?"

A gleam of infinite craft stole into those blue eyes.

"What baby?"

"Yours, yours—our own little child! who has taken it away?"

"Nobody."

"Then where is it?"

"Asleep; didn't I tell you so?"

Mrs. Allen rushed into the kitchen and searched it in every corner. The smoke had cleared away, and she discovered tracks of a small, naked foot in the loose snow that had drifted into the room. Where was the child? what could have happened? Mrs. Allen rushed distractedly into the street, just as the neighbor whom she had been in search of drove up with a load of wood on his sled.

"Hello! what's the matter, Mrs. Allen?" he called out, as she came toward the gate, pale as death, and wringing her hands.

"Our baby—my little grandchild—it is gone!"

The man stopped and emitted a low whistle.

"So there was something in all that talk," he muttered, "hard as I stood up for her."

"I only left to run down to your house—we hadn't another armful of wood. When I came back, the outdoor was open, the room full of smoke, and she all alone! Oh, God help me, what can I do!"

"Just go into the house, and let us talk it all over," said the kind-hearted farmer, leaving his oxen; "I don't understand."

"Oh, we cannot stop to talk—the child must be found. Isn't that Mr. Stokes coming up the hill? Call him— we must search—we must find it."

The farmer called out for Mr. Stokes to hurry forward, and at the same time ran to meet him. The two men stood talking together some minutes, then came toward the house in company.

Mrs. Allen had gone back to her daughter, and with tears raining down her face, was pleading with her. Poor woman! it was many years since she had cried like that, but when an infant comes to a lonely house, the fountain of tears is sure to swell afresh in the most stern bosom. The sweet word, "grandmother," had been applied to her. The baby's little heart had stirred against her own; without that child, all the stern desolation of her life would come back again.

But Katharine could not answer.

The two men came in, looking curious and excited; their presence seemed to strike Katharine dumb. She lay with her eyes wide open, staring at them. A vague smile wandered on her lips as they questioned her, but no words.

Baffled and still anxious, the men went into the kitchen again, leaving Mrs. Allen behind. They saw the tracks still imprinted on the floor, and followed them with keen observation. The tracks continued out into the yard, turned there, and led toward the orchard. One naked footprint was stamped on the top of the stone wall, as if a leap had pressed it deeply there. After this there was little trouble—broken places in the snow crust led them on till they stood by the rock under the butternut tree.

It is strange how soon a crowd will collect, if any thing unusual is going on, even in the remotest places. A good many people were on the road, some going to the stores at Chewstown or Falls Hill, some taking grists to mill, and others loitering on their way to the tavern, whose red sign swung on the river road a little beyond Rock Spring.

Before the two men, who tracked that terrible path, had touched the little white grave by the rock, some half-dozen persons had collected around it. A feeling of awe kept the first comers from touching the broken snow-crust; but now, a man in the crowd thrust it aside with his foot, and the rest set to work.

It took but little time to remove the white covering beneath, and, after a moment's work, the dead infant was found wrapped in a shawl, which was recognized by more than one present as belonging to Katharine Allen.

A feeling of profound consternation fell upon the little group of farmers, as they lifted the infant from its grave. The face, now pale and cold, was all uncovered, flakes of snow trembled in the golden hair, and the winds blew over it so sharply, that one of the men put forth his hand, and drew the shawl softly over its head, muttering, "God forgive its mother!"

No funeral ever was marked with more solemn faces than those which followed the dead infant back to the house. No word was spoken aloud, but hoarse whispers passed from lip to lip, and the hardiest man there shrunk from carrying that mournful burden into the presence of its grandmother.

A terrible presentiment of the truth had fallen upon the old woman. She had failed to win any thing from her daughter, and, with a sinking heart, listened to the men crunching the snow under their feet, as they went toward the orchard. For the world she could not have gone to the door or remained upright upon her feet. The old high-back chair stood on the hearth; she sat down. The fire flamed up and flickered over her white features. Those little tracks upon the floor fascinated her gaze. They melted and run into each other, taking uncouth shapes, but, in her eyes, there had been no change. These two little footprints, in disappearing from the floor, seemed to burn themselves into her heart.

She sat still listening, but there was no sound except the soughing of the wind among the naked apple trees. Katharine lay still in her bed, exulting in the safety which she had secured for her child, but craftily silent lest some one should find out her secret. Filled with this idea she held her breath, as if that would betray her

Thus the stillness was profound. There was no confusion in the woman's mind now. Her quick, clear intellect had seized upon the broad facts of the case. She struggled against them, but the child was gone, and those footprints on the floor were obliterating, but not dried out. After a time she heard a strange sound in the road—the heavy tramp of feet, followed by suppressed voices near the gate. With a prayer to God she arose, walked to the door, cast it wide open, and stood on the threshold with her arms extended. It was like laying a dead child into a dead woman's bosom when the man placed his burden in those arms.

CHAPTER XXVII.

THE SAILOR AND HIS TWO COMPANIONS.

In one of those common hotels, frequented by the better class of seamen who enter New York, David Rice had taken up his quarters, accompanied by little Paul and Jube. With the bravery of a Nelson, he had carried the disabled brig safely into a Southern port, with her cargo all safe; an act of heroism that had secured the warmest approbation of her owners, and what was far better, an appointment to the command of the craft he had saved.

While the repairs were going on, David, exultant and happy, had proceeded with his two friends to the commercial emporium, where he became sadly puzzled what course to take next, for two more simple hearted and helpless creatures never existed.

"Now," said David, going into a select committee of one on the subject; "now when a chap saves the life of another chap, big or little, and turns his face about from a long voyage, where all is provided for, he's in duty bound to adopt that other chap, and take good care of him so long as he can't take care of himself. Now that's just your case, David Rice. What on arth can these poor critters do without you? Nothing—that's sartin. What can you do for them?—there's the puzzler. As for work, the nigger is strong as a lion; but he's used to hot weather, and a cold snap curls him right up. As for the boy—poor little soul—no Yankee baby was ever half so helpless; and yet, how brave the little chap is! What am I to do with 'em? They can't live here when I'm away to sea; and as for working, why the nigger himself hasn't the least idee what work means!"

This consultation was held in English, while its objects sat close together, looking at the sailor as he laid down the case and expostulated with himself, pro and con, with considerable energy.

"Jube," he said, in broken French, feeling in sad want of counsel, "Jube, what do you say to living in the country?"

"Oh, anywhere Jube is ready to live—anywhere that little masser and you like!" cried the negro, eagerly.

"Well, say in a nice, cosy place up in Connecticut, with plenty of chores to do, and no hard work."

"Yes, masser Rice," said Jube, attempting English.

"Then, our little Paul, he ought to go to school—capital district school on Shrub Oak—beautiful red school-house, with the turnpike running in front, and a river back of it. You can hear the water sing all day long, behind the hemlock bushes. Besides, there's an apple tree at one end that bears splendid green apples, and a bell pear tree, that the scholars are forbid to look at. Then—keep that to yourself Paul, no one but Kate ever found it out—but, there's a hollow at one end of the school-house, and the banks are covered with strawberry vines, white in the spring, and red all under the grass where the sun has shined on 'em long enough—sich strawberries, plump as a baby's mouth, and sweet as its kisses. What do you think of that, Paul?"

The little fellow did not quite comprehend what Rice was talking about, but the subject seemed a pleasant one, so he replied, in broken English, that he should like it very much indeed.

"Yes," said Dave, kindling into enthusiasm by a remembrance of his own school days, brief as they had been, and spent in a much less pleasant place than the one he described. "Yes, I kinder see you now, with yer dinner basket on one arm—the squaws, back of Chewstown, make scrumptious little baskets, now I tell yer—and Webster's blue-covered spelling book under t'other, a marching off to that ere seat of larning which I've been telling you about. The picter is so enticing that I'm in a hurry to begin. Have you ever been to school?"

The boy looked at Jube in doubt what to answer.

"District school, I mean," said Dave, with a flourish of the hand. "Where the master or mistress boards about, and ferrules the children with a pine ruler, if they don't toe a crack every spelling time."

"No," said Paul, meekly, "I never did."

"Nor you nuther, Jube?"

Jube opened his great eyes in wonder at the question. It seemed too astonishing for any other reply.

"Then you hain't neither of you got a bit of larning?" continued Rice, patronizingly, "can't read nor write, I reckon."

Paul understood this, and brightened up.

"Oh, yes, Monsieur Rice, I read and write, and do much things in French. All my life the tutor has taught me how."

"You can, eh! then jist show us what kind of a fist you make of it. Hallo, here, waiter, bring up pen and ink, with some paper. I want to see how far this little chap has got along in his eddecation."

The orders were obeyed, and Paul sat down to the rickety table, smiling as he began to write. Rice stood with his feet wide apart and a hand in each pocket, looking over the boy's shoulder.

"By jingo, you write like a lady!" he cried, filled with exultation; "and hain't never been to school! it's 'stonishing. Now let me hear you spell. We'll skip over the abs, and plunge right into deep larning at once. Now spell Baker."

Rice plunged his hands deeper into both pockets and shook himself like a mastiff, satisfied that the boy had got a puzzler now. And so he had, for it was his first effort at English, and the word, as he tried to syllable it, was so sweetly broken that Dave shook his head.

"Isn't it right?" inquired Paul, anxiously.

"Well, no, not exactly; but don't be down-hearted. It's a tough word. I remember studying it over and over again. So keep a stiff upper lip."

"But I shall learn English?" said Paul.

"In course you shall. There's a seat in Shrub Oak school-house waiting for you now—the very one sister Kate used to set in, bless her purty face—won't she knit woollen comforters for you. The old woman, too. I say, look a here, shaver, you never saw such a home as you'll find with my women folks. No skim milk about them, now I tell you."

"Is there good fire," inquired Jube, shivering with the cold, though a bright blaze flamed on the hearth.

"A good fire? Well I should think so—back logs as big as porpoises, and fore sticks to match, trust the old woman for that."

Jube rubbed his hands, and displayed the edge of his firm, white teeth in a satisfied smile. Warmth was the thing he pined for just then.

"Now that it's settled, supposing we go out and get some good thick clothes for the shaver, Jube; them silk stockings and finefied shoes aint the thing, though you do wash and brush them when he's asleep. We must have socks and boots, and a good thick overcoat, with a seal-skin cap that turns down at the ears, and yarn mittins. But them, the old woman will knit, striped two and two, with red and white fringe around the wrist—don't I remember the pattern. Come, old chap, it aint far from here to Catharine street, we'll soon have a full rig."

Of course Jube made no objection; indeed, such was his devotion to Rice, that it is doubtful if he would have resisted any behest of his. They went out, looking weather-beaten and shabby enough, shivering with cold, and sallow from the privation of a hard sea voyage. But after a visit first to a barber's shop, and next to a clothing store, the whole aspect of things was changed. Little Paul came forth in a fur cap and an overcoat, so heavy and thick that even his movements, usually graceful as an antelope's, became a little awkward. Jube was also warmly clad, and muffled in a comforter, striped with red, green, and yellow, which had won his extremest admiration.

After providing for the comfort of his friends in this

way, Rice took them to one of the East river wharves, where a sloop, bound for the mouth of the Housatonic, lay waiting for passengers, and placed them in charge of the captain. Both Paul and Jube had learned a little broken English by this time, upon which Rice depended greatly. Besides, he sent a letter to his mother, beseeching her to receive his friends and preservers, as he named them, in her own house, and treat them as if Jube were his brother, and the boy his son—an adopted son, in every sense of the word, he certainly was. In a few crude lines he gave his mother to understand how helpless the child was, and how manfully the African had stood by him when deserted on the disabled brig, and ended by promising to come home before the vessel sailed again.

With this letter Rice gave Jube some gold pieces, which made the negro's eyes sparkle, for he recognized them as the coin circulated in his own country. Thus having provided for his friends, Rice took his way back to the disabled ship, and the sloop spread its white wings up the sound.

The deep snow, the skeleton trees, and scattering evergreens that lined the banks of the Housatonic, struck our poor fugitives from the tropics with a sense of absolute desolation. But the captain was kind, and this stood in place of sunshine and warmth with them. At the head of navigation, which brought the sloop to the mouth of the Naugatuc, the captain sent them forward with a return team, which, having deposited its load of produce, was ready to proceed up the river road, which led from Darby to the long wooden bridge below the falls.

CHAPTER XXVIII.

OUT OF HER DELIRIUM.

ALAS! it was an unhappy house. Poor Katharine! when the dead child was brought to her, wrapped in the gorgeous shawl which had been her brother's gift, she uttered a low wail, so prolonged and mournful that it never left the memory of those who heard it. As the moan died on her lips, it seemed to carry her life with it, for she fell into a state of dumb apathy, and lay for hours together gazing on the wall without a sign of animation. Then she would mutter, in a low, terrified voice, "They have found it, they have found it."

The magistrates came to the house and examined the evidences of the case, but she took no heed of them. The doctor was summoned, but his opinion, as far as it went, was all against the probabilities of a natural death. He made every exertion in his power to win the poor mother to a state of consciousness, but all in vain; she only looked in his face and muttered, "They have found it, they have found it."

Mrs. Allen was called forward. She had grown old since the day before. The hair on her temples was white as frost now, and her figure stooped, as if some ponderous weight had been laid upon it. Yet the old woman was calm and still. Had the truth struck her dead at the magistrates' feet, she would, nevertheless, have spoken it. Her old neighbors knew this, and refrained from pressing her too far. It would be hard enough, they whispered in consultation, when she was brought into court; why should they torture her when the evidence was so conclusive.

So the magistrates sat all day with the dead infant lying in its little coffin on the table before them, deliberating solemnly together; while that poor mother in the next room, harassed and demented, lay with her face turned to the wall, muttering beneath her breath, "They have found it, they have found it."

Mrs. Allen sat on the hearth in her own high-backed chair, gazing with heavy eyes on the magistrates. She was chilled and shocked to the soul. The stiff pride of her nature was broken in twain, leaving her body bent, and her soul inert. Still, such is the indomitable power of household routine, in a woman of New England, that she replenished the fire from time to time, and prepared drink for the poor creature in the next room. But no food appeared in that dwelling during forty-eight hours. The cow moaned in its stable from the pain of its abundant milk, and the pigs, in a pen back of the house, thrust their noses between the boards and begged for food, with uncouth noises that penetrated into the house without arousing the mistress. A flock of hens huddled about the door, pecking at each other and raking up the snow with their claws.

All this made no impression on the woman. When the ashes grew deep in the fireplace she mechanically shovelled them behind the back log and sat down again, unconscious of the act; when a stick of wood broke into brands on each side the andirons, she lifted the massive tongs and placed them in the midst of the fire again, but with this action her soul had no part; that seemed dead within her.

At last the magistrates brought in their verdict.

The infant had been murdered by its mother, and she was bound over for trial at the county court.

Mrs. Allen drew a deep breath when the verdict was announced, and that was all the sign she gave. The magistrates retired, leaving the house in charge of the constable. From that hour Katharine Allen was a prisoner and under arrest. Poor soul, she knew nothing about it. The officers walked in and out of her room, but she neither spoke nor looked at them. They stooped over the bed and questioned her persistently, but she took no heed; a regiment might have tramped through that little room and she would not have known it.

All that night Mrs. Allen sat by the little coffin in which the babe lay smiling in its eternal sleep. Nothing but the form of a guard was wanted for those two helpless women, so the man left in charge fell asleep upon the hearth, with his head bowed forward and his feet extended. Thus the night wore on. The grandmother never closed her eyes, and scarcely moved, but a dead numbness was closing around her heart; she began to feel the terrible position in which her child was placed —to feel that the beautiful babe which had crept into her heart, awaking all its pristine tenderness, was nothing but cold death.

As these thoughts crowded to her mind, a world of anguish gathered over that old face, 'till every feature quivered with awakening pain.

As if the anguish of this strong woman had struck some electric spark in the bosom of her child, a faint moan was heard in the next room. But that gray head had fallen forward, and the face was buried in her locked hands. The old woman was trying to pray. But she could not even send up a moan to the Almighty. For
13

that moment she had no faith. The anguish of a great trouble was upon her which shook her whole being; but the tenderness that leads to prayer had not yet descended upon her grief.

Under these awakening feelings, she began to be sensible of all the gloomy surroundings that had helped to oppress her. The tallow candle upon the table was surmounted by a long wick with a death blossom trembling at the top, which smothered half its feeble light. Thus the little coffin was filled with shadows, through which the white face gleamed mournfully.

Mrs. Allen was all alone. The officer sat sleeping soundly in his chair—the young mother lay insensible in the next room. The old woman was, nevertheless, alone, for such companionship was an added misery. She could not endure to sit still with that mournful little face reproaching her from its coffin for its mother's sin; for, as yet, its death took that shape in her mind. She had no courage to get up and search for the snuffers, wherewith that ill-omened crest could be separated from the ungainly wick. An empty cradle stood in one corner of the room. She took the coffin in her arms, and sat it reverently into this cradle, spreading the patchwork coverlet over it, thus removing the pale reality of death from her sight. This done, she sat down by the table, and let the candle smoke on, indifferent to what it revealed, so long as the thing was not death.

It is possible that she may have dropped to sleep after this, for nature was sinking within her; certain it is, her face fell upon the locked hands, while profound quiet reigned for a little time throughout that miserable dwelling.

While her face was bowed thus, a frail figure, clad in

white drapery from head to foot, came out of the bedroom and glided up to the table. She wavered in her walk, and leaned both hands on the table, or she must have undoubtedly fallen, in feeble helplessness, to the ground.

Mrs. Allen looked up and saw her daughter, worn and trembling, gazing wistfully upon her.

"Mother, what have you done with it? Who has taken my baby away?"

The voice was sweet, but troubled; the face innocent as an angel's.

"Katharine, oh, Katharine!"

It was all the poor woman could say; but the first gleam of hope shot athwart that gloomy face and thrilled through the voice. From that moment the mother felt that her child was innocent.

"Oh, Katharine, my child! my poor, poor child!"

She held out her arms, while great tears rained down her cheeks.

Katharine tottered around the table, and falling on her knees, leaned heavily on the mother's lap, lifting her face full of wistful tenderness to the troubled countenance bent over her.

"Tell me what you did with it, mother."

Mrs. Allen trembled under the wistful earnestness of those pleading eyes. She had no power of speech in her voice. It was choked up with sorrow for her daughter's inevitable anguish, with thanksgiving that she was innocent. With a tenderness which is the gift of true Christianity, link it with the sternest nature you may, she reached forth her arms and gathered the young thing to her bosom.

"Do tell me, mother, what you have done with my baby?"

"Rest a little, my child. That's right—keep your arms around me. How weak you are; and it is cold. Shall I carry you back to bed, my poor darling?"

"When you have told me. I want the baby, mother; my heart aches for it; my bosom is full of pain. If we only had it here between us, mother. Do, do tell me where it is?"

Mrs. Allen bent her face and kissed her.

"Isn't it pleasant to kiss one's own child, mother? I never thought what a comfort it was to you before."

Mrs. Allen could not answer; she only bent her withered cheek to the sweet face on her bosom, and sighed heavily.

"Come, mother."

"One minute, Katharine."

"What is that, mother?"

Katharine had heard the deep breathing of her guard, and turned her startled face toward him.

"It is a neighbor come to stay with us."

"What! in the night, mother! Why don't he go to bed, then?"

"No one has slept in this house for two nights," answered the mother, sorrowfully.

Katharine started, and began to tremble.

"Why did you sit up? Was my baby sick?"

Mrs. Allen folded her child closer, but said nothing.

"You won't tell me, mother."

"I—I cannot."

Katharine broke from her mother's arms, and stood up, white as death.

"Is my baby dead, mother?"

"Yes."

Before it left the woman's lips, Katharine had advanced to the cradle, and drawn away the coverlet. She saw what is concealed—the little coffin and her child lying coldly within it. Without a word or even a quick breath, she sank down like an image of snow which the sun has touched.

Another morning, and the stillness of death fell upon that house. While the young mother lay bereft of all strength, and scarcely alive, but with a guard of strong men at her door, the infant was carried out and reverently buried. No mourners followed it. The old woman watched by the living mother, not with the leaden despair of former days, but with calm resignation, which deepened into pathetic tenderness, whenever she approached the sufferer.

Katharine had whispered a request to see her babe before it was carried forth. It was brought to her bedside, for those who condemned her as guilty had some compassion on her youth. It was like a shadow passing near her, a pale, wan shadow, which would forever float before her vision, but was devoid of positive reality then. She had no idea of the way of its death, and suffered like any other bereaved parent, who sees the first child of love carried away after it has been folded close to the yearning heart that gave it life.

So the funeral went forth, the saddest of many years, and wound its solemn way through the snow-trodden streets down to the graveyard, which gave its white stones to the sunlight on Falls Hill. The shadow of the church steeple lay softly upon the snow as the funeral passed in, and when the tiny grave was closed, and all was white and pure as the clouds of heaven above, the broad Naugatuc sweeping toward its falls below the hill, seemed chiming a solemn requiem. Then the crowd dispersed in groups, whispering with awe over the terrible crime which no one seemed to doubt, and all regretted. A few thoughtless girls there might have been, who spoke recklessly of the sin and disgrace which had fallen upon their lovely schoolmate, but a feeling of compassion predominated, and even those who came to that little grave condemning the mother, went away subdued and doubting. Gossip there certainly was—what country village ever existed without that?—but Katharine's fault was far too serious for light comment. Even strong men held their breadth when the penalty of death was mentioned in connection with that helpless girl.

CHAPTER XXIX.

STRANGERS IN THE VILLAGE.

I HAVE forgotten one circumstance which happened that morning. Just as the funeral was turning from the highway toward the graveyard, a colored man and a young boy, both of foreign appearence, came up the hill from the bridge, where one of the river sleighs had set them down. After standing for a moment watching the procession with curiosity, they walked reverently after it, looking very sad, as if trouble were familiar to them. The negro led the boy by the hand, and both stood apart from the crowd while the funeral service was read. It was remarked that the negro seemed greatly disturbed as he looked upon the grave, and that his eyes filled with tears when he turned them on the serious face of the boy. Poor fellow! he was thinking of another funeral, where orange blossoms perfumed the air, and hosts of wild flowers brightened the turf which was laid above the dead.

When the ceremony was over, and the people began to disperse, Jube approached a little group of men who lingered by the gate, and inquired, in very imperfect English, if some one would show him the way to a place called Bungy, and if a widow lady by the name of Allen did not live there.

This was a new source of excitement. The foreign look and broken language peculiar to the strangers, were something to be wondered at and talked over, even at this solemn hour. The men drew away from the neighborhood of the burying-ground before they indulged in the curiosity which was consuming them, and for once answered a question directly, without asking another in the same breath, an instance of forbearance deserving of honorable record in these pages. But the moment they reached the road the awe of the place left them, and the direct examination of poor Jube commenced.

Mrs. Allen—of course everybody knew the widow Allen, and no wonder, after that funeral; but what did the stranger want of her—wanted to hire out, perhaps. Jube did not know what hiring out meant, and answered vaguely that perhaps he did, but wasn't quite certain.

This rather excited curiosity. What if this black fellow should prove to know something about the murder, or, at any rate, of the person who had led poor Katharine Allen into all this trouble. This idea whetted the questions that were let loose on the travellers, till both the negro and boy were thoroughly bewildered.

"Mebbe you're acquainted with Mrs. Allen—knew her afore she moved here, I dare say!" suggested a farmer from over the hill.

Jube shook his head, more to express his incapacity to understand than as a negative to the question.

"No; that's sort o' strange; but then, perhaps, you're related to some of the colored people hereabouts?"

"No, agin; stranger and stranger yet—not know Mrs. Allen, nor any of the colored population of this neighborhood. Then jist excuse me if I ask who on arth you are acquainted with?"

"We know Mr. Rice, the widow lady's son," answered Paul, in his sweet, broken language, and lifting a face to the stranger that softened every feature of his rough visage.

"You know David Rice, my little shaver! Wall, we reckon not, for he was drowned three months or more ago. Wrecked at sea. Captain Thrasher e'nmost saw him go down."

"It was on that ship we with him! Jube he help him bring her into port!" cried the boy, his great, velvety eyes filling with light as he lifted them exultingly to the negro.

The story of two persons—a negro and a boy—having insisted on sharing the fate of David Rice, on the disabled vessel, had gone the rounds of the village, and a general burst of surprise followed the boy's speech.

"Now, you don't say so! You the little shaver that sot right down by Dave Rice on that deck, and wouldn't get up on no consideration!" cried one. "Wall, now, how things du turn out. I couldn't a believed it, and sich a slender little critter, too; I swan to man, it beats all!"

Paul understood that the man was praising him for something, and in his modest innocence strove to set him right.

"No, no, no; not me; I am very little boy, very weak, and so small. I only eat great deal, and drink water, when Jube wanted it very much to keep him strong. It was Jube, my Jube, that helped save the ship. I wish you could see how him swing the pump handle—all the time, daylight and dark, no matter, Jube work, work, work, I no!"

The farmer who had been the most ardent spokesman, stepped forth now, reaching out his hands.

"I say, cuffy, give us yer hand. If you're the feller that stood by Rice when he hadn't a chance left, I'm proud to know ye. If you raly did bring him safe ashore—well, by golly, if I aint e'enamost a crying! Now, you don't say that Dave Rice is alive?"

"Left him much well in New York two days ago; me and Jube," answered the boy, smiling at the farmer's enthusiasm.

"Yes, little masser."

"Master! Now, you don't mean tu say that this little black-eyed shaver is your master, in earnest, cuffy?"

"Yes," said Jube, showing every white tooth in his head. "Reckon little masser won't say no!"

"And you're his slave—a rale, downright sarvant, ha?"

"Yes; that's it!" answered Jube, with another happy laugh. "Little masser hasn't none but me now."

"You don't say so!"

"But we both owned to Captain Rice, now. Jube, you not forgot that," said Paul, earnestly.

"What's that you're a saying! Dave Rice a bringing

home slaves into old Connecticut, and one uv 'em e'enamost white! I say, neighbors, what will the selectmen say to that?"

Instantly there was a season of whispered and eager consultation. With all their joy over the deliverance of Rice from a watery grave, the neighbors were not prepared to accept the slaves he seemed to be sending home from foreign parts.

"What do you think," said the chief speaker, "they'll perhaps become an expense to the town, and have to be bid off for their board with the other paupers—supposing we send them back."

"Wait till we've examined 'em according to law," interposed another, who was a selectman of the township. "Perhaps I'd better do it. Now jest stand by and listen"

"What do you do for a living, if I may ask," he commenced, planting himself in the road in front of Jube, "before we admit strangers, especially colored, it's as well to be sure that they wont be a town charge—what do you foller?"

Jube shook his head—the whole speech was a mystery to him.

"What do you foller?" persisted the selectman, getting impatient.

"What do I folly!" repeated Jube, with a puzzled look, then brightening up all at once, he added with a smile:

"Me folly little masser."

"But how do you get your living?"

"He's my father now, and me support him," said Paul, with dignity, for he began to comprehend a little of the conversation.

"And who supports you, my little shaver?"

"Me have money," answered Paul; "Jube, show monsieur much money there in the purse."

Jube took a heavy shot bag from his pocket, and opening it exhibited more gold than the selectman had ever seen in his life. The whole group of countrymen gathered around him, full of eager curiosity.

"I should think that satisfactory," said one of the speakers, addressing the selectman.

"No doubt on that point," was the answer; "but where on arth du they come from, I should raly like to know."

"Will you please tell us some way," said Paul, modestly. "It is much cold here, and Jube likes a fire too much."

"You want to know the road to Mrs. Allen's?"

"Yes, monsieur, that is the name!"

"Well, she lives over the hill."

"Which way we go, monsieur?"

"No, it isn't monsur, but Bungy that you're after."

"And that way, if you please?"

"Turn round that great willer tree on the corner, keep to the left of the white house back of it, and then go straight along. It's a brown house with a narrow door yard, and a shag bark walnut tree standing at one end—you can't miss it, no how."

"Thank you," said the boy, lifting his cap with the grace of a little prince, "monsieur are much kind."

Jube also lifted his cap, and stood close by his master, a good deal puzzled and disturbed by the conversation that had been forced upon them.

The men who were left behind drew together in a group

"It's a bad time for strangers to be asking the way to that house," said the selectman, looking after the travellers, "but one couldn't make them understand. With officers in charge, and that miserable girl lying at the point of death, as I may say, it will come hard on Mrs. Allen. I almost wish some of us had taken them home."

"Let them go," said the man addressed. "They bring good news from the son that was lost—poor woman, she will find that God does not altogether forsake her, though it is an awful trial she is going through."

With a parting salutation, so respectful from Jube, and so elegant from the boy, that the men stood quite confounded, the old negro and his charge passed on up the hill.

"It's the first brown house," one of the little group called out, as soon as he recovered his power of speech, which, like those of any true New Englander, were not to be checked long by any condition whatever; "the first brown house, and ask for widder Allen."

The two strangers looked back, comprehending the gesture which accompanied these words, and, with another courteous salute, disappeared along a bend in the road.

"We've almost reached our journey's end, Jube," the boy said, in their native tongue, after they had walked some distance.

"Yes, little master," said Jube, in the same tongue, "that's the house I see now up yonder."

"I wonder if she is a kind woman?" the boy continued, his thoughts reverting to all the trouble and cruelty of the past months.

"I hope so, little master; it's a woman's nature, most times; and if she have a spark of goodness in her heart, it must come out when she see that blessed young face."

"Dave's mother ought to be kind and good, I am sure."

"Very nice man, that Master Rice; Jube will never forget him, never!"

With such broken conversation, they pursued their way, and soon reached the summit of the hill. Just before them was the old farm house which once looked so cheerful and pleasant, but now a quiet so profound pervaded the whole place that it seemed like a shadow deepening under the trouble which oppressed its inmates.

With his refined instincts and sympathies, the boy felt a peculiar restlessness creep over his mind as he approached the dwelling.

"How still it is, Jube," he said, unconsciously sinking his voice to a whisper, as they lingered for an instant by the gate; "it seems as if they were all sick or dead."

"Not that, little master," replied Jube, occupied with the reflection that his beloved charge had at last reached a place of tranquillity, and incapable of the vague emotions which agitated the sensitive nerves of the child.

He opened the gate, and held it ajar for the boy to pass through. Never once, in all their sorrow and confusion, had he forgotten the respect which was due to his old master's son.

"Go in, Master Paul; don't be afeard, Jube is with you yet."

"I am not afraid; I only feel sorry for these strange people; but why, I cannot tell."

Jube made no answer to the fancies which he could not comprehend; and, after that momentary hesitation, the boy passed up the little garden path to the house, and waited, while the negro gave a quick, eager rap upon the door.

Mrs. Allen was occupied in the bedroom, and did not hear the summons, but it aroused the officer who sat over the kitchen fire, struggling with sleep and the dreary reflections to which the place and his duty gave rise.

"Come in!" he called, in a low voice; then, fearful of disturbing the sick girl, whom he had already begun to pity, in spite of the sin and guilt which he believed to be upon her, he rose from his chair, and walked to the door, starting in astonishment when he opened it, and saw the two strangers standing there.

Paul looked at Jube for assistance, and Jube looked back at him so helpless and confused, in his efforts to recall his very imperfect English, that the boy was obliged to depend upon his own courage and knowledge of the harsh tongue.

"Madame Allen live here?" he asked, while the officer, between astonishment at his grace and foreign accent, only stared the harder, instead of answering.

"Moder to Masser Rice," added Jube, coming to his young master's assistance, and after successfully pronouncing so much in his best English, he rushed into a flood of French, which completed the man's bewilderment.

"Land's sake!" he exclaimed. "What on arth does the critter mean—never heerd such a lingo in all my life!"

"*Chut!*" whispered Paul to his companion; "he doesn't understand you."

The recollection quite took Jube by surprise. He ceased at once, his mouth gaping wide, and the whites of his eyes displayed in bewildering astonishment.

"We wish Madame Allen," pursued the boy.

"De moder of her son," put in Jube, coming to his senses, and determining to assist his master by every means in his power.

"The widder Allen lives here," replied the man, "if you want her—the Lord knows she near enough crazy, anyhow," he continued, in a lower tone. "But walk in, walk in."

CHAPTER XXX.

THE WELCOME LETTER.

The guard left Paul and his black friend standing on the door step, and went toward the bedroom, calling, in a half-whisper,

"Here, Mrs. Allen, somebody wants you."

The old woman heard his voice, and came out into the kitchen, closing the bedroom door, and looking with as much astonishment at the strangers as her numbed faculties would permit her to feel.

"They want to see you," said the officer, turning toward her; "I can't make out nothing more—they talk such outlandish lingo."

Paul motioned Jube to follow, and entered the kitchen. He walked up to the old lady and removed his cap with a low bow, saying:

"It is Madame Allen—the mother of Monsieur Rice?"

"I was his mother," she replied, in a hollow voice, "but he is dead. What do you want of me, little boy?"

"This letter for you," Paul continued, taking the carefully preserved epistle from his pocket.

The old woman shrunk away, and put out her hand as if to thrust the letter aside.

"More trouble," she muttered. "What can come now?"

Paul understood, rather from the expression of her face than a comprehension of her words, that she was startled.

"Very good news," he said. "The lady much happy now."

"Happy!" she repeated. "Who is that from?"

"From him—from madame's own son!"

She only looked incredulous; she was so stunned by suffering that her mind could not readily receive any new impression.

"I haven't any son," she said; "my son is dead."

The boy glanced anxiously toward Jube, and the old negro felt bound to offer his assistance, although sadly at a loss to remember a single English word by which matters might be explained.

"No dead, lady!" he exclaimed; "bery live, Masser Rice; yes, certainement; very much so."

The old woman gave him a wild look, snatched the letter from Paul's hand, and tore it open, while the three stood gazing at her in astonishment.

"His writing," she muttered. "Oh, I must be going crazy!"

She read the page, retreated backward, and fell into a

chair, while the letter fluttered slowly to the floor. She understood the contents, but had wept so much during the past days, that no tears were left; even joy could not revivify the wasted fount.

"What is the matter, Mrs. Allen?" exclaimed the officer, frightened by her appearance. "Don't look so; don't now; it skeers a fellow!"

She pointed to the letter.

" Read it to me," she whispered; "read it, I say; maybe I shall believe it then."

The man picked up the sheet, and spelled out the tidings as well as his astonishment and Rice's crabbed writing would permit.

"My son is alive," muttered the woman. "God has not altogether forsaken me!"

"Alive!" repeated the officer; "gone another voyage, and sent these two here."

Paul had crept close to Jube, and slipped his slender fingers into the broad palm of his trusty companion, startled by the scene.

"You came from my son?" said the woman, looking earnestly at them.

"Yes," interrupted the officer; "seems to be a sort of adoptation on Dave's part; he's dreadful perticular to have the boy sent to the district school to once."

Mrs. Allen struggled with herself, managed to rise, and walked toward the chamber door.

"Stay here," she said; "sit down and wait for me."

They understood her words, and seated themselves as she directed. Her heavy tread upon the stairs echoed down into the room, and when it died away in the garret, they sat waiting, while the officer stared at them as

14

if they had been two strange birds, placed there for his observation.

When Mrs. Allen reached the cold, silent garret, she sank upon her knees on the bare boards and tried to pray. Broken and faint were the murmurs which fell from her lips; but gradually, through that silent prayer, a ray of holy happiness stole over her haggard features —God had sent one gleam of light into the terrible blackness which surrounded her.

She rose, at length, strengthened, and able more clearly to reflect upon the joy that had come so unexpectedly into the midst of her anguish.

Her son was alive—it was better that he should not be there—he could in no way aid Katharine. As for her own portion of the agony, only God could help her to endure that. But he was alive, and would come back in time to comfort her.

Nearly half an hour must have elapsed before she descended the stairs and again entered the kitchen. The strangers were still seated by the fire, and the officer had sufficiently recovered from his stupor of astonishment to overpower them with all sorts of questions, very few of which they understood; but as they made up for this lack of comprehension by a courtesy altogether new and puzzling to him, he had to make the best of matters.

"They come from 'way off, goodness knows where," he said, turning toward Mrs. Allen. "Dave's the queerest fellow to pick up odd critters!"

The woman paid no attention to his words, but went up to Paul and laid her hand on his shoulder; the look of childish comprehension and sympathy which he lifted to her face seemed to go to her heart as no expressions of kindness from another had been able to do. A faint dew gathered in her eyes, but no absolute tears.

"Are you hungry?" she asked. "I will get you something to eat."

"Madame must not trouble much," Paul said, respectfully.

"It's the natur' o' children and darkies to eat," remarked the officer, sapiently; "you'd better hunt 'em up a cold bite. I feel kinder hungry myself, Mrs. Allen."

The old woman went about her duties in a methodical way, finding a kind of relief in the occupation. She placed such food as she had prepared upon the table, and motioned Paul to sit down. Before the little fellow touched a morsel himself, he heaped a plate with great slices of gingerbread and mince pie, and carried them to Jube.

"Do look at that," muttered the officer; "wal, I never seed a little chap have so much manners afore."

"You are much kind," Paul said to Mrs. Allen; "so was good Rice—*le grand Dieu* will bless both."

"Granite do," remarked the officer; "I wonder if that's his name?"

"The letter says, Paul," returned the woman.

"Me; that me," said the boy, catching his name, and looking up with a smile.

The woman once more took up the letter, and sat down to gain a clearer knowledge of its contents.

"And you're sent here to stay," she said, with a weary sigh, as she folded the sheet. "Dear me, what a place for any one to come to!"

"Yes," replied the boy, understanding her first words; "in few months—tree, four, Monsieur Rice come too."

"His name is Dave," said the officer; "but, la! I calculate they have all sorts of queer names for folks in them out of the way countries."

When Paul had finished his meal he returned to his old place on the little stool by Jube's side, and the pair sat looking wistfully at each other, oppressed by the strangeness and gloom of the place.

Mrs. Allen paid little attention to them. She washed the dishes with her usual care, and put them away in the corner cupboard, brushed the hearth, moved restlessly about, finding that relief in constant occupation which the mind is sure to seek during a great sorrow.

Paul sat watching her with his large, wistful eyes, for she had strangely excited some inexplicable sympathy in his heart.

After a time a feeble voice called from the bedroom.

"Mother; where are you, mother?"

Katharine had awakened, and was startled to find herself alone; but at the summons the old woman went into the bedroom, and the murmur of their voices reached the kitchen faintly.

In a few moments Mrs. Allen came out with a cup in her hand. She went to the fire, took a tin basin from the hearth, and poured a portion of the contents into the cup, but her hands shook so tremulously that the hot liquid spilled over them.

Paul arose, and took the dish from her with his usual gentleness.

"Let me carry it," he said. "Madame very tired."

Poor old madame! His kindness touched her like a new pang. She followed him to the bedroom and took the cup again.

"Sick lady there?" he whispered.

Mrs. Allen bent her head, she could not speak just then.

"Paul will help," continued the boy. "Paul nursed mamma once—please let him help the sweet mademoiselle."

The boy had caught a glimpse of Katharine's face, and his own brightened.

The old woman felt as if an angel had unexpectedly been sent to aid her in her misery—the pitying light in those beautiful eyes went to her heart like a blessing.

After that, every time she went in or out, Paul watched her movements and assisted her in his unobtrusive way, then crept back to Jube, and waited to see in what manner he could next express his desire to be of use.

"He goes about as handy as a pet kitten," said the officer at last, sorely perplexed in his mind. "Got a mother, little chap?"

The negro understood these words, and put up his hands with a warning gesture.

"Hush!" said Mrs. Allen, sternly; "you know what the letter said."

"I forgot," returned the man, and he began uneasily biting his finger nails, to hide his confusion; but the nails proved very horny and tough, and he failed to get rid of much contrition in that way.

Paul made no answer to his question; he only retreated a little closer to Jube, and laid his head upon the negro's knee. The simple action wrung Mrs. Allen's heart with a new pang. Hard and severe as her nature was, it had become so softened under her grief that she was unusually observant, and touched by trifles which at another time would have passed by unheeded.

"I expect you're tired," said the officer, pointing his

finger, with its dilapidated nail, at the boy; "you're tired now, aint you?"

"A little," said Paul, without raising his head. "Only very little."

Jube knew by the sorrowful voice that the child was thinking of his mother, and had been pained by the man's thoughtless question in regard to her. He attempted no consolation in words, but laid his great hand protectingly upon the boy's shoulder. The two crept a little closer to each other, feeling a sort of safety and comfort in that silent companionship.

"I expect they feel kinder cold," remarked the officer.

Mrs. Allen heard, and remembered that there was a fireplace in the chamber where she intended them to sleep. She went out into the wood house for pine knots to kindle a fire, but Paul had followed her with that solicitude to which she was so unaccustomed, and when he saw her errand, motioned Jube to follow.

"Jube very strong," he said; "carry me—carry wood—likes to do it too much."

The old woman attempted no opposition; she allowed the negro to take up an armful of sticks, and led the way up-stairs in silence, Paul still accompanying them, from an unwillingness to remain alone with the strange man.

Jube's intentions were of the most praiseworthy description, but it must be confessed that his success in making a fire was not equal to his ambition. When Mrs. Allen saw that he only succeeded in raising a smoke instead of kindling a flame, she took the matter into her own hands, and speedily the knots and kindlings were hissing and snapping on the unused hearth at a famous rate.

"Jube learn," Paul said, smiling at both, and trying to comfort the negro's evident discomfiture, "learn very quick. *Tout suit!*"

"Yes, little masser," he replied; "Jube know how next time."

Mrs. Allen signified to them that they were to sleep in that room; there was a trundle bed for Paul, which Katharine had occupied when a child, and she improvised a very comfortable sort of couch for the attendant. She spread a bit of rag carpet before Paul's bed, and made everything homelike and tidy for the shivering strangers.

"Come down and warm," she said, when her preparations were completed, noticing that they shivered with cold.

Paul and Jube followed her down-stairs and took their former seats by the fire, while she, after stealing into the bedroom, to be certain that Katharine slept, took her station by the hearth likewise, and remained gazing drearily into the fire.

At last she seemed to remember how late it was, and, getting up, took a brass warming-pan, with its long wooden handle, which she filled with hot coals. Thus armed, she went up-stairs, came down again after an absence of ten minutes, and told her guests to go up to bed before the sheets got cold.

When the two went up-stairs, Jube found his humble bed warmed comfortably, like that of his little master.

CHAPTER XXXI.

THE RED SCHOOL-HOUSE AT SHRUB OAK

One entire week that poor girl lay upon the verge of death; but so still, so mournfully feeble, that it would have pained you to look at her. The sound of her voice must have sent you from her presence heart-broken. The doctor visited her every day. At times he attempted to arouse her with some of his droll sayings, but the voice in which they were uttered was so pitiful that she understood it only as a compassionate attempt to comfort her, and so, in truth, it was.

One day, when the fever had left her brain, and she could scarcely speak for want of strength, Katharine whispered the doctor to sit down a little while, as she had something to ask him about.

The doctor slid his crutches along the floor, and seated himself on the edge of the bed, looking very grave, for he felt what the poor thing was about to say.

"Doctor."

"Well, my child."

"What is that man always staying in the kitchen for?"

"That man—oh! he's help."

"Night and day, night and day, he's always there," murmured the unhappy girl. "He tries to keep out of sight; but every time the door opens I see his shadow on the wall."

"And it frightens you, poor child; is that it?"

"Yes, doctor, it troubles me. I want to know what it means?"

"He has been sent here to keep your mother company."

She looked at him with reproachful earnestness, tried to shake her head, but the languid eyelids only drooped over the blue orbs fastened on his face, and, directly, tears began to swell under them.

"I heard people talking in the other room, doctor; what was it about?"

"I cannot tell you, not knowing what they said."

"They were talking about my baby."

The word broke out in a sob, and tears gushed through her trembling eyelashes. The doctor laid his hand on her head, and then the convulsion of her grief became heart-rending.

"Hush, child, hush! don't cry, don't cry—it will hurt you."

"Doctor, what—what did my baby die of?"

The doctor turned white with the pain and surprise of that question.

"Won't you tell me, doctor?"

He looked at her in stern distrust. Her face was innocent as a child's. She interrogated his countenance imploringly through her tears.

"Don't you know, Katharine?"

She began to cry bitterly.

"How could I? no one tells me, and I can't remember any thing."

"Katharine, is this true?"

"Is what true, doctor?"

"Have you no knowledge how the child died?"

"No; I was in bed here, shaking with cold and burning up with fever. I wanted the baby, and got up; it was in the cradle, dead. Oh, I remember so well how white its little face was—how white and cold. I came back again, crept into bed, and wished that God would let me die, too."

"And this is all you know?"

"Yes, doctor; I was afraid to ask mother about it—she looks so strange; but you will tell me every thing."

The doctor gathered up his crutches hurriedly, and stamped his way into the next room.

"Mrs. Allen," he said, sharply, "you are a brave woman. I'm nothing but a poor, miserable coward. I'm going to sneak off, and let you talk to that poor girl. I could cut the throat of a lamb when it was looking into my eyes as soon as tell her what must come. You're a Christian, Mrs. Allen, a downright Christian, and no sham—crusty and bitter, sharp and honest. You can do it; I can't. You're a Bible woman; I'm an old sinner, and am running away—do you understand—because I'm an abominable old coward. Tell her yourself."

Mrs. Allen turned white as parchment. She understood the doctor's meaning in full.

"Has she been asking questions, doctor?"

"Yes; enough to break a commonly good heart—but mine is tough as sole leather."

"She is better?"

"Yes; a great deal better."

"And when she is well enough to be moved, they will take her away?"

"I suppose so—the hounds."

The woman stood motionless—her hands tightly clasped, and her lips stiffening with pain.

"You are right," she said; "who but her mother should take up this burden. I will tell Katharine."

"Not 'till I am out of sight!" cried the doctor, wheeling sharply on his crutches. "I tell you, woman, I can't stand it—feel like a butcher for what I have done. The law is an abomination. Why can't they let my pretty pigeon alone? As if there wasn't babies enough without making a fuss if one does drop off a little out of the common way?"

"I'll tell her. It's hard, but what is before me I can do," said the woman.

"Can't I help little?" said a sweet voice from the hearth, "or Jube? he's very strong."

The doctor looked down on little Paul with a glance half quizzical, half serious.

"You, little shoat, you?"

"Yes, if madame please," said Paul, with a sad smile; "if there's trouble, I and Jube very used to it. We've been in a boat together three days, with nothing but red hot sun and many waters to look on, till they blind us. We know how to be hungry and cold, and he knows how to be whipped on his back and never say a word. That is why we can help."

"That little trooper is what I call a pilgrim," muttered the guard, nodding at the doctor with a wink of the left eye.

Mrs. Allen laid her unsteady hand on Paul's dark curls. "He is a good boy, and God will bless him," she said.

Paul, with that touching grace that is so beautiful in highly bred children of foreign birth, took the hard hand of his benefactress and touched it to his lips.

"He ought to have been sent to school," she said, in a weary voice, addressing the doctor. "My son charged it upon me, but I could not leave her."

The doctor wheeled round, and examined Paul's face from beneath his heavy eyebrows.

"Go get your cap and great coat," he said with gruff kindness. "If you've got a wedge of mince pie or a slice of gingerbread, Mrs. Allen, drop it into a dinner basket, and I'll put the shaver on his course of studies in double-quick time. Send him out when all is ready."

It took the doctor some minutes to mount his horse. By the time he was in the saddle, Paul came forth with a painted dinner basket on his arm. A new pair of mittens imprisoned his delicate hands, while the yarn comforter that Rice had given him was twisted around his neck, and concealed the lower part of his face.

"That's right, little trooper; climb up the fence and hop on behind. That's it—sharp as a steel trap. Sit up close and hold on to my belt. All right. Here we go! Get up! Get along, I say!"

The doctor's horse had been used to carrying double in all sorts of ways, so he only threw up his head, and cast his long mane on the air like a banner, intending this action as a protest against extra burdens in general, before he started off in a heavy trot toward Falls Hill.

The doctor was heavy-hearted enough, but he took some note of the strange child under his charge, told him to hang on to his belt like a dog to a sassafras root, and expressed a decided opinion that Paul would be a man before his mother, which filled the boy's heart with sadness, as that word mother was ever sure to do.

The red school-house at Shrub Oak was half a mile out of the doctor's way, but instead of setting Paul down at the willow tree on the corner, he put his eccentric steed to its mettle, and drew up in front of that sublime seat of learning with considerable dash.

"Holloa there, Tibbles! Holloa! I say! Come out and get a new scholar."

Mr. Tibbles, the master, heard this shout while in the midst of his pupils, and laying down his ruler with dignity, moved toward the door, leaving a hum and rush of whispers behind, which might have reminded one of Babel before the inmates had ventured entirely upon their new tongues.

"How do you do, Tibbles? Young ideas shoot prosperously—ha? Give 'em the birch—give 'em the birch. Nothing like it. Whipped half out of my skin before I got through Webster's spelling-book. Did me good. Give 'em birch; and if you can't find that handy, try hemlock sprouts. Tingle beautifully."

The master took these suggestions demurely, and asked if the little boy upon the horse wanted to come to school.

"Yes. Hop down, shaver. Give him a lift, Tibbles. A little Frenchman from St. Domingo. Nothing but a nest of niggers left there. Killed all the white folks off. Nice country, that. You have heard of the boy that stuck to the wrecked brig with Dave Rice?"

"Oh, yes, doctor," answered Tibbles, brightening.

"There he is, large as life. Take good care of him, for he's worth a dozen of your common fellows. Put him through English, and give him a touch of Latin, if you remember any. Who knows but I may take him for a student one of these days?"

While the doctor was speaking, he took Paul by the hand, and swung him lightly to the ground. Mr. Tibbles took possession of the handsome boy with no little pride; for the child who had stood so manfully by David Rice had become a historical character in Shrub Oak, and the master felt the dignity of his school enhanced by Paul's advent there.

Paul was a good deal embarrassed as he entered school with thirty pairs of eyes levelled at him, sparkling with every possible degree of curiosity. He sat down on a little bench, blushing like a girl, but looking so modest and gentle withal, that the whole school felt a general and kindly impulse toward the stranger. The bluest covered spelling-book was handed to him from the master's desk. One boy volunteered to lend him a slate, and another took a new pencil from his pocket and gave it to him outright, looking triumphantly round at the little girls' bench to be sure that his intimacy with the distinguished stranger had made its impression in that quarter.

At noon time there was no limit to the hospitalities of the occasion; wonder-cakes, biscuits, and wedges of pumpkin pie, made their way into Paul's dinner basket. One pretty little girl slily offered him a rusty coated apple, and another was ambitious to teach him how to slide on a strip of ice that lay, like a mammoth looking-glass, a little distance down the turnpike.

Paul received all these kindnesses with gentle grace. His broken speech, the sweet expression of his eyes, the natural refinement which even children could feel, made him a general favorite in less than two hours. The large boys were already arranging to lend him their sleds. As for the girls, the whispering and nudging that took place among them whenever the lad lifted those splendid eyes from his book, was a scandal to the whole school and sex.

When Paul went out of school at night he felt very lonesome and forlorn, not exactly knowing his way home, and a good deal dismayed by the snow, which was getting damp and heavy, with a succession of warm, foggy days. While he was standing in the door, uncertain which way to turn, two large boys, rosy from the fresh air, came racing up harnessed to a hand sled, in their opinion a marvel of workmanship, which was expected to lift the stranger off his feet with admiration.

With cordial hospitality, the boys offered this conveyance to Paul, who accepted it in good faith, and the boys carried him away in triumph, dashing off toward Falls Hill, and up the crossroad, in splendid style.

The next day, one of these boys—the same little fellow who had given Rose Mason the string of robins' eggs, might have been seen hanging around Mrs. Allen's gate, looking wistfully at the front door. When it opened, and Paul came forth, the lad ran to meet him, and the two went away together, talking earnestly on the road to school.

CHAPTER XXXII.

A TERRIBLE DISCLOSURE.

ALAS! the sad and heavy-hearted sorrow that was left behind on the day that little Paul went forth to his school-boy life. Twice, Mrs. Allen went into Katharine's room and sat down, pale and soul-stricken, waiting to be questioned; but her daughter had been exhausted by her conversation with the doctor, and lay with her eyes closed, weary of all things. So, drawing a deep breath from a consciousness of this reprieve, the wretched woman went away again still more heavily laden with the duty that clung to her like a vampire, and so a week passed by without another attempt. At last, toward nightfall one day, Katharine spoke:

"Mother?"

"My child."

"What is it that you are all afraid of telling me?"

"A great trouble, Katharine; something that even I, who have some courage, tremble to speak of."

"Is it about my baby, mother?"

"Yes."

"I am glad you are willing to answer me; the doctor put me off."

"But I will not put you off, my poor child."

"What is it, mother? This frightens me—your voice is husky, your face strange—did my baby die a hard death?"

"Yes, very hard. It was killed."

The voice was indeed husky that uttered these words.

Katharine rose up in the bed, her eyes grew large and wild.

"Killed?"

"Yes, God help us—it was dead and buried when we found it."

"Dead and buried; mother, mother!"

The words came forth in a sharp cry, breaking the pale lips apart and leaving them so.

"I left it alive, Katharine—sleeping by your side. Can you remember when I went out that day after a man to haul some wood from Castle Rock?"

Katharine held both hands to her temples, rocking to and fro as if the effort to think cost great pain.

"Yes, mother, I remember about the wood. You put the shawl, that David sent me, over my shoulders. The baby was asleep then, with one hand to its mouth. I took the hand away just to see it nestle; its pretty lips were moving all the time."

"What then?"

"It was a noise, mother—a trumpet sounding through the house—dead leaves, white leaves flying all about me; then, mother, then immense heaps of snow rolling, heaving, and spreading everywhere. I—I cannot remember how I got in or out of this cold whiteness. It seemed to bury me in a long sleep."

"Poor child—poor little Katharine."

"Oh, I remember you called me that when I was a very small child."

"Katharine, try; can you remember nothing more?"

"Nothing more, only as one recollects that she has been miserably asleep."

"But it was in this time, while I was away to see about that wood, that our baby was killed."

"Killed!—how?"

"Strangled."

"Mother—mother!"

The anguish of this cry made the poor woman tremble; but she must speak out all her fearful knowledge or her daughter would never be prepared for the future.

"Mother, tell me—tell me!"

The poor young creature lay gasping upon her pillow. It was a terrible scene to witness.

"It had been strangled or smothered, and buried deep in the snow, by the rocks under the butternut tree, half way to Mr. Thrasher's."

"There—there in sight of his father's house!"

She writhed in anguish on her bed, weak, fragile, tortured, it seemed as if she must die before another shock reached her.

"Dead—buried in the snow," she kept repeating.

The mother knelt by the bed, holding forth her arms, which the wretched girl could not see.

"Ask God to give you strength, Katharine."

"You ask him for me, mother; my heart aches so."

"Oh, Katharine, we have greater trouble yet to come."

"Greater trouble than the death of one's little babe— that can never be!" Katharine answered with pathetic pain. "No, no, mother, that can never be!"

"Katharine, the neighbors believe that—" she paused, put a hand to her throat, as if the words strangled her, and went on in a voice so near a whisper that it sounded unearthly, "believe that you killed the child."

"Kill my child! Did they know I was its mother?"

"Killed and buried it with your own hands in the snow," persisted the woman, drearily. "This is what they charge you with, my daughter."

"No, no, mother!"

"A jury have decided so."

"A jury! What cruel thing is that?"

"It is a court."

"A court! What was that for?"

"To say if you were innocent—"

"Guilty of murdering my own baby—his and mine! Do the neighbors want a court to prove that of me?"

"It has been held, Katharine, here under my roof."

"Held here?"

"And that is why we are never alone."

"That man—you mean that man!" cried Katharine,

shrinking back in the bed with a look of affright. "Did the neighbors put him here to watch me? Why?"

"They fear you will attempt to escape!"

"Escape where? Is not this my home?"

The old woman wrung her hands in bitter agony. This scene was racking every nerve in her body. That young creature had not fully comprehended that which no mother living could have told. All her own strength was exhausted—she had no fortitude left. Katharine lay with her great, wild eyes searching her mother's face, as it fell helplessly downward upon her bosom.

"Mother, if the neighbors believe this, what will they do to me?"

"Kill you, my poor lamb!" the woman whispered.

Katharine did not seem to feel this so keenly as other things that had been said; it was beyond her comprehension—she could not realize it.

"No, mother, that can never be. God knows all things!"

The young creature almost smiled as she said this, and closing her eyes turned her face to the wall.

It was strange that, in all her trouble, she never once alluded to Thrasher with an idea of protection, or seemed to have any hope of succor from him. The letter he had sent left no impression on her memory, but some more subtle intuition possessed her soul, and this secret second-sense held all hope in check. This half supernatural feeling also had doubtless given vague after-shadowings of her child's death without absolutely awakening her consciousness, for when the terrible truth was revealed to her she seemed struggling to remember something that had gone before.

Thus the real and the visionary were so mingled in

her mind that a true realization of her danger was impossible, and knowing her innocence, a sweet trust in the Divine justice sprang up in her soul, keeping out all fear.

CHAPTER XXXIII.

THE OLD COUPLE ON THEIR SHADOWED HEARTH-STONE.

DURING the days that had followed Katharine Allen's arrest—days so terrible that their memory could never die wholly out of the neighborhood—the old couple in the farm house beyond the widow Allen's dwelling, bore their full share of the horror and grief which oppressed all who had known and loved the girl.

But both Mr. Thrasher and his wife were bowed beneath a deeper sorrow than mere commiseration for one unfortunate creature—beneath a horror more painful than any thought of her sin.

For a time neither spoke of it. They avoided looking in each other's face—those true hearts that had never had a secret before—lest the fear that haunted their minds should find utterance in their eyes.

One night, as they sat by the kitchen fire, the old lady mechanically knitting, and her husband looking mournfully into the cheerful blaze, her thoughts found an almost unconscious utterance.

"Oh, if I could only be certain—if Nelson was only here to answer for himself."

Mr. Thrasher glanced quickly at her, then back into the fire, while the old lady let her work fall, and sat with her hands clasped in her lap, that mild, womanly face darkened by a deeper shadow than it had ever before worn.

"If I could send for him, I would," replied Mr. Thrasher, with a sternness his voice seldom took in addressing his wife. "I don't want to believe wrong of any one, but if he were here, I'd question him."

"I wouldn't," broke in the mother; "my heart would break if I was sure of it."

"It's a black thing," continued he, taking no notice of her remark, although the nervous twitching about his mouth, and the tremulous movement of his hands, proved that he had heard and shared in her feelings. "If I could look him in the eyes," he continued, the sternness creeping over his face again, "I should be answered."

"Don't think harshly of him!" returned his wife. "Don't do that! If we were to hear he was dead, remember how we should blame ourselves for any wrong feeling."

"I would rather see him lying dead yonder, where he used to sit, than know that he had tempted that poor girl into sin."

"Yes, I know. But don't talk in that way, father; don't look like that! I feel as if it wasn't you, with that frown on your face."

She put out her hand and took his. He clasped his hard fingers about hers with the faithful love of a lifetime; but the determination and gloom did not leave his features.

"I want to go down to the house," pursued the old lady, "but I've put it off—I hadn't the courage, somehow."

"Nor I," replied Mr. Thrasher; "but isn't it a dreadful thing when we are dreading to ask questions, for fear we should stand face to face with our son's crime?"

"No, no, I don't believe it! I won't believe it, father! Such cruel words are unbecoming his parents!"

"I don't mean to be cruel to you or him, wife. Was I ever so?"

"Never! You have been one of the best husbands that ever lived."

She could not longer keep back her tears—they rolled down her cheeks, and fell, drop by drop, on her apron.

"I must go to the house," she said; "who knows but what Mrs. Allen is all alone. I feel as if I had been hard-hearted in not going before."

"You'd better go," he answered. "Yes; it's your duty."

"I thought of asking you to go with me, if you don't mind. I should have more courage with you by my side."

Mr. Thrasher was silent for a moment, then he said:

"Yes; we will go to-morrow morning."

They put the subject aside; nor was it again resumed. The chapter in the Bible was read, the prayer was uttered—no trouble could make those hearts forget that duty—and, in their affliction, they only turned more earnestly toward the help and comfort of their whole lives.

The next morning, when breakfast was over, and the work for the forenoon arranged, the husband and wife took their way down the hill toward Mrs. Allen's house, keeping close together, as if great comfort lay in that silent companionship.

When they reached the gate, both paused, looking anxiously at each other; when Mr. Thrasher saw the pale trouble which agitated his wife, he tried to say a few comforting words, but they broke on his lips.

He opened the gate, and they passed up the walk to the house. Mr. Thrasher knocked, but there was no response; a second time, but no better success.

"Maybe we might go in," whispered his wife, but he shook his head, and again tapped upon the door.

After another instant of suspense, which seemed very long to them, they heard footsteps, the latch was lifted from within, the door slowly opened, and Mrs. Allen stood before them, so changed by those terrible days, that the old friends of years could hardly feel that it was her.

When Mrs. Allen saw who stood there, she started a little, and the old pride gathered slowly over the anguish of her face.

"We—we came to ask how Katharine is," Mrs Thrasher said, faintly, taking it upon herself to break the silence.

"She is better," returned the widow, neither moving to give them entrance, or turning her eyes from that steady gaze.

"Do you think I could see her?" persisted the old lady, trembling all over and ready to cry aloud.

"Nobody sees her but the doctor," replied Mrs. Allen.

"I thought maybe I could do something—"

"There isn't any thing to do."

Then there was another awkward silence, which Mrs. Thrasher broke, with a timidity which she could hardly overcome.

"I should like to see Katharine," she said, "very, very much."

"She cannot see any one now—it is forbidden."

There were a few more faint remarks from Mrs. Thrasher, then the pair turned away. Mrs. Allen closed the door, they walked silently out of the yard and back toward their house, which had never appeared so cheerless to them.

As they passed the butternut tree both the old people turned away their heads, for the remembrance of that morning when they stood together and watched their son making signals from that very spot, for the wretched prisoner to whose presence they had been denied not half an hour before, filled their hearts with sensations which neither of them could ever express.

It was a mournful thing to see those two good souls in their bungling efforts to cheat each other into a belief that no terrible sorrow had fallen upon them. It was all a sad, sad failure.

CHAPTER XXXIV.

THE SNOW FRESHET.

There was rare confusion and riot at the red schoolhouse. The weather had changed suddenly, the wind blew from the south, the sun lay warm and dazzling upon the snow-drifts; but its treacherous kisses subdued their cold strength and wasted their beauty.

At last it settled into a regular "thaw"—a New England one at that. From the mud, a stranger might have thought the very foundations of the earth had been ploughed up. Every snow bank dissolved itself into a pert little rivulet, that swelled the general tide, and formed a muddy lake on each side of the road, along which horses and men passed so bespattered and stained that one could easily believe they had been formed entirely from clay, and were fast resolving themselves back to the original element.

A tiny brook, that died out in dry weather and sprung to existence on rainy days, ran along one end of the school-house. It had slept quietly for weeks under its icy bridge, but woke up with great commotion as thousands of tiny streams flowed down from the hills, and poured their excited little wavelets into its channel, swelling the brook to such a size that it evidently believed itself a stupendous sort of river. It must have been so; nothing but that idea very firmly impressed, could ever have excused the reckless conduct of that overgrown brook.

It raved, and scolded, and tore along its banks, tumbling the great stones about, uprooting the poor little frozen shrubs that had clung in fancied security to its brink. Fuming, splashing, and rioting madly across the road, the brook plunged down a gully at one end of the school-house, and set up a famous little waterfall on its own account. Then, rampant and muddy, it hurled itself forward, melting the snow as it went, and pouring over a high bank of the river, plunged in with tumultuous violence, making the deeper and slower stream swell, and eddy, and fume for a whole minute as it swallowed up the noisy affair.

The rush of this brook reached the boys caged up in the school-house, and nearly drove them frantic. They could hear the snow sliding off the roof of the school-house, and fall in heaps under the eaves, which dripped with incessant moisture. Now and then came a crash of icicles, breaking up the sunshine like splintered diamonds, and scattering broken fragments of crystal all over the snow.

This riot of waters and crashing of ice were enough to disorganize the best school in New England. The boys might be kept on the hard benches; but no power on earth would tame them down to real study. There they sat, burning with impatience, yet trying their best to look studious and quiet, whenever the master's eyes were upon them.

For some reason, there was to be a half holiday that afternoon, and the poor little sinners waited as restlessly as so many wild pigeons, with their wings tied, for the hour which should contain their release.

A plan of operation for the afternoon had been already decided upon—I do not think there was one dissenting voice—and of all the fun which the whole year might bring there would be nothing equal to that which they anticipated as soon as the school was dismissed.

But it really seemed as if twelve o'clock never would come! Those boys began to think, one and all, that the master had never been so slow in hearing the lessons. At last he became so irritated by their restlessness and inattention, that great fears arose that the holiday might be lost altogether.

When that horrible prophecy was whispered about—it originated with an unhappy-looking little Belshazzar, who was afflicted with a step-father, and who, from the vast stores of his experience, was always ready to draw out sorrowful warnings—I say, when it got whispered about, several of the larger boys nodded their heads at each other and looked ferociously rebellious, while the little ones eyed them with profound admiration. Just at that moment, the master's hand glided softly toward the great ferule that lay upon his desk; and somehow, at that sight, the mutineers became wonderfully interested in their lessons, and their small admirers retreated into their spelling-books so far that there seemed danger of their disappearing altogether.

The moment came at last. The master pulled out his silver watch, which ticked so loud and wrathfully that it could be heard all over the room—glanced at it, while every boy held his breath with anxiety. He waited an instant, in order to give due solemnity to the occasion, then down came the ferule on the desk with a grand crash. School was dismissed.

Out rushed the boys, tumbling over each other in hot haste, shrieking, hallooing, and plunging into the snow with shouts of eager delight. Even Belshazzar forgot his forebodings, and was foremost in this race after fun.

The teacher, a kind, elderly man, went to the school-house door and watched the tumult benignly from beneath the steel-bowed spectacles that had been hastily thrust across his forehead. His face, which had been severe, in a strained effort to keep up the dignity of his school, now beamed with infinite satisfaction, and rubbing his hands gleefully, he was sorely tempted to take a share in the fun himself. Damming up a torrent like that which came tumbling across the road, was something worth while, even for a man.

The boys rushed down to the swollen brook where it entered the gulley and made a tumultuous descent to the river, which was only concealed from the bulk windows of the school-house by a growth of young hemlocks that contrasted richly with the crusted snow. Here the boys were bound to make a dam big enough to drown a fellow in, neck and heels. Who cared for the mud? Who was afraid of the snow? Hurrah! hurrah! come on all hands and pitch in. There is a broken rail. Look out for the loose stones in that tumble-down, old wall. Bring up drift wood from the river, dead branches from the trees; tear loads of moss from the white oak stumps; bring any thing, every thing. Had any boy pluck enough to drag out some logs from the school wood pile? "Oh, golly! there is the master standing square in the door, and little Paul, the furrener, talking to him. Hurrah! the master is sending him off to join the fun. Isn't he a trump?"

Some of the boys stood still, knee deep in the water, frightened half to death by that wicked word—trump. But Tom Hutchins cried out with wonderful audacity, "Trump! who'se afeard? He's a high, low, jack, and the game, he is! There he goes into the school-house just to give us a chance at the wood pile. Come on, boys!"

Away the little fellows went, leaping like deer out of the mud, and directly a whole team of boys came dragging a walnut log through the snow, leaving a deep path all the way from the wood pile, which the master never could be made to see, spectacles or no spectacles, any more than he could hear the tumbling logs close under the window where he was sitting. I am inclined to think the boys were right, and that old man was a trump, though he did belong to the church.

"Hurrah! stand from under," said Tom Hutchins, looking down upon a swarm of schoolmates who were busy as bees in the mud and water of the gully. "Here comes the crowner—A number one, and no mistake. Come up here and give a boost, you chaps."

The boys sprang up the muddy sides of the gully, dripping like water-gods, reckless of wet jackets, torn trowsers, and shoes from which the water came up in gushes, and helped pitch that great, knotty log end foremost into the gully, where it was to form a line for the water to sweep over.

"Take it by the end—lift all at once—now, heave all together. Hurrah! hurrah!"

Paul had, indeed, lingered around the school-house door till the master sent him off to join the play. Then he went down to the brook and stood disconsolate on its high bank, as all this wild fun went on. He was cold and confused. No one asked him to help dam up the brook, so he stood in the snow, buried to the ears in his overcoat and comforter, and thinking that the watery sunshine was a very poor imitation of the tropical warmth in which he had formerly luxuriated.

He was at a loss how to take part in their play; besides that, the very roar of the water, and riot of the boys, reminded him of that fearful night when he was made an orphan, and so recalled his sufferings, that he longed to get beyond the sound. As for the boys, they were all too much engaged to notice his abstraction or ask his assistance.

CHAPTER XXXV.

ALL SORTS OF TREASON.

I have done a little injustice to Tom Hutchins—the warm-hearted lad who had been so in love with little Rose Mason, and was sure to be in love with every boy or girl who awoke his admiration, or needed his help. It was he who had proposed to draw Paul home on his sled, on his first lonely school day, and since that time a warm friendship had sprung up between the two lads. The first liking had been cemented by an exchange of doughnuts, wonder cakes, and red-checked apples. Then Tom had undertaken to teach Paul English in conversational lessons, and picked up a few scraps of French from the boy, fairly believing himself to be speaking a foreign language when he twisted his hard, New England tongue into imitations of Paul's pretty broken English, in which the boy could now make himself understood.

In the midst of his eager work on the dam, Tom saw Paul standing alone on the bank and called to him. But Paul shook his head, with a sad smile, and shrunk further away from the water. Then Tom gave one great heave at the log which was to complete the dam, shook the mud from his hands, and went dripping up the bank, with his face all aglow, and smiling as if he had just come out of a spring shower, and was inviting his friend down to watch the wild flowers start up in his track.

"Are you cold, Paul?" he asked, dancing about till the water splashed over the tops of his boots.

"A little," Paul said, shivering. "Only a little."

"Why, it's a'most like summer," returned Tom. "Splendid."

"Is it?" Paul asked, shivering worse than ever, as he thought what a forlorn idea of summer people must have in that frigid land.

"Why, how you do shiver," cried Tom. "Let's take a run up the hill and back, or you'll freeze solid."

"But you want to play," Paul said; "go with the boys, they are calling for you."

"Let 'em," replied Tom, philosophically, consoled at once by the idea that his playmates needed his assistance, and too full of generous kindness for any thought of leaving Paul to his loneliness. "Come along—let's see who'll get to the top first."

At the conclusion of their race Paul had got a color in his cheeks, and felt somewhat less like an icicle than before.

Then Tom paused, and looked Paul in the face quite seriously.

"Come down here among the hemlocks; I want to talk to you where the boys can't hear. We might do it in French, you know—you and I—but mebby we'd better have it out according to the spelling-book."

Paul smiled, and followed his friend to the bank of the river, where they sat down under the sheltering hemlock boughs. Tom shivered a little, but he shook the weakness off, and broke forth at once into the subject that was on his mind.

Tom's head was full of Katharine Allen and her troubles, a subject upon which he and Paul had held many earnest conversations, interspersed by mysterious hints about Rose Mason and Tom's unhappy state of mind regarding her absence in some unknown country.

"Paul, how is Katharine Allen this morning?" he said, abruptly.

Paul shook his head sadly by way of answer.

"Not any better?" asked Tom. "Wal, I'm sorry for her, anyhow. Little Rose liked her, and she was always good to Rose. It scares me to death to think what they're going to do to her."

"Who?" asked Paul.

"Why the law, of course," replied Tom, shocked at his friend's ignorance. "You know they're going to take her to prison as soon as she's well enough to be carried there."

"Yes, I know. They are wicked men, too wicked," exclaimed Paul; "why can't they leave her alone?"

"You mustn't say any thing agin the squire," returned Tom, with his New England respect for the law and its ministers. "I'm sorry for her, but you see she kinder killed the baby, poor little critter—I guess she was crazy, though, I do, but marm won't hear on it."

"Why don't her husband come and help her," Paul suggested.

"She haint got any—oh, dear no, that's the worst on it, marm says."

"Oh, she must have."

"Oh, must she!" retorted Tom, exulting in his knowledge of this world's wickedness, gained from conversations he had overheard concerning the poor girl, yet perplexed, and quite unable to settle the matter to his own satisfaction. Still he had no intention of allowing Paul to suppose that his wisdom was more than half assumed.

"I'm glad Miss Rose ain't here, anyhow," he observed; "she'd break her heart about all this. I know she would."

Paul thought the girl's heart must be colder than the weather if it would not have that effect, and nodded his approbation of Tom's sentiment.

'Katharine is getting stronger; they talk of carrying her off in a day or two," continued Tom. "I heard our folks say so this morning."

Paul's great eyes dimmed with tears, then a quick-passion turned them into fire.

"I could kill them," he said. "Yes, I could."

"'Twouldn't be no use," remarked Tom, sapiently; "'cause they'd only take you off too. I wish we could do something, though—I wish we could."

"Can't we?" questioned Paul, his face kindling with eagerness. "Oh, don't you think we could?"

"You're such a little bit of a chap," Tom replied, eyeing his companion, with a natural exultation at his own superiority in point of inches and weight.

"I'm little," Paul said, "but I am very brave—oh, you don't know! And Jube—Jube is strong like a lion, he could do any thing."

"I wonder if she couldn't run away," Tom burst out, quite overcome by his own inspiration. "I don't suppose she could run, you know, but she might get away."

"And we could help," Paul said, his quick intelligence seizing at once upon the suggestion; "I am sure we could."

"Why, my marm would kill me!" exclaimed Tom. "Wouldn't I ketch it, oh, my!"

"You would beg and pray," said Paul; "she could not refuse—she would be willing."

"Wal, I guess we wouldn't ask her—'tain't disobeyin' when you hain't been told not to do a thing, and nobody can tell you what to do when they never heerd of it."

Tom got dreadfully bewildered in his labyrinth of negatives and Paul was unable to make much of his speech, but he was certain that it harmonized with his own ideas, even if he did fail to comprehend its entire signification.

"We could help her," he kept repeating; "I am sure we could."

"I do wonder what the squire would say?" said Tom, giggling at the very idea, although somewhat frightened at its audacity. "Wouldn't there be a rumpus—oh, my golly!"

He laughed outright, and Paul joined him from sympathy with that merry face; but he became thoughtful again in a moment.

"You are certain they would take her away from home and lock her up in that dark, lonesome place you call a prison?" he inquired.

"Sure as a gun. Par says so, and he knows the squires and lawyers about here all to pieces; but that aint the worst of it, not by a jug full."

The good-hearted little fellow's voice began to choke in his throat, and he burst into a laugh to keep from sobbing outright.

"What can be worse than that?" inquired Paul, startled by his friend's demonstration.

"They'll kill her!"

Paul turned deadly pale. The horror in Tom's words had struck him dumb.

"They'll hang her up on a gallows made of two high posts, with a cross-bar on the top," continued Tom, shuddering at his own words, "and a halter fastened to the cross-bar, which they will tie round her pretty white neck, that Rose used to hug so much."

"Don't, oh, don't!" whispered Paul, putting up his hands; "it makes me tremble all over."

"And so it does me," cried Tom, dashing the tears from his blue eyes. "But you ought to know it just as it is, the burning brand and all."

"The burning brand—what is that?" asked Paul, faintly.

"The hot iron that they stamp M—that's for murderer, you know—on her hand!"

"Oh, me!" sighed Paul. "That petite white hand!"

"Sometimes the courts do that, and let 'em live in Simsbury all the rest of their lives. Sometimes they hang 'em right up. I don't know which they'll do to her."

"But they will do some of these awful things?" questioned Paul, breathing as if he was chilled through with the cold.

"Of course, they've got to do it. The law won't let 'em back out if they wanted to."

"Oh, dear, it makes me feel so wicked," cried Paul, brave thoughts kindling through the pallor of his face. "I want to cry and strike somebody at the same time."

"Strike! I want to maul some of 'em! Oh, if them courts was only little boys, and I the law, wouldn't they come down on their marrow bones and beg her pardon for thinking of such a thing. Besides, do you see, Paul, I don't believe she killed the baby. Anyway, them little creatures, with long flannel petticoats a hanging over their feet, are always doing things to torment grown folks, catching the rash, and measles, and chickenpox, to say nothing of a habit they get into of hiccuping right in a feller's face when he's told to tend 'em. Babies! They're the only thing I ever raly had agin marm—she always would be keeping one on hand, just for us to rock, and tend, and hush up. Par never would make a fuss about it, as a man aught ter with such goings on in the house."

"Perhaps he rather liked them!" suggested Paul.

"Liked 'em. Well, maybe he did, there's no saying; besides, they're well enough in their place, and that, according to my notion, is sound asleep in the cradle. Anyhow, what's the use of making sich a time about it when one of 'em stops crying for good and all, and what on airth could anybody think that ere young gal wanted with one of 'em a tagging after her?"

"I don't know," replied Paul, tenderly; "but from the way she looks at the empty cradle sometimes, it seems to me as if she wanted it there very much."

"Of course she does. It's a way of the wimmen folks have. I don't know about marm, for our cradle never is empty; but some wimmen make such fools of themselves, it's enough to set a feller agin the whole pack and boodle on 'em."

"You don't mean all the beautiful ladies," said Paul, thinking sadly of his own sweet mother.

"There's marm—she's a purty good kind of a woman after all, and Miss Mason, harnsome as a pictur. Then, little Rose—oh, my! don't you wish you could see her, with her white aprons ruffled all around, and her long curls, just like a wax doll. But then the generality of 'em—well, I don't want to say nothin'."

"That was a very nice little lady that gave me one apple with the brown coat."

"She? yes, she'll do; but we're going off the handle, you and I. What's the good of talking about the best on 'em if Katharine Allen has got to be hung! As I was a saying—when you would go on about wimmen folks in gineral, as if I cared any thing about them—as I was a saying, she never hurt that baby no more than I did. It went off and buried itself up in the snow—stealing Katy's shawl to wrap itself up in, then took cold and went into a conniption fit just out óf spite. Them little sojers are up to all sorts of tricks; don't I know 'em!"

"I am sure it died of its own accord," said Paul.

"Of course; anybody but a squire would a found that out long ago."

"And she would be much glad to have the little baby back again."

"Wall, I don't know about that," said Tom, shaking his head doubtfully; "Katharine Allen's got some sense, I reckon; squalling must come unnatral in that ar house—now I leave it to you."

"But they will hang her dead."

"No doubt about it."

"Or burn her poor petite hand."

"Both on 'em, for all what I know, without you and I stand up to the rack like men, and tell the laws, and squires, and constables to go to old scratch."

"What is old scratch?"

"Well, I don't just know; but he's a feller that's always about times like this."

"But hadn't we better let the laws, and the squires, and all the rest alone, and try very much to help her?" suggested Paul.

"In course we had; I only threw them in sort of promiscuous. Now I'll tell you what my idee is: Katharine is getting stronger every day, you know."

"Yes," said Paul; "she sat up in a chair this morning, and eat very little *déjéuner*—breakfast, I mean—and the man—that great big man that sits on the hearth always—said she was getting much strong, and the window is too near the ground—not safe."

"Did he say that?" inquired Tom, breathlessly.

"Yes; the man said that. Then madame—that is the old mother—she look frightened very much, and said, no take the poor sick child away too soon. Then the man said up-stairs was best—high from ground, very sure."

"That's bad," muttered Tom. "Ladders are scarce and heavy to lift."

"So," continued Paul, "they move my bed into another room, and take up many things for her, because the man thinks it sure."

"Well," cried Tom, coming out in force, "'what can't be cured must be endured,' as par says. There may be a ladder about Mrs. Allen's premises. To-morrow morning, when I come after you, we'll just take a survey there. About that cuffy friend of yourn, I want to have some talk with him. When there's ladders to be used, I'm afraid you and I couldn't come quite up to the scratch."

"But Jube, Jube he come right up to old scratch for us—very strong Jube—very brave, like lion."

"You're sartin that cuffy would do it; that he wouldn't slump through?"

"What, Jube? oh, yes, he do any thing I say; very good Jube, never slump."

"Well, then, we're a hull team, you and I and the nigger. Yes, and a hoss to let. If we don't get Katy Allen out of that end window, I don't know what's what; but, then, what are we to do with her when that's done?"

Paul shook his head in sudden despondency.

"Oh, dear, where can we go?"

Tom folded his arms and drooped his head. Here was a difficulty which he hadn't thought of before.

All at once Paul brightened up.

"We will take her to New York. If David Rice is there he'll be very good, and so glad Jube and we did it for his sister."

"Yes," cried Tom, "That's a genuine idee. I'll hook par's yaller wagon and drive down to the sloop atween two days, they'll never think of searching aboard a sloop. But oh, golly, golly, here's a fix. It takes money to travel in that ere genteel way, and I haint got more'n a ninepence on earth."

"Money?" cried Paul, eagerly. "What you call gold with the king's head on it?"

"I don't know about gold, never saw none of that ere money. What I mean is silver with a spread-eagle on one side and a woman's head on t'other."

"I am sure that gold is money," said Paul, recovering from his first look of disappointment, "for Jube gave it to the people as we came along, and they gave him back silver like that you speak of, more pieces than the gold, oh very much."

"And how much have you got?"

Paul put his delicate hands together.

"So much full, three, four, five times."

Tom emitted a low whistle. "Oh, golly, that's up to chalk, and you're sartin the tavern keepers and captains gave you silver money for it?"

"Sure I saw."

"And Jube will shell out—no mistake about that, ha?"

"Jube what?"

"ll hand over," persisted Tom, counting imaginary gold into his palm.

"What, give the money?"

"Yes; chink!"

"Oh, yes—sure."

"Then we're sot up in business. Three stout fellers, saddles lying about loose in some barn or other, yaller wagon standing ready, harness chucked under the seat, horses whinnering to be druv, and that ere poor gal ready to jump out of the window when we say the word. Now, Paul, this is just what you must do. Get the nigger—I mean our friend Jube—for when a darkey has his double hands full of chink to do as he pleases with, he's got a right to be treated like folks, for that makes him an individual; get him ready to toe the mark when we give the word. Jest tell her that Tom—she knows me—is on hand, and working for her like sixty, and just the minute she's well enough to cut, we'll have her out of that winder. Then you sleep with one eye open, and tell me every word that officer says."

"Yes," said Paul, "I'll do every thing; but hadn't we better say something to madam?"

"Do you mean Mrs. Allen?" answered Tom, dropping his chin into the hollow of one hand, in a thoughtful way. "No; I should rather say not. She's got strict notions about things, and might put the wrong spoke into our wheel. Now, if I was going to tell anybody, it would be the doctor; he's clear grit, he is, and wouldn't stop us if we run through his own home lot with that ere gal. Ketch him telling."

By this time the boys were chilled through with standing in the wet and cold. Tom's teeth chattered in his head as he uttered this encomium on the doctor, who was the most popular person among the juveniles in all the neighborhood, and Paul shivered in his garments like a tropical bird brought into the midst of a foreign winter. Besides, the boys had conquered the brook, which was storming its way to the river over a pile of stones and rubbish, which he triumphantly pronounced the finest dam that had ever been built on this side of creation; and Tom, though a philosopher, philanthropist, and hero, loved fun above all. So away he started, shouting hurrah, and made a rush clear through the turbulent waters of the brook, just to let the boys know that he hadn't been shirking; but amid all the noise and fun, he resolved to be faithful to his young confederate, and only hold council with the true-hearted negro.

As Paul went toiling up the hill that day, he saw Jube coming toward him—a circumstance that often happened on his way from school. How his beautiful face kindled up at the sight of his friend. His pace quickened, and the trouble went out from his eyes as he held out the little, cold hand, in its wet mitten, for Jube to lead him home, as usual.

Jube drew off the mitten, and took the chilled hand in his broad palm, caressing it as if it had been a bird.

CHAPTER XXXVI.

MRS. MASON AT HER STUDIES.

Several months had passed since the arrival of Mrs. Mason at the minister's house, in Bays Hollow.

During that time she had not been idle. When she placed herself under the quiet lady's instruction, she had announced that she wished to make all the progress possible and turn every moment to account—truly, she had done so.

Had the woman kept some good design in view, the assiduity with which she labored would have done her honor—as it was, vanity took the place of any better motive and perhaps was the strongest incentive which a nature like hers could have felt.

The facility with which she gained a knowledge of things astonished the minister's wife, whose education was thorough and solid, yet Mrs. Mason made far more show with her little accomplishments than her instructress could with all her learning. She had an excellent verbal memory, was quick to seize every movement or expression, and as Mrs. Prior was a true lady she could not have had a better model.

Among the gifts with which Thrasher had presented Mrs. Mason, there were many articles of which she did not know the use or even the name, but nobody would ever have dreamed it—she gained the knowledge so adroitly from Mrs. Prior, that the little woman had an unpleasant feeling that the wealthy Southerner considered her very ignorant, and desired to enlighten her.

She did wonders in her French lessons—she promised to make a showy, dashing performer upon the piano, and her quick ear taught her speedily to regulate any little inaccuracies of speech by the correct, although sometimes formal language, of her companion.

Yet she carried it all off with so lofty an air, that her teacher often felt that she was the only person instructed. She corrected herself with so much assurance and dignity that Mrs. Prior would color modestly, almost inclined to believe that it was she who had been guilty of false syntax, and that the stately lady opposite had set her right with good-natured insolence.

In the box of books which Thrasher sent Mrs. Mason, there were a large number of novels, principally French, and those she read with great avidity, although there were many, after she began to read the language with ease, which she did not think proper to display to the criticism of her hostess.

The little parlor had assumed quite a different aspect since the introduction of the piano and various articles of furniture which Mrs. Mason ordered from New York. Her own rooms were furnished with a degree of elegance she had never seen equaled, yet from her manner one would have thought she only endured their meagreness with the condescension of one accustomed to a very different state of affairs.

Little Rose grew prettier every day, and made herself happy, as was natural at her age. She became a great favorite with Mrs. Prior, and even with the dreary clergyman. But beyond a certain point, Mrs. Mason would not permit any intimacy to extend. She was jealous of Rose's affection for the worthy pair, as she would have been at the idea of sharing love with any one.

Neither the minister nor his wife were able to understand the character of their inmate, but they felt a sort of repulsion in regard to her which it was impossible to overcome, although they reproached themselves as if they had been guilty of a deadly sin, but after all their struggles they sunk back into the same unpleasant state of mind.

The minister really felt uneasy while going through family worship in her presence; not that she appeared irreverent, on the contrary, she was as strict in her performance of such duties as the rest of the house, but she acted all the while as if she were doing a great favor to all concerned, even to the Being to whom she prayed.

Mrs. Prior knew very well that her pupil had not always been in possession of the wealth which was evidently then under her control; yet, as weeks wore on, and Mrs. Mason grew more stylish and elegant, the little woman almost began to think that her first impressions had been false and impertinent; that, on the whole, the lady had no need of instruction, and only gave herself to study from the whim of the moment.

Every little graceful, lady-like way, every pretty habit of voice or manner which the minister's wife possessed, did Mrs. Mason assume, only she carried it off in such a showy manner that it appeared an original grace of her own, and which Mrs. Prior was imitating in a modest fashion and with indifferent success. In fact, it really seemed more as if the minister's wife were a sort of humble pattern of her dashing companion than as if Mrs. Mason had ever gained a hint from her.

One day the household was thrown into a gentle sort of confusion by the arrival of a visitor for Mrs. Mason. He was an elegant and handsome man as Mrs. Prior could have desired to see; but she shrunk instinctively from him as she had always done from her guest.

The minister's wife left this strange man in the little parlor, and went up to tell Mrs. Mason that some one desired to see her.

"Who, if you please?" the lady asked, negligently turning from her book, as if troops of visitors had been an every-day occurrence in her life, and were rather a bore than otherwise.

"Mr. Thrasher," replied the little person, still in a flutter.

"I will be down presently," was the answer; but still Mrs. Mason did not rise from her seat, or lift her eyes from the book upon which they had again fallen.

The door closed behind the bewildered lady; then Mrs. Mason sprang from her seat and began a hasty, but careful toilet.

At the beginning of her residence in that house, Mrs. Mason would have obscured and vulgarized her beauty by dress and ornaments unsuitable to the hour or place. Mrs. Prior's remarks and her own observations had already made her much wiser.

When she turned from the glass, there was an expression of triumph upon her face which plainly betrayed a consciousness of her own surpassing beauty.

She went down-stairs, opened the door of the room where Thrasher sat, and glided in as self-possessed and elegant as any city belle of three seasons, and a more dashingly beautiful woman you would not find in a day's journey.

He started forward to meet her, his face flushed and lighted up with excitement.

He caught Mrs. Mason's hand between both his own and faltered out an almost timid greeting, very unlike the usual boldness of his manner.

"Are you well?" he asked. "Have you been well and contented?"

"A fine question, truly!" she replied, putting aside his eagerness with a sort of unconcern very well assumed, and which evidently displeased and pained him.

"As if any one could be contented shut up in a bird-cage."

"Have you been anxious to go away?" he questioned, as if hoping to derive some comfort from her answer.

"I have not thought much about it; I find one thing which pleases me greatly."

"And that?"

"Nobody interferes with me; I can do just what I like."

He frowned, although he appeared more troubled than annoyed.

"Good gracious!" she exclaimed, with an affected laugh. "What a face of greeting for a man to wear—one might think you were a jailor, come to announce that the day of my execution was at hand."

He dropped her wrist and turned away; she sank negligently into a chair, in the very attitude she had admired in a picture of some forgotten French marchioness, which embellished one of her favorite novels.

"I did not expect a welcome like this," he said, bitterly.

Mrs. Mason looked at him with an expression of surprise which an actress might have envied, and laughed again, not the hearty, ringing merriment of old time, but a low, subdued sound, which did her infinite credit

"In what have I been amiss?" she asked, coolly.

"I thought, at least, you would be glad to see me."

"Oh, did you? Upon my word, the vanity of mankind is beyond all belief! Certainly, I am glad to see you"—he brightened at that—"quite so," she added, with such carelessness that he looked more annoyed than before.

"This is abominable!" he exclaimed. "Ellen, I would not have believed that you could treat me so."

"Have you come here to lecture and find fault?" she asked, gayly. "Are you sure that you have not made a mistake—wasn't it Rose you wished to scold?"

"I did not come to find fault, Ellen. For weeks I have been crazy to see you; nothing but your express commands kept me away; at last you wrote that I might come; I hurried here, and now you are as cold and distant as if I were a stranger."

"Poor boy, poor boy!"

She patted the hand which he had laid upon the arm of her chair, very much as if it had been a pet lapdog.

Thrasher looked at her, overpowered by astonishment. Where had she learned those arts—that playful manner? He had desired her to educate and improve herself in every way; but here was a change beyond any thing he could have expected.

"How handsome you have grown," he said, suddenly.

"You might as well tell me at once that I was a plain person before."

"You know I always thought you handsomer than any woman I had ever seen; but you are really beautiful now."

Mrs. Mason smiled; her insatiable vanity was gratified by his words and the glance of admiration that enforced them.

"Would you like to see Rose?" she asked

"Certainly; very much."

CHAPTER XXXVII.

SETTLING THE WEDDING DAY.

Mrs. Mason stepped into the hall, and called the little girl, who came bounding gayly in; but when she saw Thrasher, an expression of dislike, beyond her years, crossed her face, and she clung to her mother's side, as if for protection.

"Won't you come and speak to me, Rose?" he asked.

Rose only clung closer to her mother, and hid her head in her dress.

"Go and speak to Mr. Thrasher, child," said Mrs. Mason. "How foolish you are."

"Come, Rose, and see what I have got for you," he added; "such a pretty present."

"I don't want any present," replied the child, her voice sounding smothered and choked.

Thrasher looked so much displeased, that Mrs. Mason angrily commanded the little girl to go and shake hands with him, though all the while she had an evident enjoyment of his discomfiture.

"Do as I bid you, Rose, or I will shut you up for the day. Go, I am very angry with you."

Thus commanded, the child raised her head, and walked slowly toward Thrasher, still keeping her face averted.

He took her hand, spoke pleasantly, and tried to kiss her, but that she would by no means permit.

"Are you sorry I have come, Rose?" he asked.

"Yes," she replied, honestly.

"And you wont kiss me?"

"No; you can get me whipped if you want to, but it wont do any good. I wont kiss anybody but my own pa when he comes."

"Rose, Rose!" expostulated her mother, losing a little of her bright color.

"Obedience does not appear to be one of her virtues," Thrasher said, smiling even through his agitation.

"I never saw her behave so before," replied Mrs. Mason; "she is generally very tractable. Go out of the room, Rose, and don't speak to me again to-day."

The child broke away from Thrasher, and ran out of the room with a loud burst of sobs, leaving them both disconcerted.

"You should not have allowed her to dislike me so, Ellen," he said, after an instant.

"Dear me, I cannot control the child's fancies. Do you think the whole world must be in love with you?"

"I should be satisfied if I only felt certain that you cared for me," replied Thrasher, earnestly.

She rose and gave him a look of coquettish defiance.

"Where are you going?" he asked.

"To call Mrs. Prior."

"What for, I should like to know?"

"To bring you back to your senses, of course."

"You will drive me out of them!" he exclaimed, catching her hand. "Do listen to me, Ellen."

"Yes; well—I am listening."

"Tell me that you love me—even yet I cannot feel certain—you are so restless, so capricious."

"Certainly I had better call Mrs. Prior."

"Hang Mrs. Prior."

17

"That would be very cruel; besides, I should lose my French teacher."

"Let us start for Paris. You can finish your studies there."

"Thank you; I am quite comfortable where I am. I believe I am afraid of the water."

"You! the bravest woman I ever met!"

"But I have reason to dread the sea."

This time there was no affectation in the shudder with which she broke off—her husband's memory for a moment pierced even her vanity and egotism like a blow. Thrasher grew pale with jealousy and a thousand feelings more painful still.

"Let us think only of the future," he said.

"Well, what of that?" she asked, forcing those sad thoughts aside, and becoming gay and selfish once more.

"Why should we wait for its happiness?" he continued. "I am rich, far richer than you guess. We are both young. Marry me at once, Ellen, and let us go away in search of pleasure and new scenes."

"Not yet," she answered. "I cannot."

"Why should we wait?"

"I will not be married until the year is up," she replied, more seriously.

"You will die in this stupid place."

"I am used to quiet."

"But now you have had a glimpse of another life; you know what money can do for you; your books have told you what a delightful life we might lead in France or Italy."

"That may be, but——"

"What? You torment me on purpose to enjoy my distress! What were you going to say?"

"I am not certain that I had better make any change in my life."

"Not make any change! Do you mean to treat me as if I were a child?"

"What a look! A reasonable woman would certainly hesitate about placing herself in the power of a man with such a dreadful temper."

"You need have no fear on that score," he replied, subduing his passion. "Nowhere in the world, Ellen, could you find a man so devoted and patient as I would be. Remember how long I have loved you——"

"Now you are reminding me of my age."

"You are not old enough yet to dislike thinking of it."

"Well, what were you saying?"

Thrasher returned, and stood directly before her.

"Ellen," he said, firmly; "I will not be trifled with— I must have an answer."

She looked up a little startled, thinking, perhaps, she had carried her coquetry too far, but when she saw how troubled he looked, how his eyes sunk under her own, she became certain again of her own power over him, and with that security a desire to tease came back.

"I am not your slave," she replied; "how dare you address me in that tone?"

"I did not mean to offend you."

"But you have offended me seriously; if you only came here to play the tyrant, I would advise you to return at once."

It took many moments to make his peace, not that she was in the slightest degree offended, but to a woman of her character there is always great pleasure in the exercise of authority, no matter how petty it may be.

"Then you will not promise to set my mind at rest?" he asked, after a short period of more serious conversation.

She shook her head.

"I do not see why you should be otherwise than at rest now."

"You know I am not, Ellen; you know that I cannot be. At least name some period when my suspense shall end."

"Not now; the next time you come, perhaps."

She could not bear to relinquish the pleasure of torturing him. Her own heart was so little touched that she could have no pity for his troubles; indeed, it seemed somewhat to appease the few reproaches which haunted her, in spite of her vanity and selfishness, to occasion him uneasiness and pain.

"When I come a second time you will put me off with some new pretext," he said, angrily.

"Then you cannot take my word? Very well; if you will not believe me, what can I do?"

"I have never doubted you, Ellen."

"Indeed you have had no reason to think about it either way," she replied, carelessly; "we were nothing to each other more than common acquaintances."

"You know that I have loved you for years—that I have given up my home, my profession—have endured and suffered every thing on your account."

"I would not give much for affection which would be unwilling to do that much," she retorted.

"I was willing," he said; "but at least now, let there be an end to all this—tell me when you will become my wife?"

"When I am accomplished enough to set up for a lady."

"That you were always."

"*He* used to call me so," she replied, with a shade of sadness.

Thrasher turned pale.

"Don't speak of him in my presence, Ellen; it is cruel."

"To his memory, yes," she answered, with real bitterness in her voice.

Thrasher sat down irritated and pale. "Ellen," he said, "it would be far better if you would consent to take a voyage and be married at once in France or Italy. I am restless in this country—it is hard to breathe the same air with one's parents—and such parents, Ellen, without sometimes wishing to see them."

"I thought you wished to give them up as I was willing to put away all the friends who had been kind to me," answered the heartless woman. "How else could you or I hope to enjoy our new life? Besides, it was your own proposal; I never asked you to sacrifice the old folks—merely said something of how much out of place they might be, and how provoking their ways would become in a house like that we were building in the clouds."

"In reality, Ellen, the house I talked of shall be nothing to the palace I am building for my queen."

Mrs. Mason's eyes flashed triumphantly.

"I am half tempted," she said.

"Ah, my love, be wholly tempted!" he pleaded, with genuine tenderness in his voice. "No woman ever was worshipped as you shall be."

"Ah, but one gets tired of worship."

"No queen upon her throne shall have more admirers."

"But you'll be jealous as a Turk. I am sure of that."

"Try me, but do not put me off in this cruel fashion."

"Well, Thrasher," she said, seriously enough, "get every thing ready, and I'll take the time into consideration; but one thing is positive, we must be married here, in this country, in this State of Connecticut. I will have no question or mistake about that. The laws of other States, and particularly of other countries, may be different, but I know what they are here."

"I would rather be married abroad, Ellen," was the agitated reply, "for many reasons."

"But I will be married in the State of Connecticut, or not at all."

Thrasher bent his head, and the woman saw, with astonishment, that all the color left his face. It scarcely excited her suspicion, but the wanton cruelty of her nature came back, and she gave a little, mocking laugh.

"Perhaps you are afraid that our pretty Katy may hear of it, and put in a protest?"

"What do you mean, woman?" cried Thrasher, starting to his feet.

The widow drew herself up in magnificent displeasure.

"Woman, indeed."

Thrasher sat down, with his eyes fixed keenly on her.

"What did you mean, Ellen?" he said, more quietly.

"What did I mean? When you can look and talk like a gentleman, perhaps I may admit that there was no meaning at all in what I said, only that girl was dead in love with you, Thrasher, or I don't know what love is."

"We will let her alone, if you please," he answered, with a manner that checked her flippancy. "The poor girl is nothing to us."

"I should hope not," replied the widow, with a disdainful motion of her head. "In my poorest days I was always above that sort of people; and remember, Thrasher, when we are married—if I ever could make up my mind to it, you know—these old neighbors must be kept at a distance."

"Have I not promised? Is it not decided that we go by my Christian name after that?"

"Yes, I remember something was said about it. A good idea. That will be cutting them off root and branch, old folks and all; besides, Mrs. Nelson has a refined sound."

Thrasher sighed heavily.

"Yes," he said, "we shall be alone in the world then, you and I."

"But we shall go out of our old world and find a new one," she answered, proudly. "Millionaires are never alone."

"How worldly you are getting! But it becomes you."

"Worldly? No, only wise! But we are staying here a long time; Mrs. Prior will wonder what it is all for, and Rose will cry her eyes out, poor thing."

"You wish me to go?" he said, in a mortified tone.

"Why, yes; one must not risk a good name among strangers. It is something a little unusual for me to receive gentlemen."

"I am glad of that, Ellen."

"Oh, I have no desire for visitors of either sex."

"But when may I come for good? I must know that."

"Well, I cannot tell the exact time, but it shall be within a few months; weeks, perhaps, if you are good."

"Then it shall be. You promise that?" he said, kindling with delight.

"Yes, Thrasher, I promise now. Only give me time," and she held out her hand, he kissed it, and went away.

CHAPTER XXXVIII.

A DOUBLE GUARD.

It was true the officer had insisted that Katharine should be removed to one of the upper chambers. She was gradually recovering strength, and though he had not the heart to propose her removal to prison, the dangers of escape became more apparent each hour. At last he suggested the only means of safety that presented itself—Katharine must be confined in the upper story, from whence flight would be difficult, unless assistance should come from without, a thing that he considered more than improbable.

Mrs. Allen made no resistance to these arrangements, for well the poor mother knew that all protest would be in vain. In some respects she preferred the change. It would remove Katharine from the sight of her jailor whenever the door of her room was opened; a presence that had become unspeakably oppressive of late. She seemed afraid of understanding what it meant, but every time his face passed by, or his shadow appeared on the wall, a terror came into her eyes, and she would look wistfully out, as you have seen a poor little rabbit peering with his great brown eyes through the trap some cruel boy had baited for him when the snow covered all other food.

Mrs. Allen had seen this with an aching heart. The man who usurped her own high-backed chair, with his feet stretched out stolidly on the hearth, watching the door of her child's room, had become a torment to her, patient and undemonstrative as she was. So the room was prepared, and in gentle silence Katharine took possession of it. She had no courage to question her mother, but shrunk with sensitive pain from the truth, harassed with fears, yet dreading to have them confirmed.

The mother, too, shrunk from the subject, which was forever lying cold at her heart. What good would it do were she to place all the hideous danger before her child? The law would strike hard enough when its time came; she had no heart to help it by a word.

They were very silent together, those two wretched women, for—with the one subject that filled their existence held in abeyance—what could they talk about? But the mother grew so gentle, so exquisitely loving, that some gleams of joy broke through their misery; still, the tenderness of this affection almost broke her child's heart. It was the offshoot of a great sorrow, which had softened the stern character of the mother, and lifted the young girl into sudden womanhood. The hour of maternity, be it in joy or grief, breaks down all the barriers of age, and, as in this case, the extremes of womanhood meet with some degree of equality.

But a painful apprehension was always at Katharine's heart. No one told her the terrible fate of which that man, sitting forever on her mother's hearth, was the harbinger, but the the truth pressed vaguely upon her understanding, and her solitude was a perpetual terror. She grew keen in her observation. She searched even the mournful eyes of little Paul and the grieved features of Jube, in her silent quest after the knowledge she had no courage to claim in words.

Now two men kept guard in the room below. Their prisoner was getting strong, and more vigilance became advisable.

The night that this double guard was set upon her, Katharine could not sleep, for the two men conversed in low voices that penetrated to her chamber, and tortured every nerve in her body. What evil things were they saying in those muffled tones? Perhaps talking about her babe? What would they do with her in the end?

Dark ideas of the terrible truth came slowly over her. She was seized with an uncontrollable wish to hear what it was that kept her jailors in such close conversation.

Shivering with dread, yet filled with a sort of wild courage, she arose and crept from her room down-stairs. A door opened from the stairway into the kitchen—it was left slightly ajar—and through the crevice came a gleam of light from a candle that stood on the mantlepiece. Katharine sunk down on the lowest step and listened keenly.

"Yes," said one of the men, "it's a settled thing—they'll take her off in the morning. Tough, though, aint it."

"Does the old woman know it?"

"I reckon not; the constable says he can't find the heart to tell her till the last minute."

"What will they do with her in the end? Have you any idea?"

"Well, law's law, you know, and I calculate they'll hang the poor critter."

"No!"

"Sartin; the constable was saying so at the hill store only yesterday. The strangling," says he, "might a been got over; but that burying of the poor little critter in the snow was the pint that no lawyer could ixplain."

"Yes; that allus stops a feller's mouth when he sets out to defend her, and yet—"

"What was you a saying?"

"And yet I can't bleave she really did it."

"It's unnatural; but facts are facts."

"Poor critter; I wonder if she's told any thing about its father yet. The feller ought to be hung fifty times where she had once."

"I reckon not; the old woman said that her daughter was married, at the examination, but she would not name the man, and people were left to guess."

"Was it Nelson Thrasher, do you really think?"

"There's no telling, and maybe it wont come out till court day."

"And when it does, what'll the law do with him?"

"Well, I aint quite sure; but suppose it would be brought in preup terus criminus; that is, 'complice 'fore the act."

"You don't say so. Then it'll be a hanging matter for him, too?"

"Sure as Sunday."

"But how will they find him? Maybe, Katharine wont inform."

"Oh, she'll tell; women always do."

The poor young mother behind the door was quaking with fear, and chilled through and through with the cold. Her teeth chattered so loudly that she lost the next few words; but those that followed were horrible enough.

"Did you ever see a person hung?"

"Yes; once."

"Wall!"

"Don't ask me about it; the rope broke, and—"

"Hark! wasn't that a voice?"

"No; it's one of the icicles falling from the eaves."

"It seemed to come from the stairs, I thought; suppose we look."

"Oh, be still. It's the ice, I tell you. Just hand me a drink of that ginger cider. This talk about hanging makes the cold chills run over me."

There was a moment's silence, then a deep, satisfied breath, and the jingle of a pewter mug as it was set down between the andirons.

CHAPTER XXXIX.

OUT IN THE DEPTHS OF THE NIGHT.

How she got to her room, Katharine never knew; but little Paul sat with his back to the door which led from her chamber to his, and heard faint shudderings with that icy sound which had disturbed the men, for a long time after she entered the room. It troubled him so much at last that he went into the outer garret and sought Jube, who stood like a bronze statue by a window in the gable.

"Jube, I'm sure that she is up now, you can hear her tremble through the door."

Jube put a finger to his lip, and lifting Paul in his

arms, pointed through the window. The end of a ladder rested against the sill, and Tom sat perched on one of the upper rounds, motioning to Jube that he must stoop down and help him in.

The moment after he stood in a broad space of moonlight that paved the garret, whispering eagerly:

"I've come before the time, I have, and hain't got a sign of a wagon nor sleigh; for, consarn him, par locked the stable door to-night, the first time he ever did it in his life, I'm a'most sartin. But it's got to be done. Them constables will be arter her to-morrow, sartin. We'll get her out somehow this very night, and trust to luck arterward."

"What shall we do?" inquired Paul, full of generous courage. Jube has got the gold."

"That's half," answered Tom, promptly. "Now, Paul, you go into the room and tell her to get right up and huddle on all the furs, and cloaks, and things that she's got, and tell her to be still as twenty mice. Them chaps below are as wide awake as nighthawks. I've been watching 'em through the winder since twelve o'clock; but they've just begun to pitch into the hot ginger and cider, and that'll put 'em to sleep, sure."

"But if she wont come?" said Paul.

"Wont? she must, or stay here and be —— oh, I can't bear to think of it. Now get along, Paul, and do as I tell you."

Paul went softly into Katharine's room. She was sitting on the bed in her long nightgown, cold and still, frozen, as it were, in the moonlight, which fell over her from a near window.

Paul shrunk back at first, her face looked so deathly; but he found courage, and took the cold hands that lay clasped on her lap.

What he said in those low, eager whispers, the boy himself scarcely knew; but after the first words she bent down, listening greedily. Friends in the outer room, a ladder at the window, money to take her from that guarded house, life, liberty, away from the terrible shadow of those men, clear from that gaunt horror which they talked about so calmly. Yes, she would go. Life was very sweet, and she so young. Out to sea in a vessel bound for a long voyage. Thus, she would in time meet her husband, whose name her silence had saved from disgrace. She began to love herself for this thought, and, gathering fresh energy, put on her outer garments.

Paul went into the garret and told his friends that Katharine was getting ready. His voice was raised imprudently, it penetrated to a room at the other end of the garret, and might have disturbed the guards, but their deep potations at the warm cider had, as Tom predicted, thrown them into a sound sleep.

All this while Mrs. Allen had been lying in the back of her daughter's bed with her face to the wall. The wearying effect of nights without sleep and days of harassing labor lay heavily upon her. At most times she was a sound sleeper, but now it seemed as if death itself had taken possession of her faculties. She knew nothing of Katharine's absence from the room—nothing of Paul's entrance, but the first cold touch of the fugitive's hand was enough. The gray eyes opened wildly in the moonlight, and she started up in bed.

Katharine stood before her fully dressed, and with some heavy dark garment in her hand. Mrs. Allen heard Paul speaking in the garret outside, and comprehended the scene.

"Mother, I am going. They want to kill me; I am innocent, and have a right to my life. I am going away, mother."

The whispers in which Katharine spoke were broken, and came gasping from her lips. Mrs. Allen started from the bed and began to put on her clothes.

"Yes," she muttered, wildly, "I have thought of this night and day. One does not see a lamb go to the slaughter without a wish to help it. The child of one's old age is better than a lamb. I said to myself, if the instincts of innocence lead her to it, she shall escape. She has forfeited nothing—her life is her own—God gave it to her, and God will instruct her how to keep it."

Tom opened the door, and came into the room on tiptoe.

"Hush! don't, Mrs. Allen. We can hear you a muttering clear into the garret. Them men down-stairs love cider, but they ain't moles. Just give 'em a chance, and they'll be after us full split afore you know it—hish!"

Mrs. Allen did not speak again, but took a heavy cloak from the wall and folded it over the garments which she had just put on. She took Katharine's hand in her own firm grasp, and led her into the garret. The gable window was open, and a cold, sharp wind came sweeping through, while the moonlight thus let in fell half across the garret.

Jube was on the ladder outside, waiting. Paul stood aside from the light, but the eager fire of his eyes could be seen even in the darkness. The mother and child were half way across the garret, when Katharine broke away suddenly, and went back, her face uplifted, as if she were counting the rafters. She disappeared in the gloom, and her hand made a creaking noise, as it passed along the torn shingles projecting themselves from one of the rafters. But she darted back into the moonlight with a scrap of paper in her hand, which rustled to the wind like a dead leaf.

"I am ready now, mother," she whispered.

"Hist! he! he!"

It was like the lowest hiss of a serpent, the sound with which Tom warned his allies, and signified that all was ready.

Mrs. Allen lifted her daughter in both arms, held her one moment in a clinging embrace, then passed her through the window, and leaned out till Jube stood with her at the foot of the ladder. After that, she followed, while Paul and Tom crept after, noiselessly as shadows.

"Come this way," said Tom. "It's a glare of ice all around, but I scattered ashes along here, so keep straight ahead, while I take a peep, and see if them old chaps are sleeping yet."

The little group drew close together, and moved quickly along the path which Tom had made safe with wood ashes. Directly that youngster joined them, chuckling to himself, and rubbing his yarn mittens gleefully together.

"They're in for it! Oh, Miss Allen, that cider of your'n must be scrumptious stuff. They've drunk up the hull bilin of it, and there the great pewter mug lies atween 'em, upsot on the harth, a little gingery stream a running and a hissing from it into the fire. There they set, each of 'em, with his legs half way across the harth, and the toes of his boot a sticking up, sliding off from them chairs till their boots eenamost touch, and each on 'em has got his head pitched forward and his face hid in his bosom, and snoring like all nature. Oh, Paul, I'd a gin the world to have boo-hood right out as loud as I wanted to."

All this was said in a loud whisper that sounded sharp and distinct on the frosty air, but no one heeded it. The two women hurried forward in dead silence; Paul and Jube went before, making a path, for they had turned into the field, and had instinctively crept within the shadow of the stone wall which Katharine had fled along on that fearful day. They were fast approaching the old butternut tree, when Katharine, whose breath had come quick and short with each step, reeled and fell back against the wall.

"I can't go this road," she gasped, pointing to the butternut tree, which flung its gaunt skeleton shadow far out on the snow. "Take me any road but this."

Tom, who had been running along in the moonlight, came up, speaking for the first time in his full voice.

"That's right; we may as well stop and make up our minds what to do next, as Robinson Crusoe did when he reached that ere uninhabited island; for the old soger warn't much wuss off than we are, I reckon, 'specially now that we've got another woman 'tached onto the consarn."

"She's ill, the poor mademoiselle," whispered Paul.

"No, no—we havn't time for that ere; tell her she mustn't think of it."

"Mother," whispered Katharine, "take me away! It seems as if my ghost had been here before."

Mrs. Allen drew close to her child and tried to shelter

her alike from the cold and a sight of that gaunt old tree.

"What shall we do next?" inquired Tom, feeling the want of some efficient counsellor. "Miss Allen, as you've kinder broke into this ere concern without asking, I give up being leader, 'specially not knowing what on 'arth to do. I've sot her free, and that's glory enough for one little feller, so now I throw up and consign."

Mrs. Allen gathered Katharine closer in her arms, and looking in the boy's face, strove to comprehend the position in which they were placed.

"Tell me what it was you hoped to do for my daughter," she said, gently. "I know nothing more than that she was ready to escape, and I followed. The idea was in my dreams, and we are here. Was there any place you had in view where she could be safe?"

"Yes, marm, there was," answered Tom. "Jube and Paul can tell you all about it. We got it up together, us three. I meant to have brought par's hoss and wagon, but the old man locked 'em up. Besides, we did not mean to go into it till to-morrow night, only the constable let out as he'd take her off in the morning, so we had to come right up to the rack, ready or not; and now we are free and independent. But where to go? that ere is the question."

Mrs. Allen uttered a low groan; the frail form in her arms grew heavier and heavier. The desperate course they had taken presented itself to her mind in all its hopelessness.

"Oh, my God, must I take her back?" she moaned, lifting her face to heaven.

"Has madame no friends—no house where mademoiselle could hide one little day?" said Paul. "Jube has gold, great deal of gold, that people in this country like very much. People that have much gold can run away—Tom says that—oh, very far. We will take mademoiselle to Monsieur Rice; he very strong, like Jube; nobody touch him—never dare."

"Yes, marm," struck in Tom. "The sloop which goes out of New Haven twice a week, sails Saturday. Jube's got lots and lots of chink. Just send him to Dave Rice; he's the fellow to tell the constable what's what —he is."

Mrs. Allen gathered in the whole plot, and her clear judgment saw at once that it was the only means of escape left for her child. The attempt, which had seemed a moment before so rash, took consistency and wisdom in her mind. God himself seemed to have provided the means of escape for her child.

"Well, now, what do you think it's best to do?" asked Tom, flattered by her grave attention. "You are the gineral now; I'm only a soger."

"May the God of heaven bless you, my brave boy," said the mother, with deep feeling.

Tom hastily wiped the cuff of his jacket across his eyes.

"Don't, Miss Allen; don't say that ere; 'cause, you know, I was kinder diserbaying my parents, and I'm afeared he'll remember to set one agin t'other, and I might git the worst of it."

Mrs. Allen looked around along the dreary road.

"Is there no one of all our neighbors who would shelter us for one night?" she cried.

"Mother," said Katharine, struggling from her arms and trying to stand up, "*his* father. I will go to him. It was his wish. I will go to his home. Where else should a wife ask shelter?"

Mrs. Allen drew a heavy breath.

"Come, mother, come."

"Where is it you have an idea of going?" inquired Tom, forgetting that he had resigned all command of the party, and was only a "soger."

"Up yonder," answered Mrs. Allen; "we will ask them to hide us for one night, in the barn, or anywhere."

"Us? you say us?" persisted Tom, shaking his head. "Now I'm only a soger, you know, Mrs. Allen, but if I had the lead yet, I'd jest observe that one is easier hid than two. If them fellers get up, and find the house empty, they'll search like blazes, and the fust thing after daylight; but if you're there to get 'em a warm breakfast, and Jube's on hand to pile on the wood, they'd kinder be content, and not ask about anybody else mebby till noon."

"You are right," said the mother. "Let me know that she is safe and I will go home again. My child, can you walk?"

"Yes, mother."

"No, no; she trembles. Let Jube carry her—he is so strong," said Paul.

Jube came forward with his brawny arms extended. Mrs. Allen gave up her child, and she was carried away so swiftly that the boys were compelled to run in order to keep up with the negro, but Mrs. Allen walked close to him, never faltering or pausing to draw breath till the whole group stood in front of Mr. Thrasher's house.

Jube sat Katharine quietly down upon the snow, where she stood gazing wistfully toward the house, till her mother reminded her that there was no time to spare.

"Leave me," said the poor creature, "leave me here, mother. I would rather go in alone—quite alone—it will be easier."

Mrs. Allen hesitated, but Tom came up with one of his clinching arguments.

"It's nigh on to morning, Mrs. Allen, and we are only doing her hurt. If she goes in alone they wont have the heart to send her off, but if we all stand here ready to go farther, they'd tell us to keep on just as like as not."

"He is right, mother," said Katharine, faintly. "Give me one kiss—God will help me—have no fear."

The old woman pressed her cold lips to that still colder face, and went away, looking mournfully behind, from time to time, until a bend of the road took her out of sight.

CHAPTER XL.

TAKEN IN FROM THE COLD.

THE old couple were in bed, but not sleeping. Since the return of their son, weary, broken nights and most anxious days had marked the lives of these blameless people. It had been very hard to part with their son when he almost seemed domesticated with them. It had been hard to expect him back, day after day, and always with keen disappointment following the morning's hope. But more bitter than all was the news that had reached them within the last few days. Nelson had sailed again—sailed on a long voyage into those seas which take the youth out of a man before he returns.

How could they help being wakeful? Were they not worse than childless? Of the grave they knew something—its length, its depth, and how long it required for the green turf to spring up and draw the uncouth mound back into the loving bosom of nature. But what did they know of those far off waters where ships were lost in immensity, and fishes of monstrous size tempted men away from their homes. A whaling voyage—that was like a life banishment to an old couple who had so many gray hairs on their temples.

They could not sleep, though each kind heart strove to cheat the other—both were wakeful and miserably anxious.

"Father?"

The old man would not speak, but drew a long, heavy breath, which smothered a sigh, while it was intended to deceive the good soul into a belief of his sound slumber.

"Father, I say?"

Still he would not answer, for the poor mother had got a habit of keeping herself awake with midnight conversations in these days, and he was determined to put it down with masterly inactivity.

"Dear old man, I'm glad he can sleep so sound," she murmured, rising softly to her elbow and putting the gray locks back from his forehead, which she kissed with infinite tenderness. "It's a shame to wake him up."

The old man turned softly, and said with inward contrition, "I am awake, wife."

"Father, I think there's some one knocking at the window."

The old man lifted his head, and listened.

"Mrs. Thrasher! oh, Mrs. Thrasher, wont you let me in?"

There was a moan of anguish in the words that struck to the heart at once. The old man held his breath, while the wife clung to him with her head lifted from the pillow.

"It's her, it's Katy Allen," she whispered.

The old man slipped out of bed and hurried on his clothes. She, good soul, followed him, groping for her dress in the dark, but another faint knock on the glass, and a mournful voice crying, "Wont you let me in? I'm freezing! I'm freezing," sent her to the window in nothing but her long night gown and cap, with its double borders shading a very pale and startled face.

Mrs. Thrasher lifted the sash and looked out. A dark figure sat crouching on the snow where it had just fallen after losing its hold on the window sill.

"Katharine, Katharine Allen, is it you?"

The figure struggled to its feet, and clinging to the window-frame with one hand, put the other through the opening, where it touched Mrs. Thrasher on the bosom. A lump of snow could not have chilled her more completely, but nothing cold had power to reach that kind heart. She lifted her plump little hands and folded the trembling fingers to her bosom tenderly as if some stray bird had fluttered there. Then the sharp wind swept over them both, and dropping the hand with a caress, the woman said, kindly:

"Go round to the door, Katharine. Father is unbolting it now."

Katharine turned away. Mrs. Thrasher closed the window, and hurrying on a garment or two, went into the next room, where the embers of a noble hickory wood fire lay smouldering under a bed of ashes. While she was raking out the fire Mr. Thrasher came in, treading softly in his stocking feet, and with the suspenders he had forgotten to button, trailing to the floor behind him. From the darkness beyond came Katharine Allen; her hood was pushed back, and sparkles of ice shone in her hair as the ruddy light from two brands thrown hastily together flashed over her. She had been crying, but the tears had frozen to pearls on her cheeks, and filled her eyelashes with delicate frostiness.

She entered the room and sat down in Mrs. Thrasher's chair, looking wistfully at the old woman, and begging pardon with her eyes as she touched the blue and red patchwork cushion, which, in those days, was sacred to the mistress of a New England home.

"I am very cold," she said, with a wan smile; "it chilled me through standing by the gate so long."

"Poor child," said Mrs. Thrasher, gathering the stray brands together with a pair of heavy tongs. "Father, just hand in a stick or two of wood from the entry way. There, now, set up close to the andirons. Never mind us, we're not a-cold."

Katharine drew close to the fire, and held out her hands, that trembled and fluttered to the heat like half perished birds.

"I ran away," she said, piteously; "crept out of the garret window, and came off here. They want to kill me, you know."

The old people looked at each other and turned away, with their faces in shadow.

"You'll not be afraid to hide me a little while?" she questioned, anxiously.

The old lady bent over her, with tears in her soft eyes.

"Afraid, dear? no; we're not afraid, are we, father?" she said, lovingly.

A noise outside startled Katharine; she sprang up and fixed her wild eyes on the window.

"They've seen the light—they're after me."

"It's only an icicle dropping from the eaves," said the old lady, smiling. "There isn't a soul near but father and I, Katharine, dear, and you aint going to be afraid of us?"

Katharine looked at her lingeringly and sat down again.

"No; I'm not afraid of you. He told me to come, and not fear any thing."

Mrs. Thrasher drew close to the girl and bent over her.

"He, dear; tell us, father and I, you know, who it is you mean by *he?*"

Katharine looked up, and a strange light came to her face; it was as if a pearl had been suddenly illuminated at the heart.

"It was Nelson who told me to come," she said, in a tender voice.

"Nelson Thrasher—our son?" interposed the old man, almost sternly.

Katharine shrank together in her chair, and looked at him with a frightened glance.

"Did I say Nelson?" she questioned, faintly. "Not if it makes you angry with him."

The old man rose from his chair, and stood up in the fire light.

"Katharine, he said, "tell us the truth—was it our son who brought this shame and trouble on you?"

The words were stern. The old man trembled in all

his limbs, but still there was strength both in his look and utterance.

"Shame, no; it is not shame for him—you might be sure of me there," she said, with pathetic simplicity. "I never mentioned him, and never will. So don't speak of shame and Nelson in one breath. The disgrace is mine, you know; and the sorrow, he shall never hear of it—never."

The old lady looked imploringly at her husband, and shrank back into the shadows of the room, wringing her hands.

"And this is my son! He brings ruin on an innocent, thoughtless girl, and then abandons her for years—her and his parents."

"Ruin! No, not that!" cried Katharine. "Shame! No! no! It is I that somehow have brought disgrace on him! Only I never told his name—never will ask for it! Don't be afraid. I didn't come for that—only to beg a hiding-place for one day. Those men will never know that I have any right to come here. Let them search. If they tear the house down, nothing will be found under the rafters. I've got the paper here!"

CHAPTER XLI.

THE MARRIAGE CERTIFICATE.

She pressed one hand to her bosom, and smiled proudly, as if they ought to be grateful for something she had done.

"The paper—what paper?" questioned Mrs. Thrasher.

"That which the minister gave us. It is more than three months, and he told me not to wait longer than that."

"Let me read the paper, girl!"

"Yes," joined in Mrs. Thrasher, coming out of her obscurity. "Let father read the paper."

"He told me to bring it here after three months," said Katharine, looking at them doubtfully; "but he did not know how it would happen. Dreadful things have been done that he never thought of, so I must be careful. I am only a poor girl, and they have almost done the worst by me. Nothing can disgrace me more, but it hasn't reached him yet. I wouldn't even tell the doctor. Nobody ever saw the paper. That is my secret—the only thing I have left. When they have killed me I will eat the paper, and die with it in my bosom, be sure of that."

"But you will tell us—remember he is our only child, and it is hard not to know the truth—hard to think badly of him," pleaded the mother.

"Badly of him—who has a right to do that?" said Katharine, excitedly. "You ought to know better. But you are only his mother, not his—"

"His what, dear?"

Katharine shook her head, and bent her eyes on the fire.

"If you have a paper that belongs to my son, let me read it, girl. I have a right," pursued the old man.

"Right—when you can think badly of him? I never could do that; but he told me to come here and ask shelter, not knowing how much I should need it. I want to obey him—want to make you think well of him—but how can I do it?"

"Give us the paper if that will tell us the truth about our son," answered the old man, firmly.

"But you might use it to disgrace his name."

"We are his parents, girl."

"But you suspect him, what of?"

"Of wronging you—we have suspected him of this!"

"Yes, Katharine, father couldn't help it, you know. It broke his heart, but he—that is, we couldn't clear Nelson in our minds. If you can only help us, dear!"

Katharine bent toward the fire, clasping both hands around her knees, and muttering to herself, "It would be worse than death to think ill of him. They have a right."

She drew back slowly, and turned to the old man.

"Promise me something, Mr. Thrasher."

"I will promise any thing that will be for your good."

"Promise never to let any human being know what is in this paper, and I'll show it to you."

"We are his parents, and are not likely to tell any thing that would disgrace our son."

"Promise her, father; no matter what it is, promise!" pleaded the mother, creeping round to her husband's side.

The old man hesitated. Katharine bent slowly toward the fire again.

"Promise," whispered the mother. "If our son is wrong, we shall never have the heart to speak of it. If he is innocent, no one but his own parents have had the cruelty to suspect him."

"I never thought wrong of him, never in my life," murmured Katharine, gazing into the fire; "that would kill me before those dark men had a chance."

"Well, girl, what promise shall I make?" questioned

the old man, who had been listening to his wife with serious attention.

"Only that you will never mention the paper, nor what I tell you, till Nelson comes back."

"Well, I promise that."

"Yes; we promise," repeated the mother.

Katharine took a scrap of paper from her bosom, unfolded it with a loving touch, and gave it to the old man. There was no candle in the room, but his spectacles lay on the closed Bible, where he had left them on going to bed. He put them on, and knelt down by the fire, from which his wife forced a shower of sparks with the tongs. As the old man read the paper, she bent over him, and when his head fell forward and buried itself in his hands, her sobs mingled with the broken thanks that sprang from the father's heart.

At last he arose to his feet, and looked at his wife, who crept into his arms, and laying her withered cheek on his bosom, whispered:

"Remember, husband, I told you so. Told you from the first, either that it was not true, or that she was our daughter."

As the sweet words fell from her lips, the good woman looked on the girl with a countenance so heavenly, that Katharine smiled under it, and for a moment forgot what a wretched fugitive she was.

"Now," said the old man, seating himself, and stooping toward their midnight guest; "now that our son is cleared from this great guilt, tell us—for remember you are our child—tell us about this terrible thing they accuse you of."

Katharine turned cold and white, then she lifted her sweet young face, and with her eyes turned clearly to his, told him all that she knew, word for word, feeling for feeling; and from the depths of her true heart he saw how innocent she was.

The old woman listened with him, but her gentle heart gave way long before Katharine had done her story; when it was finished she gathered the poor girl in her arms and wept over her.

"What can we do? How help her?" she said, addressing the old man. "The law is like a hound—it will take her anywhere; and she is our child—our innocent, innocent daughter."

Katharine clung to the woman, as she uttered these words, and began to cry. It was sweet to be so trusted and cared for in the midst of her desolation.

"Where can we put her? What can we do, father?"

There was no answer—the old man sat looking at her very sadly and with deep thoughtfulness.

"Let us first ask what the good God intends in all this. He does not lead the young into peril, or the innocent into shame for nothing. It is a fearful risk, but let us do right."

Katharine looked on him in affright, her eyes growing wildly large, her lips falling apart, till the white teeth shone through.

"You will not give me up? They will kill me! Oh, father, they will kill me!"

She had called him father for the first time in her life, and the word came forth in a cry of anguish that made even his strong heart shrink.

"No," he said, gently. "Not for all the gold of Ophir would I do this thing."

Katharine drew a long breath. The old woman folded her in a closer embrace, and softly whispered:

That she must have no fear—God always guarded the innocent.

And so they rested a little while in silence. The old man buried in thought. The women watching him with anxious faces.

"I will take her to *his* chamber," said the mother, at last, "the blinds are down and we can find the way without light."

Mr. Thrasher said nothing, but regarded the fugitive in grave sadness.

"Stay with her till morning," he said; "she has left her mother behind, poor woman."

Katharine arose and went up to the old man.

"You are his father and believe me," she said.

"Yes, Katharine, I believe you—I will give all that I have to prove how innocent you are—I will mortgage the farm to-morrow, if that will do."

"Only tell me where I can find him. He will not let any one harm me; you know that."

"If we knew—if we only knew; but the sea is a broad desert of waters, where no man finds his fellow for seeking."

"Has Nelson gone to sea?" faltered the poor girl.

"Yes, Katharine, on a long voyage. He may not come back for years."

She stood still, dumb with pain, and thrills of awe ran through her voice when it struggled back to her.

"Who told me of this before?"

"No one, my child; it came in a letter, and we never mentioned a word of it to a living soul."

"A letter to you and none to me; but who told me, I say? or when did I dream something like it? I wish all this was clear. Nelson writes to you, and yet I know beforehand what news the letter brings. It has kept me awake nights, but in the daytime fell back into dreams again."

She stood a moment with one hand to her forehead, then dropped it, and said, quickly:

"Let me read his letter, may I?"

The old man opened the great Bible, and took the letter from between its leaves. She knelt down upon the hearth and read it through.

"Yes," she said, "it is true. He has gone. I might search the world over and never find him. They might kill me, and my husband never hear of it. This is worse than their threats, worse than death, for it shuts out all hope. Where could I go? The world is so wide, and I have not learned the way anywhere."

"Oh, if you could but stay with us till he comes!" exclaimed the old lady.

"But they will not let me. To-morrow, perhaps, those men will come here and force you to give me up."

"I never will, never on earth," cried the old woman, flushing with the generous courage that filled her heart. "They shall tear me all to pieces first."

The old man stood up. The solemn thoughtfulness had left his face, and it was sadly calm, as if some painful doubt had left his mind. He went up to Katharine and laid both hands on her head. She looked at him with her sad eyes, and almost smiled, his face was so pleasant that it reassured her.

"You have thought of some way by which we can find him?" she said, with a gush of gratitude mellowing her voice.

"No, Katharine, that is impossible. Ships that have sailed can never be overtaken; but have you forgotten, child, that the guilty alone stand in need of flight—God protects the innocent."

"Oh, he has abandoned me," sighed the poor fugitive. "Some wicked thing has woven snares about me that look so like guilt that even he turns away."

"He never turns away. By-and-by, child, his doings will be made clear. Out of the depths of tribulation great mercies are sometimes wrought."

"You do not think it wise that I escaped from those men," she faltered.

He pressed one broad hand lovingly on her head. The touch sent a holy shock through her frame. Some of the broad courage that filled his Christian heart entered hers, and it flashed upon her how cowardly her flight had been—how much like a confession of guilt it appeared.

"I have nowhere to go," she said, mournfully. "If I get away every one will think it was from a sense of guilt that I left. I am his wife, your son's wife, and must not let myself be unjustly condemned. Is that what you mean, father?"

"Go to bed, child, and before you sleep ask these questions of our Father who is in heaven. He will turn your heart aright."

She bent her head and clung for a moment to the hand which he had extended; a great pain struggled at her heart; she knew what his words portended. Like the angel who met Hagar in her extremity, he was about to warn her back to her bonds.

They parted for the night, and Katharine went up to Thrasher's chamber, led through the darkness by the gentle guidance of his mother. The moonlight lay full in the room, and she could see all the objects it con-

19

tained—his bed, the glass in which he had feared to look, and the carpet which his boyish knees had pressed.

The old lady helped her undress, and after she lay down, arranged the bed-clothes and pillows as she had a thousand times for her son.

"Shall I stay with you, child?" she said, at last, stooping down and kissing her in that sweet, motherly fashion which carries protection with it.

Katharine lay in her husband's bed overpowered by a strange tranquillity. Her face looked out sweetly through the moonlight, and both hands were folded over her bosom; she had dropped unconsciously into an attitude of prayer.

"Shall I stay with you, dear child?"

"No, it is his room, I am not afraid; go to your own bed, mother; in the morning I shall be strong."

She had called his parents father and mother more than once that evening; there was a fascination in the words that could not be conquered. It made the old woman's heart swell to be so addressed. Her son's wife —it was next to having him there in person. She kissed Katharine on the forehead, and went away through the darkness, knowing well that a violent death hovered over that young head, but feeling glows of happiness in her heart all the time; for, like her husband, she believed devoutly that God protects the innocent. He does—He does, but not always in the way His creatures are presumptuous enough to mark out for Him.

CHAPTER XLII.

ON THE FIRST STAGE TO PRISON.

"WELL now, jest tell me all about it," said Tom, hurrying little Paul away from his playmates to a corner of the school-house where a few gleams of sunshine gave some slight idea of warmth. "Tell me what them chaps did when they found out what we'd been up to. Oh, golly, but I'd a gin the last four-pence half-penny I've got to have seen 'em. Didn't they rip and tear beautifully? Didn't they rare up and fall over backward? Oh, yes, I kinder see 'em now staring at one another like 'stonished pigs, and wondering what cute little shaver did it. But you don't tell me, Paul—seem kind o' down in the mouth about something."

"No," said Paul, gently, "my mouth isn't down, but I feel sad, very much for the poor mademoiselle."

"Oh, that aint nothing; just let me get things put to rights, and she'll be in New York and crowing over 'em all. What do you shake your head for?"

"She wont go, Tom."

"She wont go?"

"No; they will kill her, but she will not run away, clear off, as we desire."

"How do you know that?"

"I think so, sure."

"Oh, bother, you've got the drag on. Now jist tell me all about what happened up yonder. How did them officer fellows act when they found out that she was gone?"

"Oh, they found out nothing at first. Madame, that is Mrs. Allen, came down-stairs so softly and made one good breakfast, very nice, and they sat down, eating plenty. Madame look very white, and her hand shook when she pour coffee into their cups, but the men very sleepy and never see that, but sit so, with eyes almost shut and opening the mouth wide two, three times, sleepy a good deal."

"Wal, I reckon it warn't for want of snoring over night. My, didn't they go it in them two chairs," cried Tom, gleefully.

"By-and-by madame began to wash cups, and do work. Then one man he say: 'Come, supposing we go up-stairs and see how that pretty bird comes on. The old woman don't mean to give her any breakfast this morning, by her washing the dishes so soon.'

"Then madame, she stop short, so, and look much frightened, very cold, and she say nothing, only look, look."

"Wal, now, I'd a thought better of that 'ere woman, she's disappinted me," said Tom, settling both hands in his pockets, and planting his feet apart on the ground. It's scandless. Wal, now, what did the fellers do arter that?"

"They go up-stairs and knock; one, two, three times, very loud, then great noise with feet, and the door open, no one there, bed empty, garret window open."

"But no ladder, darn 'em—don't say as I swore now, Paul, cause it's a lie. I didn't—Jube and I took care of that 'ere ladder between us. Golly, how I'd liked to have seen 'em looking out of that 'ere window like two foxes in a box trap. Wal, what did they do then?"

Paul smiled and looked around to see that **no one was** within hearing.

"Well, now I tell you, Mr. Tom, they come along tramp, tramp, on the floor—great noise and much talk, down the stairs—madame, she stand white, like snow, but with her eyes very sparkle. Jube, very brave, stand close by the stairs. Madame say something quick, then Jube he put his arm through the iron, so, and hold tight the door, madame go out, like lightning, and bring long piece of wood from out door. Then Jube take his arm away and make bar. Bang, bang, but the door no open, very strong."

Tom, with a spasmodic spreading of his feet and elbows, almost set himself down into the snow. "He, he, hi, hi, ho, ho-o-o-o!" he shouted, rolling about in furious glee; "I take it all back; that 'ere woman is a sneezer—I give up—own beat. She knows a thing or two, she does! Bang, did you say? I reckon it was bang! but, oh, she had 'em tight!"

"Very tight. They kick and call loud, and make great noise, but madame wash her dish and say nothing. Jube he stand by the fire and laugh; I laugh, too, very little."

"Laugh! wal, now I reckon you did. If you hadn't I'd a licked yer right where ye stand, if you be a furrener. I wonder you didn't march right up and hug the old woman—I'd a-done it."

"Madame don't like that; she keep on her work, no smile, nothing but work. The men make more noise; she no take care, but work, work."

"She's a Queen of Shebe, she is. I tell you what, Paul, I'm proud of that woman. She ought to have been my marm. Wal, so she worked on, and let 'em take it out in stomping, didn't she?"

"Yes; she work all the time; not seem to hear till

somebody open the gate, then she stop, with the broom in her hand like a staff, and held her breath, so."

"What was that for?"

"We all hold our breath, for under the heavy step come a soft one like little child walking. The door it open, and that man from next house come in, and with him mademoiselle."

"You don't say so. Paul, you furrenir, I dare you to say that over agin. If you want a licking, do it, that's all!"

"Yes; it was the poor, pretty lady," said Paul, nothing daunted by this grand threat. "She come in very softly, with the petite bonnet over her face. She looked like one angel. Madame stood still. She bear on her broom like a staff, and her eyes open wide. Mademoiselle, she go up to madame and take her hand. 'Mother,' she say, 'guilty people run away, and I am not guilty. God knows it, and He is good; so I come back!' Ah, Monsieur Tom, it broke my heart in pieces to hear her speak so sad, so sweet. I can't help it, the tears will come!"

"Now don't," said Tom, drawing the sleeve of his jacket across his eyes. "It's enough to make a feller forget that he's a man!"

Paul went on, twinkling the tears away with his black eyelashes.

"So then she come home once more like a poor little bird that flies round and round its nest. Madame said no one word, but took mademoiselle's head, so, between her hands, and kissed her very much, once, twice. I never saw madame do that till now; it made me sad very much."

"What did she come back for?" cried Tom. "I can't understand it, no how."

"She took off her petite bonnet, and sat down by the fire, holding out her hands. Then the good man from the house with trees before it, very tall, he speak to madame so kind, and say that mademoiselle is very right not to run great way off like guilty people ; that the great God was very strong to take care of her, and she must not have too much fear, but keep brave heart. Then madame began to cry ; oh, how she cry, with great sobs, like the wind in trees that give all their leaves away to winter, she say 'God help me, for I am a coward ;' and then she goes to the stairs and opens the door, and says to the men, 'Come down, my daughter has not run away, she is here.'"

"Then mademoiselle stood up and say—ah, so sweet: 'Yes, I am here, do with me as you please ;' and a smile was on her mouth like the sun on the snow, and ——"

"Don't, I tell you don't," cried Tom, stamping furiously. "It's enough to bust a feller's heart, if his jacket was buttoned ever so tight. She's a brave gal. You, and I, and Jube, may just hang up our fiddles, for the law's got her now, tight enough. That old Thrasher has done the business for her this time, anyhow. Gracious, what's that? Look a there—didn't I tell you?"

A wagon was coming up the road, slowly ploughing its way through the muddy snow: a single-seated wagon, with a rush-bottomed chair standing in front, upon which a man sat conspicuously, driving the horse. In the seat behind sat another man, with his arm thrown around a slender female, who shrunk away from his embrace, and cast wild glances toward the group of school children, that gathered in a crowd by the side of the road.

"Ah, me, it is her," said Paul, turning his eyes upon the wagon, and clasping his hands.

"Yes," said Tom, and the great tears leaped down his cheeks. "It's no mistake, them men are the keepers, and that is her. They're taking her up to the Squire's. It's all day with us, Paul; she'll never sleep in that brown house agin. Don't shake so, Paul; don't cry like a baby; I tell you it's enough to make a feller ashamed of your company!"

That moment the wagon came opposite the place where the two boys were standing: the prisoner saw them, and leaning forward tried to smile. Tom's bosom heaved, every feature in his face quivered, and then his feelings broke forth in a burst of tears that shook him from head to foot.

"Cry, Paul; cry, if you want to! I wont say a word agin it," he sobbed; "if you and I was giants, fifty feet tall, we needn't be ashamed of boo-hooing right out at a sight like that. Poor gal, poor gal, she looks like a blessed lamb between two butchers. Never mind, Paul, cry if you can't help it. I'll stand between you and the boys—they know me—by jingo, wasn't that one of 'em laughing? I'll maul him, see if I don't."

"Ah, no," said Paul, whose grief had been far less turbulent than that of his friend, "they not understand it as we do. She would not like you to fight, or think of any thing wrong. Let us be good, very much, and perhaps God will take care of her as He took care of Jube and me, when there was nothing but sky and water, very deep, all around us."

"Oh, why didn't she cut when we got her off!" cried Tom, bursting into a fresh passion of sobs. "It's like climbing a high tree after a young bird, and then seeing it flip out of your hand just as you touch ground. What's the use of being a gineral if your sojers wont work! That old Thrasher has undid us, Paul."

"Don't, please!" said Paul, listening. "I can hear the wagon yet, and it seems to be saying good-by—good-by. Oh, it is very sad, too sad, Mr. Tom."

True enough, the wagon was out of hearing, and Katharine Allen proceeded on her first stage to prison.

CHAPTER XLIII.

FRIENDS IN COUNCIL.

There was a mournful council held in Mrs. Allen's house on the morning after Katharine was carried away to prison. Old Mr. Thrasher and his wife had gone to the widow's residence early in the day, in great humility, seeking to share her sorrows, and take the burthen of Katharine's defence upon themselves. In words, they kept the promise that the poor girl had extorted, and never mentioned their son in connection with her, but the truth broke out from their innocent bosoms in every way. It breathed in their voices, and looked kindly forth from their eyes. They called Mrs. Allen sister, and there was a tenderness in the words that no common ideas of brotherhood ever possessed. They spoke of Katharine as the dear child on whom God had laid a heavy hand, but who had proved as brave as she was innocent.

All this comforted Mrs. Allen. She had great faith in the justice of God, and would not believe but that the truth must prevail even against the iron rule of law. She did not hesitate to accept the aid which Mr. Thrasher offered, and in one hour those three persons who had been so far apart two days before formed one little community of grief, and consoled each other like members of one household.

At first the two women had their secret misgivings, and, dear old cowards as they were, regretted that Katharine had even rendered herself up to the laws. Flight seemed to them the only sure way of escaping the horrors that threatened her. But the old man silenced these secret repinings with his firm Christian faith. His faith in divine goodness was perfect; believing Katharine innocent, he trusted her to the laws, certain that in some way her safety would be wrought out. Still he was not one of those men who indolently resign every thing into divine hands without individual effort. While ready to trust, he was equally ready to work for her deliverance in any way that seemed best.

The doctor came while these three persons were consulting together. A long ride was before him that day, but he scouted all ideas of fatigue, and left a host of patients to wait while he rode off to the widow Allen's in pity to her forlorn condition. Under the eccentricities which marked this man's character was a fund of sterling good sense and shrewd worldly knowledge, both of which he brought into the general council, where it was greatly needed, for three more inexperienced and single hearted creatures than he found in that kitchen seldom existed, even in New England, before stage-coaches gave way to railroads. Every face in the little group brightened when the doctor came in with his usual quaint joviality, which often covered more true benevolence than people suspected.

"That's right! all in Indian council round the fire. Something to be done; you're ready to go at it, and I'm here to help. I say, Thrasher, if you can't save that girl, don't ever dare to pray in the face of heaven again."

"It must be a greater than I who saves her," answered the old man, reverently; "but all that an honest man has power to do I am ready for."

"Well, now give me a chair, Mrs. Allen; don't keep me standing, it's bad policy; I may be a widower some of these days, can't you understand that!"

Mrs. Allen got up and placed a chair for her old friend, who dropped into it, deposited his crutches conveniently, and began to rub his hands before the fire.

"Well, now, to begin at the root of the matter, Thrasher. This thing wants money."

"I have some in the house and more out at interest. Tell me how to use it best."

"You're a prime old chap. A church full of such members would be enough to save the whole country, bad as it is. How much money in all, brother?"

I am afraid the word brother broke into a slight sarcasm on the doctor's lips, for he rather disliked these empty titles of endearment, and was apt to laugh at them a little in ordinary times. This one word had sprung from his heart in spontaneous warmth, but it was so strange to the lips that they threw it off irreverently.

Mr. Thrasher named a sum of money larger than any one could have believed at his command.

"It isn't mine," he said, noticing the look of surprise. "My son brought home all his profits and savings the last voyage, and told me to put them out at interest, and always consider them as mine if I wanted means. I shall use this money now—every cent, if needful for her safety or support."

"You think the girl innocent, then?" said the doctor.

"Innocent as I am," answered the good old man.

"As a baby," chimed in the mild voice of Mrs Thrasher.

"As the children of heaven," said Mrs. Allen, standing up, and speaking with all the authority of conviction.

"And this is why you would not let the poor thing run away?" inquired the doctor, sharply.

The two women looked at each other guiltily. They had been willing enough that she should run away. It was the sublime faith of the old man, appealing to a consciousness of innocence in the girl herself, that had wrought the noble act of self-abnegation, carried out in Katharine's return.

As for the kind-hearted women, to them Katharine's safety was the first thought; it was with heavy hearts that they had seen her return like a bird to the snare.

"Innocent or guilty she was in the hands of her God," answered the old man. "It was not for weak man like me to wrest her therefrom."

"Perhaps not; but I shall do my best to put all that stuff out of the lawyers' heads," answered the doctor, dryly.

The two women sighed heavily. Mrs. Thrasher looked a little shocked, and was troubled with vague misgivings that no lawyer of less strict principle would be tolerated by her husband.

"We must try and get a conscientious lawyer, if possible," said the old man, coloring under the doctor's words.

The doctor took up his crutches, and crossed them angrily before him.

"Look here, my old friend, we must divide this work, I see. You shall take the church and I'll take the law. You pray night and morning, I'll work morning and night; and if we don't save that poor child in the end, why it wont be for want of a suitable division of labor."

Mr. Thrasher yielded to this, for he had the great good sense which gives to every man a clear insight into his own capacities.

"I never had any thing to do with the law in my life," he said, meekly; "and for the whole world I wouldn't injure her by meddling with what I don't understand. If you'll undertake it, doctor, I'll——"

"Be content to play second fiddle—that's exactly what I am up to. Leave these law matters to me, and if you can do any thing to comfort her—if your religion can teach the poor thing to be cheerful or patient, my part wont be the most important after all. Well, now, Mrs. Allen, what are you good for? Why didn't you go with the girl?"

"I wished it; but they wouldn't let me. The jail was only for those who commit crimes, the constable said, and I had no right there."

"But you shall have a right, if I have to sin for you," said the doctor, dashing his crutch on the floor. "This is what you must arrange. Shut up the house here; take some of Thrasher's money, and go down to New Haven, take board close by the jail, and I'll answer for it you shall spend half your time with Katharine. If Thrasher and his wife could go with you, all the better —plenty of time to convert her in the prison. If the worst comes to the worst, she'll need you, and you can do more good than fifty ministers."

"Is it really your advice that I go?" said Mrs. Allen, with painful eagerness.

"It's my opinion that you should all go; nothing to do in the country at this time of year. You can comfort one another, and do her a world of good."

'I'm sure he's right," said Mrs. Thrasher, casting an appealing glance at her husband. "We might be a great comfort to her. How can we spend Nelson's money better?"

The old man arose and went out with the doctor, and the two consulted together some minutes by the gate, then Mr. Thrasher returned.

"There is a thing we have not considered," he said; "these two strangers. What can be done with them?"

Mrs. Allen went to a cupboard and took from one of the shelves a New York Journal, dated months back, in which Mrs. Prior's advertisement for scholars and boarders was conspicuous.

"These people live in my native town," she said; "it's a long time since I left it; but Paul would be much better off with this good minister than here with a broken-hearted old woman. My son has forwarded money for his support. While this trouble hangs over us, I will send the child to a happier home; as for Jube, he can stay on the place."

Jube heard this, and clasped his great hands with the sudden shock of her words. What! part from his little master—let the boy go off alone among strangers! It was more than he could bear. But obedience had been the first lesson of his life, and though every nerve of his heart protested, he uttered no complaint. Still, as he went heavily about his work that day, tears were constantly dropping from his eyes, and once he approached the window with such creeping humility that she half relented, and was tempted to let him go with his young charge.

But with a true Connecticut woman, industry is one of the leading virtues. The idea of a stalwart man passing his life in petting a little boy, was out of the question. True, it was very painful for her to separate these two singularly matched friends, but it was not in her nature to encourage idleness, so Paul's destiny for a time was decided.

CHAPTER XLIV.

THE SEPARATION.

IT was a sad night for Paul—the saddest, perhaps, of his whole life—for hitherto one friend had been with him; now he was to go forth alone. This was weary trouble; but the boy met it bravely. Being told with firmness that it was wrong to desire Jube to be always with him, he hushed down the anguish of that parting, and went away with bitter tears choked back in his heart.

This story was in the days of carriers and stage-coaches. Paul was placed in charge of a driver, and early the next morning was to be sent on his journey. He and Jube spent half an hour in the garret before he left, and a touching scene passed between those faithful hearts in that lonely place. Jube sat down on the floor and held the lad in his arms.

"You wont forget me, never, little masser?"

"Forget you, Jube, I couldn't do it; never, never; when 'sleep, it will be Jube who stands by in the dreams that our lady will send. If I pray, I will ask her to bless Jube."

"Oh, little masser, how Jube's heart aches!"

"And mine, Jube. What shall I do, all alone?"

"Yes, little masser, who will wake you up in the morning and warm your hands in his?"

"No one," sobbed Paul—"no one ever will be good to me like you, Jube."

"And you'll want Jube?"

"Want you—oh, very much."

Jube gathered the little fellow to his bosom and cried over him in forlorn silence.

"Little masser?"

"Well, Jube?" was the mournful answer.

"I'll try, little masser—I'll do very much to stay in this house when you're gone; but don't be frightened if I come often. Masser," sobbed the negro, "it does me good to say 'little masser,' but to-morrow no one will hear me."

Paul clung to his friend. "But I shall know it. In my soul I shall hear Jube's voice saying, 'little masser.'"

The rattle of wheels disturbed them. Tom Hutchins had driven up in his father's yellow wagon, and sat cracking his whip, ready to convey Paul to the stage house, where the doctor was waiting to see his youthful friend off. There was brief leave-taking between Mrs. Allen and her son's protégé. The sorrows that possessed her were so absorbing that all lesser griefs passed as nothing. She kissed the boy with a mournful farewell, and saw him driven away heavy-hearted and heavy eyed, wondering that any one, even a child, could feel sorrow for so slight a cause.

Jube, poor, faithful Jube, lifted Paul into the wagon, folded the checked blanket which draped the seat tenderly around him, and turned away, covering his face with both hands.

When Paul looked back to wave his last adieu, Jube was following down the road with long strides. He soon reached the wagon, and kept up with it, nowithstanding Tom's splendid driving, till they reached the stage house on the hill at Chewstown.

The stage was not in, and Tom sat in magnificent state by his foreign friend, snapping his whip and holding in his horse, which was made restive by the noise, with great force. What between grief at his friend's departure and the glory of driving a young horse for the first time, that precocious Jehu was in a state of wonderful excitement. But when the stage-coach came in, with its tin horn sounding over the hills, and a crack of whips that startled the whole neighborhood, Tom folded up his lash in despair, and shrinking into the insignificance of a one-horse wagon, gave way to his counter passion and became inconsolable over Paul's departure.

"I don't wonder you look so, Jube," he said, addressing the negro. "The idea of sending him off without you—it's downright scandlous. Now if it was me I'd cut. Catch a chap about this size staying behind to please an old woman! I wouldn't do it!"

"Ha, what is that? What you say, Masser Tom? Cut—what is cut?"

Before Tom could explain his meaning to the negro, the doctor rode up and shook Paul by the hand.

"Come, hop out, my little shaver—seat all ready—driver's got his orders. Here's a letter that you must give Mr. Prior, that's a good boy. Open the door, driver—lift him up, cuffy—ho, heave, ho!"

The stage took a splendid sweep, that nearly broke Tom's heart with envy, then swung down the sand banks across the bridge and away.

Paul leaned from a window, and wildly flung kisses back to his friends. Jube shaded his eyes with one hand, but tears dropped heavy and thick from under it, while Tom jumped out of his wagon, and ran after the doctor.

"Doctor, I say, you jest listen to reason. That ere nigger is breaking his consarned black heart 'cause you amongst you wont let him go with Paul. It's a burning shame of you, doctor; he'll jest pine away into a consumption; and that'll be what you have done."

"Why, Tom, what is all this about? I haven't kept your snowball; he can roll where he pleases for any thing I care about it."

"And you didn't set the widder up to this, doctor?"

"Set her up to it?—no."

"Doctor, give us your hand. I ought to have known better. If ever there was a chap that I look up to he isn't far off from this 'dentical hoss. If you'd gin orders for cuff to stay, stay he should, right or wrong; but if it's only a specimen of woman's work, then Jube is his own boss. A woman's a woman, and a nigger is a nigger—neither uv 'em can vote or train according to law. Then what right has one over 'tother, I should like to know?"

The doctor's eyes twinkled under their heavy brows.

"That is logic," he said, leading the boy on. "If women could vote, and——"

"If wimmin could vote!" exclaimed Tom, with magnificent disdain. "The idee! Who'd take care of the young ones while they trapsed about 'lection days? Well, I reckon it wouldn't be me—I've had enough of that 'ere."

"Well, Tom, as women can't vote, and have no right to order negroes, what course would you advise Jube to take?"

"Cut, doctor; that's what I'd do in this case!"

"Well, if he wants to cut, and has the money to afford it, I don't see the harm."

"You don't? Hurrah, Jube! You don't?—that's enough. Good-by, doctor."

Away the lad rushed, and sprang with a bound into the wagon.

"Come, Jube—hurry up. I've got something splendid to say to you. Jump in, and I don't mind driving you over the hill. Chirk up, old fellow, we'll be after him yet, but I'll think it over till morning."

Jube obeyed this boisterous summons, and climbed into the wagon.

The next day, Mrs. Allen left her house, and took up her lonely abode in New Haven. Old Mr. Thrasher went with her, leaving his wife behind for a few days, when she too would give up her home. Jube was left alone in the house, alone in the cruel cold, so heartbroken and desolate that he had not sufficient energy to build a fire, or cook necessary food. Tom was right—a few weeks of this life would have killed the noble fellow outright. On the third day after Paul left, he was sitting drearily on the hearth, with his feet in the ashes, when Tom came in.

"Just as I expected," he said, dropping into Mrs. Allen's high-backed chair. "Down in the mouth—clean give up—not worth salt."

Jube did not speak, but sat supporting his head with both hands, looking gloomily into the ashes.

"Look a here, cuff, to-morrow is stage day agin."

"I know it," said Jube. "The doctor stopped here and told me."

"He did?"

"Yes."

"Well, why didn't you take the hint?"

Jube looked at Tom, with a languid question in his eyes.

"Pick up your money, jump on the top of the stage, and dash away after Paul. That's what he meant by coming here."

"Ha! ha! what that?" cried Jube, starting to his feet.

"Now, don't go off the handle; but pack up your bundle, and be off in the morning. What are you skeered about? What's the use of working when you've got lots an' lots of cash? Just up and go after Paul. He's breaking his heart, and so are you; besides, this old house is enough to set a feller crazy. I couldn't stand it. Just up and go; that's my advice. The doctor'll make it all right with the old woman."

"But the animals—the poor cow and the birds—who feed them when Jube gone?"

"That's exactly what I come about. If it hadn't been for that difficulty, I'd a had you off afore this. I've been talking to par about the chores to hum, and he's kinder promised to let me off from part of 'em and give me time to stop here on my way to school and back. I'll take care of the critters and feed the chickens till some of 'em get home again; so don't worry yourself about them, but chirk up and act like a man. What are you looking away for? Don't it suit you?"

Jube turned his face upon the boy; a face all quivering and aglow with happiness.

"Oh, Masser Tom, a great rock is lifted right off from my heart. Masser Paul! Masser Paul!"

"It wont take you more than a day to get there."

"One day? to-morrow night? no more?" questioned the negro, earnestly.

"Jes so. Now pack up and I'll drive you over to the stage house, consarn me, if I wont; for, cuffy or no cuffy, you are a prime feller, Jube, and I aint ashamed of your acquaintance. It's an honor, Jube, and I feel it."

The next morning Tom sat in his father's yellow wagon in front of the stage house, while Jube, smiling till all his teeth shone, again waved an adieu from the top of the stage.

"Good-by, Jube; tell Paul not to forget old Bungy and the folks that's in it."

Jube smiled broadly.

"Tell him to come back in the spring."

Jube lost his message, for the stage went off, scattering a storm of mud from its wheels, and thundering down the sand banks with a flourish of whips that aggravated Tom's unhappiness beyond measure.

"Never mind," he muttered, turning his horse to follow on the same road. "If Rose Mason only knew I was driving this young critter that she used to consider so harnsome, she wouldn't think that stage any thing tremendous, loud as the driver cracks his whip."

With these consoling fragments of thought, Tom followed in the wake of the stage, trying his whip as he crossed the bridge in a manner that made his young steed plunge and jump on one side with a violence that brought the boy's heart into his mouth. While he was busy subduing the spirited animal the doctor rode on to the bridge and watched the conflict. It was soon over, for Tom had ignominiously given up by thrusting his whip under the seat in great dismay.

"Well, what's the news, Tom?" inquired the doctor, as he rode by.

"Nothing special sir, only Jube has cut. Going up the hill yonder on top of the stage. I say, you'll just make it all right with Mrs. Allen, doctor?"

The doctor nodded, chuckled softly, and rode on

CHAPTER XLV.

PAUL FINDS A NEW HOME.

ONCE more the stage swung to at minister Prior's gate, and this time a slender boy, with a beauty of countenance that made you hold your breath, was lifted through the door, and set carefully down upon the grass.

Mr. Prior, who had been dreaming over his sermon in the study, came out, looking bland as a summer's morning, and was accosted by the driver:

"I say, minister, I always bring luck. Here is one of the nicest little shavers that ever you saw. He wants to come to school, and I've told him that you'll be a father to him, and as for Mrs. Prior—well, there's no doing that lady justice."

Mr. Prior smiled pleasantly, and went up to Paul.

"He is indeed a fine boy."

"Thank you, monsieur," said Paul, taking a letter, which the doctor had given him, from his pocket. "When you read this perhaps you tell more sure if I can stay here."

Mr. Prior glanced over the letter, and smiled down with hospitable kindness into Paul's anxious eyes.

"It would be difficult to answer no, even if we wished it," he said, kindly; "an orphan and a stranger—it is from such I fancy that the angels come to us unawares."

"You will not find me too much trouble," said Paul, smiling. "I study English good deal—try always."

"French is your native language, I think?"

"Yes, monsieur!"

"Then we will soon find a lady who can talk with you; come, my little man."

The minister led Paul into the house, speaking to him kindly enough, although, in his shyness, he was always sadly at a loss what to say to any child, and the boy looked so sorrowful at parting with his friend that the clergyman was in doubt what manner of argument to employ by way of consolation.

He gave the little fellow a seat in the parlor, and went away to find Mrs. Prior, and inform her of the arrival of her new pupil. She hurried in at once, and her motherly kindness soon made Paul, in a measure, forget his loneliness and desolation.

Mrs. Mason and Rose had gone out to walk; so, for an hour or two, the little woman gave the boy her undivided attention. He refused dinner, saying they had dined on the road; but Mrs. Prior, out of the experience of her schoolmistress days, had great faith in the unlimited powers of children in the way of voraciousness, so she brought him all manner of quaint shaped cakes and crullers, red apples and nuts, until Paul was confused by the abundance, and sat with them on the handkerchief laid across his lap, staring ruefully at the pile, and really not knowing where to begin.

But what comforted Paul more than any thing was to hear himself addressed in his native language, which Mrs. Prior spoke with a sufficient degree of fluency.

"I have a little girl here," she said, "who will be a nice playmate for you."

"Is she a pretty little girl?" Paul asked; for he possessed a keen appreciation of beauty.

"Very pretty; her name is Rose, and she is nice and sweet, like her name."

Paul was interested at once, and poured forth a flood of questions with such volubility that it required all Mrs. Prior's knowledge of French to follow him. When he learned that it was the very Rose that Tom Hutchins had talked of so much, he felt at once that he had fallen among old friends, and his face brightened till its singular beauty became a marvel in the eyes of the minister's little wife.

Before Mrs. Mason and her daughter returned, Paul and his hostess had become the best friends imaginable. He grew very confidential, made her cry heartily with a few words which conveyed an account of his mother's death, and she brightened at the story of his rescue at sea, and in her gentle heart blessed the rough sailor of whom Paul spoke so lovingly. In the glow of these

PAUL FINDS A NEW HOME.

benevolent feelings she determined to do every thing in her power to make the child's residence in her family a happy episode in his life.

When she heard Mrs. Mason and little Rose in the hall, Mrs. Prior went out and asked them to come in.

"I want your daughter and my new charge to be good friends," she said, pleasantly, to Mrs. Mason.

"I will see him before I give any answer, if you please," replied that lady, who grew more haughty and insolent every day.

"His society could not fail to be of benefit to any child," returned Mrs. Prior, annoyed, as often happened now, by the imperious manner of her boarder. "He is the most perfect little gentleman I ever saw in my life."

Mrs. Mason made an effort to look somewhat doubtful of Mrs. Prior's judgment in such matters, but there was a certain dignity in the lady's manner which checked further insolence.

Indeed, Mrs. Mason herself was wonderfully struck with the boy's delicacy of features and refinement of manner, the moment she saw him. Her curiosity was excited, and she asked innumerable questions, which Paul answered evasively, for his childish instincts prejudiced him against the beautiful woman at once.

But the little girl and he soon opened friendly relations, after the first shyness, natural to children, had worn off. In the corner, where Paul was taken to admire her dolls, all fast asleep, as good dolls should be when visitors come on them unawares, she began to question him at once. What child would not? He told her of his perilous sea life, and of the beautiful country where he once lived, but there were scenes in that life so dark and terrible that the boy's heart shrunk away from them even in thought. To have mentioned them in childish play would have proved beyond his power. Among these were the blows that had been dealt on Jube, and all his miserable life in that brig.

Another subject which he never mentioned was the story of poor Katharine. Mrs. Allen, shrinking from the idea that her daughter's disgrace should be carried to her native town, had cautioned Paul never to mention their names, and he obeyed her faithfully.

The doctor had obtained a letter from a clergyman in New Haven to Mr. Prior, which the boy had brought as an introduction, and that was all the information necessary.

Thus, though Paul and Rose became good friends, he never spoke of the people or scenes which they knew in common.

When bedtime came, Paul went up to the pretty little room prepared for him with considerable hesitation, as he had always had Jube near for comfort and protection.

However, he was too manly for a single remonstrance, and when Mrs. Prior kissed him good-night at the door, he knelt for his prayers, and hastened to bed with all speed.

When he was safely in bed, and the warmth began to make him feel somewhat less disconsolate, Mrs. Prior came to take away the candle, through fear of imaginary accidents.

"Are you comfortable?" she asked, stopping to look at him, as he lay with his classical head visible above the clothes.

"Very," Paul said.

"Sleep well, and try to be happy," she returned, giving him another kiss, out of the tenderness of her heart.

"Thank you, madame," Paul said, touched, as he always was, by any evidence of kindness. "I like you very much, very much."

Mrs. Prior was not half way down-stairs before Paul was quietly asleep. Fatigue kept him from dwelling upon this new change. Indeed, he had grown so accustomed to removals and strangers that he received them with very different feelings from those which would formerly have troubled him.

CHAPTER XLVI.

JUBE FINDS HIS WAY TO BAYS HOLLOW.

The next morning, while Paul and Rose were playing in the dining-room—the little girl having been granted a holiday on account of the boy's arrival—there arose in the kitchen a sudden commotion, which attracted Mrs. Prior's attention. She went out, and found her little handmaiden in conversation with an immense negro, who looked so good-natured and anxious, that it was a wonder he could have frightened anybody, although the girl appeared somewhat inclined to run away.

When Mrs. Prior entered, the man turned toward her with a ponderous bow.

"What do you want, my good man?" she asked, gently.

"My young masser is here," Jube said, with another salute.

"Your young master?"

"Yes; Masser Paul."

"Are you his servant?"

"Yes, if madame pleases. Jube came with him from the old home, saw the mistress buried, and has been wandering about with little masser ever since."

"He told me about you," said Mrs. Prior.

"Yes, madame. So when madame sent masser away, Jube meant to stay there and take care of the house. But Jube would have died—came after little masser. Please take me, madame. Jube can work; he'll do any thing, big, big, strong."

He extended his stalwart arms as a proof of his words, and Mrs. Prior was touched by his earnestness.

"We have no need of any more help," she said.

"Oh, yes; Jube be great help—jis take me, madame, you see—no be sorry, no indeed."

"I would willingly, for the child's sake, but we are not rich; my husband could not afford to pay you wages."

"Jube not want wages—no good of money. Please let Jube stay, lady."

"Mrs. Prior went up to the study to hold a private consultation with her husband; while she was gone, Paul and Rose passed through the kitchen.

At the sight of the negro, the boy gave a cry of delight, and rushed into his arms, with a burst of tears and wild ejaculations. Jube sobbed aloud, and it was some time before either of them could in the least recover their composure.

Rose stood looking at them in great astonishment; but when Paul managed to explain that this was the Jube of whom he had told her, she cried and laughed also, from pure sympathy, while the handmaiden worked herself into such a state of bewilderment that she laid the forks where the spoons belonged, put an empty tin pan into the oven, instead of the pudding, which was ready for baking, and performed a variety of other wonderful feats, which brought great disgrace upon her shortly after.

When Mrs. Prior and the clergyman came down-stairs, they found Paul nestled close to his old friend, and looking so happy that the very idea of refusing the negro's request sent a pang to their hearts.

"Jube must stay," Paul cried, in his exquisitely persuasive way; "please to say yes, good madame—shan't he stay, sir?"

The clergyman looked at his wife, and she looked back at him; both were extremely perplexed.

"Jube no want wages," said the negro, "only wants to live near little masser."

"Yes, that is all," added Paul.

"We certainly cannot have the man," Mrs. Prior said to her husband.

"That is out of the question," he replied.

"But what can we do?"

"Settle it yourself, Mrs. Prior; your decision is sure to be a correct and wise one."

With these complimentary words, the minister helped himself out of his difficulty by leaving the room.

Mrs. Prior looked at the friends in great trouble; but little Paul approached her chair and put his arms about her neck; Rose clung to her hand and added her entreaties; while Jube gazed at her with his great, honest eyes.

The result of all this affair was, that Jube insisted on making himself so agreeable, and began at once to demonstrate his powers of usefulness so acceptably that there was really no turning him out of doors.

The good fellow had some mechanical genius, and exerted it to the delight of little Rose in furnishing her play-house, and building sleds and wagons for Paul, large enough for her to ride in. Then, Jube made such a splendid horse, and never got tired of carrying her or drawing the little sled on which she rode. When she expressed a wish to ride on horseback, Jube lifted her to his broad shoulders, or put out his foot, which instantly swung itself into full canter, and away she went, rushing off to "Canterbury Cross" in high glee.

To Mrs. Prior, both Jube and his little master were objects of peculiar interest. Paul was eloquent in his own language, and through its medium he conveyed many pleasant fancies to the mind of Rose, and thus, all in play, brought her through the first practice of a study her mother had greatly at heart.

As the winter snows melted, and the sweet spring days came on, it was pleasant to see Jube seated with the children—at heart, almost as much of a child as either of them—beneath a huge apple tree that stood in the meadow, and covered one of the most lovely strawberry slopes in the world with its shadow.

As the bright days came on, the favor of instruction was not altogether on one side. Rose had her own little accomplishments, which she taught in shy triumph in exchange for the sweet language and pretty names bestowed on her. She taught Paul how to curl dandelion stems into innumerable ringlets, and made an astonishing halter of daisy chains for Jube, that was not the less perfect because it broke into a shower of white blossoms at the first hard pull, and littered the grass like a snow-storm. Then she could braid rushes seven strands at a time, and weave them into such pretty green baskets that Mrs. Prior considered them the pet ornaments of her parlor.

Besides these accomplishments, Rose had a delicious voice, and sung snatches of music at her work. These wild strains so excited the robins in the apple tree boughs that they forgot nest-building and love-making, to join in a chorus that rang all over the meadow, bringing other birds to see what it was all about, who liked the premises, and built their nests also among the sweet blossoms and leaves of dainty green, till the old tree was a marvel for its feathered population.

I am afraid Rose sometimes followed Paul up into the apple tree, taking shy peeps at the pretty blue eggs which he exposed by sweeping the soft leaves back from the nest with his hands. Once or twice Mrs. Prior found her in a corner of the garret, making desperate efforts to darn a long rent in her dress, and crying bitterly because the cloth would draw into knots and gathers under her hand, more conspicuous than the original tear had been, which must have strengthened this suspicion about the apple tree very much.

Of course the good lady remedied this evil with her own deft little fingers, and Mrs. Mason was too busy with other things just then to heed torn frocks or the shamefacedness which on ordinary occasions would have betrayed them.

Thus time wore on, till Mrs. Mason had become a dashing performer on the piano, for she practiced day and night on the accomplishments that she willed to master, and in every thing made up for deficiencies by audacious self-possession. Thus, while Rose and the birds were singing out of doors, she sent a storm of music through the open windows, which were just far enough from the apple tree to excite the birds without frightening them to death.

CHAPTER XLVII.

A CHILDISH CONSULTATION.

The life which these children and their companion led at Bays Hollow was quiet and peaceful, especially to those strange beings, after the privations and bitter troubles through which they had passed. The mournful look that had seemed natural to Paul, went out from his eyes, which grew soft or bright with changing feelings, but the haggard anguish which had made their glance so painfully sad, never came back to them. As for Jube, he was like a Newfoundland dog—full of courage, strength, and cheerfulness.

The minister and Mrs. Prior were a great deal happier for having these children in the house. Indeed Mrs. P. put on the most awkward little maternal airs, like a great girl beginning to play with dolls late in life, for which the minister admired her prodigiously. Once, when they were quite alone, he observed in a dreamy way, "That it was a sad pity such talent for government should be exhausted on other people's children," at which Mrs. Prior went off in a spasm of blushes, and the minister crept out of the room, quite ashamed of himself, feeling that he had approached the verge of total depravity in that unhappy speech.

A CHILDISH CONSULTATION.

One day when Paul and Jube were busy among the strawberry vines in the meadow, searching, with great anxiety, for the first tinge of red upon the slowly ripening fruit, for the boy was eager to secure a handful for little Rose, that young lady was seen dashing through the back door of the house, and running full speed toward the strawberry hollow. Paul started up and shook his head to indicate that there was no hope of strawberries yet, while Jube, who was on all fours among the vines, lifted his broad face like an expectant dog, and laughed till all his teeth shone again, with the joyousness of her approach.

On she came, rushing through the fresh wind, her curls floating out behind her, and her face full of wild excitement.

"Something is the matter," said Paul, stepping forward to meet her. "Who has frightened Rose, I should like to know?"

"Paul, Paul, come here, under the apple tree," were the first breathless words of our little girl. "I want to tell you something."

Paul took her hand with his usual gentle kindness, and the two ran to the apple tree's shade.

"This is it," said Rose, panting for breath, while her eyes sparkled like diamonds. "He has come—that man who loves my mother so much. He's a going to marry her right off, as sure as you live. Marry her—my own, own mother—who never will love me again after that; never, never!"

Rose burst into a passion of tears, and flinging herself against the trunk of the tree wept bitterly.

Paul was greatly troubled; not that he understood

the matter, but because it grieved him to see Rose cry so bitterly.

"Oh," she exclaimed, dropping two dimpled hands from her eyes, and stamping her tiny feet on the grass, "oh dear, how I wish that Captain Thrasher was dead."

Paul started, and turned very pale. "Jube, Jube," he called out, with a cry of pain.

Jube started up from his knees, and came running toward the children.

"What is it—what is it, little masser?"

"He is here, that bad man—he wants to marry Rose's mother," cried the lad, flinging his arms around the little girl, and looking the brave, bright boy he really was.

"Who, who, little masser?" cried Jube, looking around for some enemy.

"Captain Thrasher." Paul uttered the name in a whisper.

Jube clenched his hand, looking fiercely toward the house.

"He there, Masser Paul?"

"Yes," said the angry child, shaking her little rosebud of a fist at the house. "He's there with my own mother, this minute. He'll carry her off in spite of us all."

"What can we do?" said Paul, anxiously looking at Jube.

"Couldn't you just kill him, Jube, as you did the garter snake," cried Rose, shaking the drops from her eager eyes.

Jube hesitated; the fellow had a vague idea that some one might object to this mode of settling the difficulty.

Paul drew back with affright. He had received a cruel knowledge of the laws regarding human life, and the remedy pointed out by little Rose made him shrink.

"We must not ask Jube to be wicked," he said, gently.

Rose dashed his hand away. "Isn't it wicked for that man to come here after my own mother?" she cried, indignantly.

"Yes, Rose; but it would be more wicked for Jube to harm him. The law, Rose, the law."

"Well, I don't care. What is the law? If it's a man, Jube can whip him, can't you, Jube?" cried the little damsel, going for belligerent rights with all her puny strength.

"But it isn't a man, Rose," said Paul, solemnly. "It's something that no one ever sees. It comes like death, and when a person does wrong, even if it was a beautiful lady, strikes her down till her heart breaks. It shuts people up in prison."

"Oh don't, don't," cried Rose.

"It hangs 'em by the neck between two beams."

"Oh, how you frighten me, Paul."

"It hunts after a person who has done wrong, day and night, and catches him at last. Oh, Rose, if you only knew how cruel the law can be."

Rose hushed her sobs and drew close to Paul, quite awe-stricken. "Never mind, Jube needn't do it. I'll ask the minister to pray God to help us, that will be the best thing."

"Yes," said Paul, brightening, "and I'll—no matter about that, people shouldn't talk about these things, but 'our Lady' has done great things for people in distress."

They sat down in a group under the apple tree, consulting eagerly together. After awhile the parlor window opened, and a clear, ringing voice called out:

"Rose! Rose Mason, I say."

"I must go," said the little girl, with a look of deplorable helplessness. "She'll want me to kiss him, but I wont!"

Paul lifted her little hand to his lips, and kissed it with touching grace.

"Don't be afraid, Rose. Jube wont let anybody hurt you."

"I—I aint afraid," cried Rose, tossing her golden curls. "He daren't kiss me, I know that."

She went away slowly, looking over her shoulder from time to time during her progress toward the house. The apple tree was not within sight of the parlor windows, thus both Jube and Paul remained unseen by the two people who occupied that room; an unfortunate circumstance, perhaps, for their recognition might have changed the whole course of events. As it was, both Paul and Jube were anxious to keep out of sight. When they left the meadow, Paul went to his room, and in the simplicity of his faith, put up many an orison to the Virgin, in behalf of this pretty friend. What else could the child do?

CHAPTER XLVIII.

PAUL SEES HIS MOTHER'S NECKLACE.

BEFORE Rose left the parlor she was so frightened and subdued by her mother's stern reprimands, that all idea of appealing for help forsook her. So she ran desperately into a closet connected with her mother's chamber, fell upon the floor, and cried herself to sleep, with her flushed cheeks resting on two round arms, folded helplessly on the bare boards.

Toward night, Mrs. Mason came up-stairs, looking haughty and excited. Without heeding the child, who lay just within the closet, with her curls scattered over the threshold of the door, she began to open trunks and bureaus, from which she drew first a heavy silk dress, which just escaped being white by a tinge of pearl gray, some gossamer laces, and other indications of an elaborate toilet. Then she let down her magnificent hair, brushed out its glossy waves, and began to braid it; stopping now and then to rest her arms on the table before her, and sighing heavily, as if it required all her energies to keep up that proud show of strength.

After wreathing these heavy braids around her head in the form of a coronet, she arose and went to the closet for something. Lo, there was her child prone upon the floor, disturbed by her approach, and moaning at her feet.

A person who deliberately does wrong, is almost sure to be angry at any thing calculated to touch the conscience. Mrs. Mason's cheeks flushed and her eyes flashed at the sight of little Rose. She was tempted to spurn the child with her foot, but restrained herself, only touching the bare, white shoulder, with the point of her slipper.

"Get up, child. Get up. What on earth are you doing here?"

The touch awoke Rose. She started to her feet, and tried to shrink away.

"Stop, you naughty, disobedient child!" cried the mother, seizing her by the shoulder. "You don't deserve it; but see what a beautiful present Mr. Thrasher has brought you—coral and pure gold—for your arms and neck. There, Rosey posey, don't it make your eyes dance?"

The little girl's eyes did sparkle for a moment, but directly they filled with tears.

"No, mother; it's very pretty, but I don't want anything," she said, timidly.

The mother frowned.

"Go to Mrs. Prior this instant," she said; "tell her to dress you in the India muslin frock that I gave out to be done up. Loop the sleeves with this coral. Mind and let Mr. Thrasher see it on your neck and arms. Oh, Mrs. Prior, I'm glad you've come! Please have this child properly dressed. There are the ornaments; go, Rose, I have no time to spare; be a good girl, and look pretty to please mother."

"I'll—I'll try," sobbed the child, "only don't make me wear them."

"Hush, or you'll make me angry, my dear. Mrs. Prior, if you would hurry with her, and help me a little, I really am so nervous."

"No wonder," answered Mrs. Prior, gravely, "the whole thing is so sudden."

"Not with me," was the cold answer. "The day was settled the last time Mr. Thrasher visited us; but I did not think it necessary to make it a subject of conversation with strangers."

"But we might have been better prepared," said Mrs. Prior.

"Not at all necessary, as we go away in an hour after the ceremony is performed."

"Go away, Mrs. Mason?"

"Certainly."

"And little Rose?"

The good woman's voice trembled.

"Ah, she will stay with you, heaven only knows how long! that is, if you will keep her—say at the price we have been paying for both. She will have the piano for practice, and you can keep the furniture to remember me by."

"You are very kind."

"Not at all; I know you will be good to Rose."

"Indeed I will!"

"And give her every accomplishment. Remember, money is of no consequence."

"That which you offer is more than enough to pay for all the knowledge or accomplishments I can teach," said the little woman, conscientiously.

"If it isn't, say so, and we'll double it," answered Mrs. Mason, with reckless munificence. "There is gold enough in my work-box there to pay for three or four years, if we do not send for her before that. You can take box and all after we're gone, for I shall leave all these things behind; it's too much trouble to pack them up. Use what you like, and cut over the rest for Rose—the dresses, I mean. That brown silk for travelling will be all I shall care for after the ceremony is over."

"I hardly know how to receive this liberality," said the little woman, with tears in her eyes. "It don't seem right to accept it."

"Oh, nonsense! Be a mother to Rose, and seem glad to see us when we come after her. You have been very kind to me, Mrs. Prior, and I feel it now, indeed I do."

There was a touch of genuine feeling in Mrs. Mason's voice, as she bent forward and kissed Mrs. Prior on the cheek, with lips that were red and dewy as rose-buds. In her selfishness, she had not noticed Rose, who stood clinging to Mrs. Prior's dress, growing paler and paler at each word.

"Mother, are you going to leave me all alone!"

There was so much of sorrow in the child's voice that it reached even that vain heart.

"Never mind, Rosey, dear," said the mother, kissing the pale lips of her child. "It wont be long; besides, Mrs. Prior loves you dearly, and will be very kind."

"Indeed I will, darling," sobbed the little woman. "So now cheer up, Rose, and run off to be dressed," added the mother, beginning to tire of the scene; do try and help me, Mrs. Prior, and see that your husband is ready; there must be no delay, for we have a long ride before us."

Mrs. Prior hurried off with Rose to her own private room, and in a marvellous short time the little girl came forth airy as a butterfly. The red coral glowing on her face and neck, the India muslin floating around her like a cloud.

Rose met Paul in the upper passage. He was looking sadly troubled. She went toward him and laid her hand in his.

"You are going?" he said, interpreting the act from his fears.

"No, *they* are going, Paul, but I am to be left behind."

The boy began to smile.

"And Mrs. Prior will be your mother?" he said.

"Yes."

"Ah! I'm so happy, so glad; let me go tell Jube."

He attempted to descend the stairs but came back again.

"One thing, Rose. I should like to see this gentleman, Captain Thrasher."

"Well, he's in the parlor."

"But I don't want him to see me."

"Oh, then I can't help you, Paul—there's no way."

Paul looked disappointed. That moment Mrs. Prior came toward them from Mrs. Mason's room.

"What is the matter, Paul?" she inquired, kindly.

"Oh, nothing," answered Rose, "only he wants to see that hateful man."

"For shame, Rose!"

"Well, he wants to see Captain Thrasher, and he don't want Captain Thrasher to see him!" persisted Rose, shaking her head with pretty defiance.

"He wants to see a marriage—is that it?" said Mrs. Prior, whose kind heart was always prompting her to the pleasure of others. "And you would like to have a peep at this wedding? Rose, you will go into the room; but it is to be very private, you know, and I can't let you in, Paul."

"No, no, I do not wish—I only want to see," cried the boy, eagerly; "I and Jube—one little minute, that is all."

Mrs. Prior smiled and dropped into a moment's thought.

"Well," she said, "as you have set your heart upon

it, Paul, there can be no harm in letting you see them married so long as it disturbs no one. There is the door between the parlor and dining-room; the upper half is glass. Just lift the curtain softly and look through; but remember, there must be no talking about it. The whole thing is to be kept secret."

"I will not speak to any one, be sure," said Paul.

"Well, be in your room and I will call you at the right time," said Mrs. Prior; "but hurry away, now, for she'll be going down-stairs in a minute."

Paul went to his room. Scarcely had he disappeared when Mrs. Mason came forth; the thick silken folds of her dress rustling sumptuously, and with a carcanet of gems flashing its tinted flame over the snow of her neck and shoulders.

When Rose saw her mother the color died from her face and she shivered as if with cold. Mrs. Mason was too much excited to heed this. Taking the little hand in hers, she led the child down-stairs, sweeping through the hall like a sultana.

Mrs. Prior was struck with admiration at the splendor of her beauty, but depressed by this display of magnificence for a wedding which was to be strictly private. Her own refined taste revolted at the incongruity. Indeed, Mrs. Mason herself seemed to feel something of this, for she blushed even while giving her head a proud lift, and observed, in a low voice:

"He would insist upon it. Nothing is rich enough to satisfy him."

Paul found Jube in his room when he entered it.

"Be ready," he said. "We shall soon know if it is the same man."

"But he may claim us, and say that I am his slave again," said Jube, anxiously.

"He will not see us. There, I hear the minister going down. Be ready. Madame is coming to call us."

Mrs. Prior opened the door, and said: "Come," in a quick, nervous whisper.

Paul and Jube followed her into the dining-room. A crimson curtain hung over the sash which filled the upper part of the door. Mrs. Prior drew it slightly inward, leaving a crevice on each side, through which Paul and Jube could see all that went forward in the parlor without fear of observation.

The couple who were to be married, sat out of range of the window, and at first they only saw the minister saying something in a low voice to Mrs. Prior. She went out and returned with the servant girl, who hung shyly around the door, as if doubtful of the part she was called upon to perform. Then there was a rustling of silk, a general movement, and Paul saw the tyrant of his sea-life standing before the minister, with Mrs. Mason's hand clasped in his. He saw more—for the Venetian blinds fell apart, and a gleam of sunshine quivered across the gems upon the bride's neck. A shudder passed over him, he clung to a neighboring chair for support, and breathlessly looked on. Every word of that awful ceremony—for it was awful to him—fell upon the boy's heart. When it was ended, and the woman turned to the full light, a sick faintness crept over him, and he fell into Jube's arms perfectly insensible. The sight of his mother's necklace had overpowered the boy with terrible memories.

CHAPTER XLIX.

A PALACE READY FOR ITS MISTRESS.

AT the time of our story, New York Island was not so thickly crowded with habitations as it is to-day. Men who lived on the outskirts of the city could afford grounds more or less spacious about their habitations. Gardens were no uncommon luxuries, and lawns not altogether unknown. Just far enough from the city for retirement, yet sufficiently near for easy access, stood a large mansion, which commanded a view of the Hudson, and was surrounded by forest trees, which had doubtless sheltered many an Indian encampment. Sloping lawns, flower gardens, and rustic arbors lent glow and richness to every nook and vista of these grounds. The house—a fine old family mansion—had been renovated and altered so completely, since it had fallen into the hands of the present proprietor, that the most intimate friend of the former owner must have failed to recognize it.

The solid stone walls had been faced with marble. The small paned windows had given place to broad plate glass, transparent as crystal. Wreaths of rich sculpture broke the snow-white front around the doors and windows, while heavy scrolls of marble rolled down the broad entrance steps, and antique heads enriched the balconies. Two noble lions, with slumbrous limbs and foamlike manes, crouched on the lower entrance steps, and graceful vases, overflowing with rare and flowering plants, stood on either hand by the door.

The approach to this house was by a lodge gate, and along the sweep of a gravelled carriage road, which held a beautiful flower-garden in its curve. Every thing about the dwelling was in perfect order—not a leaf disturbed the emerald richness of the grass, not a broken flower could be found in all that luxuriant waste of blossoms. The English gardener had done his work perfectly. There was not a footprint on the gravel walk, nor a stain upon the whiteness of the marble. Pure, rich, and beautiful, the house arose amid the bloom and shade of tall trees and delicate flowers, like some snow-white palace in fairy-land.

Every thing was silent within this house. Servants moved about, it is true; but they were too well trained for any thing like confusion, and a state of expectation kept them unusually quiet. The housekeeper went from room to room, anxious that nothing should be out of place, and a little nervous in her desire to please a mistress whom she had never seen.

The truth is, that the household was in a state of more general ignorance regarding the persons they were hired to serve than usually falls to people of their class; but what was more remarkable, they knew as much, and more of their master than any of the neighbors, with whom he was an object of no little curiosity.

Mr. Nelson had come upon the neighborhood suddenly, whether from the east, west, north or south, no one could pretend to say. Of course there was a great deal of conjecture. A man of vast wealth and liberal education he certainly was; fine looking too, after a peculiar style. Besides this, he appeared quite young enough to be considered a desirable match for the most fastidious belle in any one of the hundred and fifty circles that dispute the palm of aristocracy year by year, without settling the question among themselves.

He had bought the old mansion house, paid for it in cash, and taken up his residence in one wing, while the alterations we have spoken of were going on. As a bachelor his habits were very simple and his words few.

The best artisans were employed, and the most expensive books on gardening and architecture lay upon the table in his room. He studied these books night and day, for some weeks before the persons necessary to his work were called around him. When they came at last, he was prepared not only to take specifications, but to suggest them, and that with an air of knowledge that won profound respect from the persons with whom he conversed.

It was impossible to tell, by this man's manners or conversation, what his business in life had been. He was always on his guard against the intrusiveness of curiosity, always gentle, or rather stolidly quiet; but once or twice, when a man conceited in his art had ventured to contradict him, the frown upon his forehead had proved an ominous warning which no one cared to provoke a second time.

During some months he had lived entirely at the old mansion, watching its gradual transfiguration and superintending the changes with untiring assiduity. Two or three times he had been absent for several days, but no one knew where, and he gave no notice either of his intended departure or return.

CHAPTER L.

COMING HOME OF THE BRIDE.

At last, when every thing was complete, and the place stood out a paradise in comparison with the most beautiful residences of the city, circumstances arose that inflamed anew the curiosity of the household. The entrance was haunted by tradespeople, bringing packages that could only prove useful to a lady. All this was a fitting preparation for the very quiet orders which Mr. Nelson gave to his housekeeper, just as he stepped into his carriage one morning.

"Have every thing in readiness, Mrs. Ford," he said, "for on the third day from this I shall bring my wife home."

Mrs. Ford was a nice old English housekeeper, brought up with profound reverence for her employers, and early taught the useful lesson of minding her own business, one of the most valuable secrets known to society. Had this been otherwise she could have commanded no time for asking questions, for while making this announcement, Mr. Nelson stepped into the carriage, and drove off without vouchsafing another word.

Mrs. Ford went back to the quiet performance of her duties, wondering a little what kind of a person this new mistress would prove, and doubtful whether it was a bride or a wife of long standing, whom she would be called upon to obey.

The appointed days passed by, and the whole household, as I have said, was in a state of expectation. A low hum came up from the city, as if a vast hive of bees were swarming, but the sound was so distant and faint, that it rather deepened the quiet of the place. All at once the noise of wheels inside the lodge gate sounded distinct, and grew stronger, till a carriage, from which a lady looked forth with every appearance of keen interest, swept up to the front entrance.

Mr. Nelson stepped out of the carriage, looking almost nervously anxious.

"This is our home, Ellen. Tell me that you like it, and will be happy here," said the master of the mansion, holding her hand tightly as they stood on the lower step together.

The lady lifted her eyes to the beautiful *facade*, and for the moment seemed overpowered by its great beauty.

"Why, Nelson, this is a palace," she said, while a glow of triumphant vanity spread over her face.

"To what else should I bring my queen?" he answered, bending his flushed face toward her and speaking in a voice that thrilled with passionate tenderness. "Oh, Ellen, my wife, if you desired the stars of heaven I would strive to reach them for you."

"How very, very beautiful it is!" she exclaimed, gazing around with triumph beaming in her face, utterly ignoring his passionate outburst. "I have dreamed of such places, but never saw them. Nelson, we shall live like princes here!"

"Princes are not always happy," he said, smiling upon her in a way that only a naturally grave man ever smiles. "But we, Ellen, we will let neither discord or care come near us. If gold can hedge us in we will heap walls so high that nothing but love can reach us."

"Ah, these are not dreams," she said, drawing a deep

breath. "The man who has power enough to create a palace like this, makes no false boast when he talks of golden walls."

She stood a moment, drinking in the scene with greedy admiration. Then, for the first time that day, she turned her eyes full upon Nelson's face, and smiled upon him.

"You are pleased, my wife."

"I am delighted, Nelson."

"Nelson! when I call you wife?" he said, with reproachful tenderness.

"Well, husband."

As the word left her lips an unaccountable pallor spread over both their faces. Instead of the happiness he expected, the husband of two days felt a pang so heavy that it made him shrink; and the woman—she had uttered the word before, and under different surroundings!

With a sudden and heavy cloud upon them these persons turned from each other without speaking, and mounted the steps.

To have seen Mrs. Nelson passing along the tresselated floor of the vestibule, where the servants were gathered to receive her, you would have believed that she had trod on Gobelin carpets all her life. The good housekeeper, who had dwelt in the atmosphere of nobility from her cradle up, was absolutely struck dumb by the queenliness of her presence, and thought in her heart that the new mistress must have come from abroad, or at least have been educated there.

Mrs. Nelson saw the impression she had made, and this gave graciousness to her presence which completely subdued the group of dependants into admiration. She said a few patronizing words to each, and passing through the vestibule, entered upon her new life with a degree of graceful self-possession which astonished even her husband.

And now commenced a career such as few persons ever carried out so triumphantly. Mrs. Nelson had wealth, unbounded beauty, education quite sufficient for the demands of fashion, and a craving ambition for notoriety, which was sure to make its way. Gold, in America, proves a sure road to this kind of distinction, and the great lever of republican society was used without stint or measure in this singular household.

Mrs. Nelson had seized on the insinuation, half put as a question by the housekeeper, regarding her foreign appearance, and accepted it as a truth—nay, more—so absorbing was her vanity that she allowed it to be understood that the great wealth which astonished everybody came into Mr. Nelson's hands through her own munificent affection; an idea that Mr. Nelson rather encouraged by his silence and entire submission to her will in all things.

It was not many months before the beautiful Mrs. Nelson became a star of magnitude in the fashionable circles of New York. Of course she was an object of great interest; when curious persons inquired about her origin, they were answered that she was an American by birth, but had spent most of her life abroad with her first husband, who had left her a young and beautiful widow with enormous wealth. This wealth she had bestowed on Mr. Nelson, who, after travelling all over the world, had fallen in love with her at first sight, and still regarded her with a sort of adoration, as everybody could see.

If there was any thing hollow or false in all this, the most intimate person in that magnificent household never could find the proof. True, Mr. Nelson was not a gay or particularly cheerful husband, but that might be said of a thousand other men with dashing wives; it was, after all, a matter of constitution only. Certainly the lady was altogether the most popular of the two. The material style of her beauty was of that sumptuous order which wealth embellishes to its greatest perfection. She was witty, gay, and for all the superficial uses of society, a fascinating woman, whom the most ultra among the fashionable, were glad to recognize as a leader. Thus, unlimited control of wealth, and unflinching assurance, placed the widow Mason, in a few short months, in the very heart of our Metropolitan society.

CHAPTER LI.

THE DAY BEFORE TRIAL.

THERE is no unendurable sorrow which is not the outgrowth of some sin. A peaceful conscience cannot be rendered altogether miserable, place it where you will. You would not have suspected that the fair young creature who sat within those prison bars from morning till night, when her misery was lost in the darkness, had been charged with the dread crime of murder. Indeed, a person with quick sensibilities might have regarded her rather as some gentle martyr, waiting to seal her faith by sublime suffering, for a more heavenly face than hers never appeared behind the rusted gratings of a dungeon.

Up to this time, Katharine had been a bright and very beautiful girl; such graces as youth, bloom, and cheerfulness give, she had possessed in perfection, but she was something more now. The roses had died on her cheeks, but a pure whiteness rested there, more lovely by far. The dimples had faded from the corners of her mouth, but an expression of holy sweetness was left behind, that sometimes deepened to a smile when any one spoke to her with unusual kindness. But her eyes—those who have seen the original Beatrice Cenci, where it hangs an embodied sorrow in that old Roman palace, would ask no farther description of the look which slept forever in the deep blue orbs of the American girl; there was, indeed, a difference to be felt rather than portrayed. Through all the exquisite sadness in those eyes, a terrible remembrance sleeps, which leads you to forgive, but not altogether acquit, the Cenci. But with Katharine nothing but sublime innocence lay beneath the sorrow. The expression of the living eyes was mournful as those of the immortal picture, but you looked upon them with less pain.

Thus in the twilight of her prison she sat reading the family Bible, which had been brought to that place by her mother. It was an old book, worn with much handling, the paper yellow with age, and the leathern cover broke at the corners. Since Katharine's remembrance, this Bible had occupied the round candle stand by her mother's bed. When that singular woman first entered the prison, after giving up her home, she laid this most precious of her treasures upon the young girl's lap, without speaking a word. Katharine knew what this

THE DAY BEFORE TRIAL. 357

act imported, and bowed her fair head in thankfulness, for she sorely lacked the comfort those holy pages might bring.

Katharine had never been a great reader, but her intellect was clear, and her heart, rendered earnest by suffering, seized upon the solemn truths of that book as a flower absorbs the air and sunshine, until she grew strong beneath their lessons.

Not long after that Bible was laid in her lap, much of the horrible dread of death went out from her soul. In its holy pages she found how tranquilly innocence could die, how trustfully it could repose in the hands of God, and from that day the sublime beauty that I have mentioned dawned on her face.

Thus, as I said awhile ago, Katharine sat in her prison, reading. The Bible lay open on her lap; but while her eyelids drooped, and their lashes shaded those deep blue orbs, they were tinged with the depths of their color, as violets cast purple shadows where the sun touches them. The golden tresses of her hair, embraided around her head, scintillated the sunbeams that fell through her prison bars like a glory. Her dress was white dimity, a fabric much worn in those days, which fell heavily around her like the marble drapery of a statue. Thus she was surrounded with a whiteness which threw her figure out in strong relief from a background of shadows gathering on the walls of her dungeon.

As the last sunbeam left the heavy bars that rusted across the window, she lifted her eyes and waited, with one hand—alas! snow-white from confinement—resting upon the open page. A footstep near the door, and the jingle of keys, had disturbed her. She looked earnestly toward the noise until the door opened. Then the expression of her face grew animated. She laid the Bible down upon her bed, and moved forward with both hands extended.

"You have come; ah, I knew it; when did you break a promise."

The old man who entered took her hand softly between his two hard palms, and glancing at the open Bible, said:

"You were well employed, child; I can bring you no better company than that."

Katharine looked back upon the Bible, smiling faintly, the only way she ever smiled in those days.

"Yes, I know," she said; "but you look pale, have you brought news for me?"

"Yes, dear," said old Mrs. Thrasher, coming forward and kissing the prisoner, "he brings news, but keep a good heart. God is above all."

Katharine bent her head an instant and stood before them in silence, then she looked gravely up and said:

"Is it to-morrow."

"Yes, Katharine, it is to-morrow; are you ready?" answered the old man.

"Yes, father, I am ready."

Her voice was low, but clear as the fall of water-drops.

"I am ready to live or to die as God shall will it. Our Lord has told me how to do both."

"Blessed be his holy name!" broke forth the old man.

"Amen," whispered the gentle woman by his side.

Katharine clasped her hands and lifted her eyes upward, while her lips moved silently.

"We have good counsel; every thing has been done that lies within mortal power," said Mr. Thrasher.

"I know it. The lawyers were here questioning me. They told me it might be soon, but to-morrow—that is sudden."

"But it will be over in a little while," said Mrs. Thrasher, anxious to throw in her mite of consolation.

"Yes, it will be over, and then——"

Katharine's voice trembled. She was so young, poor thing, and sometimes her timid nature fell away from the faith that gave it strength, and shuddered at the death before her.

"Then and now we must put our faith in Him," answered the old man, with tender solemnity.

"I know—I do, father!"

There was something very sweet in the way she uttered this little word "father." Indeed, Katharine had been brought to trust in the old man so thoroughly that she followed him as a lamb keeps by the side of its shepherd. But for his mild, firm teachings, the poor child must have fallen under the burden of her misfortunes, and the sorrow of her young life might have taken a different course.

"What is sorrow, what is death itself, compared to the pangs of guilt, my child?"

"I know, father, but death seems terrible to me sometimes when I am alone here in the night."

Mrs. Thrasher began to sob and Mrs. Allen looked down upon her child in pale grief.

"Ah, why cannot I, who am old, and used to trouble, take her place," she said, drearily.

"Yes, mother, I want courage. At first, when they left me, I was a coward, but it is not so of late, at least not often. Something here grows stronger every day."

The girl laid one hand on her heart, while a soft glow came to her face.

"And that is faith," said Mr. Thrasher.

"It seems like a living presence; as if my babe had turned to an angel, and were folding its wings here. How can any one think I killed it—I who gloried so in being its mother."

"We know that you never harmed it," said Mrs. Allen. "That is one comfort, my child."

"No, no; we never thought it, neither your father nor your two mothers," said Mrs. Thrasher, planting herself by Mrs. Allen's side; thus suggesting her own right to be considered.

"It is strange," said Katharine, thoughtfully, "very strange that any one can believe such things of a poor girl. I am sure no woman in the world ever got this idea of herself."

"No woman would have the heart to think it," muttered Mrs. Thrasher; "but the law, that is stern and cruel enough for any thing."

"To-morrow it will prove cruel with me, I am sure," said Katharine; "when they took me away from home the little children looked after me as if there was blood on my clothes. It made my heart ache to see their frightened faces at the windows as the wagon went by. If children can judge one so harshly, what will a court full of stern men do."

"The men who look so stern are sometimes very kind at heart," said Mr. Thrasher.

Katharine lifted her eyes to his face.

"You will be there, father, and you—and you, my mothers?"

"Yes, Katharine, we will be there," said both the women at once.

"And a greater than they will be there, Katharine," added the old man, solemnly, and resting one hand on her head a moment, he turned away.

The two women saw that his lip quivered as he passed through the door, but to Katharine he was an embodiment of sublime strength, and it took away half her courage when his shadow disappeared from the threshold of her prison. Alas, she was nothing but a girl, timid from want of experience, and greatly dependent for strength on those she loved. When Katharine Allen was left alone she began to realize that the day of her great trouble was near at hand. A faintness like that of death itself crept over her, and she sat down in the midst of her dungeon chamber, sinking down upon the floor in a wild, dreary way, that would have brought tears to the eyes of her worst enemy.

By many an anxious question she had won from the jailer a general knowledge of the forms which attend a criminal trial. She knew that crowds of curious people, perhaps coarse-hearted people, would jostle her on the way to prison—that scores on scores of eyes would follow her with hate and loathing. She saw the band of jurors grasping her life in their will, listening with heavy countenances to the evidence of a crime that was not hers, but of which it seemed impossible that any human tribunal could absolve her.

Then, going to and from the trial, little children would look up at her as they had done when she passed the red school-house at Shrub Oak, some with timid pity, others with coarse amazement, and others still ready to break forth into hoots and sneers, as if some abhorrent animal had crossed their path. These thoughts were hard to endure. She had so dearly loved little children, and turned so naturally for affection toward all living things, that the edict of hate, though undeserved, made her shrink with absolute pain.

She took up her Bible and tried to read, but the letters ran together on the page, harassing her sight, but giving back no sense. Thus the evening found her going out into blank space till the darkness crept through her prison bars and fell over her like a pall.

CHAPTER LII.

THE STREETS AND THE COURT HOUSE.

THE next day found a crowd around the court house, hours before the time for opening—an eager-eyed, jostling throng, to whom a trial for life was sure to bring keen excitement of some kind. In a Puritan State, where places of amusement are seldom found, any thing calculated to excite public curiosity is an event which makes the most painful occasions a sort of holiday for the populace. The horrible fascination which a trial like that always possesses for the human mind was added to other feelings with which the people of that day frequented the courts of justice, and any trial which had a tragic interest for the people, drew crowds around the court house, full of eager curiosity, and sometimes almost ferocious excitement—crowds which watched the progress of events like men enthralled by the horror of a terrible play.

The events which caused the arrest of Katharine Al-

THE STREETS AND COURT HOUSE.

len had been a favorite theme of conversation for months. Public excitement was at its highest pitch; and, when the day of her trial came, a stranger, passing through the streets, might have believed that some event was transpiring in which the highest interests of the whole community were at stake.

A crowd gathered about the old jail, which loomed up in the midst of the town—a dark monument of human sorrow and human crime. A moving throng was in every street which led from thence to the court house— men, women, and little children, brought out as for a holiday show, all waiting, breathless and eager, for the appearance of the poor girl they were ready to hunt to an ignominious death.

Now and then you passed a face that looked grave or sad, as if the moral lesson of that trial was felt, and not without sympathy for the poor young creature who was to be its object.

The crowd had been waiting for hours, and so singularly organized is this miserable human nature of ours, so dependent are our feelings upon the position in which we are placed, so completely do our sympathies waver to and fro, according to our particular situation, that it was noticeable, as time wore on, that murmurs grew harsher and more sullen. The hard faces grew harder; even those which had expressed something akin to pity lost their softness, and wherever a knot of such women as love scenes of this kind were gathered, execrations and complaints against the criminal were the most severe and cruel.

At last there was a little bustle in the jail yard; the crowd responded by eager murmurs. Slowly the heavy gates swung open; a simultaneous rush was made toward them, and it required all the efforts of the armed constables to force back the eager mob.

At length, a passage was made down the street, and the crowd pushed back on either side. Then slowly, with a dull, ominous sound, a wagon, drawn by a single horse, rolled out of the jail yard and took its way through the street.

In this wagon, with an officer upon either side, sat Katharine Allen.

She was deadly pale, her sunny hair, too bright for a scene like that, was brushed smoothly back under her bonnet; a large shawl was thrown over her white dress, and she sat between her guards so still and silent that she hardly seemed conscious of her position, or terrified by the danger which gathered closer and closer about her.

A new murmur of pity went up from the people who thronged the sidewalks. In her statue-like quiet, the girl looked so young and fair, it appeared incredible that she could have been guilty of the crime with which she was charged.

At that sound, Katharine raised her head quickly, her great eyes wandered to and fro, hopeless, helpless, a vivid crimson swept over her whole countenance, then it faded almost as quickly as it came, leaving the features paler than before. With a low moan, the poor young creature closed her eyes, her lips moved tremulously. Amid all the terror of that scene—with judgment and death so near—a calm, such as she had not before felt, settled down upon her soul.

I do believe that in that hour of supreme agony, God sent His angels to whisper comfort and peace. By no human law could one have accounted for the change which came over her.

On through the street passed the little cortege, the constables marching in front, and pushing aside the people, who, faithful to their New England instincts, yielded almost ungrumblingly to the dictates of those armed with the power they so reverenced—that of the law.

Katharine did not look up again; the deathly pallor had left her face; but around the lips, which still moved at intervals, a smile had settled like a ray of sunlight.

It was a glorious morning; the sun lay golden and warm upon the town; it fell caressingly upon the girl in the prison wagon, revealing her broadly to the rude gaze of those curious eyes.

As they approached the court house, the crowd grew denser. The wagon moved more and more slowly, and the people grew keenly eager, as if curiosity and interest had reached a climax when the victim was about disappearing from their sight.

The court room was a bare, gloomy apartment, where every thing seemed to deepen the usual horror connected with such a place—a dark chamber where the shadows never wholly dispersed. No matter how brightly the sun shone without, the golden radiance broke against the window panes, as if frightened by the appearance of the place, and in passing through the dusty windows, seemed to lose all brilliancy and warmth.

On that day it was packed with a dense crowd, all waiting eagerly for the entrance of the girl whose conviction they had come to witness.

Every one was there—the judge upon his bench, cold and silent as a marble image of justice; the jury in their box, and, a little way off, the witnesses.

Mrs Allen sat by the side of old Mr. Thrasher; he

had taken her hand, meaning to speak some last word of consolation, but the agony in her eyes froze the words upon his lips; he could only hold fast to that withered hand, which in her anguish she wrenched away from him, impatient even of sympathy.

The dead silence of the court room was broken by a dull murmur from without, through which the rattle of the wagon wheels was distinctly audible.

A sound upon the stairs—the tread of heavy feet, and the door swung slowly upon its hinges. A shiver ran through Mrs. Allen's frame; she sank heavily back, moaning. She knew that her child had been brought in; she heard the bustle with which they placed her in the criminal's seat, but when she tried to raise her eyes it seemed as if the lids had turned to iron.

When silence was again restored she made one violent effort and looked up. Katharine was sitting still and white in her place of shame. The mother half rose, with a vague impulse to rush forward and save her child. That moment Katharine lifted her heavy eyes, and met that longing gaze—unconsciously she extended her arms.

"Mother! oh, mother!"

The words died on those white lips in a moan so faint that it failed to reach the most eager listener. Then the stern old woman leaned heavily back in her seat, and fainted away so quietly that no human soul was aware of it.

CHAPTER LIII.

THE DOCTOR'S EVIDENCE

OUT upon the steps of the court house were a couple of men who had been Mrs. Allen's neighbors, and had known Katharine from childhood. There they stood, unable to gain entrance to the court—talking one to the other in subdued voices.

At last, a man from the same neighborhood forced his way through the crowd upon the stairs and hurried up to the spot where they stood.

The men turned toward him with eager questions, while he wiped his face with a huge silk pocket handkerchief, breathing hard, like a man who had been engaged in some painful struggle.

"How do they get on, Mr. Amos?" asked one of the men.

"They've just had her mother up," he answered, in a low voice. "I couldn't stand it a minit longer—I felt as if I was choking to death."

"What did she say?"

"Oh, it wasn't that. She went toward the stand quiet enough, but just as they held the Bible out to her she looked up at Katharine, and begun to shake so that one of the constables had to take hold of her."

"What did the girl do?"

"She kind o' raised herself and looked at her mother. I can't tell you what it was like. I've seen a lamb look like it when the knife was at its throat. The old woman tried to stand up firm, but when she saw that poor cretur she just laid her head down on the railing and begun shaking and sobbing like every thing, but she didn't shed a single tear. When she lifted her head again, Katharine looked at her and smiled. She did actually, but it was enough to break a man's heart. I'd rather a seen her cry right out a thousand times."

The farmer paused here, took out his silk handkerchief again, and turned his face away.

"Poor gal," muttered one of his listeners; "it seems as if it was only yesterday I see her dancing about like a little poppet, with her curls hanging down her shoulders. I can't believe she did it, I can't, in spite of every thing; 'taint in natur."

"What's that they are saying?" cried one of the group. "The doctor's called up; I want to hear his evidence. Come, let's try and crowd in."

The two men joined forces, and elbowed their way into the court room again, not unfriendly to the poor girl, as our readers have seen, but resolved against losing a single feature of the scene they had come ten miles to witness.

It was, indeed, the doctor whose name had been called. He was enrolled among the witnesses of the prosecution; but those who knew that eccentric, but really great man, had an idea that, in attempting to criminate the poor girl by that witness, the law would find its match. The lawyers themselves partook somewhat of this feeling, and rather shrunk from the keen sarcasm and sly wit with which he was likely to retort upon any professional encroachment. As for his old neighbors, the doctor's evidence was a point in the trial which engaged their keenest interest. They held a sort of property right in the doctor's reputation for curt eccentricity, and were anxious to pit him against the lawyers in the most striking manner before the assembled wisdom of all Connecticut.

Thus, hundreds of faces, familiar about Bungy, Falls Hill, and Chewstown, brightened eagerly when the doctor's name was called out, and murmurs ran through the crowd that now those city lawyers would find their match. No mistake about it!

The doctor, who had been sitting in a corner of the court room, watching the proceedings with vigilant attention, heard his name called, and arose. You would hardly have known the man, as he made a slow progress toward the witness stand. The usual quaint smile had left his lips, and his eyes, always full of droll or sarcastic humor, were bright with the dignity of an earnest purpose. He stood upon the witness stand, leaning heavily on his crutches; but, notwithstanding this disadvantage, a dignity was imparted to his presence that no one could resist—you would not have believed that a droll saying had ever passed those lips.

The prisoner leaned forward, clasped her hands, and pressing them heavily on her lap, looked at him in wild dismay. The change in all his features struck her with terror; it seemed as if he had suddenly turned her enemy.

The doctor observed this wild astonishment, and his face softened a little; nay, those stern features began to quiver, and he was obliged to look down a moment to recover himself.

"May it please the Court," he said at length, motioning the person away who came forward to administer the oath. "I am a physician, and bound by a professional oath not to reveal the secrets of my patient. I am not sure that any knowledge which I have would bear against this poor girl, and from the depths of my heart I believe her innocent, but I ask to be excused from bearing evidence in the case."

There was a moment's consultation among the counsel. That for the prosecution sprung up as if there had been high treason in the doctor's speech, and insisted that no distinctions should be made in his favor. A great crime had been committed against the Commonwealth, an unnatural crime, and the ends of justice demanded that every means should be used for obtaining the truth. The judge yielded to, or rather sustained his argument, and the doctor was courteously desired to take the oath.

A gleam in the doctor's eye, and a keen glance at the prosecuting attorney, prepared his friends for a sharp encounter of wits, but he was a man to rise steadily with the occasion. Terrible interests were at stake here, and his true character rose out of its eccentricity. He took the oath reverently, and stated the facts already known to the reader, in a clear, impressive manner that told greatly upon the jury, but sheltering himself within the strict limits of the law, he volunteered nothing, neither did he shrink from any question propounded to him; all this struck his friends with a sort of awe. They were profoundly impressed by the dignity of his course, but a little disappointed, nevertheless. Once the doctor turned and looked anxiously on the prisoner. It was when the lawyer asked if Katharine had exhibited any anxiety to conceal the birth of her child from the neighbors—if, in fact, she had not requested the doctor to keep it a secret.

The doctor hesitated, moved uneasily, and half wheeled

around, as if determined to leave the witness stand, for he knew what effect his answer would have.

Katharine leaned more decidedly toward him, and while the court was hushed under a general anxiety to hear his reply, her sweet, clear voice penetrated through the silence.

"Speak, doctor; I did ask you not to tell—I was afraid of what they would think."

The officer stepped forward to enforce silence, and the prisoner shrunk back affrighted.

Now the doctor's stern lip began to quiver, and his keen eyes flashed sharp as steel through the tears that shot into them, for the first time, perhaps, since his manhood.

"Yes," he said, "if you will force me to it—she did make this request; but it was only for a little delay. The poor child wished her secret kept till some one should return."

"And who was that person?"

Katharine's lips parted, and she held her breath with keen interest till the answer was given.

"I do not know."

"And she never told you?"

"She never did."

"And you have no suspicion who this person was?"

"Suspicion is not evidence. I have no knowledge."

The questions now took a professional turn, and the doctor's evidence bore strongly in favor of the prisoner. His deep knowledge, and clear elucidation of medical theories bearing on the case, made a deep impresssion upon the jury, and threw out gleams of light that were adopted with avidity by the defence.

Indeed, the doctor, acting himself under a clear conviction of the prisoner's innocence, contributed more than any other person in fastening the same idea upon the court. But one terrible fact remained immovable—the burial of the child. The apparent forethought by which this had been accomplished. The time seized upon during the absence of the mother. What eloquence could sweep these fatal truths from the case? None, none!

CHAPTER LIV.

THE VERDICT.

ONCE more Mrs. Allen was put upon the stand to undergo the questions which had been so fruitless with the doctor. It was this point of the case alone which struck terror to the prisoner. When a question was asked which apparently threatened to drag her husband's name through that tortuous investigation, her lips would blanch and her eyes fill with sharp anxiety. Thus her face gleamed out white and ghastly when Mrs. Allen was put under the torture of new questions. The mother looked at her gravely, and turned to the judge; but when the attorney proceeded with his interrogations, she answered simply:

"I am her mother. Let me go."

They did let her go. The attorney had no heart to press that pale, tortured woman farther, and became generous, partly from humanity, partly because there was something in the face of his witness which warned him that nothing short of death would force her to speak.

Unfortunately he had evidence enough, and could afford to take this poor mother from the rack of his questions.

When this danger was over, the prisoner fell back into her previous state of gentle resignation. So long as her husband's reputation was safe, so long as his name was kept out of the proceedings, she had no feeling of resistance.

The business of the court went on. All the details of that strange death and burial, so far as known evidence could give them, were laid before the court. The prisoner heard them like one in a dream. Once or twice she lifted those mournful eyes as some detail struck suddenly on her remembrance; but the connecting links being deficient in her mind, baffled its consciousness. Then a change came upon the court. The witness stand was empty, and a tall, hard-faced man stood before the judge, pledging himself to prove her guilt Katharine heard him with a sort of dreary amazement How sturdily he denounced her. How bitter were his words. How cruelly sharp those dark eyes as they turned from the jury to her face. Poor thing, it seemed very cruel. What had she done that a strong man should hunt her to death with his words.

Then another man arose. She knew him, for he had visited her in prison. The look which he cast upon her was full of compassion. He pleaded for her like one inspired. His face was pale with emotion—his voice faltered and his eyes filled when he turned to make a last appeal to the twelve men who held her life in their hands. In the midst of this appeal, Katharine came out of her dream and began to weep from self pity. Her sufferings all rose vividly before her, but it seemed another person she was pitying, not herself. She met the softened glances turned toward the place where she sat with tender sympathy, as if they were all deploring the misery of some third person. Thus, a faint glow shone out from the pallor of her face, which deepened the sentiment in her behalf.

Then the judge arose with his face to the jury. His voice was slow and grave, his countenance sad. She could not comprehend him. He was neither stern like her enemy, nor pathetic like her friend. Still, under his seriousness she felt that some pity for her youth existed. When he sat down she gave him a long, sorrowful look, which he broke by lifting one hand to his face as if those eyes troubled him.

The twelve men arose and went out, one after another, like mourners at a funeral. Then a murmur ran through the court, and suppressed whispers went from lip to lip. She knew that these men held her life, but could not realize that their fiat was so near. Time went by. It might have been minutes, it might have been hours, for aught she knew, since those men had left their seats empty. The court was still thronged. The judge sat in his arm-chair, shrouding his face with one hand.

A faint bustle. The twelve men glided into their old places, and a voice, deep, solemn, and stern, spoke out:

"Prisoner, look upon the jury—jury, look upon the prisoner."

Katharine stood up. Those twelve men met her mournful gaze with shrinking glances.

"Guilty, or not guilty?"

"Guilty! But not of murder in the first degree. Not guilty unto death!"

There was a hushed tumult in the crowd. Those who

looked upon her face rejoiced that she was saved the last penalty. Some muttered bitterly against the verdict, and grew indignant with the jury for depriving them of a death spectacle; and a few said, in their hearts, this verdict is unjust—that young creature is innocent.

Katharine sat down; a band, hard and firm as iron, that had seemed tightening around her heart all the day, broke, and flooded her being with tears. Poor, poor child! she had been so afraid to die. Amid all her heroism, there was a perpetual dread, which made her gentle nature shrink from the horror before her. Besides, death would take her away from *him*, perhaps, forever and ever. This thought had been the most cruel of all. But it was over now. They would not take her life—she might see him again—he would love her all the better for having shielded his name from this trouble and disgrace; at any rate, she would not die, she would not die.

Overwhelmed with these feelings, she heard nothing that was going on in the court, but sat with her hands clasped and quivering in her lap, while the tears fell, drop by drop, down her cheeks, whispering:

"I live! I live! and shall see him again!"

A voice called forth her name, commanding her to stand up and hear the sentence of the court.

She arose, supporting herself by the railing, for the last few moments had left her very weak. Her eyes were full of tears. She saw the judge through a mist, and his words sounded from a great distance.

"Condemned to sit upon a gallows, erected on the public common of New Haven, for one hour, with a halter around your neck; and, after that, to be confined in the State's Prison, at Simsbury Mines, during eight years."

She heard words of kindly encouragement and entreaty to use the mercy extended by the court as a means of repentance. Her great sin, unnatural cruelty. Time for reformation—fragments like these floated by her, but they left no impression. She only comprehended one thing—they had given her life! life! life! life!

She sunk on her knees as the judge ceased, buried her face on the criminal's seat—and thanked God that he had permitted her to live. The old widow had sat through it all quiet—as great suffering most frequently is—pale as death, but with a certain stern fortitude which a Spartan mother might have felt without shame. When the jury came in she arose with slow unconsciousness, and stood upright in the presence of the court, her gray eyes heavy with anguish, her white lips parted in an agony of suspense. Guilty, but not unto death. She lifted her clasped hands feebly upward, and fell back, sobbing like a little child.

CHAPTER LV.

THE TRAIL OF THE SERPENT.

No more brilliant house than that of Mrs. Nelson could be found in the city of New York. This woman had flashed upon society like a meteor. Her dress—her style so original that they were taken to be foreign. Her quick wit and sumptuous beauty won hosts of admirers. Her carriage was the most splendid and nobly appointed of any that appeared in the fashionable thoroughfares. Every thing rich and unique that a prodigal taste could imagine or money obtain, was to be found in her home. All the costly adornments which her husband had prepared for her, with so much solicitude, were crowded into side rooms and entrance halls, while she filled the principal apartments after a fancy entirely her own. The great joy of her life was in spending money, and in parading the result before the world. To defy emulation and excite envy was her crowning desire. Yet, with all this prodigality, she was never generous, never felt the sweet impulses of charity, or knew the gentle bliss of self-sacrifice.

It sometimes, nay, often happens, that those who rise from poverty to sudden wealth, are more hard-hearted than persons born to affluence. This may arise from a reluctance to review painful or humiliating associations; or it may be that, with some characters, poverty has a hardening process, and, when lifted above it, they feel a sort of pleasure in seeing others suffer as they have done. This is a bad phase of human nature—but who can say that it seldom presents itself in society.

Mrs. Nelson was one of these women. She would not, knowingly, have perpetrated a crime, or done a palpable injustice; but her whole life was made up of trivial vanity and intense selfishness. What little feeling she possessed, had been sacrificed to a craving desire for wealth, and she bent all her faculties to one end, that of securing all its privileges and enjoyments to herself.

It was not long before her husband became convinced of this; for real and deep passion rendered him keen sighted. His character, naturally stern and silent, grew bitter under this one thought; but the fatal love which had led him to lavish so much upon her, still imprisoned his heart as the serpents of the laocoon coil around their victims.

A few months of married life, and this was the condition in which the Nelsons found themselves. He a lonely, sullen slave — she reckless and egotistical, at the best—sometimes insolent in her exactions, and always ungrateful. But this did not impair her popularity, or, in truth, meet public observation at all. To the world she was every thing charming. But it is at home we must seek this woman in order to judge her aright in this new phase of her strange life.

It was Mrs. Nelson's caprice to breakfast alone in a little room which opened to the sunniest nook of the flower garden. In less than three weeks after her marriage she began to separate her life from that of her husband in every possible manner, and absolutely sold the fragments of time which she doled out to him, bartering them off unblushingly for some new extravagance, until even his absorbing passion revolted at her egotism.

The room that we speak of was really an exquisite affair in its way; very cheerful and sumptuous in all its appointments. Lace curtains were looped back from the deep windows, so heavy with embroidery that they fell over the pure plate-glass like snow wreaths floating over ice. Through this transparent cloud came the cool rustle of tree boughs, the gleam of flowers, and glimpses of warm sunshine, turning the grass to a golden green. A broad mirror, surmounted by a wreath of gilded foliage, reflected back this out-door picture from its limpid surface. The carpet appeared but a continuation of the blossoming turf without; you seemed to trample upon a living flower at every step, and the foot sank luxuriously into its rich pile, as if pressing wood moss in a forest. The hangings upon the walls were of pale green clustering with golden roses. Small tables of oriental alabaster and delicate mosaic supported vases of flowers, which shed a delicate perfume through the apartment. Two easy chairs of the most elaborate construction, and a couch that yielded to pressure like down, completed the rich assemblage.

Most regally did this apartment frame in the queenly woman who formed a tableau of wonderful effect in its centre. The rare tone of her beauty demanded delicate tints, and these were in direct contrast with the colors that predominated in the room. Morning dresses, as they are now worn, were not then in vogue, but a Canton crape dress, of a glowing red, fell across her bosom in surplice folds, revealing glimpses of costly lace underneath; the sleeves fitted her symmetrical arms to the elbow, where they terminated in a fall of frost-like lace. A gossamer cap seemed to have settled like a butterfly on the lustrous tresses coiled around her proud head, which she crushed ruthlessly against the back of her chair, rather than change her idle position. She held a newspaper in her hand, while her foot rested on the ebony claw of a small table, on which the frosted silver and delicate china of a breakfast service were arranged.

Mrs. Nelson was no reader, but she loved to drone over the morning papers after breakfast, picking up such fragments of gossip and news as floated through their columns with satisfaction, so long as no effort of thought was necessary. Thus her eyes roved restlessly over the paper in her hand until they fell upon the heading of a paragraph that sent the bloom for a moment from her cheeks. It was an account of Katharine Allen's trial. She read it breathlessly from beginning to end. A cloud gathered on her fair forehead as she proceeded, which grew dark and stormy when she approached the termination.

Jealousy is more likely to spring from self-love than from pure affection. The pang which Mrs. Nelson felt was not the less keen because she had no real regard for the man whom she had married. Her arrogant vanity had been pampered till its craving could not be satisfied, and the idea that another would dare lift admiring eyes to the man it had been her pleasure to select, wounded her almost as if she had possessed a heart. She remembered Katharine Allen as she had appeared that night at her own humble home in the pine woods, and a clear conviction fell upon her that Nelson Thrasher was in some way implicated in the trouble that had fallen upon the girl. Had he—her slave, her spaniel, whom it was her right to caress or spurn, dared to swerve from his allegiance to her, even when she was the wife of another?

The question filled her heart with bitter scorn. She gloried over the fact that this girl would be degraded and crushed out of respectable life for having presumed to cross her path. She remembered the delicate beauty which had been so remarkable that evening, and bit her lips fiercely as the idea presented itself, that less adroit management on her part might have placed Katharine in the honorable possession of all she enjoyed so keenly. What if he should relent, even then? What if the knowledge of this poor girl's terrible position should touch the heart she had herself trampled down so insolently, while it was loading her with benefits!

She grasped the paper in her hand—no, no, he must never hear the news it contained. She would change her course, and strive to endure his society. He had grown sullen of late. What if his love for her should change. The crowning passion of her character revolted at this, but still a lurking fear crept in, and she reflected that the slavery of a strong heart would not last forever.

She touched a curious little bell that stood on the table, and a servant opened the door.

"Send me all the papers that have been brought this morning!"

The man went away and returned with several of the morning journals; she glanced them over hurriedly, pressing her lips hard, while each column was scanned. That paragraph was only to be found in the paper that lay crushed in her lap. She arose hurriedly, and passing through the entrance hall, swept toward the kitchen.

The cook stopped in the middle of the floor, struck with astonishment by the presence of her haughty mistress in that place. Mrs. Nelson walked toward the range, and taking up a heavy poker, thrust the newspaper into the fire, holding it down till the fragments floated in black flakes over her hand. She laid the poker down, observing that the woman was regarding her curiously.

"Send in coffee, and some of those delicate French rolls which Mr. Nelson is so fond of," she said, indifferently; "with any other nice thing you can pick up."

CHAPTER LVI.

LOVE'S GOLDEN HARVEST.

THE cook was full of regrets that madame had been compelled to give her own orders, and, amid a world of protestations, Mrs. Nelson went back to her room. Soon after she rang the bell with emphasis, and directly that exquisite breakfast service was re-arranged for two, and one of the silken easy chairs rolled opposite her own.

"Go tell Mr. Nelson that I am waiting for him to breakfast with me," she said, drawing close to the table, and forcing the clouds from her face.

She waited impatiently till the man came back, tapping the carpet with her restless foot. What if she had gone too far? If he ever could have thought of another might it not be so again? and she so completely in his power, so helpless without his wealth.

The servant came back.

"Mr. Nelson's compliments, but he had taken breakfast hours ago."

The woman absolutely turned pale. It was the first time he had ever refused an advance of any kind from her. She arose, stood in thought an instant, and then left the room.

"Master is in his office, madame," said the servant.

"Yes, I know—he was not well this morning."

She swept through the hall again, and crossing two or three rooms, entered one in the extreme southern wing of the house. In this place, Nelson had, of late, taken his meals alone. It was simply an office upon the ground floor, containing a few chairs, an oaken bookcase, heavy with carving, and a library table, which stood in the centre of a small Persian carpet. There was nothing very remarkable in this apartment, except one thing. The floor was paved like the entrance hall, with a rich mosaic pattern of variously tinted marble. Mrs. Nelson felt a chill from the stones through her thin slippers, and exclaimed:

"Dear me, Nelson, what a dreary place you have! All wood work and stone. I never observed how very comfortless it was before."

Nelson was locking something in a drawer of his writing-table, and his face was bent, but she saw the blood rush to his forehead.

"I do not find it disagreeable," he said, gravely.

"Ah, but my room is so much pleasanter," she said, approaching the table, and laying a hand caressingly on his arm.

He rose up suddenly, shaking her hand away.

The color mounted to her temples, but she controlled the temper that burned within her.

"You are out of sorts, dear husband; and I am lonesome. Come away from this cold room."

"It is not colder than usual," he answered, curtly; but a thrill ran through his frame and the blood tingled in his veins. She had never called him by that endearing name but once before, not even in the first days of their marriage.

Her hand had fallen lightly on his wrist—she felt the leap of the pulse, and smiled with inward triumph.

"Come, come. I am getting angry. How could you neglect me so? Busy, busy, all the time; about what?

and I left alone! Come—this morning I will take no refusal! You *shall* breakfast with me!"

Nelson took her hand, grasping it hard, and looked steadily in her face.

"Ellen, what is the meaning of this?"

"It means that I want to see my husband now and then, or he will forget how much I love him."

Nelson shook his head. This sweet flattery was too sudden. It lacked the ring of truth, and he felt it.

He looked at her sternly.

"Ellen!"

"Well, what is it?"

"What do you desire in exchange for these minutes of deception?"

"Nelson!"

"It is a simple question. If you have any wish ungratified, speak. This cajolery is not necessary."

"You are cruel, Nelson."

He saw the tears mount slowly to her eyes; the hand which touched his, trembled.

"You have ceased to love me, Nelson?"

She asked this question breathlessly; all the splendor of her position seemed fading away. Her lips grew white, and she leaned heavily on the table. Ambition spoke loudly as her heart should have done.

Her evident grief made his pulses leap. The white lips—the trembling of those limbs. The emotion thus betrayed must be genuine. He stood irresolute, looking at her. The thick lashes drooped over her eyes, her bosom began to heave.

"Ellen, is this real?"

She lifted those velvety eyes to his, and the man was her slave again

Three weeks from this day, two important things were concluded. A deed of gift, conveying the mansion house, was made out in favor of Ellen Nelson, and a large amount of foreign gold was deposited in one of the leading city banks, subject to her order. Those few sweet words had brought her a golden harvest; but what was that compared to the vast wealth which still remained in her husband's power? wealth that could not be brought out in the face of the world, though she had never been permitted to know its hiding-place. While her husband held this great secret back from her knowledge she could not feel altogether secure, for what was moderate wealth to a woman who had dreamed so long of millions?

In the depth of his heart, Nelson may have felt that his secret was the strongest tie that bound him to his wife. If so, it was one of those cruel thoughts that men put away from their souls only to feel them creeping back again like serpents. One thing is certain, he clung to the secret of his gold with stern tenacity, and watched all her stealthy movements toward it with the vigilance of a hound. The golden chains with which his wife was bound became more important to him every day. While he lived, that should fetter her to his side if love could not. When he died—a shudder ran through his soul as he thought of that. Was he certain that retribution would wait for him till then?

CHAPTER LVII.

ONE HOUR OF SHAME.

A VESSEL was being hauled in at the Long Wharf, at New Haven—a weather-beaten vessel—that gave evidence of a long voyage over the seas. Two men leaped from the deck, as she was slowly warped to her moorings, and stood together a few moments at the head of the wharf. They were both fine looking men, but in a different way. The one had a frank, honest countenance, that expressed great natural vigor of mind, joined with a physical organization of uncommon strength. The other was lighter, taller, and more decidedly intellectual every way. Indeed, a face like that was not met with on the same thoroughfare once in a twelvemonth.

This man seemed eager to be moving; he held a small portmanteau in his hands, while a few hurried words passed between him and his companion.

"Then you wont go into the town with me and give us both a fair start?" said the stouter of the two. "The stage starts from Buck's Tavern at daylight."

"No, no; I could not sleep, I could not rest within ten miles of home. Think how long I have been away —of all that has happened."

"But we are four hours too late for the morning stage, captain."

"I know; but what then? It is but an easy walk after all. I can be there before noon."

Rice laughed, and slily winked one eyelid.

"All right," he said; "this comes of being a married

man; a ten miles' tramp, with a heart fluttering like a partridge all the way. Well, we old bachelors have nothing to hurry for, and can afford to take it comfortably. I'll go down to Bucks, and be at the old woman's to supper. But keep dark; I want to come down upon her and Kate all of a sudden, to say nothing of that little shaver and cuff—so keep a close lip, captain."

The captain gave a happy laugh, thinking that he would be too pleasantly employed for any chance at gossip, so he promised silence very cordially, and the two shook hands.

"Good luck to you," exclaimed Rice, with hearty good will, "I'll be after you in short order."

They parted here. The man with the portmanteau walking with rapid strides toward the highway which led to the country, and our sailor friend taking a more leisurely course into the town.

He was so busy with thoughts of home at first that a certain bustle and excitement among the people upon the sidewalks failed to arrest his attention. But as he approached the heart of the city this unusual bustle aroused him. The people all seemed to be going one way, men hurried along in eager haste, women jostled against each other in their reckless movements, some dragging little children after them, and scolding their slow progress.

Rice followed the current. He, too, became anxious to see what was taking a whole population so completely in one direction, and having plenty of time, sauntered on, with the easy roll learned in his home on the rolling deep. He asked no questions, indeed he felt very little interest in the matter. Something was going on—it might be a political meeting, or "a general training," it made very little difference to him which it should prove. There seemed to be a crowd assembling somewhere, and that was all he cared about the matter.

At last the throng of people grew so thick around one of these green enclosures, common to the City of Elms, that Rice made his way onward with some difficulty. He paused to take an observation, saw the great square crowded full of people that murmured and swayed to and fro, when new crowds poured in from the streets, as he had seen the ocean in many a dangerous storm.

The general excitement fully aroused him now, and he looked keenly around while elbowing his way through the human masses, asking the crowd in general, and no one in particular, what the noise was about.

No one answered him. All were eagerly searching for commodious standing room, and his questions remained unheeded. At last he saw, looming up in the centre of the public green, a mass of timber, great, heavy oaken posts, and a cross-beam rising above a scaffold, upon which a mass of white, that possibly shrouded a human figure, was lifted above the crowd.

Rice paused, with a sudden exclamation.

"What is that?" he said, turning to a female, who elbowed him fiercely with one arm, lifting up her child with the other.

"What is it? Can't you see? Look for yourself. What should it be but a gallows, and a woman on it?" cried the mother, lifting the little, golden-haired girl on her shoulder, that she might command a view of the show.

"A gallows, and a woman on it!" exclaimed Rice,

losing half of his ruddy color. "Oh, my good woman, what has the poor thing done?"

"Done! why, where did you come from? Done enough to hang her as high as Haman, where she ought to be swinging this minute. Done, indeed!"

With these words the woman thrust herself forward, marking her rude progress by the frightened face of the child, which rose and fell in that ocean of human heads like some flower tossed upward by a storm.

A strange feeling seized upon Rice—a desperate wish to struggle through the crowd, and flee from the spot. He turned and pressed blindly against the human masses that heaved around him. But, in spite of his great strength, they bore him onward like the waters of a vortex, till he was flung, against his own will, almost at the foot of the gallows.

Yes; a woman was shrouded in that white drapery—a fair young girl, so fair and so young that the sailor's heart melted with pity at the first glance. How still and white she was. How like some of the Madonnas he had seen in the churches and cathedrals of foreign parts; those hands were folded under the cloud-like sleeves. She was very slender and frail. Rice could trace the blue veins on her temples, and see the quiver of her hands under the white drapery. A hideous thing was coiled, like a great ash-colored serpent, around that delicate neck, and fell writhing along the scaffold.

Rice uttered a cry of horror; something in that face smote all the strength from his heart. The sight of that rope made him tremble like a little child. The meek eyelids drooping over the shrinking agony of those eyes, the mouth parting now and then from its tremulous pressure, the small feet resting so helplessly on the scaffold. It was a pitiful sight.

I cannot explain why that craving desire to know who the criminal was, seized upon the strong man, whose face the unhappy creature would not have known had she lifted those heavy eyes? "Who is it? why is she here? will no one tell me?"

An old woman, or the shadow of an old woman, who leaned against the timbers of the gallows, looked up at this outcry, and her eyes settled on his face. Then her poor withered hands were slowly lifted, and fell helplessly into his.

"My son!"

"Mother—my mother, and looking so!"

"Hush!" she said, lifting her trembling finger, and pointing to the girl on the scaffold. "It is our Katharine."

CHAPTER LVIII.

THE MOTHER AND SON.

Rice did not speak—he did not move—a weight of blood fell back on his heart, turning it to stone. He felt like a drowning man, with the billows of a turbulent ocean heaving around him.

The old woman left her support against the timbers of the gallows, and rested against him. Unconsciously he circled her with one arm. She looked up in his face, and the slow relief of tears gathered in her eyes.

All this had passed very quietly. No one saw it, for but few had heeded the old woman who crept silently after the cortege when it left the jail. As the sheriff led his charge up to the scaffold, a stifled moan had made him pause, and he saw a thin hand steal forth from the crowd and touch that of the prisoner, without seeming to heed the act; for he was a kind man, and guessed who the woman was. Then the strong, brave son came up, and the old woman recognized him with sorrowful gladness; but the crowd was eager for the spectacle of human shame, and cared nothing for that.

Oh, how differently the half brother looked on that scaffold now! He saw the delicate form drooping in the presence of a great multitude. The sunlight fell around her with a soft, mocking radiance. Not even a cloud crept mercifully into the heavens to vail her with shadows. Her eyes were bent on the rough, unjoined boards beneath her feet. The tumult of popular curiosity rose and swelled around her, but she never moved or looked up. Coarse words and harsh revilings passed by her, but save a quiver of the eyelids, you would not have known that she heard them.

As she sat thus meek and still while the minutes of her punishment dropped into eternity, carrying her shame with them, the great multitude around her grew turbulent. After all, what was it to walk so far and stay so long only to see a young girl sitting upon a platform of boards, without giving a sign or lifting her eyes? They had come to see a murderess—something wild and exciting—a scene to frighten their children with in after times, and talk over with the neighbors when subjects of gossip ran low. Why did not the sheriff make her stand up and confess her crime before them all? That would be something to satisfy the law!

As the hour wore on these expressions of discontent grew strong. Men shouted for her to stand up, while the mocking voices of disappointed females scoffed at her with unwomanly fierceness.

All feelings are contagious when humanity crowds itself into masses. Lashed by these jibes the people grew coarse and cruel—the meek silence of the prisoner seemed like obstinacy to them. Her drooping face, half hidden from their eager glances, had no right to evade them thus.

These murmurs of discontent grew turbulent and surged through the crowd like the dashing of spent waves upon a rocky bank—a sea of human faces waved to and fro, white and terrified with conflicting emotions. In all that throng there was, perhaps, not one countenance which expressed indifference; a great painter might have made his name immortal could he have pictured that dense multitude as it really appeared. Men and women looked cruel and hard, as if they longed to drag the miserable young creature down from her place of shame with their own hands and put her to death. Here and there a visage appeared which seemed to express something akin to pity; but the most tender-hearted would hardly have ventured, amid that excited populace, to have expressed a word of sympathy.

In the midst of this tumult Rice heard a voice close to his elbow, which hissed in his ear like a serpent. A rough looking man stood by him with a face full of cruel mockery uplifted to the gallows. He stooped down and spoke to a lad who stood near:

"Go and give the halter a jerk, my little fellow, and I'll pay ye a ninepence the minute it's done. If you pull her off so much the better; I'll make the ninepence a shilling!"

These were the words which made Rice start, and

look fiercely around. He saw the boy, an evil-visaged imp, skulking away toward the gallows. Looking back over his shoulder, with a sly, cunning smile.

"Mother, stand alone one minute," he said, in a hoarse whisper.

The old woman could not stand without support, but she fell back against the gallows timbers, looking wildly in his face. He waited for nothing, but sprang into the crowd with the bound of a panther, grappled the lad by the throat, just as his hand touched an end of the rope which had fallen over the scaffold. With the strength of a giant he lifted the boy high in the air with both hands, and pitched him far over the heads of the multitude. Here the urchin fluttered and turned, like some uncouth bird, till he was engulfed by the crowd, amid shouts of laughter and wild exclamations of astonishment.

Pale and trembling with rage, Rice turned upon the man who had instigated this dastardly act, but the craven took prompt warning, and plunged into the crowd, which, closing upon him, left Rice with his hand clenched and specks of foam trembling on his lips. A hand was laid heavily on his shoulder. Thinking it was some constable ready to arrest him, Rice turned, but only to meet a mild and elderly face, whose placid eyes looked gently into his. It was old Mr. Thrasher.

"Stop, stop, my friend. Let the laws be fulfilled without tumult. God may be doing a great work here."

"But what is man now doing, I should like to know?" cried the angry sailor. "Can your God look down on such work as this and not hate the people He has made? Look at this girl! look at the old woman yonder! My mother and my sister!"

"Your mother—sister! Then you are David Rice?"

"Yes, I am Dave Rice, that old woman's son. I hadn't seen her for nigh upon eight years, and this is how I find her!" cried Dave, shaking all over with a burst of grief; "and that's how I find my half sister, the sweetest little child that man ever sat eyes on."

Great tears trembled in his eyes and dropped down his cheeks, he wiped them away with the cuff of his sailor's jacket, dashing his hand down in a passion of self-contempt.

"What has the girl done? What does this all mean? If you know, tell me—do tell me!"

"Be calm—be still!" aswered Thrasher, in a voice that carried soothing in its very tones. "She is innocent as a lamb."

"Innocent, and there?"

"Yes, I say it again, in spite of her trial—in spite of her sentence, just now commenced. Your sister is innocent of the murder."

"The murder! God help us!"

"The murder of her child!"

"Her child! My little sister's child!"

"Wait—wait till you see her. She has bound me by a promise, but you are her brother, and have rights. I am glad you have come. With your knowledge of sea-life he may be found. My son, Nelson Thrasher, I mean."

"Nelson Thrasher! And what has he to do with her and this?"

"Nothing with this. It would distress him as it does us, but he is away—knows nothing about it, and she—— But, hush! the time is up. The sheriff tells her to come down."

The two men moved closer to the scaffold. At the voice of the sheriff Katharine lifted her head slowly, and cast a frightened look at the crowd, which became more and more riotous as the hour closed. For the first time that day a faint flush stole to her forehead, and her eyes quailed with affright from all the eager faces uplifted toward her. The sheriff spoke again before she attempted to arise. Then a voice followed his, saying:

"Take courage, Katharine, we are here!"

She knew the voice well, arose, unsteadily, to her feet, and staggered, in a blind way, across the scaffold, with her arms held out. The changeable mob began to pity her then, for the sight of her face might have moved the very stones to compassion. More kindly murmurs reached her; you could see it by the quiver of her features and the pathetic helplessness with which she looked toward the spot whence the voices came.

David Rice could bear the scene no longer; he rushed by the sheriff, sprang upon the scaffold, and took the unhappy girl in his arms, crying out:

"Katy, Katy! God forgive them, for they are killing you! My sister, my little sister!"

She may have heard his voice, and the name by which he called her; if so, it smote the remaining strength from her frame, for she fell away in his arms, limp and dead, like a lily broken at the stalk.

The sheriff would have taken her from those strong arms, but Rice waved him back.

"Don't be afeared, don't be afeared," he said, hoarse with grief; "I shan't run away with the poor lamb; but she's dead, and no one but her brother shall touch her. Keep as close as you like. Show me the way to her prison. I aint a going to break any law; but she's my sister, and that poor old soul there is my mother. Help her along, if you've got a heart, and leave this poor lamb to me."

The sheriff had no heart to separate the prisoner from her newly-found brother; he would even have aided old Mrs. Allen, as Rice had desired, but Mr. Thrasher and his good wife were by her side, supporting her with such kindly help that any offers of assistance would have been intrusive. Thus surrounded by constables, the little group gathered in a close knot, carrying Katharine Allen from her place of shame.

The crowd fell back reverently before Rice, who followed the sheriff with the tread of a lion, while that white face rested on his shoulder. This last anguish had left her like a corpse before the crowd had changed all its impatient revilings into compassion. The children looked frightened or began to cry when they saw terror or tears upon their mother's cheeks. The men grew pale, and looked at each other upbraidingly, as the Jews must have done when the great sacrifice was urged forward by their hands.

Thus the little group passed away from the crowd and into the dark shadows of a prison, which seemed like heaven to this poor girl when she came to life, with the remembrance of all those glaring eyes and scowling faces turning their hate upon her.

CHAPTER LIX.

THE EMPTY HOUSE.

When David Rice left the jail that night, ne had the certificate of his sister's marriage in his bosom, and under it was a stern resolve to find out the man who had left her to the chance of all this suffering, and bring him to a stern account.

There was no need of his going further now; all the bright hopes of the morning were swept away. The broken household around that prison was all he could find of his old home. But the gloom of this place was too oppressive; fresh from the broad sweep of the ocean, he could not breathe in all this close misery.

The next day, Rice escaped from the contemplation of all this ruin, and took a long walk into the country, bending his way toward Hotchkistown. The rapid exercise cooled the fever of his blood, while it deepened the profound compassion excited by his sister's wrongs. As he was passing under the shadows of the East Rock, a traveller, coming from an opposite direction, appeared in the distance. Rice instantly knew the little valise and the upright figure of the man. It was the companion from whom he had parted only the day before. But why had he returned so soon? What was the meaning of that quick, almost fierce, walk?

The two men drew close to each other, and, pre-occupied as they were, stopped abruptly in mutual surprise, each astonished by the change that had come upon the other.

"Rice, my poor friend!"

"Captain, what is the matter? I know that you have heard; but my troubles can't have done this."

The stranger wrung the hand which Rice held out, but he did not speak—the encounter had come upon him suddenly.

"You found all well at home, I hope," said Rice. "Don't tell me that any thing has gone wrong there, I couldn't stand it."

The stranger wrung his friend's hand again. "Rice, I found the house empty."

"Empty! What, moved?"

"Gone, both of them; God only knows where."

"Gone!"

"No one can tell me where. The house was shut up. The grass had grown high around the gate. The bucket from long disuse had dropped to pieces on the well-pole. This is all that I can gather of a certainty."

"And did the neighbors know nothing?"

"They told me a great deal, but it led to nothing; my wife really gave no one an idea of what she intended to do. I see how it is; she was very proud, and thinking herself compelled to work for a living went off into some strange place. It was like her, but where can I go, how search her out? She left no trace. 'Surely she might have waited a few months longer!"

The proud anguish in his friend's voice drew Rice from his own troubles.

"Come," he said, "I will turn back, and we will talk this over. Some way will be found. 'Never give up the ship.' That has been our motto for many a day, captain. The storm has burst on me, and it may reach you, but we'll sail in the same boat anyhow."

"But this suspense is terrible, Rice. Does it seem possible that a man should be made so wretched in a single day? But for this hard walk I should have gone crazy."

"I know what it is, captain; all my timbers are shaking now with what happened yesterday, but I've seen many a wreck come up shipshape again. Let's keep afore the breeze, if it does blow a gale. I feel sartin that our course lies the same way, somehow. Here, give us hold of your valise. You look clean tuckered out."

The man surrendered his valise with a faint smile, saying:

"I only intended to go on a little till the stage overtook me, but forgot all about it, or that I was walking fast, till ten minutes' rest convinced me how tired I was." That moment the heavy stage-coach came swinging round a corner of the turnpike, its four horses galloping forward in a cloud of dust, through which a bright, boyish face was seen leaning out of the window.

"Hallo, there, I say, you driver, let me out—hurry—can't you hear a fellow? What are you thinking on?"

The driver heard this energetic shout above the tramp of his horses, and drew up, covering the travellers by the way-side with a storm of dust.

The lad opened the heavy stage door for himself and sprang out, telling the driver, with a magnificent flourish of the hand, that he could treat himself with the extra fare, paid in advance, from Hotchkistown to New Haven. Then he began advising two old ladies in the back seat to take a little more room and make themselves comfortable, a piece of consideration that was cut short by a sharp crash of the door, and a lurch of the stage, which set the establishment in motion again.

Left alone in the street our friend Tom took a rapid survey of the two men, and advanced toward them, lifting his new straw hat, which sported a red ribbon around the crown, after a fashion which he had admired greatly in little Paul, and regarding this a proper occasion, practiced with considerable effect. He glanced at Rice with a rather dissatisfied air, and partly turned his back on him while addressing the other person.

"I reckoned I should find you somewhere on the road, captain, and so cut after," he said, turning his back decidedly on Rice. "Expected to find you all alone, though."

"This person is my friend."

"Yes, sir, but he isn't mine, so if you'd just as lief step round back of that juniper bush, mebby I'll tell you something."

The person addressed as captain accepted this invitation, and walked to the other side of a juniper tree, which stood close by, heavy with clusters of blue berries. Tom followed the stranger with one hand thrust into his trowser's pocket, from which came a faint rustle of paper.

CHAPTER LX.

TOM HUTCHINS' LETTER.

"WHEN you was at our house, talking to par, I heard purty much all that was said, and should a heard it all if it hadn't been for the squalling of the young uns. Now he didn't know a circumstance to what I did. Just driving a person down to a sloop don't amount to nothing, if you can't tell where she was a going."

"True enough, my young friend; but what more can you tell me?"

"Well now, if you'll promise not to laugh or poke fun at me, I'll up and tell."

"Well, I promise that."

"And you wont be mad, nor nothing?"

"I think not."

"And—and—" Here Tom grew red as a winter apple, and stammered most unmerciful.

"Well, and what? I dare say you can ask nothing which I will not promise."

"Well, you wont set yourself agin me and Rose when we've grown up, and—and—"

The stranger started, and his countenance changed.

"What can you know of my—of Rose?" he said, sharply.

"Oh, now you're getting mad!"

"No, no; but you tell me nothing."

Tom withdrew his hand and buttoned up the pocket with emphasis.

"Besides that, I aint a going to. How far is it back to Bungy? I can foot it there afore dark, and no harm done."

"But you had something to tell me."

"Yes, sir. Come all this way a purpose to tell it. Now I'm going back agin—no damage to nobody."

The captain grew pale with anxiety.

"Tell me what you desire, and speak out," he said.

"Well, I don't desire nothing of nobody. Ask our doctor if I'm that sort of chap; but you come to our house and asked questions about a lady that I know, in a sort of mealy-mouthed way, as if you didn't like to speak out and say to old neighbors, 'She's gone off and I don't know where.' Par didn't know, and consequently couldn't tell. I kinder did; but with the old folks by, and the baby squalling, what could a feller do?"

"Where—where are they?"

"Now there's the question. I want to make a bargain with you."

"Boy, boy, this is too much."

Tom Hutchins looked at him earnestly.

"I'll trust you!" he exclaimed, unbuttoning his pocket in breathless haste, and drawing forth a tiny letter, folded after the peculiar fashion that school-girls affect. "Perhaps you know that ere writing—scrumptious fine hand, aint it? Jest look on the outside—*Mr. Thomas Hutchins*—don't it look splendid?"

As Tom uttered these words, he unfolded the dainty little epistle, and held it forth.

The captain's hand shook as he received the paper, and a mist came over his eyes before it was read through.

"Mr. Thomas Hutchins:

"Dear Friend:—I take up my pen to inform you that I am in good health, and hope you are enjoying the same blessing. I have got a nice gentleman and lady to live with, and am learning French like any thing. There is a colored man called Jube, and a young gentleman named Paul. They know French, and help me to speak it. I have got your robins' eggs yet, and mean to keep them all my life. Please do not let any one see this letter. I promised you to write the minute we got anywhere; but it was a long time before I knew how people sent letters; besides, I didn't know how to write fine hand then. Direct your letter to Miss Rose Mason, Bays Hollow. It will reach me; for since mother went away, there isn't any Miss Mason but me."

There seemed to be some trouble about ending the letter, for two attempts at erasure with a penknife were visible; but it finally concluded with the girlish signature of
"Your loving friend,
"ROSE MASON."

The captain read this letter over and over again, till the tears rose to his eyes and his chest began to heave.

"Will you give me this letter, boy?" he said, in a broken voice.

"Couldn't," said Tom. "Money hasn't got power to buy it. You'd think so if you only knew how much time it took for me to write the answer."

"And you think Rose is in this place now?"

"Think! Don't I know it. Haven't I reckoned up how much it would cost to get there fifty times! Only to think of hearing her talk French! My!"

The captain reached forth his hand, and shook that of Tom, with deep emotion.

"What can I do for you, my boy?" he said.

"Nothing; only if you go to the Hollow, don't forget to give my best respects to Miss Rose Mason, and tell her—no, you needn't say nothing about it—what's the use?"

"I will tell her that you are a brave, generous boy, and that I am eternally indebted to you," said the captain.

"That's very kind of you captin; but if you could only say man—now a generous man—I should be much obliged. You haven't no idea how much too short my winter trowsers are!"

"I will say any thing to prove how happy you have made me. The dear child—and this is her writing?" answered the captain, reading the letter a third time.

Tom watched him keenly, till the blood mounted into his fine face. Some great struggle was going on in his heart, that at last burst forth in words.

"Take it," he said; "keep the letter. I give it up; but when you see her remember that it bust my heart to do it. Good-by, captain. Some time or another I shall want something of you, but wait till I've stopped growing. There's all the world afore us. Good-by."

The captain called after him. Tom refused to look back, but marched off at a quick pace, waving his hand. The truth is, our youngster's face was bathed in tears. It really had almost broken his heart to give up the letter—the first and dearest epistle of his life.

CHAPTER LXI.

UNSATISFIED VANITY.

MR. NELSON had placed a Nemesis in his household, and she gave him full measure of retribution. The few days of sunshine which he had purchased, soon faded away; and he was left to wander to and fro in that splendid house, more desolate than the pauper whom his wife sent haughtily from his door.

Step by step, the woman for whom he had sacrificed

every thing, became a very tyrant in his house. Indifferent at first, then arrogant, and at last insufferably insolent, she scarcely gave him breathing room in his own home. The very tread of his foot in the vestibule filled her with a sort of resentment, as if he had no right, in any degree, to disturb the luxury of her existence. Nothing but her insatiable vanity won for him even a gleam of favor. That was the strong passion of her nature, and in its complete gratification she sometimes condescended to endure his presence with some show of cheerfulness.

True, Mrs. Nelson was now comparatively independent. A few short weeks of coquetry—for that is really the name by which her attempts at affection should be given—had won this much from her infatuated victim; but it often happens that a woman who scatters her husband's money with recklessness, proves parsimonious where her own is concerned. This was the case with Mrs. Nelson; she had no fancy for diminishing her own resources; on the contrary, she had, without consulting Nelson, placed them in a way to command more than the usual interest, at the inevitable result of more than ordinary risk.

Thus the demands of unlimited extravagance made it important that something like marital cordiality should be maintained with her husband, and from this necessity, gleams of coquettish affection would sometimes break upon his loneliness, which she foolishly believed would always prove sufficient to keep him at her feet.

It is generally the dregs of poor wine that become sour. That love can turn to hate, no one who ever felt the true passion will believe. But there are mixed feelings that combine with affection in evil natures, like foreign ingredients in the wine, and these yield to circumstances as that does to the atmosphere, turning to indifference, contempt, or hate, as the case may be.

This change was going on with Nelson. His wife did not see it, for, with a good deal of cleverness, she had not the intellect to comprehend a character like his. Her reign over him had been so complete—he had received her slightest favors with such gratitude—that any idea of revolt never entered her mind. A few blandishments had always obtained power over him to any extent, and these she had always at command.

But she too was setting up a Nemesis in the household, not the less powerful that it was slow to come.

This woman's life had become one wild commotion—nothing contented her. The desire of one day was flung off by the caprice of the next. The house was one thoroughfare of fashion. Her position once acknowledged in that world which every one talks of, but which, in a republic like ours, is never permanently defined—her hold upon it became complete; but it was maintained at great cost; morning breakfasts, evening parties, and those exquisite little suppers which are the gems of a sumptuous establishment, came and went in endless succession. Her life was a triumph of vanity—her ambition fulfilled. She had no character for higher aspirations, and only aimed at something new, something that would sweep all social competition aside.

This was altogether opposed to Nelson's ideas of domestic life. His ambition was of a sterner nature. He wanted power abroad, and domestic love at home. But the woman he had chosen overshadowed him with her dashing frivolity—put him aside with her insolent pretension. His strong nature revolted at last. Month after month he had walked through her magnificent festivities like a stranger, scarcely recognized by her guests, or approached by herself, unless the great need of money brought her smiling to his presence, and all this time one fact was brooding in his mind—for all his love the woman had given him nothing.

These thoughts hardened the rich man against the woman he had almost adored. He grew sombre and stern as a rock. No one ever saw him smile, or if he did, the gleam of a serpent stole into his eyes, revealing the venom within. This state of things might have gone on for months, perhaps years, but for a new source of excitement which the lady had searched out for herself. Hitherto the expense and ostentation of her life had been its chief objection. But display requires great genius in its arrangement not to become monotonous, and of all things on earth the routine of a merely fashionable life is the least interesting. Mrs. Nelson began to feel this. Even the triumphs of her vanity grew sickly; she wanted new fields for display. This feeling led her to the very verge of a precipice. There was one corner in Nelson's heart in which a sleeping serpent lay coiled, which even she must not dare to arouse. But with her usual audacity she trampled even there.

In New York there is always a floating population of foreigners whose business it is to be amused, and who have, with the aid of liberal travel abroad, introduced many customs into our republican society which a New Englander of any class is not quite prepared to accept.

Now Mrs. Nelson began to weary of her fashionable dissipation—the attentions of those very men made one of the chief attractions of her life. They were invited to her house; she received with pleasure their exaggerated flatteries, and gradually her whole mode of thought became so changed that the woman was scarcely to be recognized.

What Nelson suffered at first is beyond the power of description; although it wounded his pride terribly, he gave these troubles no utterance, and had scarcely expressed a word of disapproval, but his brow grew heavy with frowns and an iron pressure of the mouth became habitual. He never sought his wife's presence now, and even passed her, if they chanced to meet, with lowering avoidance.

With this new caprice Mrs. Nelson's extravagance had somewhat abated, and having no special favors to ask, she treated her husband's frowns with the utmost disdain, if for a moment they excited her attention. He took no pains to enforce his displeasure upon her, but with stolid firmness went on his way.

During her married life this woman had made many efforts to find out the sources of her husband's wealth, but except that all her expenditures were supplied in foreign gold, she could form no real idea of his resources. But this fact convinced her that he must have made vast investments abroad, and the strongest desire she had left was to ascertain the exact position and amount of these investments, which, in the end, must, she was certain, become her own, either by depletion or bequest.

But for the fixed conviction of his wife's indifference, the art of this woman would, in the end, have gained the information she craved; but Nelson felt that in this secret lay his entire hold on her. In fact he dared not trust her or divide the corroding anxieties of his existence with any human being.

At length, in the pauses of a foreign flirtation, for with her these things never approached a point beyond that of gratified vanity, she began to reflect on the persistent silence of her husband, and viewing him as the source of all her luxuries, became vaguely uneasy, as she had done once before, lest he should escape her control.

One evening, when it chanced that she had no visitors, this doubt came across her, and under its influence she went in search of her husband.

CHAPTER LXII.

ARTFUL FASCINATIONS.

Thrasher was sitting alone in the room we have spoken of, reading or appearing to read, a large book that lay open on the library table. The rustle of a purple brocaded dress as it swept over the tessellated floor, disturbed him. He raised his head and looked steadily in his wife's face as she approached, but without a sign either of gladness or anger.

"Always alone," she said, playfully leaning over his shoulder—"always studying and leaving his poor wife to her solitude."

He looked at her keenly, turning his head with a gesture of avoidance, but still reading her with his eyes.

"What do you want now, madame?"

She absolutely turned pale to the lips. There was no anger in his tone, but it cut through her flippancy like a sword.

"'What do I want, Nelson?" she faltered.

"Yes, how much?"

The tones were sharp with sarcasm; she winced under them, and slowly removed her arm from his shoulder. The massive bracelets she wore jingled faintly with the motion. Nelson glanced at them with a bitter sneer.

"Those things were not among the jewels I gave you."

She flushed to the temples.

"No," she said, with some truth; "you always seemed anxious and troubled, so——"

"So you accepted these from some one else?"

"No, I bought them. Who would give me any thing that I cannot purchase for myself? The jeweller imported them expressly to tempt me."

She resumed all her confidence now. This allusion to the jewels soothed her into the idea that it was only a spasm of jealousy which had influenced his words. She leaned her white arm on his shoulder again, and touched his cheek with her own, glancing down on the book he had been reading.

He closed the volume suddenly, and leaned his arm upon it.

"And you wont let me read?"

"No."

"Want me out of the way, perhaps?"

"Yes!"

The woman rose to her full height, and in her haughty anger would have swept from the room, but on second thought she drew a chair, and sat down opposite him, leaning her arm on the table.

"Nelson," she said, in her clear, rich voice, which, spite of herself, shook with suppressed passion, "you are angry because I have had so little time to give you of late."

He looked her steadily in the face.

"No, Ellen, I am not angry at any thing."

"Then why are you so stern with me?"

"Because I am myself again."

The woman was really frightened; the impolicy of her late conduct forced itself upon her; for a moment she sat biting her lips in silence.

"You had better go to your room," he said, quietly; "the marble floor is cold."

"Not half as cold as your heart," she answered, with a burst of tears. "Ah, Nelson, how can you treat me so cruelly? Me, who—who——"

"Who love me so dearly," he said, with one of the most cutting sneers that ever disfigured a man's countenance.

These were the very words she had been trying to utter, but they lodged in her throat. He had anticipated the falsehood with a sneer. She arose haughtily. Tears rolled down her flushed cheeks. She was really a beautiful woman; but her loveliness had no effect on him then. In her reckless vanity she had wounded him almost beyond repair, and his bosom serpent crested itself fiercely.

"I did not expect this," she said, in pale anger. "You shall never have a chance to insult me again."

"I did not seek it now. It is not my wish that you should ever come here."

"Why, what great secret do you keep in this room?" she said, speaking at random, in her anger. "One would think you had a hidden treasure here."

The sudden pallor that spread over his face struck

her dumb; what had she said to arouse this white rage? The words escaped her memory as they were uttered, but they had given him a blow on the heart. Nelson recovered himself promptly.

"Well," he said, with less of bitterness in his voice, "you have chosen to seek me without invitation and without motive, so far as I can understand. If you have any business, let me know it?"

"Cannot a woman visit her husband without special business?" retorted the wife.

"Her husband?" he repeated, in a low, sneering voice.

She burst into tears.

"Nelson, this is cruel."

"Cruel; I thought you did not understand the term!"

She could control her passion no longer, but stamped angrily on the marble floor with her foot.

"Nelson Thrasher, this is too much, after persecuting me with your attentions, begging me upon your knees to become your wife. I am insulted in my own house, sneered at almost before my own servants, neglected, trampled on——"

"Be silent, madame! these complaints are false. It is I who have been outraged and insulted; set at naught under my own roof; left to solitude, when my heart ached for the company of my wife; and all because I brought to you a devotion more perfect than man ever gave to woman; because I loved you well enough to deserve the contempt which you rain upon me."

Mrs. Nelson began to cry and wring her hands at this, and, after the fashion of widows who marry a second time, sobbed out: "It was no more than she deserved. Oh, if her first husband had only lived—never in his whole life had he spoken a harsh word to her. Alas, what a fool she had been!"

Nelson heard her impatiently; the mention of Captain Mason did not soften his heart, but closed it even against her tears and the beauty that they brightened, as dews refresh a rose.

She paused in her grief, and looked at him from under her wet eyelashes. The tears rendered her glance very tender and sorrowful. His countenance softened. She saw it; and, going round the table, leaned over his chair, fanning his cheek with her breath.

"Nelson, have you really ceased to love me?"

There was truth in the bottom of the man's heart, and he could not answer "Yes;" so he was silent, and sat beneath her caresses with downcast eyes. At last he looked up. There was forgiveness in his face, but it was stern and pale.

"Ellen, I did love you—I bought you at a fearful price. How much I gave, how much I risked, you will never know. How miserable I have been, you can never guess. All I asked was a little love and some show of respect. You gave me neither. I could not win them with entreaties or buy them with gold. You never loved me. You never liked me, Ellen."

She moved closer to him. The dew upon her cheek cooled his anger. He could not hate her quite yet. The time might come; but it was sweet to put it off, even for a little while.

"But I love you now."

As this soft whisper fell upon his heart, the serpent that had lifted his crest so angrily settled down, and went to sleep stupidly, as if it never would uncoil again.

The woman bore her triumph with caution, and would

not seem elated. She sank to his side on one knee, forcing him to support her head with his hand, which yielded to the guidance of her soft touch, as the stern heart had given way to her caressing speech.

"You have been very harsh with me," was her sweet reproach; "and all because I cannot be happy when you will not trust me."

"Trust you?"

"Yes; you keep secrets from me. You are jealous because other men admire me."

"No, Ellen; I am jealous because you have no value for my admiration, not because others think you beautiful."

"But you keep secrets from me."

"What secrets?" he faltered.

"Oh, a great many."

She dared not come to the point at once for his face was growing dark again.

She watched his face keenly—it lowered like a thunder cloud. That pretence of jealousy was only a decoy subject—she cared nothing for his early love, but was painfully intent on gaining his secret of the treasures. Without that knowledge she must be forever at his mercy—always going through scenes like the one which had just passed, or sink back into comparative poverty by abandoning him altogether. The partial independence which he had bestowed only made her more eager for new concessions.

"Then you have other secrets. Where is all the great wealth you told me of. I never saw it. I have no proof that it exists."

She spoke very naturally, but he understood her drift, and knew, in the depths of his heart, that it was this secret which chained her in that loving position at his knee. Still, with his softened feelings, it was pleasant to have her there at any cost, so he played with the question as a good angler trifles with his fly on the surface of a lake.

"You have the best of all proof, Ellen—that of spending the money."

"Yes, I know; but what is that compared to the confidence of one's husband?"

He smiled almost pleasantly, leaned forward, and opening the book which had been closed from her inspection, pointed out a page with his finger.

"What—the Bible!" she exclaimed, astonished at the nature of his studies.

"Yes," he said, quietly. "I was reading the history of Sampson."

She looked at him a moment, and the blood mounted slowly to her forehead. He saw the flush, and turned away his eyes.

Not another word was spoken. She arose from her half kneeling posture, and he stood up.

"You will not trust me now," was her gentle leavetaking, "because you think I do not love you, but time will show how mistaken you are."

She reached up her mouth to be kissed, but he touched her forehead with his lips, and she went away as she came, rustling her silks luxuriously along the mosaic floor.

He followed her with his eyes till she disappeared, then sat down, supporting his forehead with one hand.

"Ah, what a creature she is," he murmured. "If one could only buy her in selling himself to perdition, what man would shrink from the price? But who can say that he possesses her? My secret! No, Ellen Mason! that is your chain!—the shackle that keeps you here! I will never break it—never!"

A noise at the door caused him to look up. She had come back, and stood smiling upon him.

"You defy me—you liken me to that woman in the Bible, and keep secrets from me—this is a good reason for amusing myself elsewhere. I will not do that any more. Keep your secret, and hoard your treasures. I will not trouble you concerning them. Only let us be friends. There will be no happiness for either of us without that."

The woman offered her kisses again, and this time he did not avoid her lips—still she could not feel that her victory was complete.

After she had gone, Nelson cast his eyes on the floor, and started with an exclamation of dismay. When his wife fell into her passion she had stood directly over the centre ornament in the massive floor, a secret spring had yielded to the stamp of her foot, the stone had whirled from its place, leaving an opening of some inches, circling half around the centre ornament like a crescent.

"Had the woman seen this?"

The thought made him wild; great drops started to his forehead, while he fell upon his knees, and strove to replace the stone. It shot back to its groove, completing the Mosaic pattern. When all was secure, he sat down and fell into thought. A feeling of insecurity seized upon him; would this woman wrest his secrets from him after all—not by her fascinations, but through craft and watchfulness?

No; he would make sure against that. The ornament might give way again, but it should tell no secrets.

CHAPTER LXIII.

GATHERING APPLES.

Little Paul was standing under the apple tree, with Rose Mason close by. The thick grass under their feet was littered with golden apples, streaked with rosy red, which Jube had shaken from the boughs.

"Here, little missus," cried the negro, looking down through the thick leaves, and balancing a noble apple in his hand. "Hold up your apron, little missus, and down it will come so pretty into the white nest, so."

Rose lifted her little apron of ruffled dimity, and held it up, laughing and shaking her golden curls in the sunbeams, the happiest little creature alive.

"Be careful," cried Paul, looking fondly on the beautiful creature. "Don't you drop it on her head, Jube; it would almost kill her."

Jube laughed, and dropped the apple, which fell plump into the apron, but with a force that tore it from the grasp of those tiny hands; so, after all, the apple rolled away into the grass.

Both Paul and Rose made a plunge. The boy seized upon the apple first, and held it over his head, tempting Rose, with his bright eyes laughing pleasantly. She leaped after it, and danced up and down like a fairy, for her little feet scarcely trampled the grass.

Paul was taller, by a whole foot, than the little girl, so he held the fruit out of reach, smiling with his lips, and laughing with his eyes, at her graceful efforts. Jube got astride a huge limb of the apple tree, and looked down upon the fun, showing his teeth through the leaves. The minister stood at his study window, benignly regarding them, drawn from his manuscript sermon by their riotous shouts of laughter; while his wife, who was sewing on the back porch, sat with her needle half suspended, smiling brightly on the scene.

It was a pleasant sight, and the whole family enjoyed it with all the zest of innocent hearts. The good housewife loved those two children almost as if they had been her own, and as for Jube, the heart must have been hard indeed which did not turn kindly to the good negro, who brought his huge bodily strength to the aid of every thing that required it, and who was good-natured as a Newfoundland dog.

The housewife was so occupied with the pretty strife under the apple tree that she did not hear a knock at the front door, and was quite taken by surprise when the help flung open that leading to the porch, and revealed two strange men standing in the hall behind her.

When the door was opened, shouts of laughter swept through it from the orchard, and one of the men, without heeding the lady, passed by her, saying:

"Excuse me! It is my child—my little daughter!" and with quick strides he advanced toward the apple tree, leaving his companion behind.

"Don't be skeered nor nothing, marm," said Rice, looking eagerly toward the apple tree. "It's his little darter, and he's just found out where she is, arter a tough siege among the niggers in St. Domingo, where we thought he was left dead. I seed him fall down like an ox with the blow of an axe, among a hull swarm of 'em in the cellar of one of them St. Domingo houses, and arterward I saw 'em carry him off to be buried. They took him up into the mountains, marm, and his goodness saved his life arter all; for one of the niggers that he'd saved from a flogging once knew him, and when the rest wanted to kill him over agin, this 'ere chap jest begged him off and took him away to his own hut and kinder nussed him up, you see; but it was a good while afore he got well, and he had a tough time getting away—had to take a vessel going 'round the Horn.

The minister had been disturbed by the knock which his wife had failed to hear, and now stood in the back door listening to this rapid narrative with a look of wonder in his face, while his wife sat with her breath suspended, and the color dying gradually from her cheek, appalled by the first glimpse of a crime in which she felt almost like a participant.

Meanwhile, Captain Mason reached the apple tree, and paused a few feet from Rose, with his arms extended, striving to call out, "My daughter, my daughter," but the words died on his lips, and broke up in tears; thus he stood before the child trembling like a criminal, and with his noble features all in a tumult of tender agitation.

Rose had just succeeded in coaxing the apple from Paul, and tossing it into the air, was intent on catching it with her hands, but her eyes fell upon the stranger, and the sight seemed to harden her into stone. The apple fell through her half-lifted hands, the laughter froze on her lips, and her blue eyes opened wide and wild.

"Rose, my own little Rose, have you forgotten me so soon?"

The child uttered a faint wail; her hands fell down; she stood before him like a flower withering at the stalk.

"Father! oh, father!"

The words came forth in a cry of pain, yet joy shone in her face.

He knelt down on the grass and folded her close to his heart, raining kisses on her forehead, her hair, and her pretty hands. "My child, my child," he murmured, with eager tenderness. "She is frightened. She believed me dead. She has not had time to be glad. Oh, Rose, it is your father; kiss me, kiss me, little Rose."

The child trembled in his arms, but reached up her lips and kissed him over and over again.

"Now," said Mason, putting her away from his bosom, and examining her with tears of proud fondness in his eye, "now, my little Rose, go with me to your mother; is she in the house?"

Again that shiver came over the child; she bent her eyes to the earth, and seemed to wither under his look.

"Oh, father, father, don't."

What is the matter, Rose—why are you afraid? Come, come, go with me to your mother."

"Mother isn't here," faltered the child.

A look of keen disappointment swept Mason's face. "Not here! Not with her child! Then, where is she?"

"I don't know, father, indeed I don't; she would marry Captain Thrasher, and go away. I begged and begged her not to; but she would do it."

Rose began to cry bitterly, in the midst of these words. Captain Mason put her away with horror.

"Would marry Captain Thrasher! Captain Thrasher!" He spoke in a hoarse whisper, as if the words chilled him.

"Oh, I couldn't help it!" pleaded poor Rose, dropping on her knees, and holding up both hands like an infant Samuel.

"No, sir; Rose tells the truth. She tried and tried, but madame would go," said Paul, dropping on one knee by Rose, and pleading for her with his eyes. "That bad man came after madame, and put my mother's jewels on her neck. It was them which carried her away from Rose."

"Married to Captain Thrasher!" The words came forth hoarsely from his white lips. "My wife!"

Rice came up at the moment, looking fierce and agitated.

"Come away, captin, come away; this isn't no place for us," he said. "I will search the rascal out, though he were hid away in the icebergs of the frozen ocean. I'll neither eat nor sleep till he's handcuffed and shackled down in jail."

"Is this thing true, Rice?" inquired Mason, in a deadly whisper.

"True as the gospel, captin. He married 'em both —your wife and my sister. Oh!"

The sailor ground his teeth, and clenched his hand until it looked like a mass of iron.

"Married to your sister?"

"Yes, captin; it was his name she wouldn't give up. She sot there on the gallows with that marriage writing in her bosom, and let the women sneer at her without a word, all to save that villain from disgrace. When she fainted away in my arms after they took her down, the old woman found this a lying agin her heart. I took it out, and swore an oath to search the sarpent out; but his father told me that he'd gone off on a whaling ship afore she was took up, and didn't know nothing about it, so I waited. But I'm on his track now. He's on this 'ere continent, and I'll find him, or die on the hunt. Don't look so skeered, little Paul; you haint got nothing to do with this; so you needn't look at a chap in that 'ere pitiful way, no how. I aint mad with you, if I didn't shake hands."

"But Rose, poor Rose," pleaded the boy.

Rice looked kindly on the little girl. "Poor gal, poor little critter," he muttered, shaking his head; but what is her suffering to his'n, I should like to know. If his heart isn't broke, I don't know the signs. Come, captin, don't look so down in the mouth; we've both got a job afore us, and had better be a doing uv it."

Mason stood with his back to the group, gazing heavily on the earth.

"She thought I was dead; he told her so; and, perhaps, believed it. The wretch persecuted her before she was married. She was alone and destitute—a widow—very proud, and so helpless. Poor Ellen."

"Come, captin, my heart burns like a live coal. I long to be after the villain," said Rice.

"Be after him—oh, yes; but where? He is your sister's husband—that paper proves it. Legally married—and yet—and yet——"

He paused—cold shudders crept through his frame—tears of agony heaved his chest—then the might of his grief broke forth, and covering his face with both hands, he wept like a little child.

"Captin—Captin Mason, I say, look up—don't, don't—I can't stand it," cried Rice. "It's bad enough to see a woman cry; but this 'ere is more than I can bear, darn me if it aint."

CHAPTER LXIV.

MARRIED AGAIN.

Captain Mason removed his hands, and turned his face, white and tear-stained, upon his friend.

"Rice, I loved that woman."

"True enough, captin; but don't think about that; there are as good fish in the sea as ever were taken out. Jest let us get hold of that scoundrel. We've got him tight now. This 'ere thing of marrying two wives is biggermy, and all the lawyers in Connecticut couldn't keep a man from State's prison if that 'ere crime is brought agin him. Come on, captin, I'll expose him."

"And Ellen—the mother of my child!" said Mason, sadly.

Rice took off his hat, and began to brush it with the sleeve of his coat.

"Yes, captin, I'm afeard we couldn't do one without the other; but the woman desarves it."

"Rice, Rice, her child is looking at you."

"And my sister is moaning her heart out in Simsbury Mines—my innocent sister. If the court had known that she was a married woman it wouldn't have been so hard with her. It was to get rid of her disgrace, they said, that she killed her child. If they had but known that there wasn't no disgrace she wouldn't have been sent to that prison. Mebby, if I was to show this certificate to the governor now, he'd let her out, and put Thrasher in her place."

Mason looked at him with heavy eyes.

"His guilt would do nothing to prove her innocent; and she, the woman who was my wife, had no share in this guilt; but the disgrace will fall on her. She believed herself a widow."

"And was in a mighty hurry to get clear of the name," muttered Rice, under his breath.

Mason did not hear him, but had relapsed into the pain of his thoughts. Meantime, Jube had come slowly down from the apple tree, and stood before them, smiling and softly rubbing his hands. This cheerful unconsciousness of every thing but joy, at seeing his best friends, in the negro, was a new pang to Mason. He spoke kindly to the poor fellow, and that was all. In a moment he had relapsed into gloom again. Paul pulled Jube by his garments, and drew him on one side. When the two came back Jube's face was sombre like the rest. He could not comprehend the entire case, but knew that some wrong had been done to his benefactor, and this wounded his heart to the core.

Rice came closer to Mason, and drew him aside.

"Captin, will it make you happier if I let this villain go, and never say a word about it?"

Mason started.

"I don't know, Rice. I am so bewildered nothing seems real; not even my child there."

"I can search him out. He's in this country, that I feel sure about. They must be living together somewhere, either in York State or——"

Mason started as if an adder had stung him.

"Living together!"

There was fire enough in his heart then. It flashed from his eyes, and made every nerve in his body tremble.

"Living together!" he repeated, with sickening pain. "Tear them apart, Rice. She has no moral guilt now, but it may come to that. Tear him from her side. He is your sister's husband—she *was* my wife! Drag them asunder! I could not see her living with that man, without tearing him all to pieces! No, no; if the choice is guilt or disgrace, let the shame come. I can bear it. My little girl—God help us—she can bear it."

Rose began to cry, and creeping up to her father, nestled her little hand in his.

"Don't, father; she'll come back again, if you only ask her!"

Mason grasped the little hand till Rose almost cried out with the pain, but she was a brave child, and gave no sign that she was hurt.

At last Mason addressed Rice more composedly, but still in a trembling voice.

"Where was this thing done, Rice?"

"In that house. The minister himself married them. All the family saw it, Jube and Paul among the rest."

"Is there a register?"

"Yes, you can read it."

"I will."

They went into the house together, slowly, like men walking at a funeral, Jube and the children followed with downcast looks, wondering what terrible thing had happened, when Rose ought to be so glad now that her father had come back.

The minister and his little wife were in great trouble when their guests came back to the house, she had evidently been weeping, and really felt as if some inevitable disgrace had fallen upon the sacred character of her husband. He was terribly bewildered, and with the fragments of a half finished sermon in his head, found great difficulty in comprehending the true state of the case. When it really got fastened on his intelligence, the shock was powerful in its effects; he could not be persuaded that some stain might not rest upon him, and that he ought not on the very next Sunday to acknowledge himself a grave sinner before the entire congregation.

It was a sad visit, both to the father and child. At the moment they sprang to each others' embrace, this fearful intelligence had thrust them apart, and after this, all their endearments were given in tears. Rose felt as if there were something wrong in claiming the caresses of her own father, and it seemed as though her little heart would break when he put her aside, afraid that she would be terrified by the groans that no effort of his could entirely suppress.

They parted in sadness, for years, if not for ever. During all her sweet girlhood, the minister's wife was all the mother Rose must henceforth know; as for the father, how bitterly did he regret the kindness which had spared his life, and healed his wounds among the negroes of St. Domingo. What was he now but a wronged, desolate man, worse than widowed, worse than childless, for to him the very memory of affection had become a pain.

As they went from the house, Rice wrung his captain's hand. "You will let me punish the man?" he said, pleading for the justice that was his by right.

"Punish him, but spare her—spare my child. Separate them quietly; and if it must be—if she is not willing to leave him—tell her that I am alive. If she falls dead at your feet, tell her the truth. But if she gives him up, leave her in peace."

CHAPTER LXV.

THE FANCY BALL.

THE result of Mrs. Mason's latest reconciliation with the man she honestly believed to be her husband, was soon made visible in more lavish expenditure, and a display in her entertainments never attempted before.

An exuberant taste kept her always on the alert. The constant suggestion of some extravagant novelty became an habitual stimulant, now that home affection had become a hopeless thing with her.

During the season of moroseful discontent which we have described, Nelson had checked this wanton craving for display by less liberal supplies of money; but now that he was grateful and generous again, the fever burst forth in new vigor. One of her fashionable friends had just given a fancy ball, where the flowers alone cost a little fortune. Mrs. Nelson was not to be distanced thus in extravagance. She would give an entertainment before which that of her rival should wither into insignificance, like the roses swept from her banqueting hall the morning after that great triumph. This had been a leading motive for the interview described in another chapter. With a few smiles and caressing words she had won a new hold upon the purse, which opened grudgingly only when she grew neglectful or insolent by a repletion of her wishes.

Mrs. Nelson's rival had given a fancy ball at one of the principal watering-places, which certainly had proved the great success of the season. She would do something better than that. Her ball should rival royalty. It should be quoted in our republican society as the charming entertainments of Maria Antoinette, in her little palace in the Park at Versailles, became the conversation of all France.

The weather was lovely. Summer had just melted into the golden autumn. The atmosphere was delicious with fruity odors, in which the breath of late flowers mingled in sensuous richness. This was the season for her grand effort. Society had just come back from the springs and the fashionable watering-places, eager for something new. Her friends should be gratified; nay, astonished. She would throw that entire mansion open. Its rich draperies, its statues and bronzes, the frescoed ceilings, and rare pictures. All should flash upon the world at once. She would illuminate the grounds, weigh down the old forest trees with a fruitage of lights, build pavilions and rustic bridges. Nothing should be omitted to turn her residence into a paradise.

This was all accomplished. As if to crown her triumph, a moon, just swelling from its crescent, came out among the bright stars, and shone with peculiar radiance that evening. Every thing smiled upon this woman. Officious menials in livery crowded her halls —her supper room was one bower of blossoms; delicious fruits nestled in them, and mingled still more ruddy tints with their bloom; cut-glass shone through their leaves like gushes of water; silver glittered through them like frost work; and heavy garlands clambered up the pillars that supported the frescoed ceiling, forming light colonnades on each side, where mirrors reflected every thing, as lovely landscapes are seen sleeping in a lake—the shadows more beautiful than the substance.

Down from her dressing-room, rustling in white silk, embroidered with silver flowers, that shimmered like moonlight among the heavy folds, came the mistress of this festival, superb in her own beauty, with jewels flashing on her bare neck and arms, and lighting up her heavy tresses like clustering stars.

Nelson met her on the broad staircase. He was grave and sad. These ostentatious entertainments were against his taste, and always displeased him. This evening a heavier weight than usual fell upon his spirits; even the rare loveliness of his wife failed to win a smile to his lips.

She held out her hand, smiling radiantly upon him. Her triumph was certain. Nothing like the scene that broke upon her through the open door had met her eye before. She could afford to smile on the man whose gold had opened this paradise to her ambition. He made no response, but sighing heavily, turned at her request and walked by her side through the sumptuous rooms. She was exultant; the effect surpassed her expectations. The tread of her silken-clad feet on the marble floor and moss-like carpets was like that of an empress, but it annoyed her that Nelson took no part in her joy. She observed that he turned away with uneasiness whenever she lifted her arm to point out a beautiful object or some peculiar effect. She did not know that the flash of those jewels which clasped her snow-white arm was like the glitter of a serpent to him. A thousand times he had wished those diamonds at the bottom of the ocean.

Those jewels reminded him of so much that he would have given worlds to forget. They brought to his mind that palace home at Port au Prince, where he had stolen at night in search of the treasures which, in the end, tempted that woman to become his wife. He remembered the horrid scene in that cellar. He remembered the descent of Captain Mason upon him just as he was breaking open the vault where the wealth of many a rich man lay buried—the honest indignation of that noble face—the cold protest. Then the crowd of negro fiends that rushed upon them, reeling with drunkenness, gnashing their white teeth, and emitting gleams of hatred from their bloodshot eyes. He remembered how the crowbar had fallen from his hands, and felt anew the thrill with which he had pointed out Captain Mason to the vengeance of these demons.

No wonder he shuddered and turned away sick with loathing of the jewels. By eternal tortures, such as pressed upon him now, he had bought them, and, through them, the woman whose cold beauty they adorned.

They were the embodiment of his crimes. Why would she wear them? Could she not guess that every rainbow flash that came from her person filled his brain with pictures of blood? Would she never permit him to forget the riot of that awful night, when the brave man, whose wife she had been, was dragged lifeless along the muddy floor of the cellar, and carried off to be flung in the heaps of slain humanity which blocked up the streets of Port au Prince after the carnage which makes men shudder yet, even in remembrance?

She wanted him to be happy, and yet persisted in wearing those things. True, he had never dared to object, they were hers. He had bought her with them; what excuse could he make for the loathing with which he regarded their display?

She saw the pallor of his countenance and laughed.

"How strange," she said, surveying herself in a mirror, and changing one of the ornaments in her hair, "how strange, Nelson, that you never can accustom yourself to society. The very expectation of doing the honors of your own house to a fashionable crowd makes a coward of you; while I—well, it is true we ladies do adapt ourselves to circumstances better than men. Confess this, husband, and I will permit you to tie the laces of this slipper; see, they have broken loose."

Nelson, still grave and sad, dropped on one knee, and tied the laces around that exquisitely turned ankle. She laughed at his awkwardness, and spurned him playfully with her foot when the task was done.

"Come, now, I hear a carriage. It is early, but our guests are impatient, I suppose. No wonder; it is not often they will see any thing like this. Come, you must help me receive, or people will think I am ashamed of my husband."

CHAPTER LXVI.

STRANGE GUESTS.

She was very playful and charming that night. He looked into her eyes as they flashed down upon him, and forgot the jewels. They walked together into the vast drawing-rooms, and waited for the guests, whose footsteps could be heard plainly on the marble floor of the entrance hall. The steps were heavy, and seemed out of place in that dwelling. The master of all that splendor was strangely impressed by the sound of those footsteps. His breath came slowly and his restless eyes sought the door with a species of vague dread in their glance.

His wife stood careless and smiling, always graceful and ready to enjoy the surprise of her first guests. They came forward slowly, the heavy footsteps smothered in the carpets, and looking around in vague wonder, as if frightened at finding themselves in the midst of such splendor.

"Who can they be, dressed in that fashion?" muttered the lady. "I do not know them!"

Nelson watched the two men anxiously as they approached. They were strangers, and certainly could not be invited guests. The men saw him, and advanced up the room.

"Is your name Nelson?" inquired the foremost, speaking almost in a whisper, for he was awed by the splendor around him.

"Yes," answered Nelson; "that is my name."

"Nelson Thrasher?"

The woman by his side gave a little scream as the words fell on her ear, but controlled herself instantly, though the smile left her lips, and the gorgeous fan trembled in her grasp.

"Yes," said a third person, coming up the room with a heavy, rolling gate, such as seafaring men attain in long voyages. "It is Nelson Thrasher. Arrest him here and now."

Every vestige of color left Thrasher's face—he stood trembling before the two men like a coward. But the woman by his side drew her magnificent figure to its proudest height, and turned scornfully upon them.

"You are mistaken; his name is not Thrasher. This gentleman is my husband!"

The seafaring man looked at her steadily; there was nothing in her words or appearance to excite compassion, so he spoke out bluntly.

"No, marm, *you* are mistaken. His name is Thrasher, and he is not your husband, having been married to another woman long before you left the pine woods."

The color fled from her proud face, till the jewels, flashing their light across it, gave her features the appearance of marble. She turned upon Thrasher with deadly hate in her eyes.

"Is this thing true?" The words hissed through her white lips.

He did not answer, but stood before her dumb and sullen.

"Is this thing true?" she repeated, turning to the sailor.

"True as judgment, marm."

"And the woman, her name, I say!"

"His wife is my own sister, Katharine Allen."

"His wife!" she cried, fiercely turning upon Thrasher again. "Man, have you nothing to say?"

Thrasher lifted his eyes, heavy and sad as death. "I loved you, Ellen."

"Loved me!"

The bitter scorn in her voice made him shrink like a hound when it feels the lash.

"It is the truth. God only knows how I loved you, how I do love you."

Her face fairly contracted with the loathing that had slept in her bosom so long.

"And God only knows how I hate you—how I hated you then, and shall forever and ever."

"But you married me."

"No, I married these, and these, and these!"

She dashed one hand against the jewels on her bosom, hair, and arms, then pointed to the supper room, with its flowers, and the long vista of saloons opening into each other.

Thrasher shrunk into himself, standing before her white and cold. She had no mercy on his wretchedness; no control over her own rage.

"Take him away," she said, addressing the men. "If you have a warrant, use it quickly. Drag him from my sight, anywhere, so that he is taken far enough, and buried deep enough."

"Ellen! Ellen!"

The cry of his anguish would have touched a stone with mercy, but she only drew a sob, and went on, bitter as death, and sharp as steel. He knew that venomous truth was speaking up through her rage, and while she was treading him to the earth, the viper in his nature crested itself against her.

You married me for these," he said, pointing to her bosom, which heaved with rage under its flaming ornaments. "I may be guilty, but not more guilty than you are, Ellen."

"Take him away—take him away," she cried, "or I shall die."

"One moment," exclaimed Thrasher, desperately; "Ellen speak to me alone. It may be my last request."

Had she been alone, I think the woman would have refused him—but with all those eyes turned upon her, she could only step aside to one of those little boudoirs that his wealth had fitted up for her.

"Well?" she said, haughtily turning upon him as he stood before her, pale and shrinking.

"Ellen—Ellen, do not be so cruel to me; if I have sinned, it was from the love that made me desperate. If I have wronged you, think what I gave up for your sake—how much I risked—how much I have endured."

"Well?" she repeated, growing hard and stern with each word, "what more?"

"Oh, Ellen," he pleaded, "unsay those cutting words, they pierce me to the heart—never loved me—hate—oh, do not strike me so hard!"

"Hate!" sneered the woman. "No, no, that is not the word, it does not express enough; I want a stronger language, something that will combine loathing, detestation, and scorn, all in one word, that I may fling it at you, and go!"

"Ellen, Ellen!"

She took no heed of this agonized cry, but went on, her cheeks blanched, and her eyes aflame with passion. "The only drop of comfort I have," she raved, "is, that I can for once speak out, and throw off the load of hate that has fevered every drop of blood in my veins since the day I married you."

He did not attempt to answer her now. The scathing words she had uttered seemed to freeze the life from his whole system. He stood looking upon her with wild, dreary eyes, his whole face so coldly white that she paused, drawing a sharp breath, even in the headlong passion that possessed her.

At last he spoke, but the hollow sound of his voice made her shiver.

"You hate me—and I, who loved you better than truth, better than honor, better than my own soul—hate you, Ellen Mason!"

She was petrified. The fearful violence of her passion had borne her too far—fallen as he was, the man possessed power. There was his secret; with all her patient craft she had failed to win that, and now it would be buried with him in the prison to which he must inevitably go. She looked keenly in his face; it was hard as granite, and his eyes seemed scarcely human from the fire that smouldered in them, giving dusky force to the circles underneath. She knew that at last her power had been wholly swept away. She saw this with a pang. The whole scene had come upon her so suddenly, that she could not yet realize her true position—that he was not, and never had been her husband; that before the world she was a disgraced woman. She remembered, with a thrill of terror, how the measures taken only to protect her pride, and save her from the intrusions of Thrasher's family, would now tell against her. The name partially suppressed, the false history of her position, all would go to prove complicity with the criminal whom she had just exasperated into a bitter enemy.

Stung with this conviction, she stood before Thrasher in the full humiliation of a haughty spirit overthrown.

A stern sneer crept to his lips as he looked upon her. He turned and moved toward the door.

"Where are you going?" she questioned, in a hoarse whisper.

"I am going to proclaim myself a criminal, and you Captain Mason's widow!" he said.

"To whom?"

"To your guests as they come in!"

"You will not be so cruel!"

He laughed like a fiend.

"Cruel!"

"So base, then!"

"Base! I bought you with money; sold myself for love—both were cheated!"

He passed out of the room, smiling upon her as he went. She was a sharp-willed woman, crafty and prompt. The danger was imminent, but she had the intellect to meet it. Quick as lightning her plan was matured. She followed him out, and touching one of the officers on the arm, whispered:

"A hundred dollars in gold if you get that man clear of the house in ten minutes."

"Can't be done, marm. Mr. Rice has gone for more help. No moving a peg till he comes back."

"But you can lock him up; put a guard over him; do something to save us from this disgrace! If one hundred is not enough you shall have five!"

"But where shall we put him—every room in the house seems turned into a garden?"

"In the south wing, along that hall, you will find a room. It has but one door. Iron shutters are concealed under the ornamental work. Secure them, and it is impossible for him to escape. Hark! that is a carriage! A thousand dollars if you get him off before it reaches the entrance!"

She was pale as death, and her whispers sounded like the hiss of a reptile.

The two men consulted together a moment, and directly one of them touched Thrasher on the arm.

"Come, go with us into another room."

"What room?"

"That in the south wing, with iron shutters and only one door. It will do."

"No," he said, doggedly; "my house isn't a prison.

You have a warrant, execute it. I will pass those people as they come in."

The men began to expostulate. Ellen Mason trembled with terror, for the carriage was already setting down its burden at her door.

One of the men came to her for counsel.

"Shall we take him away by force, marm?"

"Yes, if it must be—quick."

To her surprise, Thrasher came forward. The expression of his face had changed—there was a gleam of malicious triumph in it.

"Madame," he said, "I consent to remain your guest a little longer." Then, turning to the men, he said: "How many hours shall I be detained in this room with one door and iron shutters?"

"All night," replied the man.

"All night?" There was something more than a question in his voice.

"Yes, yes; we shan't run the risk of taking you out in a crowd—depend on it. Too smart a chap for any risks of that sort."

"No chance of getting off before morning?" he questioned again, very earnestly.

"Not the ghost of one—even if Rice himself comes back. We have all the responsibility."

"Well, I am ready. Farewell, madame."

Ellen Mason followed him, with affrighted looks. Her guests were coming up the entrance hall in groups. Thrasher stood immovable, smiling maliciously upon her. This exasperated the two officers, and they seized him each by an arm. He shook them off at once, and moved close to the lady.

"Ellen Mason, if I leave you one more night of triumph, it is because the blow that I strike shall be for life, not for an hour."

She drew back, and stood, with a forced smile in her eyes, looking toward the advancing guests. He, too, smiled, and walked on, bowing low as he passed the groups of revellers that now half filled the entrance hall. The two officers rushed eagerly after him, and seized him by the arms in the midst of his guests. Again he shook them off, and, turning toward the south wing, disappeared.

With a wild glitter in her eyes, the mistress of the mansion watched him till he was lost in the incoming crowd. Then drawing a heavy breath, she turned to receive the brilliant throng that surged into her rooms.

CHAPTER LXVII.

TOGETHER, YET SEPARATED.

DIRECTLY, that magnificent suite of rooms was full. The house had given up its gay company group by group, when the vast apartments overflowed, and the illuminated grounds grew brilliant as fairy land. It was remarked that Mrs. Nelson had never received with such queenly grace before. That superb toilet surpassed her usual sumptuousness; the glow of her jewels scarcely matched the wild light that came and went in her eyes. Her spirits were unusually brilliant throughout the whole entertainment; the scarlet of excitement burned on her cheeks; she seemed lifted out of herself by the success of this unique fete.

This was the general opinion of her guests. They could account for the brilliant beauty of her presence in no other way.

How could strangers guess at the quivering fear that trembled at her heart when any unusual noise arose in the crowd which surrounded her with flattery and soft adulation? How was it possible for them to know that the brilliant beauty of her face was lighted by the fever of anxiety so terrible that her heart quailed under it.

A few of the guests remarked upon the absence of Mr. Nelson. At first she evaded these inquiries, but, as the evening drew near its close, she whispered to one of her most intimate friends a secret that soon spread through the vast crowd:

Mr. Nelson was insane. The men that had been remarked with him in the hall were his keepers. The malady had been growing upon him for months, and could be kept secret no longer. She had done her best to conceal it, but of late his eccentricities had become so uncontrollable that a private asylum had been decided on. This it was which had made her so restless and excited all the evening. People thought it high spirits, but alas! how little the world knows of human suffering.

It had been against her will that the party had gone on. Indeed, her husband's malady had never become really violent until after the invitations were given out, but he was quite unfit to appear. It was a great affliction, but Mrs. Nelson was afraid of her life, and had with painful reluctance compelled herself to consign her dear husband entirely into medical hands. Early in the morning he would leave home.

These were the remarks which floated from lip to lip when the guests broke into groups after supper, and the dear friends who had met the lady of the mansion with congratulations, left with compassionate words of consolation, which she received with gentle grace, more attractive than her previous high spirits had been.

Ellen Mason was a magnificent actress—few women on the stage ever went through a difficult *role* so triumphantly. But when her guests were all gone, the facts of her position came upon her mind with bitter force. She looked around on the luxurious ruin of the supper table, the withered garlands, the groups of glasses stained with amber, or ruddy wine, the broken pyramids, and silver baskets heaped with dying flowers and rejected fruit, with a feeling of absolute disgust. The glittering confusion made her faint. She longed to rush by the servants, who were closing the house, and seek the open air, late as it was. This impulse seized upon her with such force that she gathered up the scarf of Brussels point, which had fallen like frost-work over her dress, and vailing her head with it, stepped through an open window into the grounds.

The moon was down, but hundreds of colored lamps still burned in the trees, looking only the more brilliant from the deep shadows that lay in the leaves. The cool night air chilled the fever in her veins and gave her more vivid power of reflection. There is no time when the emptiness of fashionable life strikes the mind so forcibly as that which follows a successful entertainment. The ruins of a feast are always oppressive.

The hollowness of her whole life struck Ellen Mason full upon the heart. What was she after all but a gross impostor forced to work out the problem of her own falsehood without help? She began to realize the i. sufficiency of all that had been gained to her life. She thought of the honest love that had made her humble home in the pine wood so pleasant. In that home how often had she thought of scenes like the one before her, and longed to act a part in them. But these had been only dreams. They had never deepened to ambitious hopes till Thrasher came with his brilliant temptations and won her from that honest roof. What a worthless life hers had proved since then! would it always be so? had she tied herself forever and ever to all this emptiness? Would she indeed be permitted to revel still among these golden husks? That man had threatened her with his speech and more fiercely still with his eyes. Oh, how she dreaded him.

Lost in these thoughts she sat down on a garden chair, and clasping both hands in her lap, began to cry. This was an unusual weakness. She had wept when the news of her husband's death came, but seldom since then. Vanity thrives best in the sunshine, tears are unnecessary to its growth. And now Ellen Mason's life was all vanity.

But Ellen wept now. The excitement of the evening had left her in a state of utter exhaustion. She gathered the lace scarf over her eyes, and it fell away damp, like a cobweb heavy with dew.

A slight noise upon the turf made her look up with some impatience. What servant had dared to follow and disturb her?

It was no servant, but a tall man, with the light from a cluster of lamps lying full upon his face. She arose, stood upright a moment, and fell back again, her lips apart, her eyes closed tight, as if to shut out some terrible object. Her lips trembled as if words were struggling through them, but they gave forth no sound, and she fell away with her head resting against the hard iron fruit and clustering leaves of the garden chair.

The man drew close to her side, when he found that she was insensible, and bent over her with a countenance full of unutterable grief. There she lay beneath his eyes like a broken statue. The mother of his child —the wife of his youth, with the burning shame of a second and illegal marriage flashing from the jewels on her bosom and in her hair. But she was the mother of his child, the object of his first and only love, and that pale, cold face was wet with tears. His own hands had aided in separating her from that man. It was a solemn duty, but he had no wish of revenge beyond that. This task accomplished he would go away and struggle against his bereavement as a strong man should. He had not expected, nor perhaps wished to see that woman's face again, but as it lay beneath his gaze so like death, something of the solemn tenderness which death claims came over him. It was not love. It was not forgiveness—he had never condemned her enough for that—but the wronged man could not forget that she had been his wife, and that great sorrow and bitter shame had fallen upon her that night. He knelt upon the grass, and lifting her head from its iron resting-place, drew it to his bosom. The heart beneath scarcely quickened a pulse. To him she was not a living woman, but a memory that had turned to marble under his eyes and lay like marble against his heart.

It was terrible to see a human being so perfectly lifeless and yet feel that vitality existed in the pulseless heart. He did not touch that forehead with his lips, but passed one hand tenderly over it, muttering:

"Poor Ellen—poor lost Ellen."

She did not move; his words failed to reach her. He felt how cold she was growing, and lifting her in his arms carried her into the house; for the window through which she had passed was still open, the light of a chandelier poured through it, and was exhausted in the flower beds underneath.

In passing through the shrubbery the lace scarf caught on a rose-bush and was torn in fragments. He remembered how the drapery which had shrouded Paul's mother had been swept from the dead, and sighed heavily, as if composing this one also for the grave.

Mason passed through the window and stood in the little breakfast room, which has already been described. Through the open doors he caught a glimpse of the supper room, from which the scent of luscious fruits and dying flowers came with sickening force. On the other hand was a long vista of drawing-rooms, with the lights half extinguished, and a host of glittering objects visible through the semi-darkness, as lightning breaks through a cloud surcharged with electricity.

A sadness like that of death fell upon Mason as he saw these things. They told, in one glance, the history of her involuntary sin. Why should he wait there to cover her with new anguish and more living shame when life came back? He laid her down among the silken cushions of a couch whose crimson warmth only made her face more deathly, and went away forever. What more was there for him to do? Already he had persuaded Rice to spare that proud woman the last humiliation of her rashness, and keep her name, as it was now recognized, out of all legal proceedings necessary to the conviction of Nelson Thrasher. Beyond this, magnanimity itself was powerless.

CHAPTER LXVIII.

THE TREASURE VAULT.

MEANTIME Thrasher entered the room which had always been considered as particularly his own. The officers went after him, found out the iron shutters, and fastened them securely. Then looking complacently around this impromptu prison, they went into the hall, locking the door securely outside.

Thrasher sat down in his easy chair, and leaning one hand on the table, waited patiently till they were gone. When all was quiet, he got up, crossed the room softly, and drew a couple of bolts, hidden in the elaborate carving of the door frame. He fastened the shutters in the same way, so that it was impossible for any one to gain entrance to the apartment against his desire.

When every thing was safe, he pushed the library table aside, and kneeling upon the mosaic floor, wheeled the centre ornament from its place. He descended to a flight of steps that led from the opening, and with a touch of the finger wheeled the pavement into place again, closing himself into a deep vault, apparently of solid mason work. Casks, evidently filled with choice wines, for the name of some rare vintage was marked on each, were piled on one side of the vault; a rack filled with bottles rose to the ceiling opposite. It was, after all, only a wine vault that he had taken so much pains to conceal. This would have been the first conclusion had any one followed Thrasher into that recess. But his actions spoke of something more.

Previous to entering the vault, he had lighted a lamp, which he now placed on the pavement. With a quick wrench of the hand, he swung the wine rack from its place, and busied himself with one of the slabs of granite which composed the wall. That too swung open, and exposed an inner compartment, or square chamber, from which came a flash of precious metals, and iron-clamped boxes, piled in heaps within. A broad glow, given back to the light, streamed into the outer vault, filling it with golden gleams.

Thrasher stepped into the recess, and dragged out a bronze box, scarcely larger than that which held the jewels entrusted to Captain Mason, and which now blazed on the person of his wife. He opened this box carefully, and took out a heavy block of gold, evidently pure metal, but polished smoothly. It was shaped like a common house brick, and weighed so heavily that the strong hand of Thrasher sunk under it, and it fell to the stone floor, giving out a ringing sound that made him start, notwithstanding all his precautions, and the fact that he was now deep in the bosom of the earth.

There were many lines of fine engraving on one of the flat surfaces of the brick; the writing was in French, with which Thrasher seemed familiar, but he read it over with great care more than once. Then sitting down, with the brick before him, he took out a graver and began to cut some rude letters on the opposite side.

The gold was very soft, in its pure state, and he made rapid progress; but the record, whatever it was, took more than two hours in the completion. When it was finished he dropped the brick into its box, leaving it unlocked. This he placed just within the mouth of the recess, muttering, "it will be the first thing to catch the eye."

After this, Thrasher opened another box and took out what seemed, by their glitter, to be some unset diamonds. These he placed in his bosom. Then filling his pockets with a weight of the gold coin, he stepped into the outer vault, swung the granite slab into place, and proceeded to cement it into the wall with some material which he took from one of the casks.

When this was accomplished he stole softly up the steps again, let himself into the upper room, and proceeded to undraw the bolts, which had given the doors and windows a double fastening. There was nothing more for him to do. Unconsciously the woman who was his fate, had placed him in a position to accomplish all that was needful to protect his wealth, and even if it should be found, to save it from her rapacity. Once satisfied of this, he became less excited; for during his work, great drops of perspiration had stood on his forehead, and a wild eagerness burned in his eyes; now he sat down in his easy chair for the last time, and sternly awaited the coming of his captors.

About daybreak they opened his prison and took him forth. He turned a fierce look on the paradise his wild love had created for a woman who now loaded his misfortunes with scorn, and muttered such bitter words under his breath that their venom turned his lips white as it passed them. In these words the last remnant of his love for Ellen Mason went out, poisoning the sweet breath of the flowers over which it swept.

CHAPTER LXIX.

SIMSBURY MINES.

At the base of Greenstown mountains, in the town of Granby, stands an old ruin, surrounded perhaps by more fearful associations than any one spot in the United States. The very tread of a stranger's foot on the soil arouses painful thoughts, for it awakens the reverberations which haunt those cavernous ruins, and every sound seems weighed down with moans, such as were for many years common to the place.

It is an old ruined prison I am writing about—one of the most terrible places of confinement ever known to this free country. A copper mine, which failed to yield its rich metal in the abundance demanded by capitalists, had been abandoned, and over the caverns hollowed out from the bosom of the earth, the authorities of Connecticut erected a prison for criminals. Thank God the place is a ruin now.

Humanity has dragged the wretched sinners from their burrowing places under ground, and given them at least pure air and the sunshine which God created alike for the innocent and the guilty. The spot is deathly silent, but you cannot pass it without an aching heart, for the misery once crowded in those caverns gathers around the imagination, and settles upon it in a heavy cloud, surcharged with groans. You know that human misery has been crowded there in masses, without air to breathe, or such light as God gives to his meanest animal. You think of this till the hollows of the mountains seem gorged with groans, and the cry of suffering souls comes up through the very pores of the earth, making the wild flowers tremble beneath the doleful misery that grew desperate beneath their roots.

A group of rambling wooden buildings thrown promiscuously together, at the foot of a range of hills, standing out bleak and bare, form the ruthless feature of a lovely landscape. One building, lifted from the abrupt descent of the mountain by a double terrace of rocks, commanding a view of the country, which contrasted its rich cultivation, pleasant homesteads, and well-filled barns with that narrow roof and meagre belfry, rose beneath the wild beauty of the mountains. This was the aspect of Newgate built over the Simsbury Mines, at the time Katharine Allen first recognized it from the highway, which she must not tread again for eight weary years.

The front building alone was visible. That long attachment which runs back toward the hills, with its range of narrow windows, and the smaller buildings crowded against it, lay in shadow, but from the distance there was something imposing in the uncouth pile. The sun was approaching its rest, and flung increasing light around the old prison, giving it gleams of false cheerfulness that never entered its walls.

Katharine, who sat in the heavy country wagon, between her guards, chained to the seat, and with her delicate wrists chafed by the iron that weighed those little hands down to her lap, looked toward the gaunt pile with a feeling of sad speculation. Why had she—an innocent woman—been sent to a place like that? for it was terrible, even in the glory of sunset. In her whole life she had committed no wrong worthy of more than gentle punishment. Was it not enough that her husband had abandoned her? that her child was dead? that her name had become a by-word in the land? Not enough that she had gone through the first and most bitter portion of her sentence—had suffered that hour of public scorn on the gallows at New Haven—a more terrible penance than if her life had been exacted, for the memory was with her always? Must the laws be forever warring at her young life? Was that huge pile to be her home for eight long years? They would crowd her down among the desperate criminals who burrowed their lives out in the bosom of that mountain, and leave her to die there.

But could she die? Would the principles of life ever give way? When the sentence had been pronounced upon her, and the judge had condemned her to go through all the forms of an ignominious death without its last horrible pangs, she had said to herself, "It is well. I shall not live through that hour. They will not kill me; but I shall drop dead on the scaffold. It is thus our Lord will be merciful, and save me from all this misery."

But, alas! we cannot die of our own will. She had outlived that hour, and now stood before her second fate, and no signs of death came to snatch her from it. The anguish of this thought broke upon her as her eyes fell upon that gloomy pile, and she cried out in the depths of her soul.

"My God! my God! why hast thou forsaken me?"

As the cry left her lips, she lifted her chained hands to her face, and shut out the prison from her sight, moaning because God would not let her die.

The two men heard this outburst of misery, and looked on each other in silence. One turned his head aside, and drew the cuff of his coat across his eyes, and the other spoke sharply to his horses and began to lash them; but his voice and arm failed, and he, too, turned away his face.

"Look up, my poor gal," he said, at last, pointing toward the mountain with his whip. "It doesn't look so tarnal gloomy now."

Katharine dropped her hands, and the iron clashed down to her lap again. The sun was now at its full setting, and flung a thousand gorgeous tints on the old prison. Its windows sent back a blaze of gold, the cupola seemed brimming over with crimson radiance, and rich lights slanted down the terraces of the mountain.

"Yes," she said, thoughtfully. "God is everywhere—even in that place. If He will not let me die it is because there is work for me to do. I shall find it among poor souls yonder—more miserable still than I am, for they struggle under a weight of guilt; and I—God help us all. I shall find some one to tend and comfort there."

Katharine grew resigned under these good thoughts, and a sweet tranquillity stole into her eyes. She was innocent. God knew that, and she knew it, for had not her babe gone to Him pure from her own heart? Why should she question His graciousness? If He permitted her home to be in that prison, what right had she to rebel against it? In this frame of mind she entered Newgate.

It was that sad hour which consigned the prisoners, whose toil lay above ground, to this living tomb, deep in the earth. The crash of hammers and clank of iron had ceased in the workshops, and the prisoners were assembled in the main building, ready to descend into the mines in search of such rest as that terrible place could afford.

The officers of the prison were occupied. Guards leaned idly on their muskets, and a group of keepers kept strict watch over the terrible group. They had no time for newcomers, so Katharine stood between her guards, drooping wearily under her irons, and looked on, forgetting herself in compassion for those lost wretches.

A trap-door, scarcely large enough to admit a healthy man, led to the subterranean dungeons. Around this the prisoners crowded, some swearing fiercely, others laughing in fiendish glee, a few humble and broken-hearted, all hustling each other like wild animals crowded on a precipice. The guards and keepers looked on impatiently. The clank of chains and those haggard prison faces were familiar to them. They were only impatient to urge the crowd down that narrow passage, and seal the unhappy wretches deep in the bowels of the earth, when their duty ceased till morning.

Down through this narrow trap the prisoners forced themselves, cursing as they went, and jesting at their own misery. At last all had disappeared save a little band of women in "linsey-woolsey" dresses cut very scant, who had waited in one corner of the room, under a guard, for their turn to descend. As they passed

Katharine, these women lifted their heavy eyes to her face, too miserable for pity or wonder; but her beauty and the strange expression of her features made them pause and look upon her as if they could not believe that she was one of themselves.

Some formalities passed. Katharine's name, age, and sentence were written down in the black records of the prison: "Katharine Allen, aged twenty-two, found guilty of manslaughter in the first degree; sentenced to sit upon a gallows in the public square of New Haven for one hour, and serve eight years at hard labor in the State Prison at Simsbury."

Twice as the warden made this record he stopped to look at the prisoner. Her presence troubled him with vague compassion. He took the irons from her arms himself, and rubbed the chafed wrists gently with his palm, muttering, "Poor wretch, poor wretch. It's hard to put her down among them."

It was not often that this dignitary visited the subterranean prison, but he called the keeper most remarkable for kindliness of heart and bade him take her away. His voice was gentle and Katharine looked at him gratefully, but she was afraid to speak, for while standing near the trap-door she had seen a keeper strike one of the women who presumed to answer him.

A rude ladder, which stood almost perpendicular, led from the trap-door to the dark caverns underneath. At the first glance Katharine drew back sick and appalled by the black gulf into which they were urging her. The warden came forward and strove to reassure her, but she trembled violently and reeled back from the door, holding out her hands with a piteous cry for mercy.

There was no help for it; she must descend like the rest, sleep and suffer like the rest, notwithstanding her beauty and the pure magnetism of her goodness. She clung to the kind hand reached forth by the warden, and shutting her eyes sunk through the trap and placed her trembling feet on the ladder. The keeper was just below encouraging her. The iron lamp which he held only served to make the darkness horrible. The blackness into which she was passing seemed to cover her soul and body.

At last her feet touched the earth. The skeleton ladder seemed melting away in the darkness overhead. The keeper's lamp flickered fitfully; a mouldy scent floated around her. "This," she murmured, "this must, indeed, be the valley and shadow of death."

The man opened a door sunk into the walls of the cavern, and there was a rude cell, occupied by a wooden bench, over which some straw was scattered; a slanting board, also covered with straw, rose a few inches above the level at one end, and this was all the pillow that beautiful head would know for eight years. The keeper carried a coarse gray blanket on his arm, which he laid down on the bench. Katharine took up the blanket, but her hands trembled so violently that she could not unfold it. He saw this; set his lamp on the earth, and spread the blanket over the straw. She tried to thank him, but could not speak.

The lamp light, faint as it was, revealed drops of moisture glistening thickly on the walls around her, and she detected the dull sound of water falling in perpetual rain from the low ceiling. This was the end of her journey; this was her home. The man left her alone; no light, no voice; the dull dropping of water from the roof was all the sound she heard. No wonder that she cried out again, "My God, my God! why hast Thou forsaken me?"

CHAPTER LXX.

THE PRISON ANGEL.

THERE is no cavern so deep, no darkness so profound that the Holy One cannot penetrate it with his mercy. It is unrepentant and stubborn guilt alone which resists Him. Soon as the cry left her lips, Katharine found her answer. Notwithstanding the hardness of her bed and the damp air which floated heavily around her, she grew calm; some heavenly strength fell upon her, and, folding her hands peacefully over her bosom, she fell asleep. The water kept dropping from the roof, monotonous and cold; the fresh straw grew moist under her cheek, but she smiled in the darkness and whispered softly of a little child that had come from a pleasant, happy place to comfort her, and which would visit that hard couch nightly, and tell her of the heavenly home where it had found a resting-place for them both.

When Katharine awoke in the morning, she was surprised to feel how strong the night had made her, and she went forth to the life which had seemed so terrible, with the firm resolve to find out her duty and do it.

What human being ever turned resolutely to the performance of a duty without finding some comfort growing up under it?

The gentleness and sweet obedience which marked Katharine Allen's conduct in the prison, won many a kind word and act from her keepers. Perhaps her beauty had something to do with this; but it was not her beauty which made those rude men respect her in the cells of that copper mine, as if she had been in the chambers of a palace. It was not her beauty which checked the curses on the convict's lips, or led them to some rude efforts of politeness as she passed in her humble prison garb.

After awhile, Katharine began to see how wise and good the Almighty had been in sending her to that gloomy place; how all unconsciously she had been led to a great work through sorrows that prepared her for it, step by step. If ever woman has a mission except that of performing the duties which come naturally before her day by day, and hour by hour, it is that of nursing the sick, and comforting the afflicted. Women were intended for the gentler works of humanity, and who shall say that the great reformers of the earth can surpass her in this mission of love, or find a channel in all society through which her womanhood can be so beautifully perfected?

It is guilt which makes the convict repulsive; attach a firm conviction of innocence, or even repentance to the prisoner and his coarse dress becomes picturesque, his hard fare sublime. When I describe Katharine Allen in prison she is lifted out of all real convict life, but seems to me like an angel wandering through those dark places, as one of old sought out and unlocked the dungeon of the apostle. Suffering had done a heavenly work with this young creature. Certainly, she had been unjustly punished, but had not this chain of events brought her into a field of great usefulness! Of her own accord would she ever have sought that place, or descended that ladder? Yet where on earth was there a spot in which humanity suffered so much, or where the influence of a good woman could so surely bring comfort.

In her solitude, Katharine remembered many a wise lesson and kindly precept that old Mr. Thrasher had taught her when she was restive in her first imprisonment. It was wonderful how deeply the sayings of this good old man had impressed her.

It was not long before Katharine was lifted out of the deepest misery of her prison life and placed in the hospital as head nurse of that most horrible place. The unwholesome position of the prison, the dreary darkness of its mines, and the damps that trickled down their walls, engendered diseases of all kinds with frightful rapidity, and that bleak hospital room was always full. Those who know only of the common anguish of comfortably appointed sick chambers can have little idea of the terrible duties which fell upon this young creature. Instead of prayers she heard little but raving curses of the past and eager cries for release from that awful life, which was worse, these poor wretches protested, over and over again, than any punishment which could await their souls beyond the grave. Some would jest desperately about the ways and means of this escape; laugh about the scant shrouds and pine boxes in which they must set forth on the long journey. Others bore their pain with stolid obstinacy, fearing to die, but dreading to get well, for death gave them to the grave, health back into those damp mines, which was a living burial.

With the sweet calm of one who finds an unexpected duty to be performed, Katharine entered this place. Her very presence had a holy effect upon the suffering convicts. Cruelty only hardens sin, and in those days moral kindness to a convict was almost considered an offence against the law. Men were convicted to be punished, not with any idea of reformation, and being thrust utterly beyond the pale of mercy, grew desperate and reviled one another when the evil spirit tortured within them could find no other means of expression.

But the sweet goodness of this young woman, their fellow-prisoner, softened all this. She comforted them with her gentle ways; soothed down the profane spirit that gave out curses instead of groans, and dropped softer feelings into those uneasy souls as Heaven gives dew to weeds trampled along the dusty highway. She never preached, never exhorted them, never forced the prison Bible upon their rejection; but the simple promises of Scripture fell like poetry from her lips, at times when the hungry soul of some poor convict, not utterly lost, seemed to crave comfort at her hands. Sometimes, too, when a sick man, won by her goodness, would ask where she found the beautiful words with which she was striving to comfort him, Katharine would open the Bible and read aloud to convince him of their reality. Then some patient in the next cot would whisper her to read louder, and when her silvery voice was lifted those sick men would turn wearily on the hard pillows and listen.

It is no great hardship to read or pray with the sick. Many a dainty person can be found to perform such duties punctiliously; but to work for the sick, to watch with them, wait on them, and with little means supply great wants—this is a noble work even for the patience and endurance of a woman. This is charity in its perfect work, mingling prayers, kindness, and stern labor in one beautiful phase of Christianity. This work Katharine performed so well that the fiend which she found brooding over the pillow of many a wretched fellow-creature, stole away under the sound of her comfortings, and a pitying angel came in his place. This was a work of slow growth, but alas! Katharine had plenty of time—eight long years.

You ask me if this young girl was unhappy in her dreary life, and I answer *no*. Those who confer great good on humanity by self-sacrifice, cannot be made utterly miserable. To such hope never dies. No, I say again, the slumber which Catharine found in her pauses of rest was very sweet. At such times the dreary sound of those water-drops trickling down the walls of her prison, seemed like the bell-like murmurs of a fountain, around which a baby child—one that always came in her dreams—was hovering and waiting for her to finish her work in that prison and see how beautiful the world was beyond it.

I cannot pause now to give the details of her strange life, or tell you how many touching events rose each day to interest her best feelings. The prisoners, young and old, began to look upon her with affection. Even the women, whose hearts are not always easy of access to a sister woman, received her little kindnesses, when she found power to offer them, with something like gratitude. All this won upon the officers of the institution. With her they began to enforce the discipline of the prison less rigidly than they had ever done before; employed her in lighter tasks; gave their own needle-work to her deft fingers; and frequently supplied her with better food than was awarded to her fellow sufferers. She received every favor with thankfulness, but took no benefit to herself. The food which she appeared to carry off and consume in private, went to the nourishing of some poor invalid, whose grateful eyes thanked her and told of gentler feelings growing up in his heart.

Thus, through her favor with the prison officers and her influence with the convicts, this young woman won for herself a power of good, which those terrible walls had never witnessed since their foundation.

CHAPTER LXXI.

THE SWEATING OVEN.

Down in the depths of those prison mines many a terrible scene took place at which humanity shuddered. Once huddled under ground and sealed in with the massive iron bars that crossed that small trap-door, little care was needed for the safety of the prisoners. So, like wild cattle hustled into a pound, they were left to their own vicious instincts, and those often led to riot and revolt. Sometimes the terrible monotony of this life was broken by a new gang of prisoners, who, shocked and outraged in every manly feeling by the degradation heaped upon them, fiercely resisted the rules which levelled them below the common brutes of the field, and, like wild animals just lassoed on the prairies, turned fiercely upon their tormentors.

Cases of horrible cruelty often occurred in the prison; Katharine knew of it only from the fierce noises that echoed through her cell at night, and by the frightened faces that passed before her during the next day. It was enough to shock the most hardened human soul, to know that any of those terrible means of punishment, invented as the curse of our prisons, was in progress. The very idea was enough to drive the blood from Katharine's heart. But she was helpless—had not even the power of protest—all she could do was to turn her pitying eyes on the poor wretch when his sufferings were over, and thus prove that compassion existed even in that terrible place. Usually these scenes of punishment ended in the hospital, then her sweet ministry made itself deeply felt, and many a hard heart yielded itself to her kindness which the most bitter correction had failed to reach.

Something of this kind had just transpired in the prison. A new convict had been sent in from the courts, and his first resistance of the prison laws had been met with unusual rigor. That night Katharine heard low groans, but no cries followed the crack of the lash, which fell so sharply and lasted so long that every nerve in her body quivered and shrunk with that keen sympathy which made the anguish of a fellow-creature her own.

She arose in the morning literally sore at heart, wounded with more tender anxiety than had ever affected her before regarding the man who had borne those awful lashes so bravely. Her duties for a time lay under ground, where much of the prison work was done. She went about them with a heavy heart. The damp, the close atmosphere, and absence of all sunlight deepened the despondency that had seized upon her. In these subterranean vaults is a vast oven, in which the prisoners' bread was baked, and here her duties for the morning were appointed. A woman stood before this oven casting wood into the red caverns of fire that glowed behind the rolling smoke. The woman paused with a huge stick of pitch pine half lifted to the oven, and balancing it a moment in her hands, she cast it to the earth, and sitting down upon it began to cry.

Katharine advanced that moment, and touched her on the arm.

"I can't—I can't! Whip me, if you like—put me in with him, but I can't do it!"

The woman evidently thought it one of the keepers, who had watched her rebellious movement. Katharine bent over her.

"What is the matter, Jones? It is only I. Can I help you?"

The woman looked up, relieved by the voice.

"No," she said, heavily. "It is the old story. You heard the lash last night—it kept us all awake. It is a new prisoner they are breaking in; a handsome, fine fellow; but he stood them out like a lion, and now—"

The woman paused and looked toward the oven with a sort of terror in her eyes.

"And now—oh! Jane, is he dead?" whispered Katharine. "Did they kill him?"

The woman pointed to a narrow door built close to the mouth of the oven, and whispered—

"He is in there!"

Katharine recoiled.

"In there, and that fire raging so; God have mercy upon us! it is death!"

"No, not always; not often, I think," answered the woman; "but I never did this work before. The sweat oven has not been used in my time till now. It's awful!"

A smothered moan, which rose above the roar and crackle of the fire, curdled the very blood in Katharine's veins.

"What is it? What is the horrible thing they are doing?" she cried, wildly. "What is that place?"

"You see the door—how narrow it is—a poor creature can hardly push through. Inside, it is just as narrow; stone walls pressing close up against the wretch, heated from the oven hot as life can bear."

"Oh, my God, my God, is this thing true?" cried Katharine, cowering down, and covering her face with both hands.

"I wont heap on the wood," cried the woman, bitterly. "They haven't the power to make me."

"Hush, hush; some one is coming."

It was a keeper to whom the terrible punishment had been entrusted. Katharine rose slowly to her feet and stood before him, her hands clasped, and the pale anguish of her face revealed by the fire light, which illuminated the darkness all around them.

"What are you women talking about? Go to your work, Katharine Allen."

She could not speak, but fell upon her knees, beseeching him with those wild eyes.

"What is all this about?" said the man, softening his voice.

"She wants you to let that poor man out—that's it," answered the woman, resting both elbows on her knees, and looking up from her seat on the wood. "She knows it aint human to treat any of God's creatures in this way, and wants to tell you so, only them groans has frightened the soul out of her body."

The man looked down at the young creature kneeling at his feet, and a shade of sympathy swept over his face.

"Get up," he said, almost kindly. "I have just come to see about him. This sort of thing don't gibe with my feelings more than it does with yours, but the fellow was obstinate as a mule—wanted a little of the proud blood sweated out of him, and I reckon he's got enough of it by this time."

"Oh, be quick, be quick, or he may die!" cried Katharine, gaining her voice. "How faint the moans are! Open the door! open the door!—hear how his poor hands beat against it!"

"Well, go away—this is no place for you. Run to the well, and have some water dipped up ready. They always make a dive for that first."

Katharine sprang to her feet, and darting across the space illuminated by the oven, made her way toward the well, which gushed out pure and crystalline in the depths of the mine, the only untainted thing in those subterranean regions. An iron lamp swung in the walls of the cavern near this outgush of pure water, which turned all the wavelets it touched to gold.

This was the spot to which the prisoners came when athirst, like cattle to a spring; and to this place, as the keeper truly said, the man who had suffered from the flames of that hot oven would surely come.

Katharine took an iron dipper, which was chained to the stones of the well, and filling it with water, held it till the weight bore down her hand, then she filled it once more from the centre of the well, and again held it ready. This time she had not long to wait, for she saw a human figure coming through the darkness with desperate effort, but slow progress—making futile attempts at speed, and giving broken leaps that brought him reeling and staggering every instant against the sides of the cavern.

Katharine poured out the water, and dipped it up afresh, as if that little effort could make it cooler. She would have gone forward to meet the man, but the chain would not permit it, and thus she stood waiting till he came up. He saw the vessel in her hand, dripping over with a rain of cool drops, and seizing upon it before she could look up, drained it off in wild, greedy haste.

"More! more!" he cried, dropping the dipper, and sweeping the perspiration from his face. "More! more!"

Katharine plunged the dipper into the well again. He would have snatched it from her but she lifted it to his lips. In this position the lamp-light fell upon her face. She dropped the iron vessel from between her two hands, as he fell forward with his face to the earth. She did not breathe—for her life she could not have uttered a sound—but dropping on her knees beside the prostrate man, she lifted his head from the earth. The light lay full upon his face. His eyes looked piteously into hers. She drew him up to her bosom; with the folds of her prison dress she wiped the rain of perspiration from his forehead and left tender kisses in its place; soft words came to her lips, tears swelled into her eyes; she had but one thought—holy thanksgiving to Heaven.

Directly the keeper came up, wondering that his victim should remain so long at the well.

"Halloo!" he said, "what is this? I thought you were half dead, my fine fellow!"

Katharine looked up; her face was radiant, and yet a tender pity beamed there.

"Hush!" she said; "he is my husband."

The keeper gave a prolonged whistle that echoed mournfully through the caverns, but Katharine repeated:

"Yes, it is my husband."

Thrasher did not speak, but she felt him trembling in her arms; his head rested more heavily on her bosom; he scarcely breathed.

The keeper felt some gleams of sympathy swelling in his bosom. With him Katharine had always been a favorite. He took compassion on her now.

"Poor fellow! he has had a tough job of it," he said; "weak as a kitten—why, see how he trembles; I'll just go to the warden and have him sent up to the hospital, where you can tend him till he picks up again."

Katharine smiled gratefully, and they were left alone, the woman and her husband. She bent down and kissed him.

"Nelson, my husband, speak one word—say that you know me."

He whispered hoarsely, "Yes, Katharine, I know you."

"And love me yet?"

The proud man was shorn of his strength, and burst into tears. When the keeper returned, her hand was locked in that of her husband. He was talking to her in a feeble voice, broken with grief; telling her things which made even that dark place still darker—of his unfaithfulness and its stern retribution. His heart was broken up, he kept nothing back. His crimes were great, but the record was given in few words, saddening the poor wife, who had been so happy a moment before, in spite of her bonds. She heard him through, wondering that so much of joy should lie underneath these facts, and whispering to herself: "He will be here seven years, and I with him. Oh, how much can be done in seven years!"

The keeper had compassion on them; he led Thrasher away to that portion of the prison devoted to the sick, and there the heaven of Katharine's convict life grew bright, for she saw the path of her duty clear, and knew, in her soul, that a holy work lay in her hands, a work of comfort and regeneration, which should lead her husband into the sunlight again.

She forgave him from the depths of her own pure heart; she forgave him all the wrong he had done, and all the hopes he had destroyed. Her care, her gentleness, and the holy faith that pervaded her words and acts, had its effect on this iron-hearted man. I cannot describe that which is beyond words, or tell how this gentle martyr reached the stern man's heart; but it softened day by day under her patient tending, and when he went back to the dreary duties of those prison mines, it was with a changed aspect. She had taught him, not only how beautiful a thing human love is, but through that most sacred of earthly feelings, led him to the holy source of all love, all honor, all the glory of life.

And so, as the years of their imprisonment wore on, these two people bore their fate with something better than mere resignation. They were content to work out the duties before them, feeling it recompense enough if they could smile on each other in passing down to their places of rest, or exchange a word of comfort and encouragement now and then by the well, where they had first met.

Do not pity these people overmuch; where true love and faith exists, there is little need of compassion. Out of the depths of his penitence sprang up that perfect love which makes a heaven of any place. As for Katharine, was not her prison life made bright and beautiful. What was seven years of toil, hunger, and thirst to her if it redeemed the husband who had been lost?

CHAPTER LXXII.

UNDER THE APPLE TREE.

Years had passed—seven long years—and in that time many a pleasant change had taken place around the minister's dwelling. Little twigs of rose bushes had grown into blossoming thickets; the big apple tree in the meadow had dry spray among its branches, like gray hairs on the head of a strong man; tiny honeysuckle shoots had spread into luxuriant vines; a row of red cherry trees along the fence was beginning to glow with fruit in season. Every thing inside and out of the minister's dwelling had prospered. He had scarcely grown a day older in his own person. Indeed, with his home comforts so cared for, and his wardrobe in order, he seemed a younger man than we found him, when, standing between the two deacons, counselling about the meadow lot, which now bloomed Eden-like around him.

As for the minister's wife, she had never looked so young, and it seemed impossible that she should ever grow old; a few almost imperceptible wrinkles marked the corners of her prim little mouth, but that was all.

Still, youth knows rapid changes, and other things than honeysuckles and roses had bloomed into perfection at the parsonage. There was a lovely girl sitting under the apple tree, not gathering fruit or blossoms, as of old, but busy with her crochet needle and a ball of crimson worsted, that would keep rolling from her lap into the grass in the most provoking manner. By her side, half lying on the ground, was a youth, the most splendid specimen of early manhood you ever saw, looking at her as she worked, with an expression in those dark eyes which could only have sprung from the one great passion of life.

'As Rose worked, a smile dimpled the fresh mouth, and she glanced sideways at Paul from under those long, brown lashes, coquetting with him in her innocent way, but with a grace that was enough to bring the youth's heart into his eyes. Jube was at work in the garden at a distance, singing to himself, and pausing now and then to regard the scene going on under the apple tree.

This was what was passing between the young people. Rose paused a moment with her crochet hook in a half-looped stitch, and the smile trembled on her sweet mouth. Paul had asked a question, expressed a thousand times before, but never with that intonation and significance.

" Rose, do you love me ?"

Now the bloom of roses mounted to her forehead, and swept down the snow of her neck! Paul saw it, and blushed also—the lashes drooped over those great velvety eyes, and a strange thrill, too sweet for pain, too new for entire pleasure, ran through his whole system.

"Rose, do you love me?"

As I have said, she had answered that question a thousand times before, but now it took away her voice. She bent her head and commenced her work again, looping up the worsted with desperate haste.

"Why don't you speak, Rose?"

"I don't know what to say," she replied, trembling all over.

"Don't know what to say!" repeated Paul, sitting upright, and turning his startled eyes full upon her. "I ask if you love me, and—oh, Rose, is there a doubt?"

Rose shook her head and bent over her work.

"If I ask this now," said Paul, very earnestly, "it is because I wish to be certain that—that—oh, Rose, why can't you answer me?"

"I have answered, Paul."

"But you turn away. You will not look at me."

"Yes—see, I do."

His face brightened all over; taking her hand, which he tangled up in the crimson thread in his impetuosity, he pressed it to his lips.

"I am going away, Rose."

"Going away—oh, Paul!"

"Yes; don't turn so white. I shall come back again in a few months—it is not so far off."

"Where, where?"

She could not complete the sentence, her tears rose so quick and fast.

"I am going back to my old home, Rose, in St. Domingo. My father was a rich man there—one of the first and highest in the island. I can remember that without help, but Jube has told me more than this. He and his brothers, a large family, were all killed in that awful massacre. They had great riches in gold and jewels. I saw piles and piles of gold brought into my father's house that last week, and heard those gentlemen, my father and his brothers, pledge themselves to defend it each for the other, so long as one of them should live. This compact was not written, but engraved on a brick of gold, that it might be permanent, and carry its own record wherever the treasures went. I was a boy, and too young for a trust of so much magnitude. Where these treasures were put I never knew. My uncles were all killed. My father, my mother—oh, Rose, you know about that. I alone was left of the family. Jube, dear old Jube yonder, is all the servant of our great household. My mother entrusted him with her jewels. They fell into the hands of Captain Thrasher."

Rose uttered a faint cry, and covered her face to hide its shame.

"Don't, Rose, don't," said Paul; "I am not blaming any one. Only telling you how it happened that Jube and I became so poor. There was some gold with the jewels, and that Rice made Thrasher give up. It has supported us ever since, for Rice traded with it, and kept it growing, good fellow. But that is very little, Rose. It kept us from being a burden here, but what would it amount to when—when—"

"When what, Paul?"

"When you and I are married, Rose."

The young girl drew a quick breath. The crochet hook fell from her hand—her arms, neck and face were bathed in blushes.

"Have you never thought of this, Rose?" said Paul, tenderly.

"I don't—don't know, Paul."

"But you will think of it?"

"Yes—yes."

"All the while I am gone?"

"Gone!" The tears that had been trembling in her eyes dropped to the roses on her cheek. He saw her grief and exulted in it.

"Jube knows where those treasures were buried. It was a safe place, deep in the vaults under my father's house. The negroes would never search there. Jube will go with me; we shall find all this gold, and then, Rose, then—"

She looked up, piteously.

"I don't care for gold; I hate jewels; from that day I have hated them. Don't go, Paul; I shall die before you come back."

"But we must live. When your father comes from the Indies, I cannot ask for his daughter without some way of earning or giving her bread. Those treasures belong to me. I am the last heir of our house. It is for your sake I shall search for them."

"No, no; I am afraid. There may be another shipwreck," cried the young girl, wringing her hands.

"Hush, hush, Rose! Jube is looking this way; the old fellow will wonder what we are talking about."

"But—but you wont go, Paul? It is too cruel."

"Not till you consent. You are my queen now, Rose, and shall keep or send me as you like."

She brightened with a sudden thought.

"Wait till father comes," she said, dashing her tears right and left with those white hands, "and then we can all go together—that is, if father has not money enough of his own."

Paul pressed her hand again gratefully, as if she had indeed reigned his queen, and once more they sunk into the old attitude, save that she did not pretend to work, and Paul no longer vailed the joy in his eyes.

They did not hear the rattle of wheels, or know that a wagon had stopped at the parsonage; thus when Jube came hurriedly from his work in the garden, with intelligence in his face, Rose received him with a pretty pout, and Paul inquired rather sharply what he wanted coming upon them in that rude way.

Poor Jube was quite taken aback. Never in his whole life had he been so received by the young people; the joyful words were driven from his lips, and he stood mutely gazing at them like a Newfoundland dog rebuked for too much spirit.

"What did you want?" inquired Paul, self-rebuked and softened.

"Why, nothing, master, only Tom has just got out of the wagon and is coming this way."

"Tom! What—Tom Hutchins?"

"Yes, master; that's him coming through the kitchen door."

Rose started up all in commotion. The idea of meeting her rustic boy lover just then filled her with dismay. But there was no escape. He was half across the meadow, making directly for the apple tree. A fine, powerful young fellow he certainly was—broad-chested and stout of limb—but there was the same frank face, the same freckles on the cheeks, the same laughing blue eyes. He came up a little awkwardly, not exactly knowing how to use his arms in walking, and halted a few yards from Rose in blank astonishment at her beauty. She went toward him at once holding out her hands.

CHAPTER LXXIII.

OUT OF A SCRAPE.

"Mr. Hutchins, I am so glad to see you!"

He took her outstretched hands and pressed them together between his two hard palms.

"Jest as sweet as ever; and oh, lots handsomer!" he said, with awkward gallantry.

"This is Paul," said Rose, embarrassed by his rough compliment. "He has not forgotten you."

"Nor I him, by a long shot," answered Tom, with energy. "How are you, old fellow? Know how to speak English, hey?"

Paul laughed, and lost his slender hand in Tom's grasp.

"I've got a little business with you, by-and-by," said Tom; "something terrible mysterious; and nothing would do but I must come right across from Simsbury and bring it myself. You guess, I reckon, what took me out there?"

"To see her?" inquired Paul, in a low voice.

"Yes, nothing else. The old people are getting infirm, and can't travel no more. That trial kinder did them up for going journeys, yet they aint content without hearing all about her every few months. So this time I went up. Had a little chore of my own in that 'ere region, and wasn't backward to go; besides, I raly du feel sorry for them old folks. Not one word have they heard from Nelse Thrasher yet—think he's lost at sea, and that has nigh about broke their hearts. They are getting old now, I tell you."

"And you have been to see Katharine—that was very kind, Tom. If ever a good woman lived, she is one. How did you find her?"

"Handsomer than ever. I swan to man! she looked like an angel just come down, for all that linsey-woolsey dress. She's soft and still as a dove in brooding-time —never complains—never sheds no tears, but goes about like—like—oh, it aint of the least use trying to give you any idea of it."

"But her time is nearly up; she'll be coming out soon."

"Not jest to the day, I reckon. She told me not to let them send arter her, for she'd got a duty beyond her freedom day, and must wait till some one else was set free; then she would start for home, and stay with the old people all her life."

"It is like her, poor soul," said Paul, with deep feeling; "but who is the person for whose liberation she is waiting?"

"Jest step this way a minute, and I'll tell you."

Paul stepped aside, and walked reluctantly away from Rose.

"Look-a-here—she didn't tell me nothing, only in her sweet way asked me not to give the old folks any news that would trouble them, as if she kinder thought I knew; but if I didn't see Nelse Thrasher in that 'ere prison, that fellow has got a twin brother that's been tried and convicted."

Paul started. Had Thrasher indeed been punished? Was he now atoning his crime in prison? A moment's thought, and he understood it all. The generous privacy with which the trial had been kept, that disgrace need not reach Rose or her mother. He remembered now that soon after Mason's visit, the minister and his wife had been absent at the county town several days, and no one could tell why. How well the secret had been kept!

"We must not mention this before Rose," he said, thoughtfully.

"Nor the old people neither," replied Tom. "In this case the least said is soonest mended; but it was him, no mistake about that. To own up, he gin me this letter with his own hands, and a little heap of shiney stones that he dug out from the wall of his cell, where they'd been hid ever since he went to the prison. Katharine told him he could trust me, and he did; but you never seen a feller so altered—he's grown steady and sober-looking, and has a soft, kind way of speaking that makes your heart rise up to meet him. I never did see any thing like it. He's learned to smile, and it does you good to see it. I raly believe he'll live to be a comfort to them old people at last—that is when his time is up."

"I hope so," answered Paul, thoughtfully; "but you had a letter—is it for Rose?"

"No; for you."

"For me."

"Yes—do you know that the chap raly thought that you was dead and drowned in the salt sea, till a little while ago, when Katharine happened to tell him about your coming up to Bungy with Jube, and how you tried to help her, poor young critter. You remember that night?"

"Yes, I shall never forget it,"

"Well, it seems he was thankful to know that you hadn't gone down with the wreck—you and the nigger; and he's been a trying to get this 'ere letter to you by safe hands ever since, but couldn't light on a downright honest chap till now."

Paul reached forth his hand to receive the letter, thinking, in his kind heart, "Poor man! he was cruel to me, and repents of it. I am glad for his own sake."

With these thoughts he broke the seal and began to read:

"Paul De Varney, I have wronged you, and would make restitution so far as human will can atone for crime. You are, *I* know, the only living heir of that proud old house which the Revolution destroyed. The treasures which were concealed by the males of your family, in a solemn compact, and buried in the vaults of your father's house, are in this country. I brought them in the vessel which Captain Mason had commanded from Port au Prince, removed them safely from the Floyd when she was abandoned, and the great bulk of them has never passed from my hands. In the vicinity of New York is a large mansion house, purchased some years ago by a Mr. Nelson. If you ask for this man Nelson, they will tell you that he is of unsound mind, and has been safely housed for years in an insane asylum. But this is the truth—I, Nelson Thrasher, am the man to whom that house belonged. In the depths of a secret vault, which you will find under the south wing, I have concealed the treasures which are yours. There is a room in that wing, furnished as a gentleman's study, the floor is a mosaic of colored marble.

"I send you a drawing of the design. The centre ornament, marked A, will yield if you touch the fourth curve of the arabasque pattern. You descend into a wine vault; the rack of bottles swings on hinges. Behind it; five feet from the corner, each way, is a slab of granite cemented into the wall; remove that, and lying in the entrance of a small inner vault you will find a Gold Brick, upon which the males of your house have engraved their compact, their names, and those of their descendants. All are dead except yourself. The treasure is yours. How I became possessed of it, the amount expended, and a solemn renunciation, you will find rudely cut on the lower side of the brick. Take possession of this wealth; no one will dare to question your right. All that I have in possession, and all that I can restore, is herewith forwarded. If you can only feel the joy in receiving this wealth that I do in casting it from me, the day that you read this will be a happy one, the first that ever resulted from this hoarded gold.

"NELSON THRASHER."

Paul read the letter over and over again. The contents seemed unreal; but for the clear description of the Gold Brick he would not have given it credence. But he remembered that well. The night when the seething metal had been poured into its mould, every member of the family had been summoned to stand by. The scene rose vividly before him. The red heat of the furnace glaring on the vault, the piles of gold throwing back its light, that group of aristocratic men stooping one after another to engrave a name on the dead gold of the brick, till he, the youngest and the last was called upon to take the graver in his young hand, and under his father's direction, record his name on the golden record.

Paul had not understood the danger which prompted his kinsmen to gather up their treasures and make this singular record on the brick, but the storm came upon them at once.

In a single week that whole household had been swept away—father, mother, home. Is it wonderful that the young man grew pale, and shuddered, when Thrasher's letter reminded him of these things?

Paul had no heart to return to Rose. For the moment he thought of nothing but that terrible scene which had left him an orphan. He walked slowly away, and entering the house, sought the minister's study.

Tom Hutchins went back to the spot where Rose was standing.

"Miss Rose," he said, shuffling his feet in the grass, "you remember when I gave you a string of robins' eggs, and what I said about 'em?"

"Yes," answered Rose, blushing quietly, for the poor string of eggs had been smashed to atoms in a romping chase with Jube years ago.

"Yes, Mr. Hutchins—I—I hope you don't want them back again."

Tom looked rather crestfallen, colored violently, and relieved his right foot by standing heavily on the left.

"No, Miss Rose," he burst out at length, "I aint going to ask for 'em back, but—but the truth is, I was a scamp for giving you them 'ere eggs; not at the time, you know, but arterwards, when I kinder forgot you and took a shine to another gal. There, now, it's out, and I suppose you'll just hate and despise me for a mean heart-breaker all the rest of your life. But I could not help it, consarn me if I could. If the gal hadn't looked kinder like you, in the way of curls, and been a match for the best on 'em, I never should have gin in; but it's done, and can't be undone, without you insist on holding me to that bargain when I give the eggs. If you do, why speak out, and I'm ready to stand up to the rack, fodder or no fodder."

Rose did not laugh, but her eyes were brimful of fun, and her lips dimpled threateningly.

"Don't—don't cry; it 'ud break my heart. I aint downright engaged, nor nothing, and I waited to see if you'd give me up afore that—but—but if you'd just as lives, 'thar is as good fish in the sea as ever come out,' you know; still, as I said, if you didn't seem to mind it, I—I—"

Rose shook with the rush of laughter that was forbidden to her lips, but she felt a sort of respect for the honest purpose which had brought the youth to her presence, and answered him with gentle kindness:

"Have no trouble about me, Mr. Hutchins—we were only children then."

"True enough—so we were."

"You were very kind to us, and I can never forget it."

"Oh, don't—don't, Miss Rose—you make me feel what a scoundrel I was ever to think of anybody else."

"Ah, but it was impossible to help it."

"Do you think so now—really?"

"Indeed I do."

"And you wont hate me?"

"Not at all."

"Nor think me fickle?"

"Oh, children are always fickle; but we meet as

grown people, now, and there will be no more change. You are content, and so am I."

"In downright arnest?"

"In downright earnest."

"Miss Rose."

"Well."

"If I was not over head and heels in love—well, it's no use talking; but there aint your match this side creation, except her."

CHAPTER LXXIV.

THE LONELY HOUSE.

That noble mansion had changed greatly. The beauty of its grounds was all run to waste. The snowy walls of the house were tinged with the damp of many winters, which no careful hand had swept away. Rose thickets had grown into jungles. The honeysuckles and clematis vines had leaped from the windows and clambered rudely up the forest trees. Long grass waved along the carriage walks and tufted the gravel. That delicate moss, which seems like the first green breath of decay, was creeping over the broad marble steps, and clothing the stone vases with gloomy richness.

It was very lonely and quiet, that dreary mansion, a mournful contrast to its appearance on the night we saw it last, in pristine freshness, blazing with lights, resonant with music, and all aglow with flowers.

Four persons, who stood in the wilderness which had

grown around it, felt this desolation with infinite melancholy.

"Was this my mother's house?" whispered Rose Mason, sadly. "Oh! Paul, where is she now? Not one word from her in all these years."

"Hush, my child," said the minister; "it may have been that trouble has fallen upon her so heavily that, like a poor worried deer, she has crept away to hide her wounds."

"My poor, poor mother," whispered Rose; "but for that man, how happy we might all be now."

"Be patient, my child, be patient."

"How can I be patient, knowing that she lives—at least, feeling the mournful hope—and yet with no certainty? How can I be patient, when my father is away where I cannot see him, wandering from country to country, trying to forget his wrongs—trying, in vain, to forget her?"

The minister looked troubled. This rebellion in his spoiled pet, wounded him like a reproach. He felt how deep were her causes for regret, and left the anguish to exhaust itself.

"There must be some one at the house who will know where she is living. The mansion is evidently inhabited. Let us go forward and inquire. We are legally authorized to enter," said Paul.

"Yes," rejoined the minister, looking at a strange man who was walking down the carriage street with Jube, "here comes our authority; but let us use it with delicacy; soft words are better than warrants; by them our Rose may gain some knowledge of her mother."

The group moved forward; that is, Paul, the minister, and Rose, leaving the stranger and Jube in the grounds.

The broad steps had a disused look, as if foot-prints were seldom left upon them; the huge knocker was dim, and grated harshly as the minister lifted it. When it fell, the noise struck them with a shock, its reverberations sounded so startling. It was a long time before any one came to the door; but at last it opened, and an ill-dressed, unshaven man looked out with unwelcoming eyes.

"Do you want any thing?" he said, curtly; "nobody comes to this door. We never see company."

"But we wish to enter the house, and have business which cannot be put off," said Paul.

"Who is it you want to see?"

"Any one who has authority to admit us to an examination of one of the rooms."

"There is no such person here."

The answer was brusque enough, like that which the keeper of a prison gives to troublesome visitors.

"Let us see your master, if you please," said the minister, blandly.

"I have no master!"

"Nor mistress?"

"No, nor mistress. I am *her* master!"

Rose started, and looked mournfully at Paul.

"What is the lady's name?" she inquired.

"She has fifty names. To-day I believe she is the Empress of Russia."

"But she has a name?"

"Not for strangers. If you have any business here but to ask questions let me hear what it is; no one else will get a say in the matter, I can tell you."

Paul beckoned to the man who lingered in the shrubbery. He came up and held a few words of conversation with the servant, who seemed greatly disturbed, and at once attempted to close the door forcibly. The officer opposed him, and, placing a paper in his hands, bade him make way.

He read the paper with a bewildered look, which changed to something like consternation in the end. He flung the door wide open, and, retreating down the entrance-hall, unlocked a door which led to the south wing.

"You will find the office in yonder," he said, pointing through the door. "I don't know what condition it is in, for no one has entered it, that I know of, for years."

The party passed in, all except Rose, who remained to question the man. But her distress was so great that it took away her voice.

"Well, what is it you want?" he asked, with a tone of kindness, for the agitation in her lovely face impressed even him.

"Tell me her name. The lady of the house, I mean."

"And what good if I do? She's nobody now—that is to any one but us. What on earth is her name to you?"

"I think—I fear—ah, sir, she may be my own mother."

"What is your name?"

"Mason."

"That is not her name, anyhow; but the other name—is it Rose?"

"Yes, yes—Rose!"

"Not Rose Nelson?"

"No, no!"

"It's of no use then: she's nothing to you."

"Oh, if you would but let me speak with her! only look on her face!" pleaded the poor girl, wild with the hopes his questions had raised.

"I could not do it. It is against the doctor's orders. Company is worse than any thing."

"Is she ill?"

He now looked on her with contemptuous astonishment.

"You call yourself her daughter, and don't know that?"

"Oh, sir, this is cruel! I have not had a letter or heard from her in nearly seven years! I never knew that this had been her home till within a week; and now you will not let me even look at her!"

The poor girl began to sob and wring her hands. The idea that she was so close by her mother, whom she was forbidden to look upon, overwhelmed her with anguish.

The man seemed touched. "Wait a moment," he said, "I will talk with Mrs. Brown about it. I command the house, but she has charge of the lady."

After this concession, the man went away, leaving Rose seated upon one of the hall chairs, breathless and anxious, for every moment convinced her more and more that she was in the house with her mother.

The man was absent some time. Suspense became intolerable to that young heart. She arose and walked the hall, but the noise of her own footsteps became irksome, as it prevented her listening to the first sound of his approach. She stood still and held her breath. Would he never return? What if he had seemed to relent only to escape her importunity? She started. Yes, yes—there was a sound—a footstep—lighter than his, though—a woman's footstep, accompanied with the rustle of silk and a perfume that penetrated pleasantly to her senses, a perfume that she recognized, and grew faint from the consciousness.

Trembling in all her limbs, she stood still, with her eyes penetrating the distance. There was a perpetual twilight in that house. The blinds were all closed, and in some places heavy shutters made the darkness complete. Thus the figure which advanced upon Rose, from what seemed a large drawing-room, moved vaguely through the dusk of the dwelling. It was a lady in full dress, sweeping through the rooms in quick haste, and huddling something to her bosom.

CHAPTER LXXV.

THE MANIAC'S TOILET.

Rose Mason caught her breath. It was her mother. She knew the face, and that proud, sweeping walk. Wild as the face was—rapid as the walk had become—she could not mistake them.

The woman saw her standing in the hall, and came eagerly forward.

"I have found them—I have found them," she cried, breathlessly. "What is an empress without her jewels? They don't understand these things—but you, my maid of honor, know better. They told me that you and all the court would keep away. That was to persuade me from wearing these; but I have got them safe—come, come, we must make haste, or force the people to wait, which should never be. My hair is to be braided yet—come this way—this way."

Rose followed her, pale as death, heart-stricken from

that moment. The woman entered the little breakfast room, where we have seen her before. It was not much changed; the sumptuous appointments had faded somewhat by time, but they retained all their elegance. In spite of her agitation, Rose remarked that behind the rich window draperies were immovable blinds of iron, deceptive, but firm as prison bars. Through the lattices of these blinds, sufficient light came to fill the room, and now Rose saw her mother clearly. Alas! the change! That beautiful face was worn and troubled; the splendid eyes were full of eager fire; the mouth was always in motion; and the whole aspect vigilant, as if her fears were eternally upon the watch.

"Come," she said, throwing herself into an easy chair, and arranging the folds of a purple brocade dress, with an exaggeration of her old, queenly grace, after she had placed the heavy bronze box, which she had carried, on an ottoman by her side, "come, put them on quick, before they break up my toilet—go to work—go to work."

With eager wildness, she snatched the comb from her hair and shook its long tresses over her shoulders. Rose saw that there was scarcely a dark thread in the mass, and her eyes filled with tears.

"What are you crying for?" asked her mother, sharply. "It is only powdered pearls that my people dust over my hair morning and night! Cleopatra, she was queen of Egypt, you know, and beautiful as I am—she drank her pearls in vinegar; I grind mine! Now braid away! braid away!"

Rose took the heavy tresses which the woman tossed into her hands, and, for a moment, her trembling fingers wandered among them, in vague efforts at obedience, but all at once her strength gave way, and dropping into a chair, she burst into a passion of tears.

Her mother started up fiercely, coiled the hair around her head in a rude crown, and dashed the lid of the bronze box open. Rose knew the gleam of those jewels, and shuddered. The woman tore the diamonds from their satin cushions, and began to huddle them in masses upon her arms and bosom. She then proceeded to tangle them in her gray hair, looking at her daughter with fierce reproach all the time.

Rose made a motion to arise—her mother saw it, and shut the box suddenly.

"Don't touch them! don't dare to touch them! Do you know how much they cost?"

The young girl retreated, pale and trembling.

"I bought them," cried the mother, in a hoarse whisper, "with my soul and body—soul and body! Understand that! But the fiend cheated me, and kept back the price!—treasures! gold! gold! gold! He hid it! but I kept these! They were the first price! It was putting them here where my little Rose used to sleep! and here where they burn like hot coals—that brought Mason back with those eyes——"

The woman laid a hand upon her bosom, and swept it across her forehead as she spoke, while poor Rose began to weep bitterly, as she heard her own sweet name uttered, for the first time in years, by those insane lips.

"No wonder you cry," said the woman. "It's enough to break one's heart! Loads and loads of money hid away, and no finding it! I've searched, and searched, and searched; but it's of no use! They lock the door and chain the windows; but there is a place!"

She paused, drew close to Rose, and bending down, whispered in her ear:

"The south wing; he was always there; always brooding over something in that room with one door and iron shutters. Once I saw a hole in the floor—an open half-moon—just under my feet. It closed up, and I forgot it till Mason came, and they began to lock the doors; then I thought and thought, such fiery hot thoughts, and up came that open half-moon from the marble floor! Oh, if I could but get there! Say, couldn't you draw the bolts? They hurt my hands! they hurt my hands!"

The poor creature shook her head, and wrung her hands, with tears and moans, piteous to hear.

Rose took the poor struggling hands in hers.

"Oh, mother! mother!" she cried out.

The woman stopped wringing her hands, and bent her wild eyes on the young girl's face.

"Rose had sweet eyes—my little Rose. She was so pretty—handsome almost as her mother. But what is the use of beauty if it cannot bring gold from its hiding-places? I like that face; there are emeralds and sapphires in the box. Besides, I have lovely pink coral that the queen of Naples gave me on my coronation. You shall wear them sometimes, for I love you for looking like little Rose. There, you may kiss my hand."

Rose took the hand, on which she pressed her quivering lips.

"Don't be afraid of me—imperial women are always gracious. You shall stay at the court. Only one thing I must tell you. That woman, Brown, shall be exiled to Siberia—that is where I get the ermine for my mantles, you know; but cold, oh, so cold! Good enough for her, though. Come close and I will tell you something. She ties my arms—she straps me down in bed—the false traitoress! But she shall go, and I will give you her place. Only don't speak loud, she might hear us. Hush —hush—hist!"

A slight noise broke the stillness of the house, and hushed the maniac's whispers. Putting a finger to her lips she moved into the hall on tiptoe. The door leading to the south wing was open. With a cry that brought an echo of affright from her child, she darted through and rushed toward the room where Thrasher had been confined that night—her garments fluttering wildly, and the jewels with their innumerable pendants tinkling against each other in her hair and on her bosom.

Rose followed, striving to cry out, but terror deprived her of the power.

The room was dark, for the bolts of those shutters had rusted in their sockets—dark, except a circle of red light that lay like a fiery wheel in the centre of the room. Ellen Mason rushed toward this opening, and swooping down upon her knees, like an evil-omened bird greedy for prey, looked down into the vault beneath. She saw the glitter of gold heaped on the stone floor, with a blaze of lamp light pouring over it. Heard the clink as it was drawn from the inner vault. She saw several persons busy with the gold piling it in heaps. The most prominent figure was a young man with jet black hair and eyes full of trouble, examining a block of gold which lay on the top of that glittering heap.

With a shriek from which the words, "It is mine—mine—all mine!" broke fiercely out, the woman half rose, flung out her arms, and made a plunge. Rose Mason came up that instant and grasped desperately at her dress. A fragment of the old brocade was left in her hand—a low, dull sound, a simultaneous shriek of dismay from the people in the vault, and all was still as death.

Rose had fallen with her face to the floor, white as the marble on which she lay, and almost as lifeless.

Paul, disturbed by the noise overhead, had retreated from the treasures, dropped the brick, and was looking up when that unhappy woman plunged downward upon the gold. Her hands were extended, and made one grasp into the heap. The old coins rattled down to the pavement—her temple struck a corner of the Gold Brick, and a cluster of diamonds which she had fastened there was driven through deep into the brain. She struggled a little, gasped once or twice, stretched her limbs out upon the treasure, and died there.

CHAPTER LXXVI.

THE DOCTOR'S RIDE.

IF the doctor was an eccentric man, he could be, when the occasion demanded it, both kind and thoughtful. More than once during Katharine's confinement he had ridden far beyond his circuit, and visited her in that lonely prison. No one was ever made aware of the fact, and he alone, of all that neighborhood, with one exception, was informed that Nelson Thrasher was also an inmate of the same prison. From the good old people it had been kept with religious delicacy. They knew that Katharine had a right to her freedom, and could now return home at pleasure; but she had written to ask more time. Duties, she said, to her fellow-prisoners kept her among them yet a little longer. She was free to depart, but the hospital needed her, and with the warden's consent she remained in voluntary service, teaching those whom she would soon leave behind how to tend and comfort the sick as she had done. This was an appeal that the old people could understand, so the lone mother submitted quietly to a few more months of solitude, and the Thrashers said to each other:

"Who knows but Nelson may come back before then?"

But time creeps on, even in a prison, and at last Thrasher was set free. The doctor knew the time, and had the harness put on his old friend that morning at an early hour. The horse did not exactly like this proceeding. He objected to any long ride without the saddle-bags. Indeed, he did not feel exactly like a respectable doctor's horse without that appendage, and remonstrated against the indignity of reins, thills, and whiffle-trees, with vigorous shakes of the head, and even a vicious kick or two. But the doctor came out and expostulated with him after his own quaint fashion, and directly the two went off in harmony, one at each end of the reins.

For two whole days the sick of that neighborhood for fifteen miles around took care of themselves, and grumbled accordingly.

On the evening of the second day, there was a terrible rumbling of loose wheels along the Derby turnpike, for the brown horse had caught sight of his home, and instantly went off in a rickety series of leaps that almost tossed the doctor from his seat in front of the wagon.

"Don't be afraid," he said, turning to the back seat, where a man and woman were seated, with the light of a crescent moon lying tenderly on their faces. "It's his way when things go to suit him. The sight of home always sets him off."

"Oh, I am not afraid," said a sweet female voice "It's a long time since either of us have known what fear was. Isn't it, Nelson?"

The man thus addressed clasped the little hand which stole into his with tender force, but said nothing. His heart was too full. The trial that lay before him at the end of that ride might have taxed the courage of any man.

They rode on to the doctor's house. He got out of the wagon, removed the temporary seat which had accommodated him from Simsbury, and held a silent counsel with his horse, patting the old fellow on the neck, and using all the conciliatory blandishments for deluding horseflesh into obedience, which have since been dignified into a science.

"There now, get along," he said, moving toward the gate. "He'll go ahead without balking. No need of a whip. The old chap wont stand that from anybody but me. Drive on, and God be with you."

The strange man leaned heavily on his crutches, and gently lifted his hat as he uttered these words. The soft moonlight fell upon his head, and a grander one seldom bared itself in reverence to a noble sentiment.

As the doctor wheeled around he saw the members of his family coming out to welcome him home. His manner changed at once. Inwardly delighted with their prompt affection he put the children aside with good-natured rebukes of their clamorous joy, and stalking into the room, which served as an office, sunk quietly into a leathern easy chair, and desired the eldest boy to hand down his fiddle.

The boy took an old violin from its place on the wall and gave it into his father's hand. The doctor drew a lump of rosin from his pocket, rasped the bow with it for a full minute, then lifting the instrument to his shoulder began to play; directly the children came rushing in from the hall and kitchen, astonished, for some of the wildest and most invigorating music heard for many a day, rang out from the dark old violin, filling the whole house with cheerfulness.

The doctor's wife—a fine woman, of the Connecticut stamp—came softly into the room with word that his supper was on the table; but he only answered with a dash at Yankee Doodle, and revelled in it with a zest ten thousand suppers could not have excited. The good housewife never urged her husband to any thing; she knew the folly of that too well; so she sat down pleasantly and listened to his music. It was well worth the trouble, for the doctor threw off a world of generous thankfulness in those erratic notes, and when music comes from the soul it is always good. She asked no questions, but knew very well that something satisfactory had happened to her husband, for he always expressed these feelings through his violin.

Meantime the two travellers kept on up the turnpike. They passed the rock spring, which sparkled out from the shadows cast over it from the dogwood thickets; all cut up root and branch in these days, and moved slowly over the old bridge. They could see the white spire of the Episcopal church, rising into the moonlight from the high bank opposite, and, with the sight, Katharine's heart melted within her. She lifted her eyes to Thrasher; the moonlight lay full upon his face. It was pale and troubled. In that church he had been baptized.

Katharine took his hand with touching gentleness, and pressed it to her lips. Her face was so heavenly that he bent down and kissed it, leaving a heavy tear on her cheek, which she would not have wiped away for the world.

"Ah, Nelson!" she said, clasping her hands and lifting her eyes from the church spire to the heavens, which it seemed to penetrate—" how plainly I see the great goodness of God in all that has happened. At first it was very dark, and I struggled against the cruelty of that arrest, and the unjust sentence which branded me before the world. I forgot that the Son of God was thus assailed, thus branded! and worse still, put to death, that Christianity might be our inheritance. I did not know what great happiness might spring out of this degradation; how holy a work lay waiting for me in that prison!"

"My poor girl, it was a terrible life for you. Can God forgive me for bringing you there?"

"Nelson, this is wrong—it is unkind! It was to be; God knew what was best, and sent me in the path of a great duty against my will, or I never should have found it. He had compassion on those poor creatures so barbarously cut off from everything sweet and good in life. They were perishing or turning to demons for the want of a little care, a few kind words, a smile of pity now and then. I was poor as poor could be, helpless as a child, but these things I could give them; so he thought it best that I should go.

"I was rebellious at first, Nelson, and wondered how it could be that I, an innocent woman, should suffer among the guilty. I was so young, so weak, and miserably selfish. Besides, I hoped so fondly that you would come back and save me. But they were dragging me away from all possibility of seeing you."

"My poor Katharine!"

"Oh, it was hard! it was hard!" she said, laying her forehead on his shoulder; "for I thought you loved me! I thought you loved me!"

He drew her head close to his bosom, but said nothing; self-reproach held his heart in silence.

"With this hope of seeing you again, rising above every thing, it was a cruel thought that you might come home and find me there, think perhaps that I had harmed your child."

"No, Katharine—no, I never could have believed that. In my most insane moments I knew and felt how good you were."

"But these thoughts would come to me in my prison, Nelson; I could not help that. So I struggled against that hard fate and wanted to die. The people were wrong and harsh with me, the law was wrong, the judges were wrong, but God was right."

"I—I was the most cruel of all," said Thrasher, in a low, pained voice.

"Still it was all needful. What else would have won me from home to live among those poor convicts, to help them and feel for them, till a beautiful happiness sprang up to me out of those dreary mines. Then, then," she added, with a gush of tender gratitude, "just as I had learned to live and endure for others, knowing that God's wisdom was higher than man's justice, you came, my husband, and I had the power to help you. I so weak, and you so strong! From that day I knew how great a blessing had been won for me, out of what seemed the deadly ruin of a life. In that black depth I found the heart of my husband."

"Oh, a worthless, wicked heart, Katharine!"

"But it was mine—all mine!"

He girded her closer with his arm, and that was answer enough.

"Then you began to trust me, and believe in me, Nelson; as a strong man lets some little child lead him, because of its very helplessness; you listened to me and loved me—for you do love me, Nelson!"

"The God you worship so beautifully, Katharine, only knows how much I love you!"

"Oh, we shall be very happy!" answered the young woman, bowing her head, while a soft rain of tears fell down her cheeks. "Every soul in the prison loved us. God has forgiven us!"

"Not us, Katharine! It is I that have need of His pardon; not you, my wife!"

But in her sweet humility she would not have it so, and protested against it. "No, no; I was untamed, impatient, disobedient to my mother. In a woman these are great sins. We are equal there as in the mercies which fall around us now."

Thrasher was a man of few words, but his wife understood this, and saw, by the emotion in his face, how deeply his spirit was touched.

They fell into silence after this, and rode on slowly, thinking of those they were about to meet. The wagon rolled heavily up Falls Hill, turned at the old willow tree, and passed up the Bungy road approaching the old homestead.

They came to Mrs. Allen's house first. It was dark and still as the grave. Why was this? The hour did not warrant such dreary darkness, such utter solitude.

Katharine, who was leaning eagerly forward, fell

back with a heavy sigh. Was her mother dead? Had sorrow broken her heart at last? Was it a tomb to which she had come, after eight long years of imprisonment?

They left the wagon, and knocked at the door. There was no footstep within. No answering voice. Not even a gleam of fire light to speak of an existing household.

They returned to the wagon without speaking, and drove slowly over the hill; very slowly, for that empty house had filled them with painful forebodings.

From the butternut tree they got a first sight of the old homestead. From the sitting room window a steady light was burning, which fell upon a great snowball bush, turning the huge white blossoms that covered it into globes of gold. "They are alive; they are at home!" said Thrasher. "God be thanked!"

CHAPTER LXXVII.

THE CONVICT'S RETURN.

OLD Mr. Thrasher and his wife sat together that night in the very room in which they had been blessed by the first return of their son. He had been away weary, weary years now, and not a word of tidings had ever reached them. But the old hope was there. The faith which nothing but a certainty of his death could destroy. There they sat, as on that night, waiting for him, not with absolute hope, but from that tender unbelief which will not give up a loved one.

This evening they were not alone. An old woman, very thin and withered, but with a certain hard stateliness hanging around her, sat near the hearth. A hood and shawl, lying on the table near the door, proved that she had only come in for a brief visit. There was not much conversation among them. Mrs. Allen had just received a letter from her son, who had shipped in the India trade from Liverpool, and had not been home for years. Now he was on a return voyage, and having saved money enough, was resolved to leave the sea and take to farming with his mother.

It was a kind letter, and spoke most affectionately of the young sister who was, as he thought, pining to death in the prison mines at Simsbury.

The old man put on his spectacles and read the letter aloud. Mrs. Allen listened with interest, as if she had not already got the contents by heart. Old Mrs. Thrasher stopped short in her knitting, and sighed heavily. What a comfort it was to get a letter from one's son! Would she ever see another from Nelson? Just then the sound of wagon wheels coming over the hill reached them. He stopped reading and listened; why, no one could tell, for wagons passed that road every half hour in the twenty-four. As the wagon approached, these three old people looked at each other with vague bewilderment, and listened like persons in expectation. It stopped before the house. The gate opened. Mrs. Thrasher leaned forward, listening. "It is his step!"

That good woman had said exactly these same words years before, when some brown threads darkened her hair, which was white as snow now.

The old man now arose, so did Mrs. Allen, for she heard a step beyond that which sounded on the gravel walk—something so light that it could have reached no intelligence save the ever-watchful love of a mother.

They all stood and listened—no one of them had

strength enough to move. The door was opened—those steps advanced up the entry way, and paused there. Then a hand, which shook the latch it touched, opened the door, and the old people saw their son, and behind him, the sweet, pale face of Katharine, his wife. The lamp light lay full upon them, but the old people were blinded by a sweet rush of love that made their hearts swell again, and could not see distinctly. The old man went forward.

"My son, my son!"

They were strong men, this father and son, but they fell into each other's arms and wept like children.

Then the old man gave way to his wife, and taking Katharine from her mother's bosom, laid both hands on her head and blessed her.

After the first outgush of welcome, Nelson Thrasher turned to his wife.

"Father," he said, " it is this woman, my wife, whom you must thank—she who suffered innocently, that I might be given back to my home. It was for your son she waited after they had set her free, for I have been her fellow-prisoner. Oh, father! I have sinned against Heaven, and in thy sight, and am no longer worthy to be called thy son."

Tears were raining down the old man's face—his arms were extended, and he cried out:

"Oh, my son, my son! what is thy innocence or guilt to us, when God has forgiven?" Again the old man fell upon his son's bosom and wept.

When Katharine's head was uncovered, and the old people had wiped away their tears, the change which had taken place in that young couple struck them with fresh thrills of tenderness. Thrasher's hair was threaded with silver, and the face it shadowed bore proofs of suffering which no after time could efface, but the serene strength which sprang out of his new life, gave something of grandeur to his features. There was no look of concealment in it now, but he met his father's eyes with the open frankness of boyhood.

The dear old lady could not be satisfied with one embrace, but hovered around her son in a birdlike flutter, smoothed his hair with her plump little palm, and laid her cheek lovingly against it, whispering, "My poor boy, my poor dear boy."

Katharine had been whispering to her mother; her face became anxious; she was evidently pleading for something. At last the stiff old woman arose, and going up to Thrasher laid one hand on his shoulder.

"Nelson Thrasher, I know the wrong you have done my daughter. My son told me all before he went his voyage to the Indies. He charged me to keep it secret, and I have. She begs me to pardon it, and I will. Nelson Thrasher, I forgive you, as I pray God to forgive my own sins."

Thrasher bowed his head; the solemnity of the old woman went to his soul. After a moment his face was slowly lifted, and his eyes looked into hers.

"I thank you," he said, gently. "Katharine, tell her that she can trust you with me now."

Katharine came to his side, smiling.

"Yes, mother; for he loves me; and I, oh, you know how it was always with me."

"And now you will live with us," said Mrs. Thrasher, hovering around her son, troubled in her heart that any one should claim a word or look.

"Yes, mother. we have come to the homestead to end our days. Here, among our old neighbors, we will redeem the good name which has been forfeited by your son, and innocently lost by this dear girl. Where else can we turn? Let our neighbors know all; we will have nothing to do with concealments, but meet their kindness or condemnation fairly. In time they will learn to like us again—for her sake I hope it, and will toil for it."

"We will always stand by our children; wont we Mrs. Allen?"

It was the soft, cooing voice of Mrs. Thrasher which uttered these words. "The neighbors like us, and wont be harsh with them. If they should, you know we are company among ourselves." The dear old woman turned her mild brown eyes from Mrs. Allen to her husband, questioning them both.

The old man smiled.

"Our son is right; let him start life once more among his old neighbors."

And so it was settled among them, in the stillness of that night, after Nelson Thrasher had revealed every thing to his parents.

CHAPTER LXXVIII.

TOM HUTCHINS' QUARREL.

THE church bell was ringing cheerfully on Falls Hill. Indeed, on a day like that, every sound took a jubilant tone. The sunshine was so bright, the meadows and foliage so richly green, that one breathed deeply with a keen sense of enjoyment.

The birds in the pine woods made a perfect riot of music among the trees, and built their nests lovingly, in defiance of blue laws, and forgetful—as birds will be sometimes—that it was the Sabbath day. Even pretty little humming-birds came out in force that morning, and shook the trumpet honeysuckles like mad things, buzzing their wings, and setting the great bumble bees that haunted the clover fields a most indecorous example. Such quantities of fennel as was cut from the green stalks that morning and tied into dainty bunches, ready to be nibbled at in church. Such pretty bouquets of violets and wild roses were made—such lovely new bonnets and muslin dresses as appeared that day for the first time—I can neither describe or enumerate.

"What was it all about?"

Why a confirmation, a wedding, and a double baptism were to come off that day, performed by the bishop himself. No wonder all Chewstown came over from that side of the river. No wonder that Falls Hill, Bungy, and Shrub Oak—to say nothing of the factory flats—should be one scene of commotion! The wedding of itself would have been enough to set people wild. Why the bride was pretty Rose Mason, that little girl who used to live with her handsome mother down in the pine woods; the sweetest creature that the sun ever shone upon, and just as beautiful now; in fact, more so.

"Who was she going to marry?"

Did any one remember a remarkably handsome little fellow who came to board with Mrs. Allen, in Bungy, about the time that Katy Allen—well, they would not say any thing about that; poor thing, she had suffered enough—but he went to school at Shrub Oak, and was a perfect little gentleman. His name was Paul De Varney, and he had come out so rich that no one could count his gold.

There was but one thing that could be said against

the match—young De Varney brought a black slave with him when he first came into the State, and kept him still, for the poor fellow had been about Bungy not two days ago, and no doubt was there yet. The bishop might have something to say about that before he would marry the young man; but it was to be hoped that it would not quite break up the match. Still, a slave in old Connecticut! that could not be thought of a moment by any Christian community. Certainly Nelson Thrasher and his wife would be confirmed—that was all settled with the bishop, who had been informed about the case thoroughly by Thrasher himself; as for his wife, people were beginning to think that after all she had been innocent about that affair. A woman that could kill her own child never yet made a wife like her. Why those old people fairly worshipped her. When old Mrs. Thrasher was sick, she never had her clothes off for weeks together. Then she was so good in sickness; always the first to offer herself, if watchers were wanted. Why Tom Hutchins might have lost his young wife if it had not been for her care. Night and day, night and day, that faithful woman was by her bedside, till the fever left her. The doctor had been heard to declare, over and over again, that he should not know how to get along with his patients if it were not for Mrs. Nelson Thrasher. Then Nelson had turned out such a sensible, steady man, for all his hard life. Yes, yes; the thing was certain; both he and his wife would be confirmed. No doubt of that.

Then about the baptism; of course that was for Tom Hutchins' twins—a girl and a boy that you could not tell apart to save your life. Tom and his wife were so proud of those young ones they never would be content till all the town had seen them in their long white christening dresses. That young fellow did make such a fool of himself. Just as if nobody had ever had twins to baptize before him.

All this gossip was pretty nearly true. The bishop had come, and was stopping at the square white house near the willow tree. Paul De Varney was staying at Mrs. Allen's with Jube. David Rice had built a large side building to the old house, since he settled on the farm, and it was plenty large enough to accommodate half a dozen guests if they could have been persuaded to stay. But when Mr. Prior the minister, and his little wife, came from Bays Hollow, bringing Rose Mason back to be married in her native village, they went directly up to old Mrs. Thrasher's and made the homestead cheerful with company.

Since the arrival of all these people in the village, Tom Hutchins, who lived in Mrs. Mason's cottage in the pine woods, had been wonderfully busy, and gave himself up to his friends more completely than could be expected of a young married man, not two months before made the father of healthy twins, good as gold and plump as partridges.

Notwithstanding this paternal drawback, Tom had made all arrangements with regard to the bishop; had seen the publishment properly laid on the pulpit cushion, ready for use, three legal Sundays, and had twice driven his steel colored colt into New Haven, to get a pair of satin slippers and a certain kind of ribbon for Rose, at which his wife pouted, and the twins, partaking of her ill humor, kept the poor fellow walking the chamber floor half the night, now with one, and then with the other, in his arms.

I am afraid Mrs. Hutchins did not, on that occasion, take quite her share of the nursing. When Tom asked her, in his distress, if she wouldn't get up and make a little fennel seed tea for the poor little things, she desired to know if it wouldn't be just as well to make that request of Rose Mason, with her curls and her gipsy hat on one side, at which Tom broke forth with energy:

"Talk about Rose Mason," he said; "the girl that was going to marry his earliest friend, one of the finest fellows on earth— a girl that was good as gold, and generous as— Oh it was too bad; he wouldn't have thought it of a wife of his—a woman that he had loved so."

"*Had* loved!" Mrs. Hutchins murmured, faintly. "*Had* loved!"

Tom's heart melted within him as he heard the low protest, but he contented himself by kissing each of the twins, while their little heads rested on his shoulders, and went on making an iron-hearted fellow of himself.

Yes, Tom meant *had*. No love in the world could stand such venomous attacks on that nice girl, who had given him up so handsomely. Where would she have been but for that? Breaking her heart, and pining herself to death, instead of taking her place as a respectable married person and the head of a thriving family. There was the twins, too, precious dears. Par wasn't scolding them. Where in the world would they have been if Rose had kept him to his word, as any other girl would have done?

Here Mrs. Hutchins began to sob, and said, penitently, that she hadn't meant any thing of the kind—in fact, hadn't said a single thing against Miss Rose Mason, who was breaking her heart though; and—and—oh, dear, if she'd only stayed at home with her own dear par and mar, instead of marrying a man that didn't love her, and was keeping her poor babies out in the cold just to break her heart.

"There, there! just snuggle the little shavers up to you, that's a darling!" cried Tom, huddling the two babies into their mother's arms, and leaving a penitential kiss somewhere in the borders of her cap. "I'll kindle the fire and make some tea myself—I know you didn't mean it."

"Indeed I didn't, Tom. But you mustn't do it; I will."

"There now, keep quiet, or you'll set 'em a-going again."

"No, Tom, they're both sound asleep."

"You don't say so. Well, they've got me wide awake, anyhow; so I'll just light a candle and show you what I really was doing in New Haven, and what Rose Mason wanted me to buy for her."

Tom unlocked a closet that held his cravats and sunday clothes, from which he took a long, deep paper box, and carried it to the bed.

"See here!" he cried, lifting up a garment so white and soft that it seemed woven from snow-flakes. "Two of 'em, just alike; India muslin that her father sent from Calcutta, she told me to tell you. See how they are worked round the bottom, and cut up with lace. Then, here's the caps! One of 'em just fits my fist. It was to get the ribbon for these cockades she sent me to New Haven—white for the gal, and blue for the boy. Now what do you think about it?"

Mrs. Hutchins thought that she was the most silly, unreasonable, good-for-nothing creature that ever lived; but she hoped, for all, that Tom wouldn't say *had* again. It was too cruel, even if she was to blame.

Tom admitted that he was a hard-hearted, cruel,

tiger of a fellow, and not worth half the love she gave him; and so the young couple were reconciled.

CHAPTER LXXIX.

THE WEDDING AND THE BAPTISM.

Notwithstanding this little domestic scene, Tom stood by his friends bravely; "he was bound to see this wedding put through in style, let what would come." Mrs. Hutchins was a wise little lady in her day, and kept quiet after this; but she insisted on having a new straw bonnet with white ribbons, and would have worn her own wedding dress only Tom objected, and said it would be like putting on airs, and she the head of a family; that dove-colored silk would do beautifully.

So the afternoon came, as I have said, and the bell rang out loud and cheerfully, sounding out an invitation to every lady from Rock Rimmond to Castle Rock. Then the people came pouring in from Bungy, Shrub Oak, Chewstown, and Pine Island in a perpetual storm. The old barn-like Presbyterian meeting-house in Chewstown was deserted by all except the most aged members, and the school-house where the little handful of Methodists worshipped, had to close its doors, for no one but the class leader presented himself for admission. So the church was crowded.

Those who could not gain access were scattered in groups on the green in front, and a crowd took shelter under the old willow at the crossroads, determined to get a good view of that young foreigner who was going to marry pretty Rose Mason. People said he was handsome as a lord, and rich as a prince. Of course he should be all that to carry off the prettiest girl that ever lived in the town, to say nothing of her goodness. Of course everybody remembered Captain Mason and his handsome wife. She was dead, poor woman; but Captain Mason had given up his ship, and was going to France with his daughter and her young husband. Wasn't it strange that Captain Rice should have got into company like that? And Tom Hutchins. The young couple are going to take tea at Tom's house after the ceremony. Strange, wasn't it? But then Tom always was stumbling into some good fortune.

While these remarks were going on the people within the church were lost in admiration of the rare flowers—white roses and white lilies—that shed their fragrance over the altar. The same perfume which was to float around the bride would first consecrate the penitents who came forward for confirmation.

They came up the broad aisle slowly and with downcast eyes—a man and his wife, only those two. The bishop stood ready. Every eye was upon them; some turned away in hard contempt, some looked pitifully on the young woman who, innocent or guilty, had suffered so much. How beautiful she was. With what meek grace she knelt down and bowed her head where the shadow of her trouble had fallen so early. And the man, how quiet and self-centered he was, giving his soul up to its holy work, without a thought of those who looked on. Handsome; yes, he was more than handsome, with that glow upon his face; but it only came once, when her eyes were uplifted to his, after that a solemn sadness fell upon him.

That group of old people, and that open-faced seafaring man, standing near the altar. Certainly that was her mother, and the little woman standing close to the old man, was his mother, and the seafaring man was Captain Rice, her half brother. How completely they seemed absorbed by the kneeling couple. Well, after all there must be some excuse—crime did not seem natural to such people, or to the children of that honest couple. God must have touched their hearts.

Thus the prejudices of the congregation softened, and gave way under the spiritual influence of that holy rite which stamped those who had been condemned criminals as Christians before the Lord.

When Katharine arose from her consecration and moved back, some of her old schoolmates looked kindly upon her, and one opened the pew door, thus inviting her to a seat. At this a flush came over her pale face, and you could see quick tears swelling under her eyelids.

After these two people were lost sight of, another group appeared in the aisle. A noble young man, with those soft, velvety eyes, that are at once so languid and so bright, and a fair young creature, crowned with white jessamines, and floating in a cloud of gossamer lace, whose cheeks wore a flush of wild roses, and whose lips trembled between smiles and tears. No bridesmaids were in attendance, but a tall, grave man, whom everybody recognized as the bride's father, walked with them to the altar, and gave her away, with a look of tender sadness that seemed habitual to his noble face.

The bridal party stepped aside from the altar to make room for another couple, and then Tom Hutchins and his wife came up the broad aisle with blushes and smiles chasing each other across their faces as pride and strength shone in those young hearts. The man

THE WEDDING AND BAPTISM.

carried an infant in his arms, whose soft face dimpled in response to its father's smiles, and which wore a blue rosette in the mass of soft lace that formed its cap. The woman looked fresh as a wild rose in her bonnet with white ribbons and a dove-colored silk adown which the long white christening dress of the girl baby floated mistily, while the rosette on its cap fluttered like a white poppy in the wind.

Paul and Rose, these names were duplicated at the altar with due sprinkling of water-drops from a fount wreathed with flowers. Then Tom Hutchins and his wife walked down the aisle again, looking grave and thoughtful, as if they had just begun to realize what it was to be the father and mother of human souls, whose pilgrimage is through all eternity.

In violation of the usual custom, a colored man was accommodated with a seat near the door, whose glowing face and genial smile made every one in his vicinity brighten with pleasant sympathy. He was so occupied with the ceremony that he had not regarded a little group of persons who stood just outside the church, conversing eagerly together. At last one of these men came and touched him on the shoulder.

Jube, used to obedience, arose and followed the man into the centre of the group that was evidently waiting for him, and looked around in some surprise, for they were all strangers.

"I say," said one of the men, making mysterious signals with his fingers, "now's your time, while everybody is looking on the christening. There's my horse and wagon; take you to New Haven in an hour; steamboat ready. We've made a little contribution. Here's two silver dollars, and you'll find some doughnuts in the wagon seat with a chunk of cheese. Liberty's the word. Leave the horse at Buck's tavern in Chapel street, till sent for."

Jube turned from one face to another, wondering what they wanted of him.

"Don't be skeered, and look so wild," said the first speaker, "we'll stand by you; it's our bounden duty as Christians. So jump in while you have a chance."

Of course Jube had learned a good deal of English in all the years that he had been in America; but he spoke brokenly, and had some difficulty in commanding words when taken by surprise.

"What you want ob Jube? Where shall he jump?"

"Out of slavery into liberty," was the answer. "Run away from the young man who owns you for his slave."

"Slave! slave!—what for Jube run away from young master? What for who says so—Jube happy very much."

"But you are a slave!"

Jube laughed till all his white teeth shone again:

"Jube like slave."

"He makes you work for nothing!"

Jube looked down at his brawny frame, and laughed again.

"Come, cuff, make haste!" cried the man whose wagon was waiting, "you've no time to lose. They'll be coming out soon, and then it's all day with your chance."

In his eager philanthropy, the man put his arm through Jube's, and attempted to drag him toward the willow tree, where his horse was fastened, but Jube shook him off.

"Jube ride behind young masser and Miss Rose. He happy there."

"Poor fellow," said the man, in a broken-hearted

THE WEDDING AND BAPTISM.

voice. "He don't know what freedom is. Let him go. It's too late now; they're coming."

True enough, Paul De Varney and his bride were walking down the broad aisle of the church—he with a smile on his lips, and she with a warm flush of roses on her cheeks. Behind them came Hutchins and his family.

A carriage was drawn up at the door, ready to carry the bridal pair to Tom Hutchins' house, in the pine woods. Jube sprang forward to open the carriage door, and held his arm down to save that snowy bridal dress from a contact with the wheels.

Rose smiled upon him as she entered the carriage, and touched his shoulder, as if for support, which brought a blessing upon her in Jube's broken English.

When Paul took his seat, Jube seized his hand and kissed it, thus giving his congratulations before those who would have lured him away in the kindness of their ignorance. The faithful fellow felt as if his master had been slandered when these men called him a slave, and so he was.

Directly after the carriage drove off, a smart, little one-horse wagon, yellow as an orange, took its place, and over the wheel leaped our friend Tom Hutchins, who waited, with the reins in his hand, till a little woman, with an infant on each arm, came out of the crowd. Tom took the boy baby in one arm, and held his horse with the other, till the little woman clambered over the front wheel to her seat. Then, after smoothing down its complication of garments, he settled the little trooper, as he called it, by its twin in their young mother's lap, gave a leap to her side, and, with an old-fashioned crack of the whip, dashed after the wedding carriage.

Not till most of the congregation had left the church

did Nelson Thrasher come forth with his wife, circled, as it were, by the old people, and supported by Captain Rice.

The bishop left his vestry and came with them, talking in a low, kind voice to Katharine for some moments on the steps of the church, when he left her with a fatherly shake of the hand. Several of the matrons and girls who had held aloof till then, came up and gave both Nelson and herself a cordial greeting. It was known that they had been invited to join the wedding party, and that young De Varney had left Thrasher in charge of his property during his proposed absence in Europe. This proof of confidence had a wonderful effect on the old neighbors, and quite a little group gathered around the husband and wife, giving them generous God speed.

Neither Katharine or her husband cared to join that bridal party down in the pine woods. The day had been too impressive and solemn for that. But with serene faces and hearts full of gratitude, they entered the one-horse wagon that waited for them and followed the old folks slowly over the Bungy hills.

THE END.

www.ingramcontent.com/pod-product-compliance
Lightning Source LLC
Chambersburg PA
CBHW051201300426
44116CB00006B/402